Romans in the Hambleden

Edited by J. E. Eyers

Cover image:
The Yewden villa complex, nestled in the Hambleden Valley, near the River Thames. Designed by Alison Jewsbury and Tony Eustace

Frontispiece image:
Yewden villa – the main villa building within the complex, as seen from the front gates. Drawn by Tony Eustace.

Published by:
J. Eyers, Chiltern Archaeology,
13 Pusey Way,
Lane End,
High Wycombe,
Bucks,
HP14 3LG
www.chilternarchaeology.com

Chiltern Archaeology Monograph 1

The Romans in the Hambleden Valley

© J. Eyers 2011

© Alison Jewsbury (cover and computerized building reconstructions)

ISBN 978-1-904898-12-2

This monograph is dedicated to the volunteer team

Contents

| List of Figures | List of Tables | Contributors | Acknowledgements |

Preface		page 1
Chapter 1: Introduction		5
1.1 Introduction and context of the project		
1.2 Site location		
1.3 Geology, topography and present land use		
1.4 Archaeological background		
1.5 Project archive		
1.6 What's in a name?		
1.7 Bibliography		

Chapter 2: The fieldwork 2008-2010 — 13
    2.1 Resistivity
    2.2 Magnetometry
    2.3 Aerial photographs
    2.4 Woodland surveys: Ridge Wood, Northcot Wood & Chalk Pit Wood

Chapter 3: The villa complex and the 1912 excavation   J. Eyers & A. Jewsbury   26
    3.1 Introduction
    3.2 Site description: the buildings
    3.3 Site description: the pits
    3.4 Site description: the furnaces
    3.5 Site description: the walls and enclosure, the yard and other buildings

Chapter 4 The artefacts (except pottery and bone) — 76

4.1 The coins	Brett Thorn	
4.2 Worked stone objects:	Jill Eyers	80
Whetstones; Querns and millstones; Building materials		
4.3 Flint		97
4.4 Copper alloy	Sandie Williams	101
4.5 Iron	Brian Gilmour	128
4.6 Glass	Jill Eyers	131
4.7 Worked bone objects	Raihana Ehsanullah	136
4.8 Miscellaneous: Small finds	Raihana Ehsanullah	146
Residue	David Dungworth	150

Chapter 5: The pottery:

5.1 Iron Age	Jonathon Dicks	151
5.2 Roman coarse & fine wares	Jill Eyers	155
5.3 Roman Samian ware	Jill Eyers	181
5.4 Potters stamps	J. Eyers & G. Monteil	197
5.5 Decorated Samian	Jill Eyers	203
5.6 Vessel repair	Rick Magaldi	233

Chapter 6: The human remains   S. Mays, S.Vincent, K. Robson-Brown and A. Roberts
    147

Chapter 7 The environmental evidence
    7.1 Animal bone   259
    7.2 Charred grain   Gill Campbell   261

Chapter 8 Discussion and conclusions — 263

Appendices:
1. Catalogue of glass from Yewden — 281
2. Catalogue of Iron Age Pottery — 289
3. Catalogue of named Samian potters — 290
4. (a) Catalogue of Samian forms at Yewden for each region, vessel numbers — 292
4. (b) Catalogue of Samian forms at Yewden for each region, as EVEs
5. Catalogue of Roman Pottery fabrics (non-Samian) — 295

List of Figures

Preface: Alfred Heneage Cocks at age 14 years
            Alfred with a group of bell ringers from Great Marlow in 1899
            Miss Glassbrook in 1912

Figure 1.1 The location of Hambleden, Buckinghamshire
Figure 1.2 The Hambleden valley – a Chiltern's dry valley
Figure 1.3 Location of the two Roman villas: the Yewden villa complex and Mill End
Figure 1.4 Mill End Villa as shown by the resistance survey of 2008
Figure 1.5 Find spots within the 1 km radius of SU 785 856, Hambleden Valley
Figure 2.1 Resistance grid locations in the Hambleden Valley
Figure 2.2 Resistance results for Hog Pit field, Hambleden
Figure 2.3 The resistance survey results for Horseleys and Middle Couch Fields
Figure 2.4 Interpretive sketch of the resistance result for Horseleys field
Figure 2.5 Magnetometer results for Hog Pit field and field west of Hog Pit.
Figure 2.6 Interpretive summary of magnetometer results for the Hog Pit field survey
Figure 2.7 Magnetometer results for Horseleys Field, Hambleden
Figure 2.8 Interpretive summary of the magnetometer results for Horseleys Field
Figure 2.9 Aerial photograph of the fields around the Yewden complex, Hambleden
Figure 2.10 Map locations of Ridge Wood and Northcot to Chalk Pit Woods
Figure 2.11 The large ditch and bank, Ridge Wood - early Medieval (?Norman)
Figure 3.1 Site plan and building materials, Yewden Villa
Figure 3.2 Floor plan of the 1st House, Yewden
Figure 3.3 The 1st House from the SW showing the stoke hole to the hypocaust of room C
Figure 3.4 The 1st House from the SE corner.
Figure 3.5 The 1st House from the NE.
Figure 3.6 The 1st House from the NW
Figure 3.7 The 1st House corridor (M) from the north showing terracotta tesserae
Figure 3.8 The 1st House: the two bath areas A and B
Figure 3.9 Butting relationship of the foundation walls for rooms A and B, 1st House
Figure 3.10 a The 1st House end 3rd to early 4th century, Phase I
Figure 3.10 b The 1st House Phase 2
Figure 3.10 c The 1st House during the 4th century
Figure 3.11 An architectural sketch of the structure for the 1st House, Yewden Villa
Figure 3.12 A reconstruction of the 1st House
Figure 3.13 Reconstruction of the 2nd House during the early 4th century
Figure 3.14 The 3rd House looking east
Figure 3.15 Areas containing large quantities of burnt pottery
Figure 3.16 The mortar floor exposed during the 1912 excavations, looking north
Figure 3.17 Reconstruction of the 3rd House. © Alison Jewsbury
Figure 3.18 The 'Little House' or 4th House of Cocks 1921
Figure 3.19 Samian mortarium (DR43) from Rheinzabern 140-260 AD
Figure 3.20 Siitomina's pot: a graffito of a Romano-British female name
Figure 3.21 New Forest mortarium 260-370 AD in the top fill of Pit 3
Figure 3.22a Flint and gravel floor levels sealing the well (Pit 6)
Figure 3.22b Chalk/Mortar floor indicating a former larger building for the 3rd House
Figure 3.23 The profile of Pit 8
Figure 3.24 The Multiple T furnace (a) looking south & (b) showing flues, looking W
Figure 3.25 The well and the Gridiron Furnace, looking *c.* southeast
Figure 3.26 The Single T furnace, east of the 1st House, looking north
Figure 3.27 The South Cream Pan Furnace, looking *c.* NW
Figure 3.28 The North Cream Pan Furnace, looking north
Figure 3.29 The East Twin furnace looking north
Figure 3.30 The Hybrid Furnace in the east side of the yard, looking NNE

Figure 3.31 The Tuning Fork furnace, north of the 3rd House, looking E
Figure 3.32 Shears Furnace, looking northwest
Figure 3.33 Middle of the North Wall looking W. Building or enclosure wall?
Figure 3.34 The Northwest Wall looking approximately northeast
Figure 3.35 The eastern enclosure wall from the southeast corner
Figure 3.36 The piers for entrance gates to the enclosure through the east wall
Figure 3.37 Yewden during the 1st century AD
Figure 3.38 Yewden during the 2nd to early 3rd century
Figure 3.39 Yewden during the mid to end 3rd century
Figure 3.40 Yewden during the 4th century
Figure 4.1.1 Number of coins per 1000 from Yewden and comparative sites
Figure 4.2.1 Whetstones from the Yewden villa complex
Figure 4.2.2 A rotary quern, Millstone Grit
Figure 4.2.3 A rotary quern, Lodsworth Stone
Figure 4.2.4 A rotary quern, Millstone Grit
Figure 4.2.5 Rotary quern ST70, Quartz Conglomerate base and profile view
Figure 4.2.6 Rotary Quern ST78, Millstone Grit
Figure 4.2.7 Beehive quern, Hertfordshire Puddingstone
Figure 4.2.8 Oolitic limestone building stone, window surround
Figure 4.2.9 Concrete for keying in stone like window surrounds
Figure 4.2.10 Mortar, Burr Stone
Figure 4.2.11 Distribution of worked stone at Yewden
Figure 4.3.1 Palaeolithic hand axes
Figure 4.3.2 Mesolithic tools: (a) an adze (F.87) and (b) 3 bladelets (F.187)
Figure 4.3.3 Mesolithic-Neolithic tools: a scraper and a pick/chisel
Figure 4.3.4 A Mesolithic-Neolithic axe, elongate and rectangular
Figure 4.5.1 Distribution of iron styli at Yewden
Figure 4.5.2 Distribution of iron chisels, clamps, saws and other tools at Yewden
Figure 4.6.1 Glass artefacts from Yewden, window fragments and vessels
Figure 4.6.2 Glass vessels from Yewden
Figure 4.7.1: Finds distribution map of worked bone objects
Figure 4.7.2 The bone pins. Types 1 and 2 (scale 1:1)
Figure 4.7.3 The bone pins. Types 3 to 7 (scale 1:1)
Figure 4.7.4 Bone objects (scale 1:1)
Figure 4.7.5 Gaming counter
Figure 4.7.6 Decorated ornament, with incision top right for attachment
Figure 4.7.7 Double sided bone comb
Figure 4.7.8 Carved bone knife handle
Figure 4.8.1 Carved scarab beetle
Figure 4.8.2 The Yewden *Dea Nutrix*
Figure 4.8.3 Baldock *Dea Nutrix*
Figure 4.8.4 Venus head, front and rear view
Figure 4.8.5 Spindle whorl
Figure 4.8.6 Finds distribution map of spindle whorls
Figure 4.8.7 A Samian gaming counter
Figure 5.2.1 Distribution of the Oxford Colour coated pottery (F51) at Yewden
Figure 5.2.2 Distribution of the Nene Valley and 2nd century Oxford Colour Coated ware
Figure 5.2.3 Distribution of the Verulamium and the Oxford white mortaria at Yewden
Figure 5.2.4 Distribution of the shelly ware C11 and C13
Figure 5.3.1 Proportion of each of the main Samian source areas
Figure 5.3.2 Average percentage loss of Samian
Figure 5.3.3 Forms from La Graufesenque (as percent of total rim EVEs)
Figure 5.3.4 Forms from Les Martres-de-Veyre (as percent of total rim EVEs)
Figure 5.3.5 Forms from Lezoux (as percent of total rim EVEs)
Figure 5.3.6 Forms from East Gaul (Rheinzabern & undifferentiated) as % rim EVEs

Figure 5.3.7 Percent of plain and decorated Samian for each of the three source areas
Figure 5.3.8 Finds plot of the South Gaulish (La Graufesenque) Samian pottery, Yewden
Figure 5.3.9 Finds plot of Les Martres-de-Veyres Samian pottery across Yewden.
Figure 5.3.10 Finds plot of Lezoux Samian pottery across Yewden.
Figure 5.3.11 Finds plot of East Gaulish Samian pottery across Yewden.
Figure 5.5.1 Iron Age pottery from Yewden
Figure 5.5.2 Distribution of Iron Age pottery from the Yewden complex and surrounds
Figure 5.4.1 Stamps of Privatus iii (left) and Albucius ii (right).
Figure 5.4.2 Stamp of Peculiaris
Figure 5.4.3 (a) Mould mark, in reverse (P.7) REP on decorated sherd; (b) illiterate stamp (P.11); (c) Lezoux potter BIGA (P.1265); (d) Aeternus (P.1773).
Figure 5.4.4 Makers marks from Yewden villa Samian pottery
Figure 5.5.1 Dr 37 bowl, restored. Paternus Group, Lezoux.
Figure 5.5.2 Dr37 bowl restored. Lezoux, Trajan-Hadrian
Figure 5.5.3 (a) to (e) La Graufesenque
Figure 5.5.4 (a) to (d) Les Martres-de-Veyre
Figure 5.5.5 (a) Lezoux
Figure 5.6.1 Eutectic temperatures of the Lead alloys of Tin, Antimony and Bismuth
Figure 5.6.2 Spirit lamp and blowpipe arrangement used for small pottery repairs
Figure 5.6.3 Hole and clamp repair on Yewden Samian sherd 1994.57.P.1391. A Dr37 decorated bowl from La Graufesenque
Figure 5.6.4 A possible *in situ* method of casting a staple during pottery repair.
Figure 5.6.5 The completed repair after casting and surface finishing (plain riveted holes)
Figure 5.6.6 The completed repair after casting and surface finishing (countersunk)
Figure 5.6.7 A basic hole and clamp repair, the staple legs are bent double and hammered
Figure 5.6.8 Single mortise and tenon repair Yewden villa Samian ware sherd
Figure 5.6.9 Double mortise and tenon repair
Figure 5.6.10 Initial stages of terracotta pot repair preparation and replication
Figure 5.6.11 Preparation of clay moulds prior to metal pouring
Figure 5.6.12 Metal casting and the removal of clay moulds
Figure 5.6.13 Repair finishing by filing to the exterior contours of the vessel
Figure 5.6.14 Preparation of moulds for the casting of lead dowel
Figure 5.6.15 Casting of lead dowel
Figure 5.6.16 Open mould casting of lead dowel
Figure 5.6.17 A staple that clamps the cracked/broken parts of a vessel together
Figure 5.6.18 The hole and clamp method showing both the internal and external feature of the repair method
Figure 5.6.19 A summary of the pottery repair stages and processes employed in the replication of Roman pottery repair techniques
Figure 6.1 Distribution of gestational ages at death of the Hambleden perinatal infants (N=32) aged from long-bone lengths using the Scheuer et al. (1980) BCH equations
Figure 6.2 Burial 38 posterior surface of the subtrochanteric region of the right femur showing cut-marks and two examples of their cross-sections generated from the μCT scan
Figure 8.1 Map of the roads and tracks linking Yewden to the Thames and wider landscape
Figure 8.2 Reconstruction of the view to the field west of Yewden villa with temple
Figure 8.3 Distribution plot of the infant burials
Figure 8.4 Reconstruction of the Yewden villa complex looking northwest
Figure 8.5 Reconstruction of the Yewden villa complex looking southeast

List of Tables
Table 4.1.1 Number of coins per Reece period from Yewden villa
Table 4.1.2 Number of coins per 1000 from comparative sites
Table 4.2.1 Fragment count and lithology of worked stone objects fro Yewden villa
Table 4.2.2 Types of worked stone objects found at Yewden and the range of lithologies.

Table 4.3.1 Worked flint items for each chronological division from the Palaeolithic to the Bronze Age
Table 4.6.1 Analysis of glass by type
Table 4.6.2 Analysis of glass by colour
Table 5.2.1 Total quantity of pottery at Yewden Villa, Hambleden as major categories
Table 5.2.2 Fine ware – fabric quantities by sherd count, weight and EVEs
Table 5.2.3 Mortaria fabric quantities by sherd count, weight and EVEs
Table 5.2.4 White ware fabric quantities by sherd count, weight and EVEs.
Table 5.2.5 White slipped ware (not mortaria) fabric quantities by sherd, wt and EVEs
Table 5.2.6 Oxidised ware fabric quantities by sherd count, weight and EVEs
Table 5.2.7 Reduced ware fabric quantities by sherd count, weight and EVEs
Table 5.2.8 Calcareous tempered fabric quantity by sherd count, weight & EVEs
Table 5.2.9 Early Roman-late Iron Age 'Belgic' fabric quantities by sherd count, weight and EVEs
Table 5.3.1 Samian statistics: sherd count, weight, minimum vessels, EVEs
Table 5.3.2 Samian statistics as percentages of the whole Samian assemblage
Table 5.3.3 Yewden Samian ware as functional categories displayed by source area
Table 5.3.4 An assessment of post-depositional processes affecting the Yewden Samian assemblage.
Table 5.3.5 Comparison of overall relative frequency of the different Samian functional categories at different types of Romano-British sites.
Table 5.3.6 Comparative sites with recorded Samian assemblages
Table 5.6.1 The relative melting points of some pure base metals
Table 5.6.2 Eutectic characteristics of various lead alloys
Table 6.1 Osteological data for perinatal skeletons
Table 6.2 Diaphyseal long-bone lengths for perinatal burials
Table 7.2.1 Charred grain samples from Yewden villa

Contributors

The contributors to this volume are:

Jill Eyers (Chiltern Archaeology) 13 Pusey Way, Lane End, Bucks, HP14 3LG
Gwladys Monteil (University of Nottingham)
Gill Campbell (English Heritage) Fort Cumberland, Portsmouth, PO4 9LD
Simon Mays (English Heritage) Fort Cumberland, Portsmouth, PO4 9LD
Stephanie Vincent (English Heritage) Fort Cumberland, Portsmouth, PO4 9LD
David Dungworth (English Heritage) Fort Cumberland, Portsmouth, PO4 9LD
Jonathon Dicks, 40 Links Lane, Rowlands Castle, Hampshire, PO9 6AE
Brian Gilmour, 20 Squitchey Lane, Summertown, Oxford, OX2 7LB
Sandie Williams, 84 Hithercroft Road, Downley, Bucks
Brett Thorn, Keeper of Archaeology, Buckinghamshire County Museum Resource Centre, Tring Road, Halton, Bucks, HP22 5PN.
Alison Jewsbury, Little Orchard, Loudhams Wood Lane, Chalfont St Giles, Bucks, HP8 4AR
Alice Roberts, NHS Severn Deanery School of Surgery & Department of Archaeology & Anthropology, University of Bristol.
Kate Robson-Brown, Dept of Archaeology & Anthropology, University of Bristol.
Rick Magaldi, 7 Malham Gardens, Hatch Warren, Basingstoke, Hampshire, RG22 4XG
Raihana Elsanullah c/o Chiltern Archaeology

Acknowledgements

Funding was crucial to the success of this project, and indeed could not even have been contemplated without the assistance of the start-up funds received from the Wycombe District Council's Community Support Grant, followed by the major funding by the Heritage Lottery, and finally assistance for the monograph printing from the Chilterns Conservation Board.

However, no amount of funding could have paid for the enthusiastic contributions of the volunteer team. Field teams were out in all weather and during the surveys we encountered drought, floods, searing heat and arctic cold and some very memorable thunder and lightening. The team undertook what can only be described as 'extreme archaeology' where surveys took us into streams, over barbed wire fences, through nettles and fields of rape-seed stems, cows that knocked down marking poles, plus the memorable freshly manured field! It is a sign of a crack team to get through the obstacles, get good results, and come back the next week. Fieldwork skills were greatly enhanced by magnetometer training provided by English Heritage via Andy Payne and we are grateful for the loan of equipment and advice offered for our continued surveys. BARG under the leadership of Andrew Hutt assisted in magnetometer work as well as final processing of the data.

Not all the team activity was in the field, there was significant input into finds ID, photography, drawing and computerization. Special thanks are due to Alison Jewsbury for her talented input to computerized villa reconstructions and base maps, to John Clutterbuck for exceptionally efficient proof-reading throughout the volume, and also to Judy Barber for skilled research and organizing as well as providing space for volunteer pottery groups.

There were several experts who helped at various times with advice and methods suitable for the project. Special thanks are due to Paul Booth who helped us set up the pottery type series and to Gwladys Monteil whose excellent training opened up the wonderful world of Samian pottery for us. Also assisting with advice at crucial moments: Gary Lock, Sandy Kidd, Chris Welch, Felicity Wild, Kevin Hayward, Dominique de Moulins, Martin Henig and Jon Cotton. We are grateful to Brett Thorn (Keeper of Archaeology, BCM) for continued access to the museum collections throughout the project.

The landowners: The Hon A, B, L and N Smith (Hambleden Side Estate) and Mr Schwarzenbach (Culdenfaw Estate), as well as the tenant farmer Oliver Bowden, were very helpful and gave us the flexible access we needed to complete a variety of tasks in the fields and woods of the Hambleden Valley.

Last, but not least, we are grateful to WHS Archives for permission to reproduce the 1912 archive photographs of the excavation.

Preface

The monograph presented here covers fieldwork undertaken during 2008 to 2010 in the Hambleden Valley by Chiltern Archaeology, as well as an evaluation of the finds from the 1912 excavation of the Yewden villa complex undertaken by Mr A. H. Cocks.

The Roman site of Yewden villa was brought to the attention of Mr Cocks during 1911 by a local resident, Miss Glassbrook. Miss Glassbrook had found significant pieces of Roman pottery and tile in Hog Pit Field, Hambleden and took them to the Buckinghamshire County Museum in Aylesbury. Mr Cocks was the curator of the museum and became very interested in these finds. His assessment of the site was that it "contained extensive foundations with Roman tiles, mosaic flooring, Samian and other pottery". Realising the potential importance of such a site to archaeological knowledge, he secured funding for an excavation from the landowner, the Hon. W. F. D. Smith. This funding was substantial enough to pay for a full workforce to excavate the site and much post-excavation work. During the period of this one year Mr Cocks employed a number of local workmen to act as labourers and he put them under the supervision of Mr A.G.K. Haytor and Dr A.E. Peake, who divided the supervision into two 6 month sessions, with Mr Cocks in overall charge. There were also sufficient funds to pay for a potter to restore many vessels and also to pay for a team of experts who identified and interpreted the selected categories of finds. Funding was finally secured from the same source to build a museum in Hambleden and to keep it open to the public for many years. The museum housed a selection of the 'special' artefacts. However, the vast majority of the bulk material from the excavation was simply placed into boxes and stored, with no identification, sorting or interpretation. This project re-investigated the museum artefacts and then sorted, identified, labelled and interpreted the vast quantity of finds that had not been touched by Cocks' team. This amounted to many hundreds of boxes and they have provided a valuable resource to inform us much more about life (and death) in Roman Hambleden.

During the 1912 excavation Yewden villa was completely excavated up to the enclosing wall of the complex and also beyond this 'enclosure wall' northwards across a yard to a second, older set of walls. All finds were collected from this area, even the smallest. These artefacts were labelled with the date and their location on the site, and some were also annotated with their depth. This information was valuable to the current project – the details of which were entered onto several databases. The extensive databases have allowed a sequence of finds plots to be produced both horizontally and vertically, hence allowing a stratigraphic interpretation to be introduced to the site almost 100 years after the excavation took place. Although no notebooks or other original written records of the excavation have been located, there is much information in Cocks' 1921 report, as well as numerous notes accompanying the finds boxes or on the finds themselves, and also a high quality, significant photograph collection in the BCM archive. (The photographs were taken during the process of the 1912 excavation by Mr T.P. Barlow of Henley).

The information within this monograph uses all the available archive information (the 1912 report, photographs and finds) along with finds on the PAS database from recent years, and from the Chiltern Archaeology team field walking of 2008-2009. This information was assessed in the light of new knowledge and investigative techniques and full identifications of all the artefacts (not just the Hambleden Museum and

Archaeologia report specimens). This amounted to a massive task which became beyond the reach of the limited budget. Some finds categories have been worked on to a high standard (e.g. Samian pottery, iron, copper alloy, human bone) while others were not attempted in detail due to a lack of funds (amphora, black burnished ware, CBM, and animal bone), although they have been separated, partly identified, and quantified. For a full account see the section on 'Potential for future research'.

A short biography of the two key players in the 1912 excavations:

Mr Alfred Heneage Cocks FSA

Mr Cocks' family line emanates from two distinguished families, the Cocks and the Somers. The Cocks family moved to Eastnor at the end of the 16th century. They bought the Manor of Castleditch and over the following 200 years gradually gained further land in the area. The Cocks' married into the Worcester Somers' family and it was the combination of their estates – including the valuable inheritance left by Lord Chancellor Somers in the early 18th century and the banking wealth of the Cocks Biddulph Bank (now incorporated into Barclays Bank) - that gave the 1st Earl Somers the finances to begin reconstruction of Eastnor in 1810. His cause was also aided by a judicious marriage to the daughter of the eminent and wealthy Worcestershire historian Dr Treadaway Nash.

Alfred Heneage Cocks as a boy of about 14 years

Alfred's father, Thomas Somers Cocks, was a banker and a J.P. Alfred was born in Great Marlow and the family home during Alfred's formative years was Thames Bank in Marlow (now called Thames Lawn). Alfred went to Eton in 1864, leaving two years later at which point he had private tuition until attending Christ Church, Oxford in 1869, where he was seen to have a strong natural history bent. This could be seen by the many notes contained in the 1912 archive boxes which refer to him acquiring recently dead animals for stuffing – many of them currently held in the BCM. It is also clear that he kept many unusual animals as pets including eagle owls, wild cats, otters, badgers, and many other animals including a herd of White Chartley cattle. There is a family story that Alfred kept a pet seal in the bath, which was allowed to swim in the river at Thames Bank. It is said that on one occasion he put it in a sink in the housemaid's pantry while the family attended church. Unfortunately, the animal managed to turn on the tap so that, on their return, the family were greeted by a small waterfall coming down the stairs! In 1891 Alfred Cocks is described on the census as being 39 years old, living alone in Thames Bank, Marlow with two servants. He is recorded as the son of the house, born in London, and living on his own means.

Alfred later moved to Poynett's in Skirmett, which is north of Hambleden. One of his many interests was church bells and his monumental work *The Church Bells of Buckinghamshire* was published in 1897 (Figure ii). Alfred became an active member of the Buckinghamshire Archaeological Society from 1890 becoming Honorary Secretary by 1893, remaining as Secretary and curator to the museum for 16 years. He resigned in 1908 due to a 'difference of opinion with the executive' (Records of Bucks, Obituary). In his obituary there is more than a sense of Alfred not mingling with people in general, rather a loner, a hard worker, but without the ability to take criticism, noted as being "someone who would not gladly tolerate opinions which differed from his own."

In later years he was considered rather eccentric; for example, he used to sleep with a device rigged up so that if an intruder opened his bedroom door at night a shotgun would automatically be discharged. Fortunately for all concerned this never happened.

Alfred with a group of bell ringers from the Great Marlow Belfry 1899

Miss Janet Glassbrook

Miss Glassbrook was born in 1870 in Wigton, Cumberland, the daughter of George and Janet Glassbrook, both from Scotland. George was a farm bailiff, first in Wigton and then in Milton Abbas, Dorset. By 1891 George and Janet had moved into Yewden Farm, Hambleden, where a job of farm bailiff was found, but their daughter was not on this census. However, she appears on the 1901 census as single, aged 30, living with her newly widowed mother (of independent means) in one of the Yewden cottages. She remained in this five bedroomed cottage throughout her life, which was later re-named Janet's cottage.

Her part in the 1912 excavations was vital. It was within a gravel pit on the Skirmett Road between Mill End and Hambleden that Miss Glassbrook observed a V-shaped ditch. The ditch was completely infilled and within the fill Roman, 'Celtic' and Iron Age pottery was visible. Collecting some of this pottery was the first step in many walks across the fields of Hambleden. Many of the museum finds boxes contain items labelled 'Miss G' and they date between 1911 to 1914. In addition to the pottery that she collected and brought to the attention of Mr Cocks (it appears through Mr and Mrs E Payton at first), she also accumulated a substantial collection of flint tools.

Miss Glassbrook, trowel in hand, at the V ditch within the gravel pit 1912

Present residents report their memories of Miss Glassbrook as being a very stern lady who was active in the community. She played a role within the church where it is reported that she frightened many a child she was in charge of. As she became older, and could not leave the house, it became a tradition for children to be summoned to her cottage for tea on Sunday afternoon. Janet Glassbrook remained a spinster, understandable after the First World War. When asking a local resident about this aspect of her life there came the response " do not worry about Miss Glassbrook, she had a good life – her last days were spent very happily walking her many dogs, placing bets on many horses and drinking many bottles of whisky"! She would have made an excellent archaeologist.

Acknowledgement: many thanks for information on Mr Cocks and Miss Glassbrook from Mrs Jane Somers Cocks and Ms Pam Knight.

Chapter 1: Introduction and context of the project

1.1 Introduction and context of project

The project was planned as two phases. Phase I was completed September 2008 and a report printed and distributed during October 2008 (Eyers, 2008). Phase I involved a desk-based study, an extensive resistance survey, limited field walking and metal detecting surveys, and the commencement of the assessment of the 1912 excavation finds from Yewden Villa, which are housed at the Buckinghamshire County Museum.

Also undertaken during this time was a variety of workshops and field training events for the volunteer workforce (numbering over 200 by the end of the year) with funding provided from the Heritage Lottery Fund. A pottery type series for the Yewden Romano-British pottery was set up with assistance from Paul Booth (Oxford Archaeology) and this system was in use throughout the pottery assessment. A database was also designed and set up in collaboration with the BCM to record finds both newly acquired and from the 1912 excavation collection.

The findings that emerged from Phase I proved that there is extensive archaeology in the valley, which is multi-phase and undoubtedly includes many Romano-British and Iron Age structures and field boundaries. The evidence suggested that the Romano-British archaeology included agricultural practice, habitation, industrial activities and religion. Specifically the results clarified the following points:

- The geographical extent for archaeological features, including the relationships between some, were established from the wide variety of techniques used.
- A more detailed layout of the Mill End villa structure (adjacent to the River Thames) was achieved by resistance surveying. Resolution was good enough to show the position of roof support posts and the presence of a hard floor (potentially mosaic), and confirming the villa boundary ditch. However, disturbed ground causing faint images in parts of the villa layout means that these results could be improved by further work using different techniques.
- The Yewden villa complex was precisely located with grid coordinates and the archaeology was proved to extend beyond the 2008 surveyed area.
- A variety of features were shown by resistance to occur in Horseleys field, east of the Yewden complex, where a number of field boundaries intersect with the Romano-British track leading past Yewden. Also, several discrete structures were proved and these are highly worthy of further investigation.
- Archive photographs allowed an approach to phasing of the Yewden buildings in the images, notably building phases for the '1st House'.

The questions that were then addressed in Phase II and (with Phase I results) are reported in this monograph were:
- What date was Mill End villa built and occupied?
- What status is Mill End villa and are there similarities in building construction and artefact types to Yewden?
- What was the prime function of Mill End villa (e.g. agricultural or linked to river transportation and trade, or other?)
- Considering the close proximity of Mill End and Yewden, what is the link between the two villas?

- Were the villas and the archaeology present in the other fields active at the same time, or during what periods?
- What is the relative building order, or precise dating where possible, for each of the building phases seen at Yewden?
- What activities were being carried out at Yewden in terms of types of agriculture and industry, and what is the likely size of the household?
- Are all the 97 Yewden infant skeletons newborn, what is the ratio of male to female, what information is there on cultural background from aDNA, and what inferences might be made from this information?
- What is the nature and date of the 'tanning pit' in Horseleys Field?
- What is the nature of the double square feature in Middle Couch/Horseleys Field (Romano-Celtic temple, malting area, or other?)
- What are the relationships and the dates of the field boundaries (ditches) determined by the geophysics?
- Are there structures (habitation or workshops) along the E-W gravel track alongside the Yewden villa complex, as indicated by finds and crop marks, but not seen by resistance methods? If so, what are their dates and for what purpose were they built?
- Can environmental evidence be gained from excavation that might yield information on industrial and agricultural activities, as well as the area's natural landscape character (e.g. wooded, grassland, etc)?

This monograph will address all of these points, except those relating to Mill End villa which is to be the subject of a future paper.

1.2 Site location

Hambleden is a small Buckinghamshire village located in the Chiltern Hills, just north of the River Thames between the towns of Henley and Marlow (Figure 1.1). It lies in a dry valley of the Chilterns, the sinuous nature of which is marked by the Hamble Brook (Figure 1.2). The valley lies within the Chilterns Area of Natural Beauty and is within Green Belt. There are two Roman sites within the valley (Fig. 1.3) and these are in an unusually close proximity. Five zones within the project area are scheduled (Figure 1.4). The project location centre grid reference is SU 785 856, and extended N-S from the Thames to the village of Hambleden and included the surrounding hilltop woodland.

1.3 Geology, topography and present land use

The Hambleden Valley is cut into Middle and Upper Chalk (the Lewes Nodular Chalk, the Seaford and the Newhaven Chalk Formations, undifferentiated). This has provided the source for some of the building materials on site. The Thames Valley has cut down into the southernmost section (the river cutting through approximately E-W here) with the Hamble Brook occupying a N-S orientated dry valley which was cut during the Quaternary. The highest points are the hill tops flanking the valley at up to 115 mOD and the lowest points are the valleys from 45 mOD in the dry valley to 32 mOD on the banks

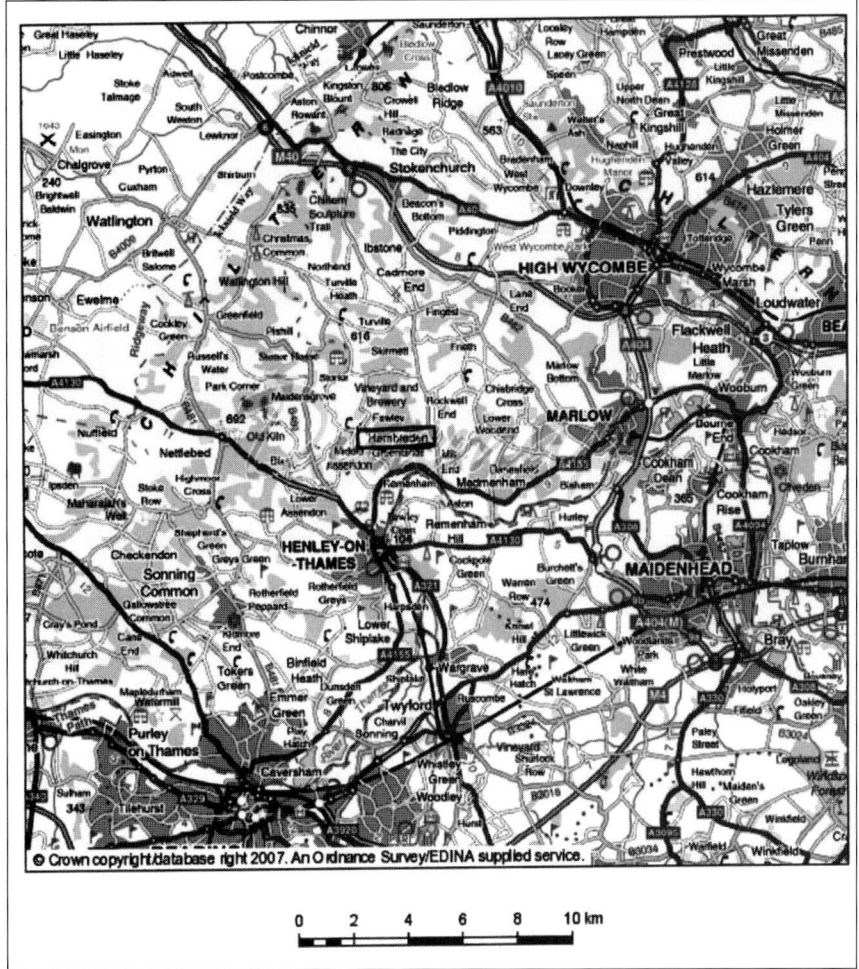

Figure 1.1 The location of Hambleden, Buckinghamshire between the towns of Henley and Marlow and in close proximity to the River Thames.

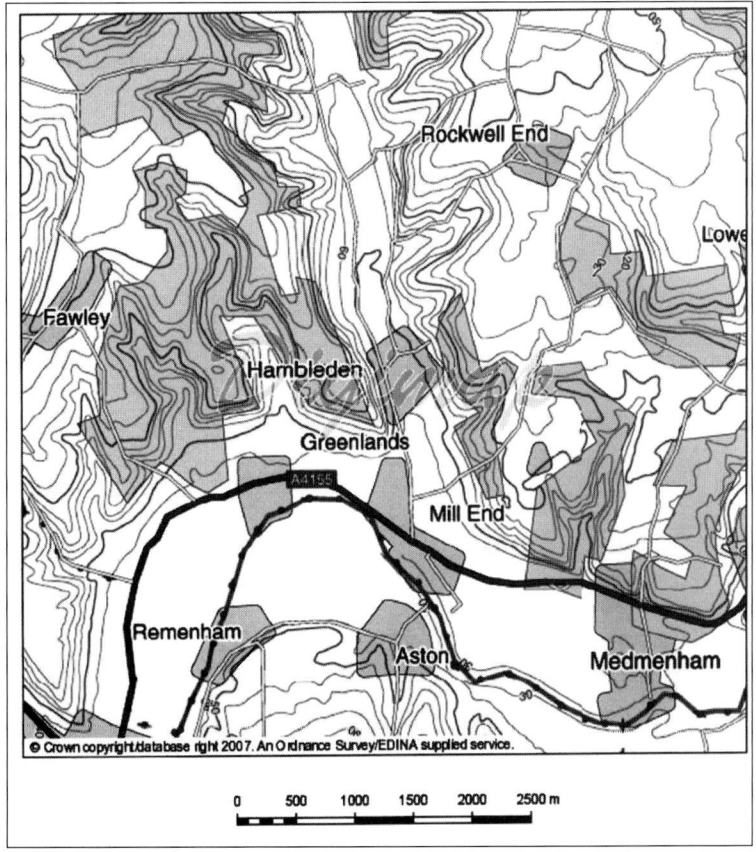

Figure 1.2 The Hambleden valley – a Chilterns dry valley which provides the landscape that has ensured human activity from the Palaeolithic to the present-day. The natural landscape has a major river (the Thames), a small spring-fed stream (the Hamble Brook) which floods to give a rich water meadow, fertile fields with the surrounding hills offering woodland and chalkland grazing. There are also a number of other natural springs along the length of the valley.

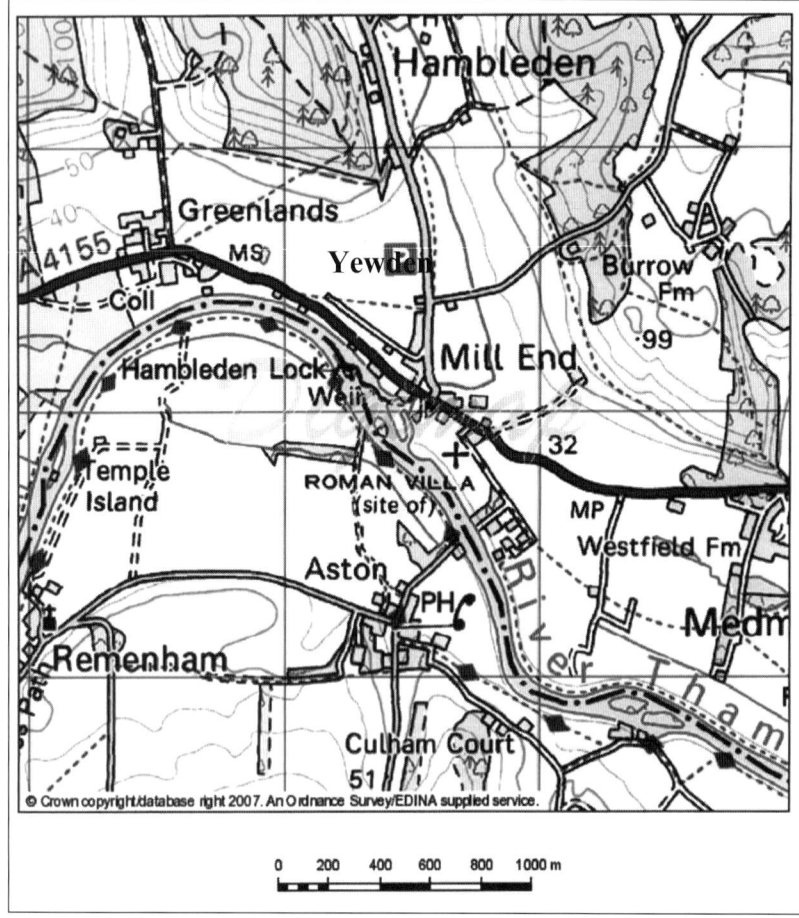

Figure 1.3 The location of the two Roman villas: Yewden (excavated by Cocks, 1921) in the area of the car park (P), and Mill End villa (marked with +)
Both are located on the north side of the River Thames in Bucks.

of the Thames. Superficial deposits are variable. The dry valley has a layer of head (slope deposits) with patchy gravels. The Thames Valley section changes from head to a mix of clay, silt, sands and gravels to the alluvium of the river floodplain. On the hill tops, such as on Ridge Wood on the west side of the valley, there is the sandy gravel of the Beaconsfield gravels. On the eastern hilltops there is the Gerrards Cross Gravels – both deposits of the ancient Thames.

The area is predominantly agricultural, being divided between two estates. Farming is mixed arable on the lower slopes to grazing (mostly dairy cattle, with some sheep) on the valley bottom. The stream has been prone to flooding the pastures in the past, but in recent years is prone to drying up. The stream was diverted from its original position during the mid-1860s as part of the enclosures and other boundary changes. The hill tops are wooded and maintained in parts for sustainable tree felling, in other parts for game rearing. Public footpaths provide access to many parts of the lower and upper valley.

1.4 Archaeological background

There are archaeological finds or features present from all eras in the Hambleden Valley, but the most numerous are from the Mesolithic, Neolithic and Romano-British Periods. This does not necessarily indicate the comparative level of activity in the valley, as this is also strongly influenced by recognition of the artefacts for each period. The Romano-British finds are numerous due to the Yewden villa excavation in 1912 and by the activities of metal detectorists in more recent years. The find spots for the Hambleden Valley area forming this study (south of the village to the River Thames) are shown in Figure 1.5, along with the scheduled areas.

In the Hambleden Parish only two **Palaeolithic** flakes have been recorded via PAS, both found in the stream bed. There are more prolific finds relating to **Mesolithic** activity – with 19 find spots of a variety of tools from tranchet axes to microburins, scrapers and cores. These are concentrated in the banks of, or close to, the river Thames and the Hamble Brook. Hence they may reflect 'visibility' of the finds. Work during this project has located many more finds falling into these eras (Chapter 4.3), which indicates a closer search with a trained team would be beneficial to our full understanding of this period.

There are numerous **Neolithic** artefacts (58 find spots with multiple objects in many of these records), which are very likely to be a true increase in activity during this period. They include axes, scrapers, cores and flakes and in a variety of locations, on hillsides and not solely close to the stream or River Thames.

In contrast, the **Bronze Age** finds are represented by only two reported items – a socketed axehead and a Palstave, both just north of Yewden. Similarly, the Iron Age is represented by only three finds – a bronze razor, 2 strap unions (near Yewden) and 'metalwork' in the Thames. However, there were two horse brasses sold at Sotherby's for £59,000 and £3,000 (Feacham, 1991) which date to the end of this period found at 'unknown locality in the Hambleden Valley'. There are likely to have been many more unreported metal finds from the valley.

The **Roman** archaeology is discussed in full in this monograph and is the subject of several subsequent papers (and Phase I is also summarized in Eyers, 2008). Hambleden is well-known for its two Romano-British villas. The famous Yewden villa was excavated in 1912 and a description and interpretation was written by the excavator A. H. Cocks (1921). During this work the villa was shown to be in use from the 1st to the 4th centuries. It is an intriguing site with a villa complex and surrounding boundary wall, tessellated pavements, bathroom suites, a well, 26 pits (interpreted as refuse pits), 14 furnaces (interpreted as corn-drying ovens), 97 infant burials, and a wealth of high status finds. Coins are numerous and include a hoard of 294 coins, at present being re-evaluated. Pottery is also abundant and includes plain and decorated Samian, Rhenish, New Forest, Oxford Colour Coat and Oxford fine and white wares, Belgic and much coarse pottery. Some of the finds are unusual such as the 70 styli indicating literacy and a recording role or manufacture of these items on site. More detailed information can be obtained from Cocks (1921) and a detailed assessment of the importance of this site within the Scheduling documentation (English Heritage SM27160).

A second villa at Mill End (Figures 1.3 and 1.4) is known by parch marks which appear in times of drought. They have been traced and interpreted by Farley (1983) and proved during the 2008 Phase I resistivity survey of Thames Field containing the villa (Fig. 1.4).

For the **Anglo-Saxon** period there is only one record of a potential barrow (outside the valley on the County boundary with Oxfordshire). The **Norman** period onwards is represented within the village of Hambleden itself (e.g. the church shows several periods from the Normans onwards). The **Medieval** period only boasts 3 find sites although one is a hoard - a beautiful collection of 59 annular brooches.

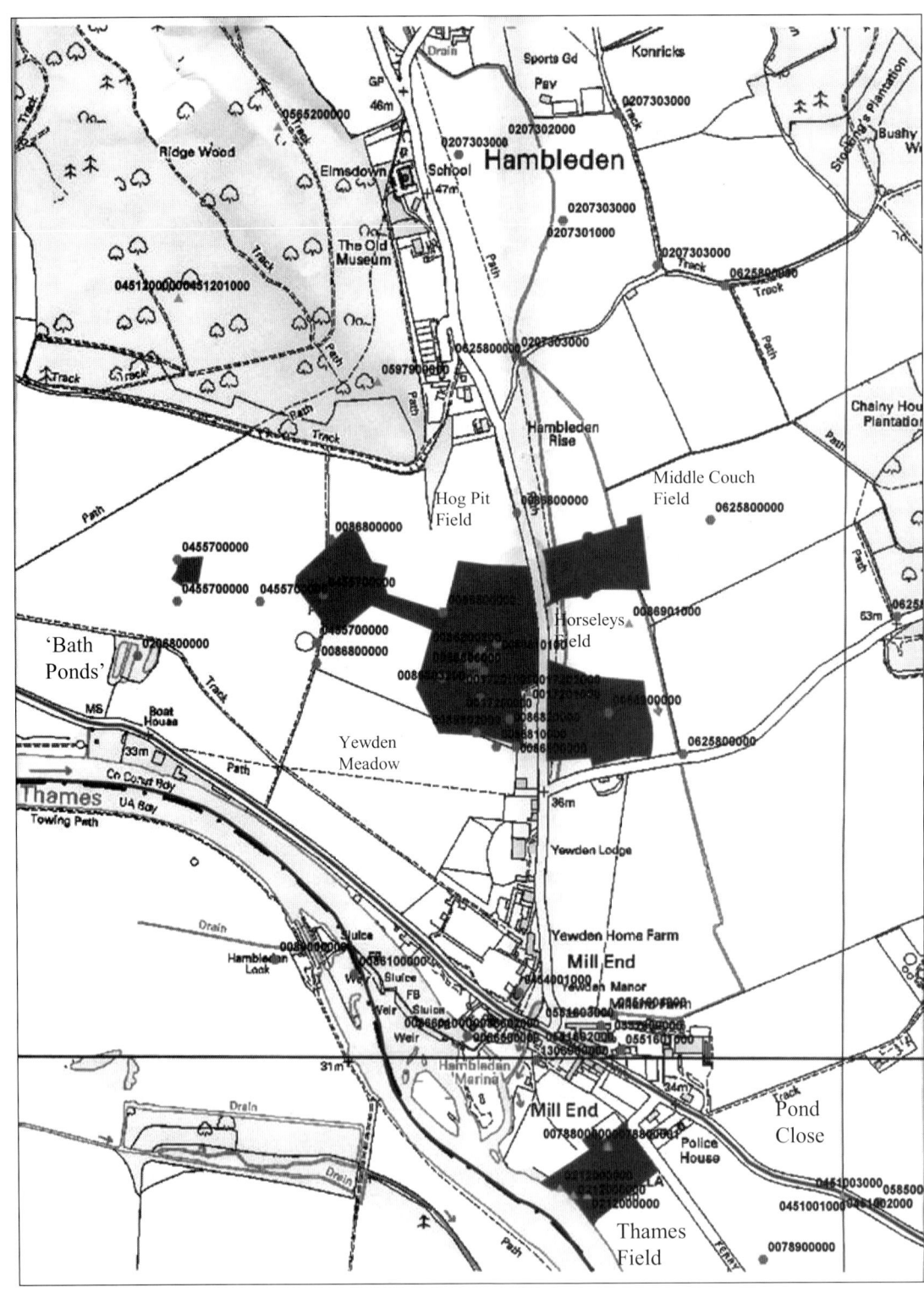

Figure 1.5 Find spots within the 1 km radius of SU 785 856. Triangles and spots = find spots and monuments; and the shaded blocks show the scheduled monument areas. © HER 2007.

Chapter 2: The fieldwork 2008-2010

2.1 Resistivity

All surveys conformed to English Heritage guidelines within: *Geophysical survey in archaeological field evaluation.* Research and Professional Services Guideline No. 1. The equipment used was a TR Systems resistance meter. The equipment was set to the following parameters:

- 20 m x 20 m grids
- Pitch 1.0 m
- Filter 1.5 s (semi-rural)
- Logging mode: automatic

Grids were merged within the TR System software package, and images were processed with the minimum of enhancement within the TR Systems software.

In addition to the normal resistance surveys, certain features were selected for a further survey to produce a 2D vertical profile and so determine the shape and depth of the feature, which is particularly useful for ditches. The kit involved a short traverse across the feature using the TR resistance meter and 20 probes. The resulting data was downloaded and processed in the 'Res2Dinv' program, supplied for the TR meter, and a profile obtained. The 20 probes used can image to a depth of about 3 m. This technique was employed for Ridge Wood and Mill End and reported in accompanying Chiltern Archaeology reports.

1. Hog Pit Field (the site of Yewden Villa Complex)

The resistance survey was undertaken in this field (Figs. 1.5 and 2.1 below) to locate the edge of the excavated site by Cocks in 1912 and to extend outwards from that point to assess further archaeology in the surrounding unexcavated area. The results are affected by noise produced by the rubble incorporated into the soil from the excavation (including large amounts of CBM and building stone such as chalk and flint) and by deep plough ridges. The weather dramatically changed during the survey from very dry to water saturated, which resulted in difficulties in balancing the results between grids. Resolution in some areas is faint, but the structure of solid features (such as Yewden villa) is nonetheless very clear.

Although continuing poor weather halted further surveying into the fields surrounding the Yewden villa complex during the time available, it can be determined from the resistance results and from aerial photographs that there appear to be no further structures or features such as pits and ditches in the immediate vicinity of the villa buildings. However, further into the surrounding fields there are features warranting closer investigation. For instance, the gravel track noted by Cocks during the 1912 excavation as running behind the outer wall of the 3rd House, continues in a northwesterly direction. From this a path diverts close to what appears to be a faint 7 m x 4 m structure. A second path leaves the edge of the annexe to the 3rd House, joined by a sideshoot from the 4th House. Path 2 continues northwest which would take it directly to a small building in the adjacent field tentatively recorded on the HER record as a temple*, but not yet surveyed at that time. This location is the precise spot where a pipeline traverses (shown by magnetometry Fig. 2.5). It is assumed the structure has now been destroyed.

[* A votive miniature axe head was found and reported by a metal detectorist *c.* 200 m N from the location of this building at SU 7809 8580 in August 2007, which is supportive evidence. Verbal evidence (M. Bird) of a statue resembling Harporates (the Roman equivalent of Horas, son of Isis) and metal detectorists have reportedly found a great number of coins in the vicinity.]

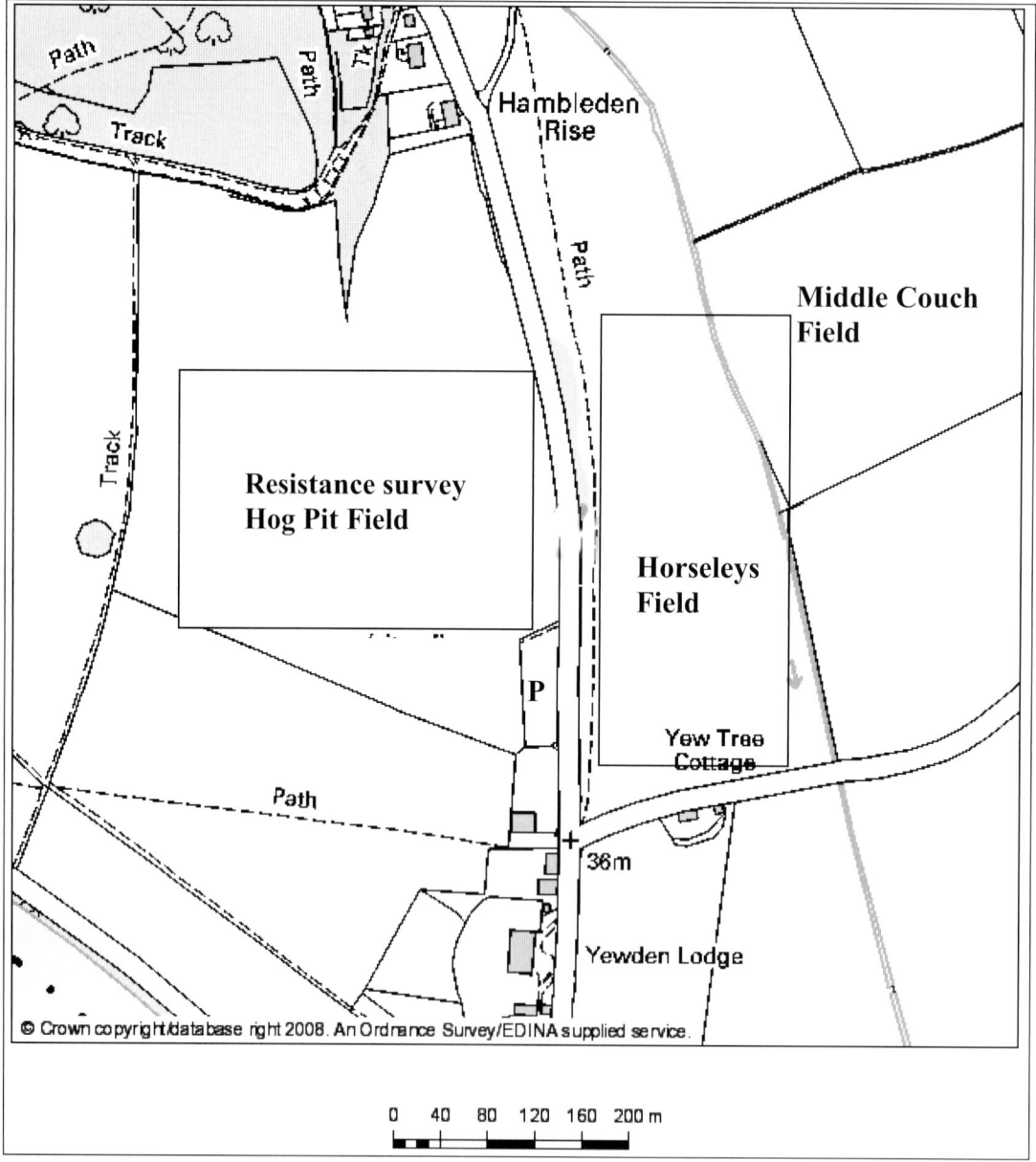

Figure 2.1 Resistance grids in the Hambleden Valley: Hog Pit Field, Horseleys Field and Middle Couch Field. P = car park.

The precise villa location was found during this initial work and further structures hinted at from these results. However, the quality of the results, due to the prevailing weather conditions and deep furrows in the field did not warrant extending the survey and the magnetometer was employed (Section 2.2 below). The interpretation of the resistance is combined with the magnetometry in Figure 2.6.

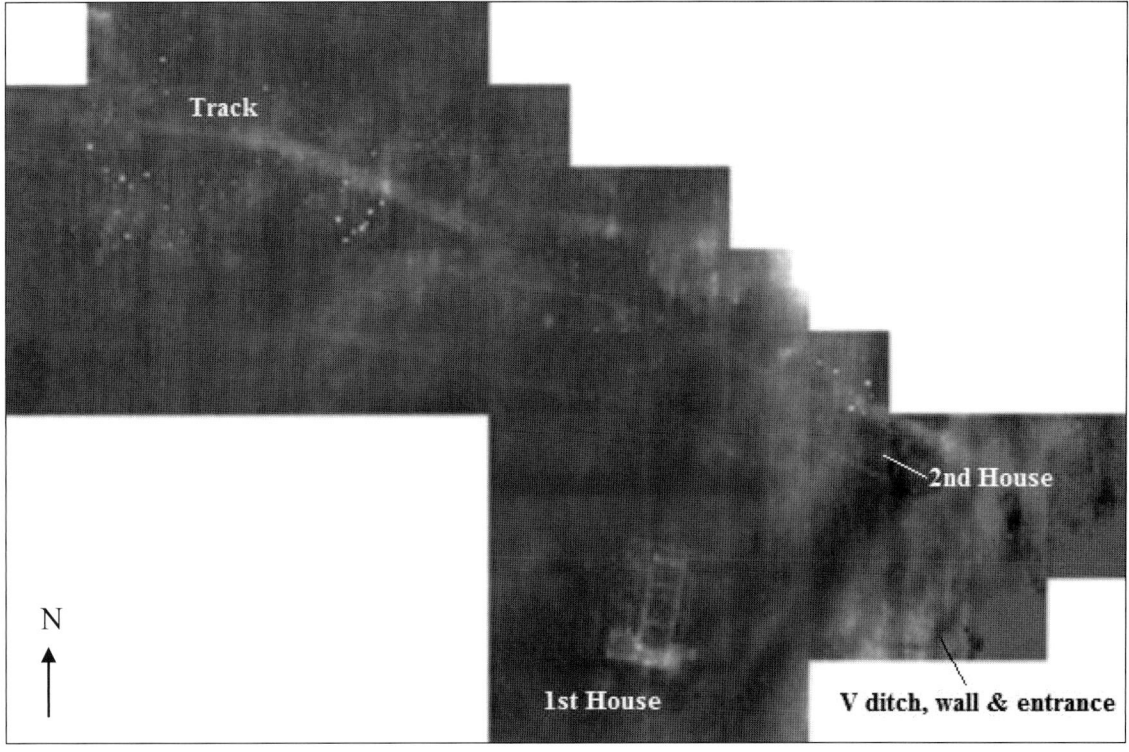

Figure 2.2 Resistance results for Hog Pit Field, Hambleden. See the site plan of Figure 3.1 to relate the 1st House to the whole site.

2. Horseleys Field

There were many features seen in this field representing a combination of field boundaries, enclosures, structures and pathways. The resistance results are shown in Figure 2.3 with an interpretive sketch in Figure 2.4. The double square feature at the north end of the site has been cut by the relocation of the stream (the Hamble Brook) during the mid-1800s. The edge of this building originally lay close to the edge or overhung the original stream. The shape is very characteristic of a Romano-Celtic temple. The outer section is a 44 m square and the inner one 34 m square. In this form of temple the inner square is usually the *cella* and the outer square is the edge of the portico. If this interpretation is correct then there are two interesting features to this building. Firstly, the *cella* has a circular 1.5 m diameter feature centrally placed with low resistance linears leading into it. It is suggested that this is drainage into a water feature or a well. There is also a second low resistance feature outside the east side of the building, also appearing to hold water – another well? The two potential wells or water features, with drainage channels, and with a building (portico) overhanging the stream makes this feature a perfect layout for worship of a water deity. However, there are no reported coins or other finds (although the site has clearly been metal detected. Fresh pits were seen whilst surveying was being undertaken). As this site has not been excavated, and it is within the scheduling, there are no artefacts to support an interpretation. Examples of similar temple layouts can be seen at Gosbecks Farm (Colchester), Carrawburgh (Northumbria) and Bourton Ground (Bucks). At Bourton Ground the temple had a timber facing with a rubble core. The large number of iron nails seen in the area disturbed around this site, and the style of building in the adjacent Yewden villa complex, would indicate that this structure was also likely to have been a timber frame over a mortared flint base.

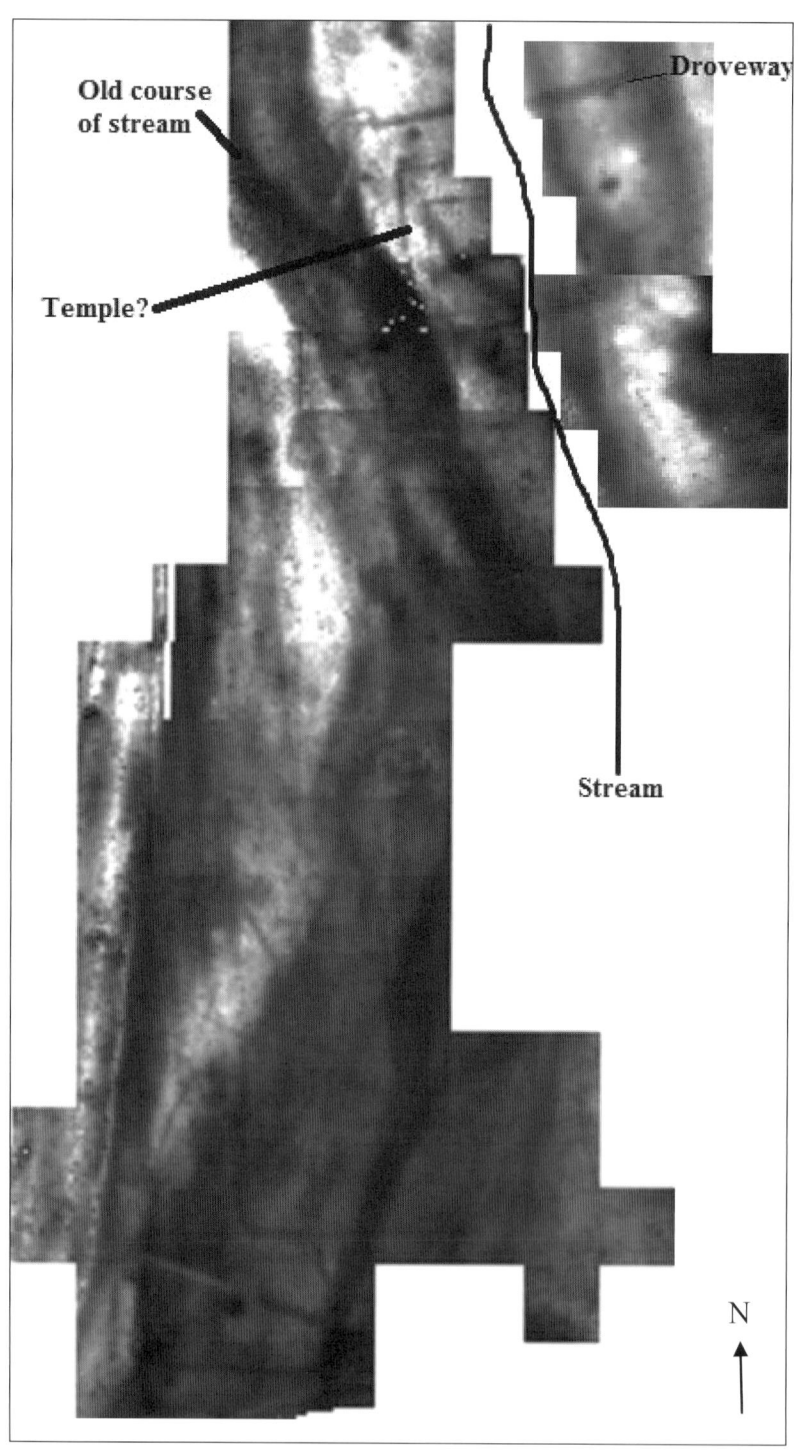

Figure 2.3 The resistance survey results for Horseleys Field and Middle Couch Field, Hambleden

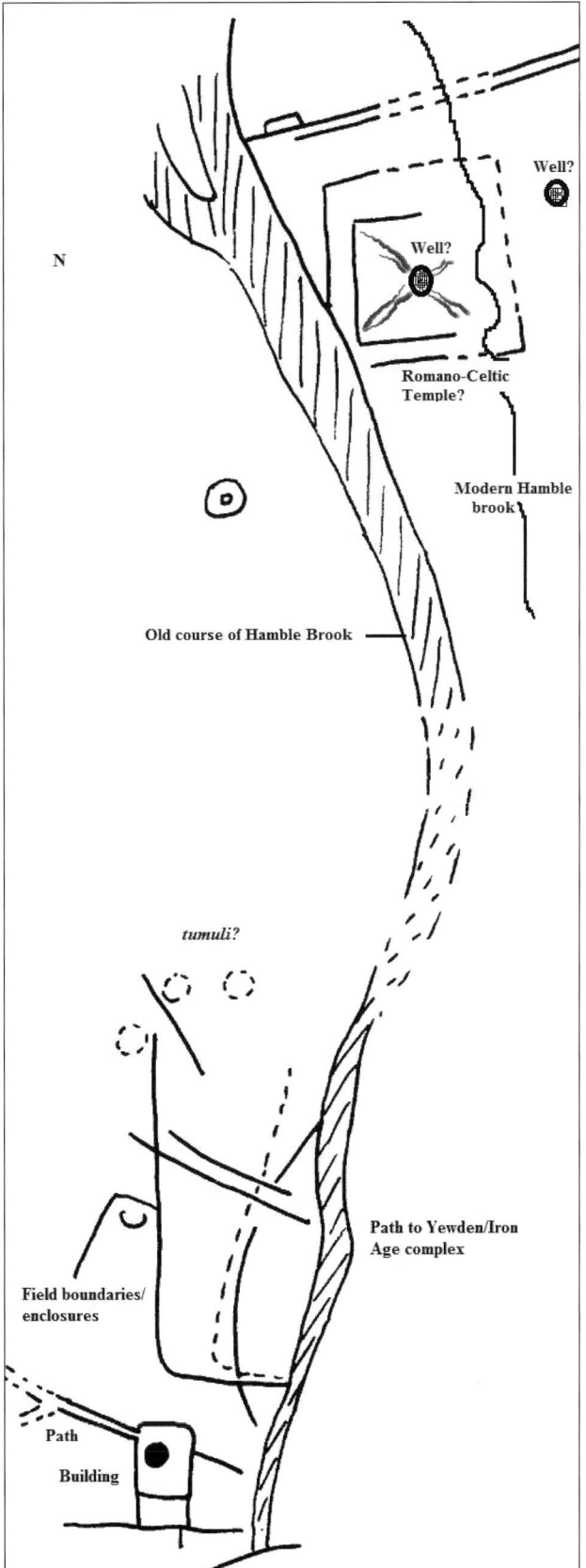

Figure 2.4 Sketch summary of important features shown by the resistance survey

Figure 2.5 Magnetometer results for Hog Pit Field and the field west of Hog Pit.

2.2 Magnetometry

The magnetometry was a collaborative survey with English Heritage (Horseleys Field), Chiltern Archaeology volunteer team (Hog Pit Field and Horseleys) and Berkshire Archaeological research Group (field west of Hog Pit). English Heritage and Chiltern Archaeology surveys were undertaken with fluxgate magnetometers (Geoscan) and BARG surveys used the Bartington 601 gradiometer. Horseleys field was processed by English Heritage (Payne 2010) using the Geoscan software (Geoplot). Due to incompatability problems with the Geoscan and Bartington datasets the surveys for Hog Pit and west of Hog Pit field were combined by Geoplot, and processed by Andrew Hutt of BARG using Snuffler.

The results are shown in Figs. 2.5 and 2.6 below. The two very high resistance spots in the east on Fig 2.5 are due to corrugated iron sheets put in place over wells by Mr Cocks.

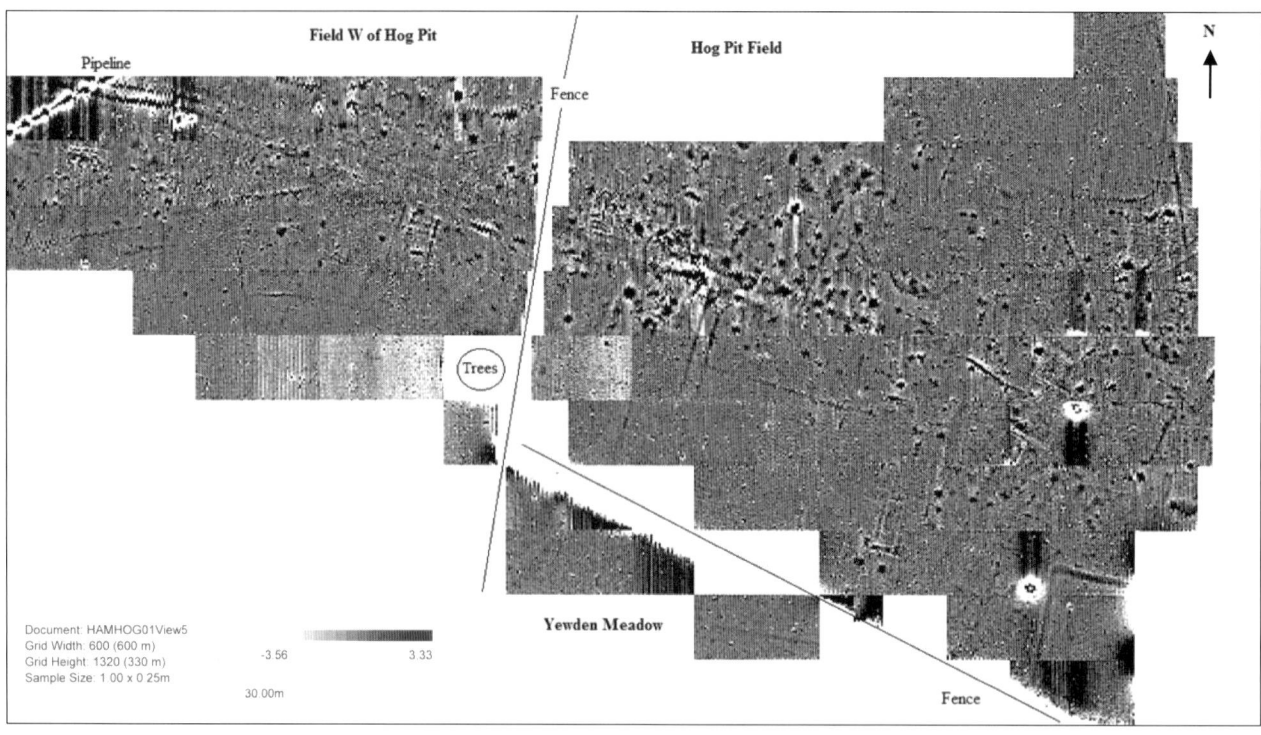

Figure 2.5 Magnetometer results for Hog Pit field and field west of Hog Pit.

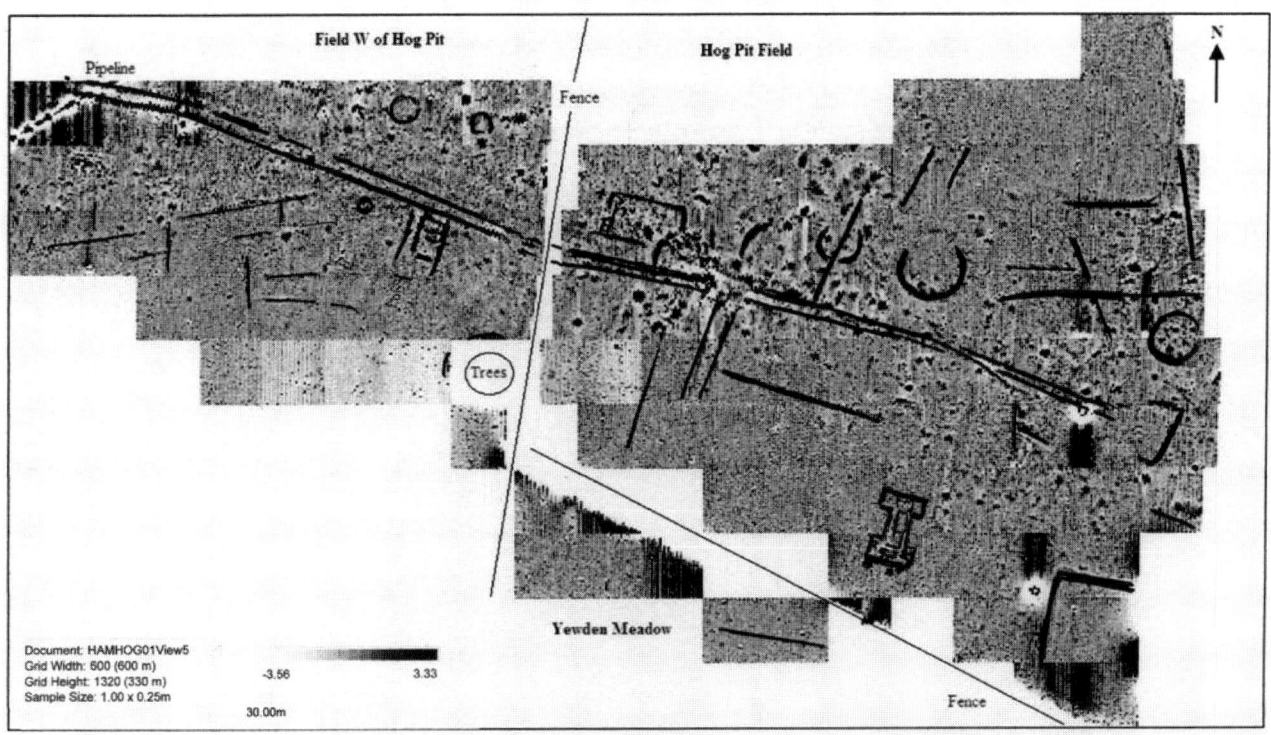

Figure 2.6 Interpretive summary of magnetometer results for the Hog Pit Field survey

2.2 Aerial photographs

There are a number of aerial photographs available from the National Monuments Record centre, Swindon. Figure 2.9 shows the villa and adjacent field archaeological features. The view shows Hog Pit Field (bottom right quarter, 1), Horseleys Field (the long field left of centre, 2) and Middle Couch Field (bottom left, 3).

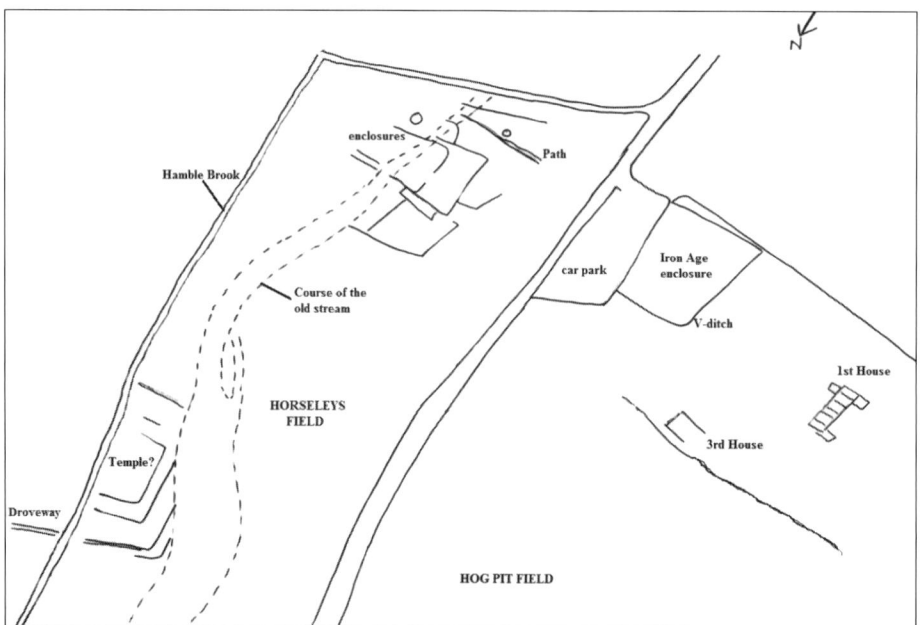

Figure 2.9 Aerial photograph and interpretaion of the fields around and containing the Yewden villa complex. Note that the view is to the southeast, and north is towards lower left. © English Heritage/NMR 2008, Photo ref. NMR4632.

2.4 Woodland surveys: Ridge Wood, Northcot Wood & Chalk Pit Wood

Three woodland surveys were carried out as part of the Your Heritage project. Ridge Wood (north of the Yewden villa complex) was surveyed in 2008 and Northcot Wood with Chalk Pit Wood (to the east of Yewden) was part of the 2009 programme. These reports have been written up in full (Eyers, 2009 and 2010) and can be obtained from Chiltern Archaeology or Bucks HER offices. A summary of points is included here.

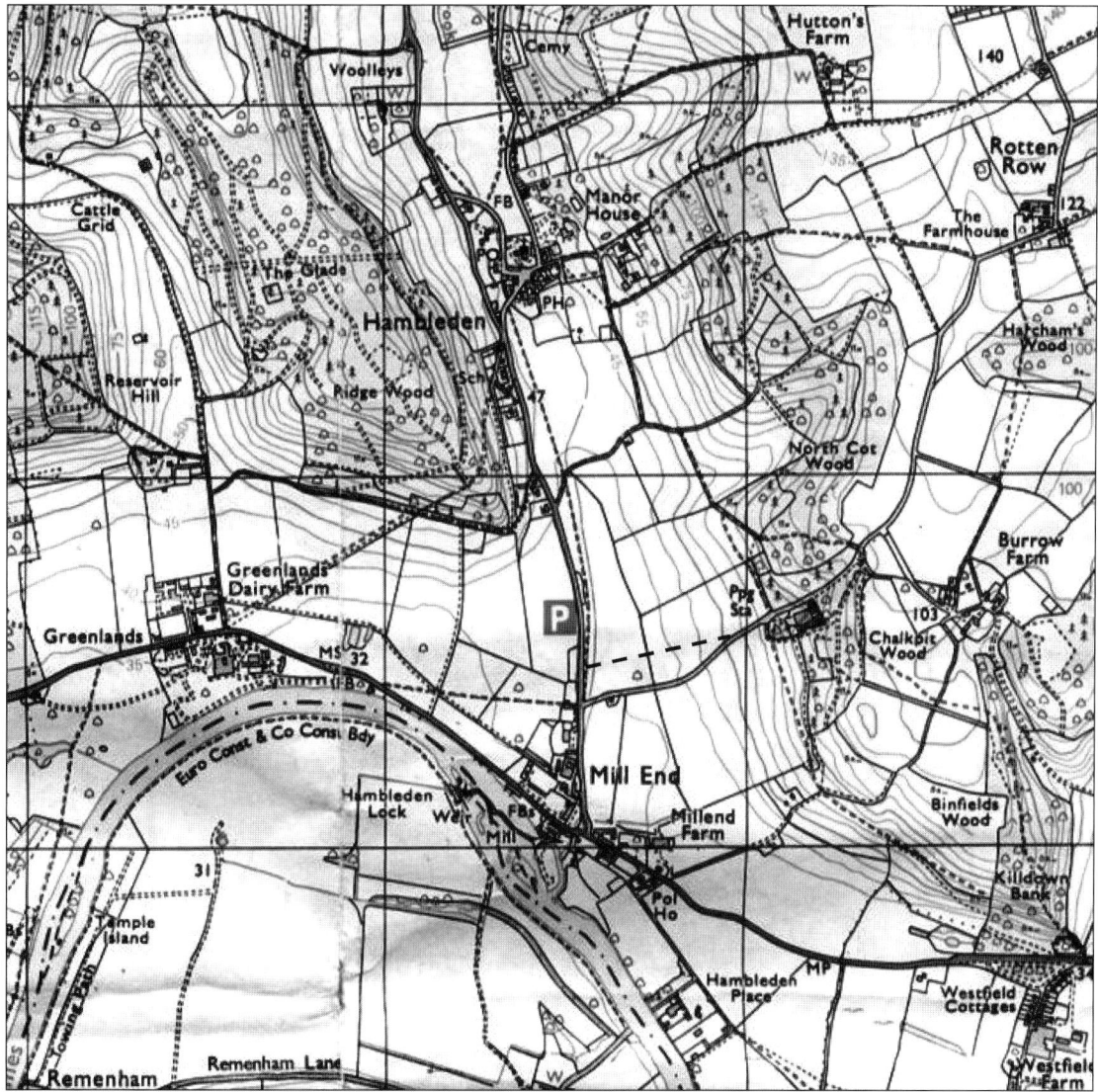

Figure 2.10 Map of the Hambleden Valley showing Ridge Wood in the NW segment and the elongate strip of woodland making up Northcot to Chalk Pit Woods in the east. Yewden villa is located immediately south of the parking sign P. The dashed line east of the car park is indicating the ancient continuation of the Rotten Row road Holloway – directly into the Iron Age enclosure proved during this project.
© Crown copyright and Landmark Information Group Limited (2009). All rights reserved (2008).

Ridge Wood summary

Grid reference (central point): SU 778 865.

There are enough species of ancient flora in the south and southeast to indicate this woodland (Ridge Wood) has been in existence for a considerable time, although with changes and disturbance (e.g. laying out the yew-lined tracks in this area as formal paths or bridleways in the 1800s). Ridge Wood is present as woodland on the earliest map of the area (1761, John Roques' map) and it remains woodland from this time to the present-day. In contrast, the north and west parts of the wood (Great Wood) show no such ancient indicator species and show evidence of much replanting, including the modern plantations of oak and pine. The 1761 map shows Great Wood largely cleared of trees and under cultivation or grazing. Large areas of the Great Wood began to regenerate during the early to late 1800s. The redwood lined, wide formal bridleway, known as the Glade, was laid out at some time between 1883 and 1898. The Glade and other Victorian tracks then became the main routes through the woods and previous pathways (such as the deep worn Holloways and other now faint ancient paths) became disused. The size and sinuous nature of the largest enclosing ditch and bank, with the relatively deep (up to 1.8 m) ditch is characteristic of a woodland boundary feature from the early Medieval period (Figure 2.11). Indeed, the most northerly Holloway respects this feature, and hence puts the ditch and bank as the most ancient structure seen in the woodland survey. It separates an area of woodland for the village which is known to have been inhabited since the Norman (and maybe the Saxon) period. The Iron Age and Roman centres of habitation are at the southern edge of the wood.

Figure 2.11 The large ditch and bank feature, Ridge Wood which is early Medieval and may be Norman. Looking east towards Hambleden village.

Other features, such as the saw pits, are close to the Holloways, indicating these paths were still the dominant entry and exit points when the pits were in use. This would indicate, although not prove, that they are before the Victorian formalising of the footpaths. There are 7 saw pits and these are all along the east side of Ridge Wood indicating they were used for the village of Hambleden. This is also the only area where notable coppicing was observed, although at a low level. Woodland management as a domestic resource seems to have had an even lower importance for Great Wood than for Ridge Wood. It is clear that the Tithe apportionment of Ridge Wood runs coincident with the ancient ditch and bank woodland boundary in some parts, but deviates significantly in others. Both the apportionment area and the original ditch and bank both support the same function – a woodland ownership boundary. This tentatively places the division of parts of this woodland into two ownerships (now the Manors of Hambleden and Yewden) and for a considerable period of time – since the early Medieval period.

Northcot Wood and Chalk Pit Wood summary

There are a variety of features within this section of woodland including at least 6 gravel pits, 5 chalk pits, 6 sawpits, 5 field boundaries, a charcoal hearth and 2 unknown features (which are also likely to be for gravel extraction). Chalk extraction is confined to Chalk Pit Wood and gravel extraction to North Cot Wood. There were more sawpits in Chalk Pit Wood. This was the location for the only charcoal hearth recognised. Four lengths of old field boundaries and tracks were recognised in North Cot Wood. There was only one short section of ancient field boundary visible in Chalk Pit Wood, and this was aligned to a current large field boundary to the north, on the other side of the Rotten Row road. Neither of these two woods showed any ancient flora which, together with some of the map evidence, shows that these areas have not been under continuous woodland management long enough to allow this flora to develop and be retained. The woods have been cultivated from time to time, becoming replanted in regular increments from about the 1880s.

Features such as the sawpits, the gravel and chalk pits, are unlikely to be older than the 1700s and may date to the 1800s, or even early 1900s. However, the field boundaries are likely to be older, and the Holloways are much older.

The main Holloway (the Rotten Row road) divides the two woodland areas. It leads down from the hill tops and farms which are located at Burrow and Rotten Row (but it also links to other farms and hamlets). The main track is worn deep into the hillside, and has only been slightly widened to allow access to modern tarmac and vehicles. The lesser Holloway to Burrow Farm diverts from this main track and it has also dissected the landscape considerably, showing this farm was a main user of the Rotten Row Holloway, but not the sole user. As the Holloway descends into the Hambleden Valley, it becomes less pronounced due to the lower incline and has become covered with alluvium in the lower sections. On reaching the valley bottom, the modern track leads across the valley to the Thames edge and to Greenlands Manor, thus marking a well used medieval pathway. However, the depth of the Holloway would indicate a much longer use, and geophysics results obtained 2008-10 show the original path took a more direct route rather than the 'kink' of the current road, leading directly into an Iron Age enclosure, part of the pre-Roman Yewden complex (Chapters 2.1 and 2.2).

Bibliography

Eyers, J. 2009. *Woodland Archaeology Survey: Ridge Wood, Hambleden, Bucks.* Chiltern Archaeology Report 120.

Eyers, J. 2010. *Woodland Archaeology Survey: Northcot Wood and Chalk Pit Wood, Hambleden, Bucks.* Chiltern Archaeology Report 121.

Hutt, A.T. F. 2009. *Fieldwork report for work done in the fields west of Yewden Roman Villa, Hambleden.* Berkshire Archaeological Research Group, Wokingham.

Payne, A. 2010. *Horseleys Field, Hambleden, Buckinghamshire. Report on geophysical survey July 2009.* Research Department Report Series No. 61-2010.

Chapter 3 Yewden villa complex and the 1912 excavation

Jill Eyers and Alison Jewsbury

3.1 Introduction

A collection of archive photographs depicting the 1912 excavations was discovered during this research project. Some of these images appear in the 1921 report. The photographs were in extremely good condition and all have been scanned at a high resolution to allow definition of small features. The originals are held at the Buckinghamshire County Museum (BCM).

Cocks' terminology and naming of the areas of the site have been maintained in this account to allow easy access of the project information with the original finds, although the names he chose are not ideal. The term 'houses' is used by Cocks for buildings, which he numbered in order of discovery. The images from the archive collection show the 1st, 3rd and 4th houses, along with other walls, gates and a ditch. These images appear below. There was only one image of the second house currently known and this appeared as Plate XVIII, Figure 2 of Cocks 1921. Unfortunately, this image is not in the archive collection. There is also evidence of four other buildings inside the complex, two of which Cocks reported as wattle and daub structures. These were located on the east side of the enclosure. There is also evidence (from furnaces and finds) for a further four, or perhaps five, buildings outside the enclosure walls. The nature of all these structures and their dates of use are discussed further here. Following the discussion of the site evidence, the final interpretation of phasing for Yewden is presented in Figs 3.37-40, at the end of the chapter.

Information on the building materials for the house wall foundations, for the perimeter wall, various floors and 16 furnaces is contained within Cocks' 1921 report and is also supported by materials held in the collections at the BCM. Figure 3.1 shows the site plan with the building materials shown as:

- Foundation walls or footings to buildings - nearly all mortared flint, but these could include portions with chalk or flint, with a mud or mortar binding.
- Floors were either concrete, pounded chalk, flint or tessellated (as discussed for the individual buildings below).
- Building walls comprised wooden frames with wattle and daub infill.
- Roofing materials were either tiles or thatch.

The overall style of building was fairly simple, continuing some of the Iron Age building traditions and apparently containing virtually no stone other than flint and chalk blocks. Stone (notably Cotswold Limestone) could have been imported to the site via the Thames. However, other than two Cotswold Stone window pieces, no stone blocks were seemingly incorporated into the Yewden complex buildings, but it is possible that these may have been removed from the site at any time from the 5th century.

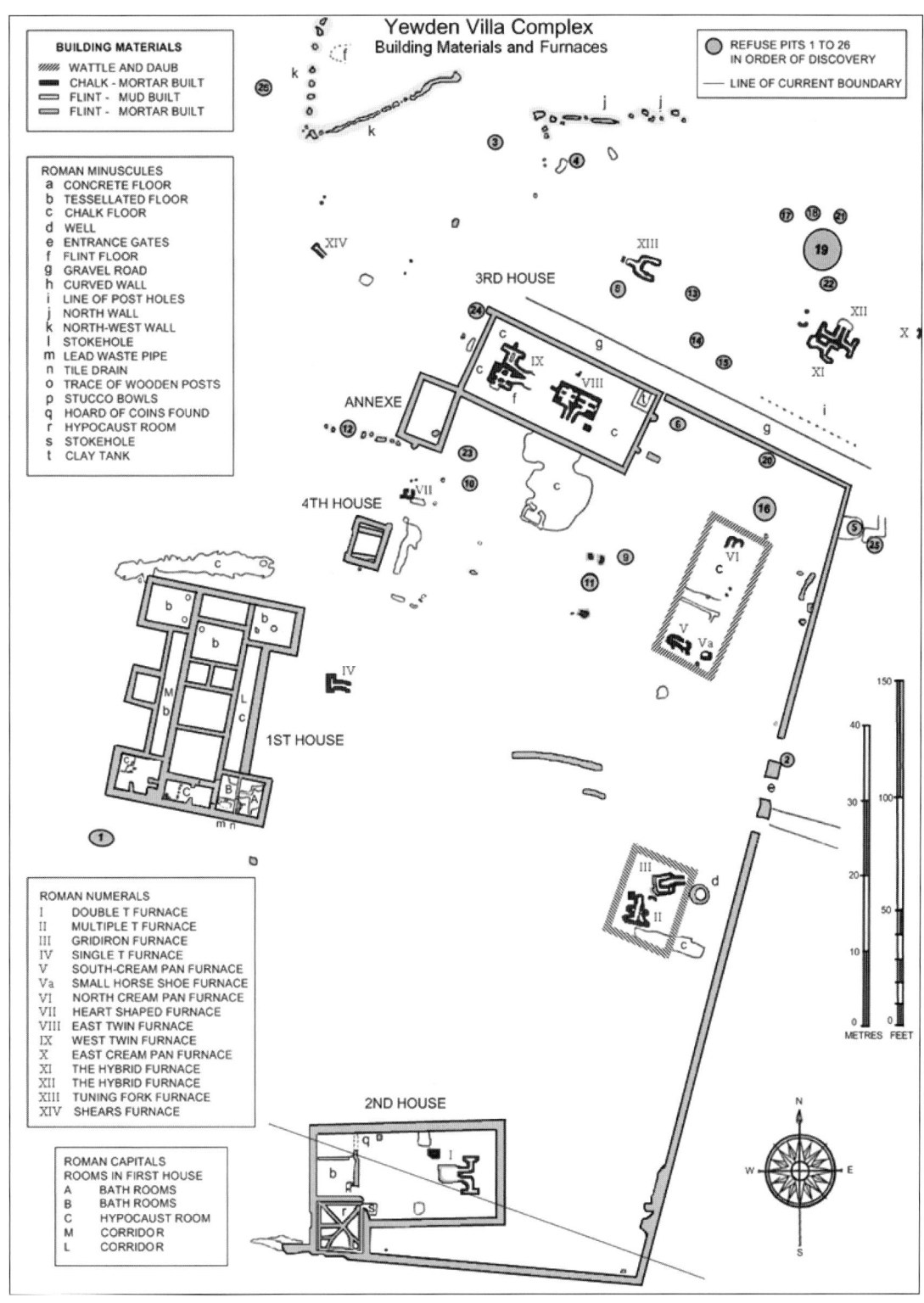

Figure 3.1 Site plan and building materials for foundations of the Yewden Villa Complex. A re-interpretation based on the site plan of Cocks, 1921.

3.2 The buildings: 1st, 2nd, 3rd and 4th Houses

The 1st House

Summary: a winged villa with 2 corridors and 13 rooms which was sited to the west of the Yewden complex enclosure. Pit 1 lay immediately to the S of the SW wing. The building dates from the end 3rd to the early 5th century, and it was built in three phases.

The 1st House conforms to the traditional layout of a Romano-British villa and becomes the main habitation of the Yewden complex from the end of the 3rd century until the early 5th century. There is no evidence for use of the building during the succeeding Saxon period. In his 1921 report Cocks describes this building in greater detail than any of the other buildings or areas of the Romano-British complex. He calls it the 'principal dwelling house', which we now know was true only from the 4th century onwards.

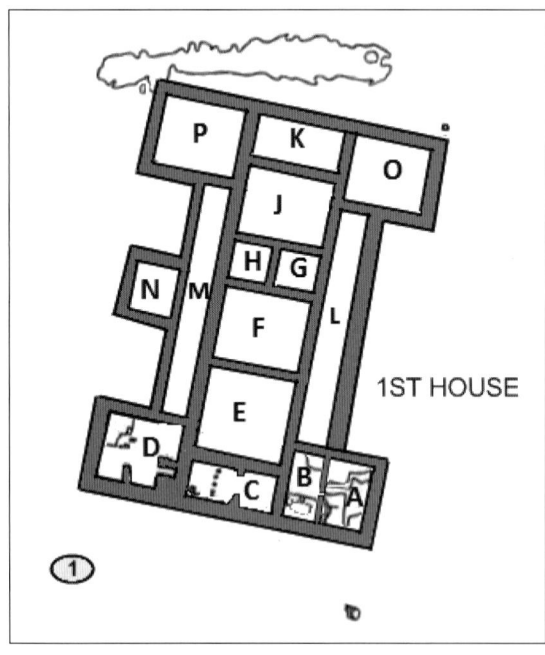

The building measures 29.3 m x 25 m with the final layout showing 13 rooms and two corridors (indicated by letters A to P of Cocks, 1921 and Figure 3.2). The building was photographed during the 1912 excavation. Figures 3.3 to 3.9 show the 1st House from different angles with the rooms and their relationships indicated.

Figure 3.2 Floor plan of the 1st House, Yewden complex, showing Rooms A to P, Pit 1 to the SW and an older area of flint floor to the north.

The mortared flint foundations underlay a wattle and daub structure with a tiled roof. Many iron nails and tile fragments are still to be found in the surrounding areas of ploughed field. Many nails were reported by Cocks as being found during the excavation. Cocks also reported that much plaster and some daub was also located here. Plastering a wooden structure with a wattle frame was a common form of building in the Chilterns and was often chosen for any location where stone building materials were scarce (e.g. the Rye villa, High Wycombe, Payne, 1870; Hartley, 1959). Brightly coloured washes were commonly applied to the plaster and Cocks reported many brightly coloured plaster fragments (maroon red, yellow, orange, beige, sage green and white) with a decoration of dots and stripes.

The roof was undoubtedly terracotta tiles as a huge number of large roof tiles were found during the 1912 excavation. Many tile fragments were left and still lie on site. There were shallow arch lintels and/or ledges for the window openings with capillary grooves to divert rainwater to the sides. These were made of Cotswold oolitic limestone (Kevin Hayward, *pers comm*.). These lintels and ledges could all butt together as a complete window surround and would act as a robust weather resistant structure. This would seem to indicate side masonry supports at either side of the window, which could be square and keyed into side (flint?) panels or simply butt to the timber frame and wattle/daub construction. Concrete sections were also found (ST78 in Chapter 4.2) which would seem to accommodate the oolitic limestone ledge. The frames may therefore have been keyed in with concrete. The windows of this building had glass. This is also true of the earlier phase as window glass was found beneath the floor of Room H and beneath the walls of the NE wing.

Cocks did not date the building phases during this earlier work. However, from the structure in Cocks' plan and from the archive photographs, it can be seen that an initial simple house had substantial wings and corridors added during later phases. A strip house being converted into a winged corridor plan became common from the second century onwards (e.g. Wycombe Rye, Bucks; Cox Green, Oxfordshire; and Lockleys and Park Street villas, both in Hertfordshire).

Figure 3.3 Yewden: The 1st House from the SW corner showing the stoke hole to the hypocaust of room C. The wall foundations are flint with mortar. The visible floor in the foreground (room D) is made of pounded chalk. M is a tessellated corridor.
All 1912 archive photographs are reproduced with permission from WHS Archives.

Figure 3.4 The 1st House from the SE corner. A and B are bathrooms and C a hypocaust room. L is a chalk floor corridor.

Figure 3.5 Yewden: The 1st House from the NE. Rooms O and J have tessellated floors and corridor L has a chalk floor.

Figure 3.6 The 1st House from the NW. Room P is a wing room with tessellated flooring and leads via the tessellated corridor (M) to rooms N and D.

Figure 3.7 The 1st House corridor (M) from the north showing terracotta tesserae.

Figure 3.8 The 1st House: the two bath areas A and B of Cocks with a lead pipe built into a mortared flint wall.

Figure 3.9 Butting relationship of the foundation walls for rooms A and B, 1st House, Yewden

The dividing wall between rooms A and B, enlarged as Figure 3.9, shows a butting relationship and confirms that A is a later addition to B.

The finds associated with each of these rooms can be used to date the phases of building and are summarized as follows:

General - no room specified: coins from one Nero as (AD 54-68, residual), and other coins dating from 268 AD through to 12 House of Theodosius folles (AD 388-402); an architectural fragment of a limestone window surround (Chapter 4.2); quantities of reduced, shell tempered and white ware pottery; a bronze stylus in the drain outside. There were also personal items such as a copper alloy bracelet and rings.

Room A: No pottery or other artefacts. One coin dated 330-348 AD. Mosaic found in the area of Rooms A and B. Bath area.

Room B: No pottery or other artefacts. One coin dated 348-360 AD. Bath area.

Room C: This room had walls of white plaster with an orange-tan decoration in places, which were described as thick stripes or a geometric design. The flooring was of terracotta tesserae. There was a hypocaust in this room, close to the adjacent bath areas A and B. In keeping with proximity to a bath area there were finds of bone and iron combs, and bronze rings. However, this room was also the site of numerous pottery and oyster shell finds, indicating use as a kitchen area during its earlier history (the bathrooms being a later extension). The pottery assemblage included:
- Reduced wares (fabrics R20, R30, R90, R39).
- Oxidised wares (O20 and Overwey 'Porchester D' type O24 dated AD 330-350).
- Fine wares (abundant Oxford Colour Coated ware F51 which dates AD 240-410 and Nene Valley wares F52 dating AD 150-400).
- Mortaria (numerous Oxfordshire white ware mortaria fabric M22 and the red slipped oxidised vessels M41, with some M31) all with wide-ranging dates 240-410 AD.

Room D: a kitchen or serving preparation area is indicated for this room as there was a quantity of pottery table wares, with relatively few storage vessels: reduced wares (fabrics R10, R20, R30), shell tempered ware (C13), white wares and Oxford mortaria (180/240-400 AD). There was a small quantity of Lezoux and East Gaulish Samian (150-260 AD), minor Nene Valley ware (200-370 AD) and a good deal of Oxford Colour Coated ware (240-410 AD). Other finds included a bronze stud with a medusa head (decoration for a vessel) and a scarab beetle (carved stone (Fig.4.8.1, Chapter 4.8)).

Room E: no finds recorded, but Cocks reported a tessellated floor where a worn track in the tesserae lay at the centre of the wall area into corridor M.

Room F: pottery from this room resembled the assemblage from room D, with the addition of minor black burnished ware. There was also an iron spear head. This room had white plastered walls.

Rooms G and H: Pottery finds included Samian from Rheinzabern (120-260 AD), reduced wares (R20 and R30), and a white slipped flagon (Q21, 200-400 AD). Oxford Colour Coat sherds were built into the wall (*TPQ* of 240-410 AD). Reduced ware sherds and a colour coated ware vessel were found beneath the floor indicating that a new floor was laid when the rooms were divided from an earlier larger room, but no date has been defined for this alteration.

Room J: pottery was the only find recorded from this room: Nene Valley ware (150-400 AD) and reduced ware jars (fabric R20). There was a tessellated floor.

Room K: substantial pottery was located in this room including R90 storage jars and substantial black burnished wares, and also reduced wares (R20 and R30), Oxford white wares (100-410 AD) and substantial Oxford Colour Coated wares (240-410 AD), along with an iron knife handle. Cocks mentioned that this room may have had an external door. This may have been the second phase kitchen and food storage area.

Corridors L and M: M was tessellated and L was a chalk floor. The only finds reported are one coin dating 117-138 AD, an R30 fabric reduced ware vessel and a copper alloy buckle (no date possible).

Room N: pottery finds were the only find recorded in this small area. These included Verulamium? white ware, sandy reduced ware and black burnished ware, and some sherds, such as the Oxford Colour Coated ware (240-410 AD) were abraded.

Room O: reduced ware pottery was found beneath the wall of this wing (including R20, R30, black burnished ware and Alice Holt fabrics, and one fine ware – an Oxford Colour Coat vessel (240-410 AD). This room also has a tessellated floor.

Room P: pottery jars and dishes (reduced ware fabrics R20, Alice Holt and black burnished wares) and abraded Oxford Colour Coat (240-410 AD) were found in this room.

The area around the 1st House

Cocks stated in his report (1921, p.143) that the areas to the east, south and southwest of the 1st House were scarce of finds. The finds plots for each of the categories supports this, so much so that it led to an early impression during this study that he may not have excavated this part of the site. This seems not to have been the case as finds from several parts have now emerged and, in addition, he put exploratory trenches across parts of this inner courtyard.

Furnace IV (the Single T) lay just to the east of the villa building and belonged to an earlier structure (1st to earlier 2nd century). There were small portions of mortared flint wall found closer to the 1st House, and relate to an earlier structure in this area, which may have linked to the Single T furnace.

On the west side of the 1st House two ornamental 'stucco' bowls were described by Cocks and these were found on the outside west and outside south walls to Room N. They were presumably garden features – for water or plants.

Phases and interpretation for the 1st House

Using information on the building structure from the footprint plans, the 1912 excavation photographs, as well as examining building materials and finds, the phasing can be deduced for the building of the 1st House during the latest 3rd and 4th century (Figures 3.10 a, b and c):

Phase 1: Rooms C, E, F, H/G, J and K were built (end 3rd or earliest 4th century)
Phase 2: Rooms P, D, M and N were added (early 4th century)
Phase 3: Rooms B, A, O, and L were added (mid to end 4th century)

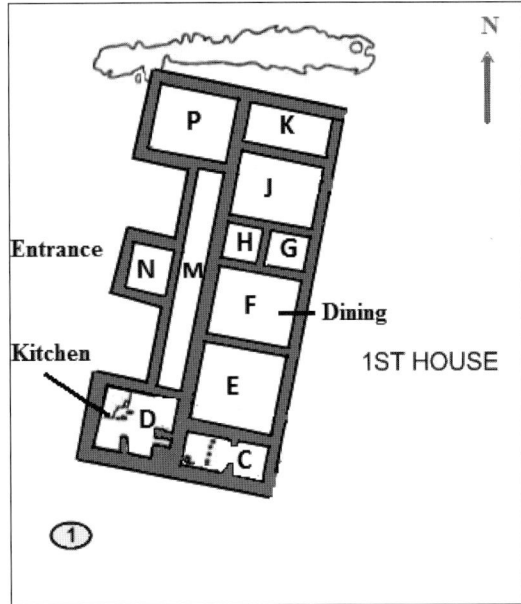

Figure 3.10 a Phase I
The 1st House end 3rd to early 4th century

Figure 3.10 b. Phase 2 The 1st House

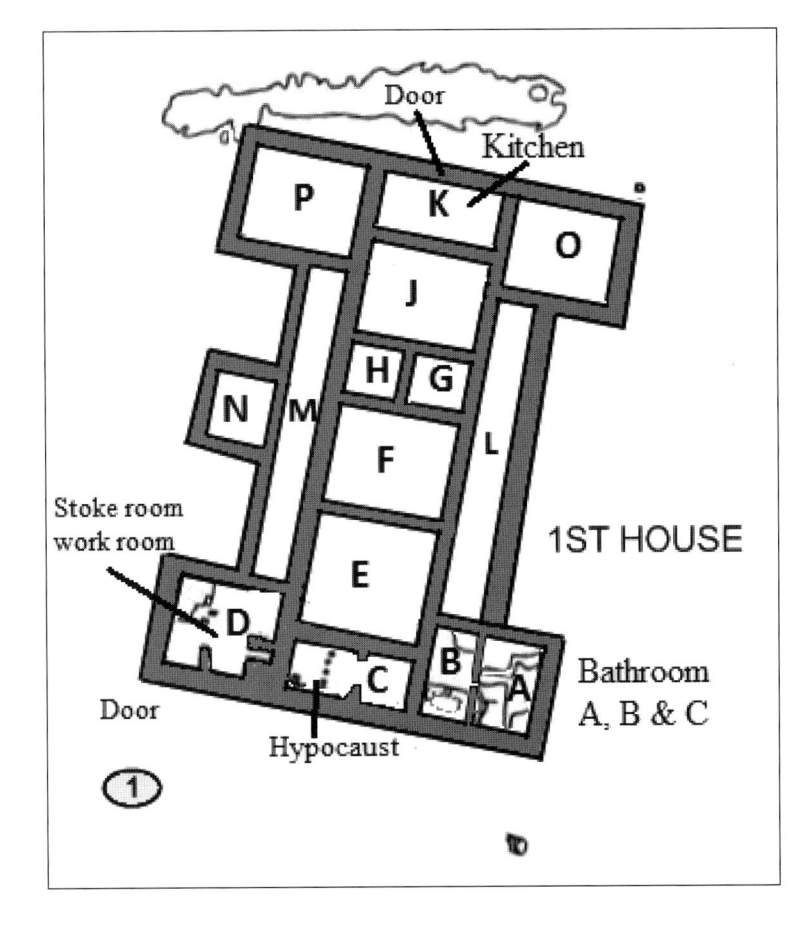

**Figure 3.10 c.
The 1st House during the 4th century.**

From this information a reconstruction of the 1st House is possible, firstly, as an architectural sketch (Figure 3.11) and, secondly, using computer software to provide a 3-D representation (Figure 3.12).

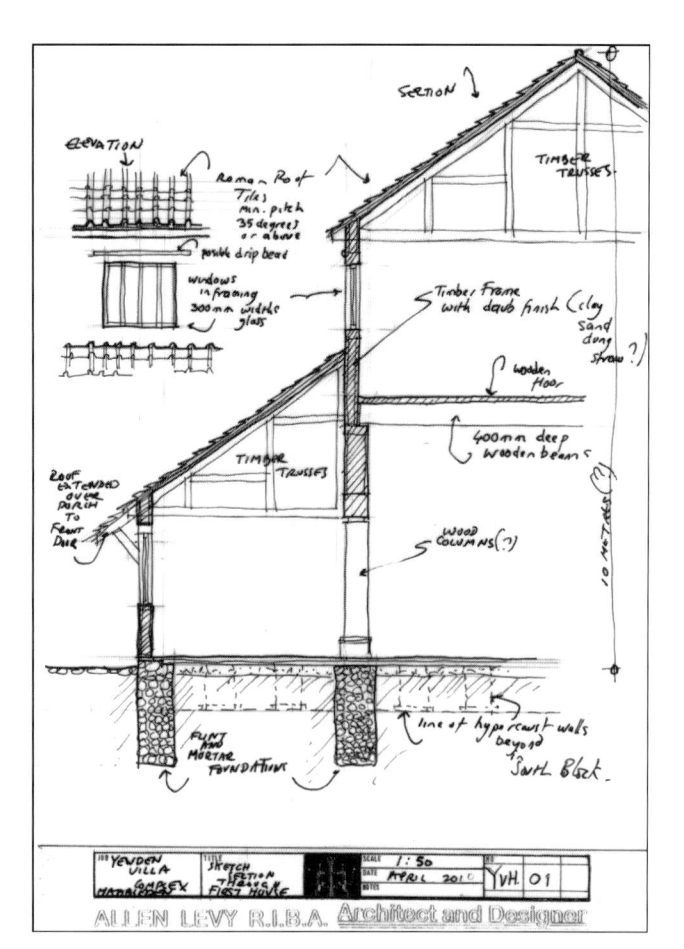

Figure 3.11 An architectural sketch interpretation of the structure for the 1st House, Yewden Villa.

Figure 3.12 A reconstruction of the 1st House, below
© Alison Jewsbury

2nd House

Summary: a wood framed building with wattle and daub infill on a mortared flint wall foundation. It had a hypocaust adjoining a side room with both a clay and a tessellated floor. There is a later furnace. A hoard of coins was located against the north wall of the building. There were 2 infant burials near the coin hoard. Date of the building: based on the coin, pottery and personal assemblage finds this building was functioning as a small domestic residence during the 1st to mid-end 3rd century. From the end 3rd or earliest 4th century it was converted to a grain drying and processing area.

The 2nd House was located within the Yewden enclosure in the south of the complex (Figure 3.1 above and 3.13 below). It had a mortared flint base for support of the wattle and daub walls. Some internal wall plaster has survived (17 pieces) which shows a simply decorated interior in red and grey. The pigments are identical to those used in the 3rd House. There is some worked stone (Cotswolds oolitic limestone 1994.57.ST26, Chapter 4.2) which is interpreted as an architectural window surround and is very similar to the window surrounds of the 1st House. This stone is not datable, but it is very likely to be part of the early (residential) structure of this building. As the 1st House is younger, it is likely that a similar stone had been imported for the same purpose, or was re-used.

The **floors** within the building were recorded as a tessellated floor, a flint floor and a prepared clay floor. The tessellated floor was found in the room at the west side of the building and in a hypocaust room. The tesserae were plain terracotta. The stoke hole to the hypocaust room was sited within the building outer wall. The clay floor was laid from the north wall of the building and there is Roman pottery found both above and below it and this is likely to be the floor laid for the second use of the building as a workshop. Dates below the floor range from 1st century up to around 200-250 AD. Above the floor dates of 240+ AD occur for pottery and 268 AD (a *terminus post quem*) from coins. There was a furnace to the eastern end of the building, surrounded by the clay floor called the 'Double T furnace' by Cocks (1921). Two coin *TPQ* dates for the furnace are 293 and 330 AD.

The hoard of **coins** consisted of 294 coins held within a sandy reduced ware pot. The coin hoard was buried about 20 cm beneath the floor level and it was covered by tile. Cocks recorded adjacent Oxford colour coat pottery (a C45 type bowl sherd of Young, 1977 dated to 270-400 AD with coins of Victorinus and Carausius –268-270 and 286-293 AD respectively). There were also around 30 or so coins found within the building floor, the hypocaust and the furnace. These indicate a date range of mid-1st century to end 4th century (the earliest coin is a Marcus Aurelius (138-161 AD) and the latest is a House of Constantine (348-360 AD). Coins associated with the double T furnace date to post 330 AD.

The **pottery** includes a wide range of local reduced, oxidized, white and imported wares. There is a large quantity of reduced wares including Alice Holt and Black Burnished wares. Fine wares include Moselkeramik (200-275 AD), Central Gaulish Colour Coated ware (150-250 AD), Oxfordshire mortaria (white ware and red-slipped, AD 180+), Oxford Colour Coat (240+ AD), and black burnished wares. The Samian pottery includes both South Gaul (Dragendorf 29 vessel 40-85 AD) and Central Gaul (Dragendorf 38 bowls and also mortaria AD 120-200). The pottery assemblage indicates dates from the 1st to mid-3rd century for use of this building as a domestic residence.

The type of workshop is not clear from finds evidence. However, the millstone grit quernstone and the whetstone, when considered with the shape of the Double T furnace, provide indications that the building was converted to a grain drying function by the beginning of the 4th century, with some grinding of grain for household use.

There was remarkably little **copper alloy** associated with the 2nd House compared to other areas of the site. A 1st Century fibula brooch was found with a nail cleaner, some unidentifiable rolls, pieces of bronze and a bronze boss. These items belong to the domestic phase.

Two **infant burials** lay within the building (1994.57.3606.16 and .19). The depth of these was not recorded and there were no associated artefacts from which to date the burials. However, their burial within the structure limits their date to within the building dates.

Figure 3.13 Reconstruction of the 2nd House during the 4th century (above).

Right - the floor plan of the building:
Hypocaust (1); coin hoard (2); Furnace (3); tessellated floor (4)
© **Alison Jewsbury**

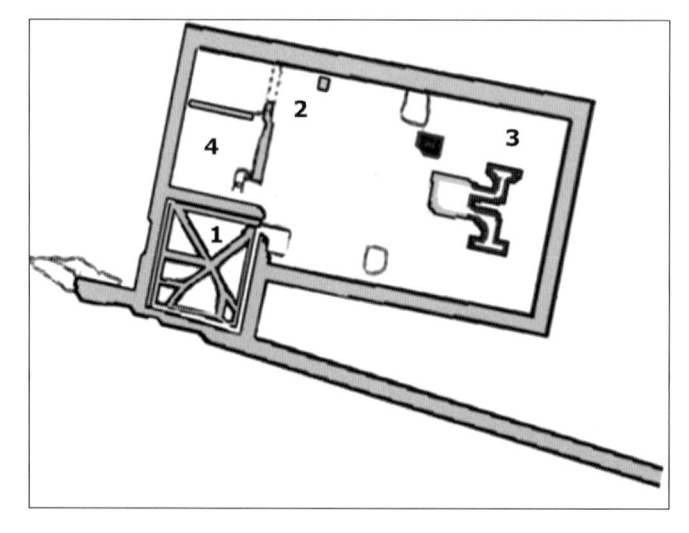

The 3rd House

Summary: a simple residence which was converted to a grain drier and malting area. It was located at the north end of the Yewden enclosure - the north wall of the building also formed the 4th century north wall of the enclosure. There were 3 phases of construction: the 1st to end 2nd century was residential; a fire at around the beginning of the C3rd (c. 200 AD) resulted in the demolition of the southern part of the house, followed by a partial rebuild of an area with a mortar floor mid- C3rd. This might have been a threshing and workshop area. Finally, from the end 3rd century onwards the south end of the building was removed, with the south wall to the 3rd House either reconstructed or just exposed. This building became a grain drying and malting area. Two furnaces were emplaced as part of this final phase.

The building called the 3rd House during the 1912 excavations measured 26 m x 12.3 m (Figs 3.1, 3.5 and 3.14). It was a wooden framed building supporting wattle and daub walling based on a mortared flint footing. Wall plaster remained sufficiently intact to display colours and simple patterns – the same red and greenish grey colours of the 2nd House. Samples of daub have preserved some of the wattle impressions.

There was an annexe attached to the southwest corner measuring 9.8 m x 6 m. There is also evidence of a further small structure attached to the east wall which has a flint floor and is similar to, and possibly an extension of, the flint floor of the 3rd House.

Figure 3.14 The 3rd House (looking east) showing the flint base for the walls and the two furnaces.

The original area of the 3rd House in the 1st century was much larger and extended southwards, at least double the living area seen in the final footings of Cocks' excavation. There was a fire dated to *c.* 200 AD or the very earliest 3rd century (evidence is from pottery finds from this area and within nearby pits, including the well called 'Pit 6', Fig. 3.15). The bodies in Pit 6 are unlikely to be victims of the fire, quickly disposed of, as the fire post-dates the gravel floor which seals Pit 6. This leads to the supposition that the bodies had been thrown into the well as victims of murder. The material in the well was accumulated so quickly that there is no tight dating possible, but is c. 150-200 AD. The assemblage of finds within the area to the south of the 3rd House indicates a re-build of some kind of structure with a mortar floor from the mid-3rd century (defined by coins and Samian pottery which occur below, within and above the floor layer). This structure was finally removed around the end 3rd century, allowing the mortar floor to become worn as an open area within the enclosure. A new south wall may have been built for the 3rd House as Cocks (1921, p.149) described as "having a possible re-built south wall as this was in better condition than the other walls"). However, the 'better condition' may simply have been afforded by protection by the earlier building extension. By the final phase, the smaller 3rd house reverted to workshop activities, mostly related to corn drying and malting.

There were two furnaces (fXIII and fIX) inside the building relating to this final phase. These occupied a large space and made an efficient and gentle heat transfer over the widest floor area – perfect for grain drying or malting. Charred grain was located in this building (Chapter 7.2) showing a mix of wheat and barley, confirming the use of the building for this purpose. In addition, Cocks describes a clay feature in the northeast corner of the 3rd House measuring 1.9 m x 1.2 m (which he notes as an 'obvious water tank'). The sides were of variable thickness (60 cm for the west side, 30 cm east, with a base of 15 cm). The feature was around 40 cm deep. There is no dating evidence for the feature, which might be related to the earlier residential phase and not the grain drying or malting phase. However, as water is required for the malting process, this feature may be contemporaneous with the final phase.

In his report, Cocks noted a large amount of charcoal, ashes, soot and roofing tile 'indicating that the roof or entire house had been destroyed by fire at one point'. This is an incorrect assumption for this northern part of the building, as finds within the 3rd House as defined by Cocks, do not show evidence of a fire. As indicated above, the final phase from the end-3rd century has a grain drying and/or malting function where much ash and charcoal would be expected. The southern part of this building however did experience a fire, and burnt pottery is associated with this south end within/on the gravel floor.

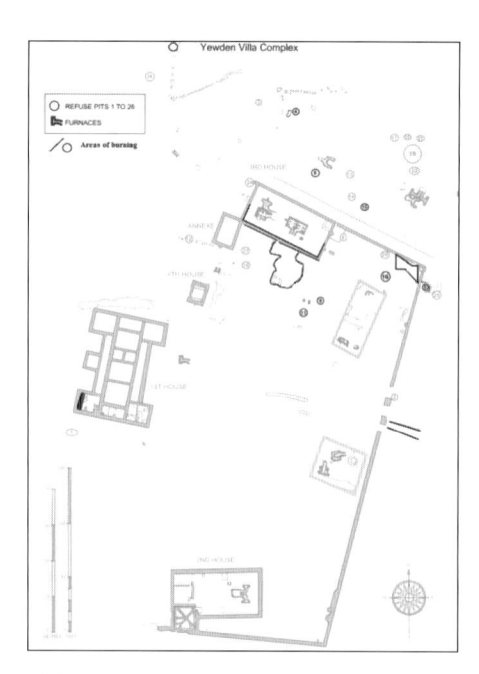

Figure 3.15 Areas containing large quantities of burnt pottery (in bold lines) and used as an indication of the likely location for a major fire. A fire is indicated as occurring to a southerly section of the 3rd House, in place prior to this plan, and related to the mortar floor. The fire can be dated to *c.* 200 AD or very early in the 3rd century.

Three floor levels were described by Cocks either in the 1921 report or indirectly with find labels – a gravel floor overlain by a flint floor, in turn covered by a mortar or chalk floor. These contained many datable finds. The older gravel and flint floors extended outside the east wall of the building and sealed the well (Pit 6). The flint floor within the main building was described as being laid at different levels. Cocks inferred that this was due to the floor being laid down separately within different rooms. This floor relates to the residential phase, so this is entirely likely. The 'rooms' he conjectured would therefore have been separated by wooden partitions (as there was no archaeological evidence of footings for more substantial walls). A door was indicated in the west wall by a layer of concrete paving.

Finds associated with the floors surrounding, and within, the 3rd House:

Gravel floor

This contains a substantial quantity of domestic finds with dates indicating mid 2nd to early 3rd century (a *terminus post quem* of 150 AD within the floor and 240 AD associated with the overlying flint floor) defined by coins, Samian and Oxford ware pottery. Many of the pottery finds within the gravel floor are abraded and indicate a source for the gravel which has included reworked pottery. A suitable source of gravel lies adjacent to the site.

Flint floor

The flint floor was emplaced in the mid-3rd century (*c.* 240-270 AD) defined by a *terminus post quem* on the underlying gravel floor, within the flint floor and under the overlying mortar/chalk floor of the 3rd House and southerly extension to this building. Burnt pottery lay under and was incorporated into this floor, indicating that there had been a fire some time after the gravel floor, but before the flint and mortar floors were emplaced. This indicates a date for the fire *c.* 200 AD.

Mortar/chalk floor

The mortar floor (also noted as a chalk floor on some finds and the 1921 plan) was present in the 3rd House and extended southwards indicating the presence of a larger building on the south side of the 3rd House. Dates are well defined by Samian and Oxford ware pottery as well as coins. The dating indicates the emplacement of the floor after *c.* 270 AD (a *terminus post quem* from a Tetricus II coin 268-274 AD). Pottery finds below and within this floor support this date. Burnt pottery occurred beneath the floor. There were further coins and pottery overlying the flooring dating from early abraded and residual items to a Helena follis 337-341 AD.

3rd House finds

Large quantities of Samian **pottery** were found within the 3rd House and the areas immediately surrounding it (Chapter 5.3). The Samian assemblage included substantial amounts of La Graufesenque pottery not seen anywhere else on site. There was also a large quantity of vessels from Central Gaul (both Les Martres and Lezoux) and a smaller amount from East Gaul. Cups, decorated and plain bowls, mortaria and dishes dominated the assemblage. Other forms of pottery included hundreds of sherds of reduced and grog-tempered kitchen wares and fine table wares from local and imported sources. A pipe-clay figurine, the *Dea Nutrix*, was also found in the 3rd House (Fig.4.8.3, Chapter 4.8).

The pottery information, together with the personal items (such as worked **bone** hair pins and **copper alloy** brooches, toiletry items and jewellery) indicate the residential use of the 3rd House from the 1st to the mid- or end-3rd century.

The finds assemblage changes drastically during the middle of the 3rd century, after the mortar/chalk floor was laid, seemingly as a short-term re-build of the southern end of the building. This southern extension is likely to have had a mixed workshop and grain processing function. There are a number of **iron** implements such as hooks, rods, rings, chisels, clamps, a stylus and a sickle associated with this extension, along with iron slag and a 'clay construction' of unknown purpose - Cocks described it as being 'full of ash and puddled clay' (Fig. 3.16). Hence, there was possibly some small-scale iron working and repairing occurring in this area. There was also a quantity of querns, rubbing stones and whetstones associated with the extension as well as within the final phase of the 3rd House indicating grain processing in both areas (see Chapter 4.2, Fig. 4.2.11).

It is certain that this southerly extension was no longer an enclosed building by the end of the 3rd century. A new wall was built for the south side of the 3rd House and this was converted into a grain processing and corn drying and/or malting area. Two furnaces (the East Twin and the West Twin furnaces of Cocks, fVIII and fIX) would have given an even and gentle heat distribution effectively over the whole floor area

Figure 3.16 The mortar floor exposed during the 1912 excavations, looking north. The flint base to the south wall of the 3rd House is visible in the distance and in the foreground is the excavated 'clay construction' that was filled with ash and puddled clay.

Figure 3.17 Reconstruction of the 3rd House looking southeast across the enclosure. © Alison Jewsbury

The Annexe to the 3rd House

The relatively few finds in the annexe secure a date of post mid-3rd century for this extension. There was no South Gaulish Samian, but Lezoux and East Gaulish forms are found within the structure (combined dates of 120-250 AD). A radiate coin of Tetricus I provides a *terminus post quem* at 1.5 ft deep of 270-274 AD. Oxford Colour Coat pottery, in addition to a Central Gaulish beaker, provide additional dates of 240-400 and 150-200 AD respectively. The remaining pottery comprised an average kitchen assemblage of sandy reduced ware jars (fabrics R20 and R90 are the most numerous) as well as white slipped vessels (both oxidized and reduced forms). Other finds included 1 bronze stylus, an iron fragment, 1 whetstone and a worked bone knife handle all close to the building (Fig. 4.7.8, Chapter 4.7).

The 4th House

Summary: the 4th House lay between the 1st House and the Annexe of the 3rd House within the Yewden enclosure. Two phases of building or repair, with a flint foundation for the walls and a tessellated floor. Date: as part of another building from 2nd century; as ?shrine mid-3rd to end 4th century.

Cocks suggested that this single roomed building may have been a shrine (1921, p.143; Fig. 3.18). Finds are not conclusive, but neither do they refute the interpretation. Two sets of walls were evident – the newer east and west walls were laid on old foundations and possibly belong to another structure entirely (related to the 'Heart Furnace' which is most likely a hearth for a residential building). The final phase of the building had a tessellated terracotta floor of the type found along the corridors of the 1st House.

Figure 3.18 The 'Little House' or 4th House of Cocks during the 1912 excavation, looking northeast. Two phases of walls can be seen.

The few sherds of La Graufesenque **pottery** recorded from this location appear to be residual, with one burnt and they are likely to have been sourced from the adjacent 3rd House and its southerly extension. The same is true for the kitchen wares: reduced wares (R90 and R20 jar), white ware sherds and oxidized grog tempered (O80) vessels. Therefore it is assumed that these finds are associated with the adjacent building, becoming scattered in this general area.

The reduced fine ware beakers (R10) looked less abraded, but no depth was given. These are inferred to form part of the Little House context. The remaining Samian pottery from Les Martres (100-120 AD), Lezoux (150-200 AD) and East Gaul (150-250 AD) also looks less abraded or show no abrasion. The Samian assemblage only includes cups (Dr27) and bowls (the Dr31 and the decorated Dr37s). There was also a mortarium (a Dr45) from Lezoux (170-200 AD).

Other finds include a **copper alloy** ligula and a sword or dagger pommel, 2 **iron** styli and 1 iron handle, and one coin "in the fill" a House of Theodosius follis 388-402 AD. There was no stone, worked bone or glass.

On the basis of the finds and the size, shape and location for this structure, it is highly likely that this building functioned as a small shrine. The date can be estimated as mid-3rd to end 4th or early 5th century.

3.3 The pits

There were 26 recorded pits which appear on Cocks' plan (1921), but he noted that there were 3 or 4 shallow pits that were not included in the plan or recorded in other ways. The pits were all very different shapes and sizes, and their dates span the whole of the Iron Age through to the late Roman period. Pottery finds from the same vessel in different pits indicate more than one pit was in use at any one time. Most pits had datable finds. Sometimes, Cocks recorded the depth of finds on attached labels. Where this is the case, these objects have been used in determining an approximate stratigraphy for the deposits. Cocks' measuring was not precise and on occasions his field supervisors chose to lump finds at certain levels. Hence finds sometimes cluster at certain depths, e.g. at 2ft, 4ft, 8 ft, etc, which means that finds within each of these categories really represents finds from 'surface to 2ft' and '2ft to 4ft', etc. Although this method does not give the refinement to stratigraphical interpretation as per modern methods, Cocks' recording nonetheless provides real insight to phases and also provides overall dates of use for the site.

The pits are described in number order and for ease in reporting and correlating thousands of finds with their location depths on labels and in records, the imperial measurements made by Cocks of inches, feet and yards are maintained here rather than converting each to metric.

Pit 1
Summary: Associated with 1st House; contained 1 baby burial. Date: end 3rd to end 4th century. The pit is 14 ft deep and is an oval shape approximately 10 ft x 8 ft

Pit 1 is about 15 feet south of Room D of the 1st House (Figure 3.1). Cocks reports (192, p.148) that "There is a reasonable probability that the position of Pit 1 shows there was a back door opposite it in the south or west wall of Room D of the 1st House, but there was no indication of one".

The fill included a substantial quantity of amphora, grey reduced wares, Oxford Colour Coated wares and Oxford white ware mortaria (several types). Pottery also included Black Burnished ware, Nene Valley colour coat, oxidised grog tempered ware (O80), Alice Holt grey ware, shelly ware (C13), coarse tempered ware (R90), white slipped reduced ware, white ware and a little oxidized ware. There were glass fragments from green vessels and a colourless glass cup. Iron included numerous nails and a lynch pin. There was no worked bone and no copper alloy items except for a small piece of bronze metal working residue at 11 ft. There were rotary querns (quartz conglomerate) as well as rubbing stones and whetstones. Coins, together with minor Samian fragments and datable Oxford mortaria, occurred from 8ft to the surface layers. Dating is good and defines the use of the pit as from the end of the 3rd to the end 4th Century. The pit is clearly for household waste from the 1st House.

Pit 2

Summary: located close to the villa entrance gateway in the east enclosure wall. The pit was c. 8 ft diameter and c. 10 ft deep. A domestic pit filling from the mid 2nd to mid-3rd century and deduced to be associated with the Northeast Building of the enclosure.

Finds: Samian ware at the bottom of the pit provided a date of post 140 AD. The fill contained iron nails and a small iron key, a knife handle made from worked bone and some copper alloy toilet items (an ear scoop and pairs of tweezers). There was also a piece of slag with possible copper working residue. The pottery assemblage contained sandy reduced ware and sandy white ware, with lesser amounts of coarse tempered storage jars (fabric R90), oxidised grog tempered ware (O80) and grog and sand tempered ware (E810) with 1 single piece of Oxford Colour Coat. Samian included vessels from La Graufesenque, Les Martres-de-Veyre and Lezoux throughout the fill. The pottery, along with one residual Trajan Sestertius, dates the fill from 140 AD to at least 240 AD. Fragments of Lodsworth Stone and Quartz Conglomerate quernstones were also present, although many objects in this pit did not have depths recorded. A pit taking domestic waste from the residential phase of the Northeast Building of the enclosure area.

Pit 3

Summary: located between the NW wall and the north wall in the yard; Sitomina's pot and much high status Samian pottery including a Rheinzabern mortarium, abundant Oxford mortaria and other local wares. Domestic pit with 2nd to 3rd century fill.

This pit was located between the NW wall and the north wall of the yard, in the northern end of the 1912 site excavation. There was a significant amount of pottery in this pit including masses of local wares used in domestic kitchens such as sandy reduced ware vessels, Alice Holt, Oxford Colour Coated ware and mortaria of many types (Oxford white ware, New Forest and Samian). There was also other Samian ware of exceptional quality and in a very good state of preservation (dishes, plates, bowls and cups). There were no finds of worked bone, animal or human bone, no iron, spindle whorls or glass. A rotary quern fragment (Millstone grit) and some bronze fragments were found. There were several unusual items found in this pit. For instance, a beautiful Samian mortarium, which shows no sign of wear, but was broken and placed near the top of the pit (Fig. 3.19 and back cover). This is interpreted as being a pit closure offering. There is also a grey reduced ware jar base with a graffiti name 'Siitomina' (Fig. 3.20) and a New Forest mortarium, a vessel which is rare outside the New Forest (Fig.3.21). These will be further discussed in Chapter 8.

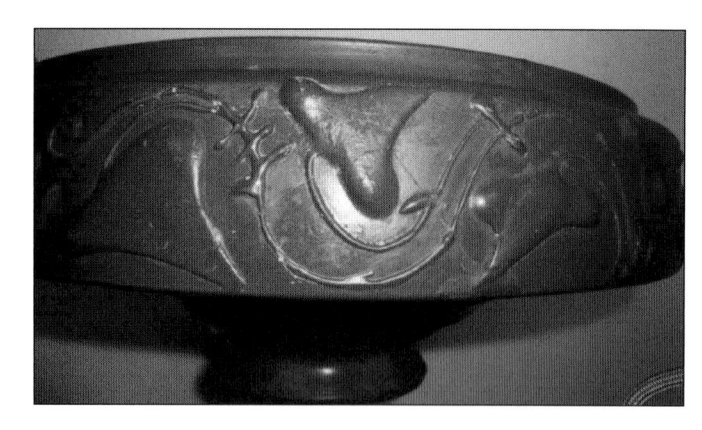

Figure 3.19 Samian mortarium (DR43) from Rheinzabern 140-260 AD. Broken into 3 pieces and within the top fill of Pit 3. Grits not worn. Peacocks and vines are often associated with Juno. A ritual 'sealing' of the pit?

Figure 3.20 Siitomina's pot: a graffito of a Romano-British female name, scratched onto a reduced ware base with a stylus.

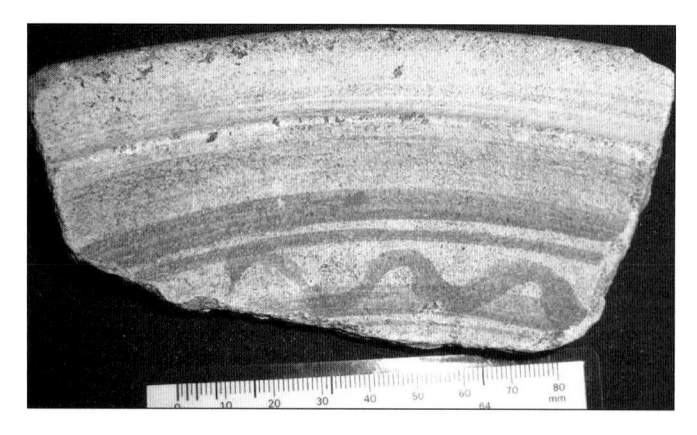

Figure 3.21 New Forest mortarium 260-370 AD in the top fill of Pit 3

Pit 4

Summary: just south of the north wall, which was an earlier enclosure. Pit diameter c. 7 ft and 11 ft in depth. Third century domestic pit.

Pit 4 was located just south of the north wall and east of Pit 3 (Figure 3.1). A substantial variety of domestic pottery was found which includes Samian from all three regions, a wide variety of reduced wares (R10, R30, R20, Alice Holt, and black burnished ware) and oxidized grog tempered ware, shelly ware and Oxford Colour Coat, amongst others.

There were fragments of green and colourless glass vessels (and one lump interpreted as cullet) and 1 pair of copper alloy tweezers at 4 ft depth, but no spindle whorls, worked stone, or other worked items. There were only 2 iron nails.

Unfortunately depths of finds were not noted except for a few items as being within the top fill. Also in the top fill was one (possibly two) pine martin skeletons and a broken Samian mortarium. Similar to Pit 3 it is suggested that this was a 'sealing' offering for the closure of the pit.

Although dating is not tight due to little depth information, the majority of datable pottery items have a minimum date of 240 AD including Oxford Colour Coat in the top layers and also the mortarium 160-260 AD. Coin evidence from the database (finds with the BM) gives two coins (a Claudius II radiate and a Valentinium follis) as being 388-402 AD. However, the location details are very hazy. The note that they are from Pit 4 is vague, with a question mark. and may not be correct. Pit 4 comprised mainly 3rd century fill on the basis of dates attributable to pottery.

Pit 5

Summary: located immediately east (outside) the eastern enclosure wall of the villa complex. Diameter c. 7 ft and a depth of more than 14 ft. Mid-2nd to 4th century domestic and workshop fill.

Pit 5 is outside the enclosure wall of Fig 3.1 on the east side of the site. It had a significant proportion of burnt pottery. Burnt sherds obtained from 'below 14ft' from Cocks' labels had been burnt at a very high temperature. As many pottery sherds were also obtained at this level without signs of burning it is interpreted that the fire was a building fire and not within the pit itself.

Domestic kitchen pottery was found throughout the pit (reduced wares R10, R30 and R20. Also present were Black Burnished ware, grog tempered ware (E30), shelly ware (C13) fine oxidized and white ware, some local and where datable all early *c.*100-200/240. Samian pottery from south, central and east Gaul was present throughout the pit, but some was abraded and clearly residual. Copper alloy brooch pins occurred at 12 ft and toiletry items were present. Iron hasps, links, rings, hooks, wire and latch lifters occurred at several levels. A pottery spindle whorl at 4.5 ft as well as quernstone fragments (quartz conglomerate and Lodsworth Stone) and a whetstone are evidence of some nearby workshop activity (the Northeast building?). Using the datable pottery and the coin at 5 ft (268-286 AD), the entire pit fill can be dated between 150-300 AD.

Pit 6

Summary*: Cocks called this a pit, but it is more likely to be a well located within the north end of the villa enclosure adjacent to the 3rd House; there were 5 skeletons at 4.3 m depth and masses of building materials above the skeletons. There were 3 newborn infant burials (one in the top of the pit at 43 cm depth and two infants 0.6 m south of the pit). Date: the pit fill dates up to c. 150-200 AD; a gravel floor level sealed the pit and was emplaced c. 150-240 A, followed by the upper flint floor 240 + AD.*

Pit 6 was found next to the east wall of the 3rd House. Cocks reported (1921) that "there was a flint floor found here, about 12 ft (3.7 m) square, which seemed to belong to a small shed (Figure 3.22). About 9 inches (23 cm) below it was a gravel floor, gradually dying out at about 30 ft. (9 m) square, and which probably indicated a previous, larger shed". This floor is also described within the 3rd House, which assists with dating. There was a large quantity of high status finds which indicate the 3rd House to have been residential during the 1st to end 2nd century. 'Pit 6' was more likely to have been a well associated with this house. This suggestion is based on the size and location - on the scale drawn on Cocks' 1921 plan it is *c.* 8ft or 2.4 m in diameter, but it is more than 14ft (4.3 m) deep and reached the June 1912 water table. The profile therefore much more resembles a well than a pit.

The date of the fill of 'Pit 6' is difficult to define any closer than between 150-200 AD, as there are very few finds throughout. The upper fill consisted of much heavy building material, including "tons of large flints, and many roofing and other tiles, some with mortar adhering to them" (Cocks, 1921, p.149). An infant burial (1994.57.3606.60) was also recorded as found at the top of the pit at 43 cm depth, beneath the gravel floor. (Note that there are two further infant burials under the gravel floor within the adjacent 3rd House, but these skeletons were not located during the study). Two further infants (1994.57.3606.17 and .18) were found 0.6 m from the south edge of the pit, depth not specified.

Cocks described how he was about the give up excavating Pit 6 as the work seemed to be very "unprofitable". But luckily he decided to continue, eventually discovering five skeletons. There were two adult males, one adult female and two children found lying together (Chapter 6). They were found at 14 ft (4.3 m), just below the water-table at the time (June). Cocks (1921, p.150) reports

"As the bones had to be felt for, under water, it was impossible to say much about the positions, except that they were all more or less in contact. The people, whether dead or alive, had evidently been thrown in without ceremony, and tons of heavy building material heaped on them."

Pottery: Samian pottery from La Graufesenque, Lezoux and East Gaul occurred under the flint floor indicating mixed stratigraphy and no doubt items brought in with the flooring materials. One piece of East Gaulish pottery (Dr31) suggests dates for the top fill as 150- 260 AD. The Central and East Gaulish dates are supported by Central Gaulish Colour coat (F43, 150-260 AD), Oxford white ware mortaria (180+ and 240+ AD) and colour coated ware (F51, 240+ AD) all found within the layer under the flint floor and over Pit 6. Reduced wares and grog tempered wares also occur under the flint floor.
Coins: One coin was located at 51 cm depth within the pit. It is either Lucilla (150-182 AD) or Faustina II (died 175 or 176 AD), the coin is too worn to be certain.
Copper Alloy: Some bronze fragments of a brooch, pin and a ring were found with the skeletons at 4.3 m (1994.57.2542), which have stained the bones of one skeleton, otherwise no other copper alloy was recorded from this pit.

Flint floor AD 240+   Gravel floor 150-200 AD

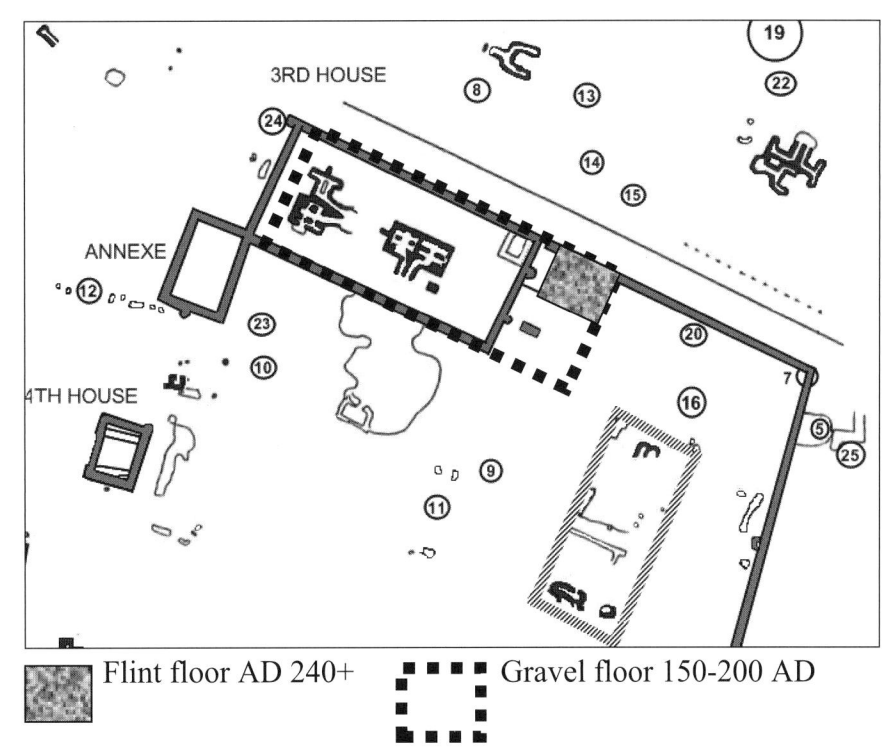

Figure 3.22a Flint and gravel floor levels sealing the well (Pit 6).

Chalk floor areas 270 +

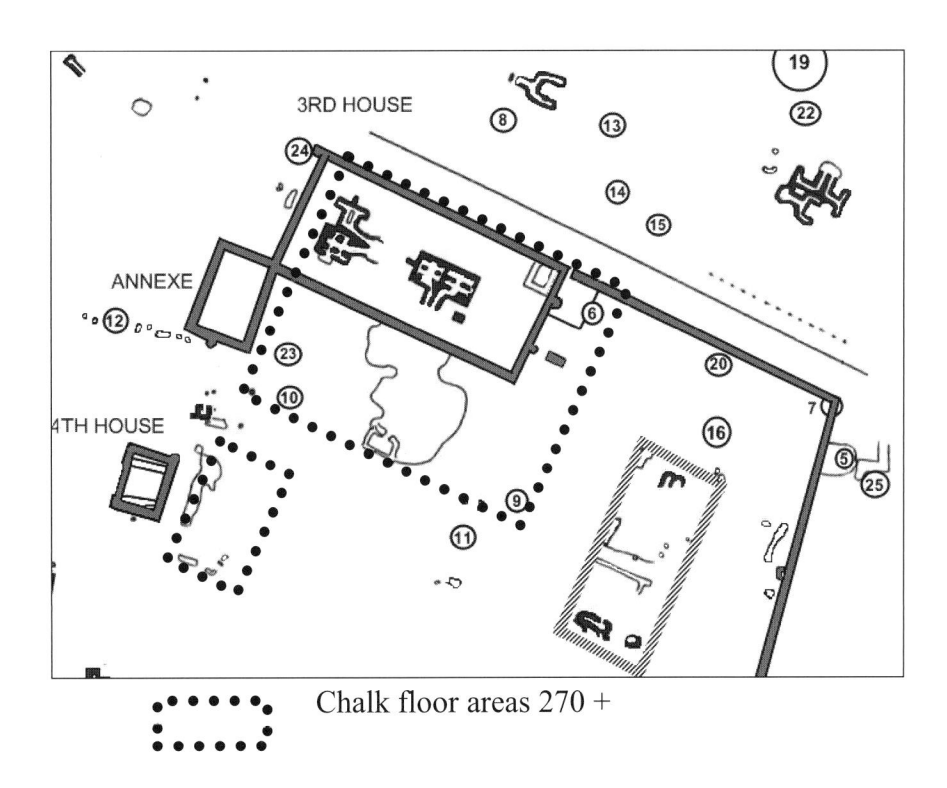

Figure 3.22b Chalk floor (sometimes called the 'Mortar floor') indicating a former larger building, lying partly south of, and within, the 3rd House.

The sequence of fill and overlying floors can be summarized as:

[**Chalk 'Mortar' floor** over the adjacent area of the same gravel floor within, and south of, the 3rd House 270+ AD]

Then, over Pit 6:

Flint floor of *c.* 25 cm thick for building of *c.* 3.7 m square (240+ AD)
Gravel floor of *c.* 9 m square building (*c.*150-200 AD)
Top of Pit 6, with infant burial, (*c.* 150-200 AD)
Pit fill to 4.3 m a mass of building material
Pit 6 **at 4.3 m** contained 5 skeletons (below water table)
Final depth not recorded.

Given the short date range for 'Pit 6' with the rapid infill of this well with building materials over the 5 bodies at the bottom of the sequence, the conclusion is that the bodies were likely to have been murder victims.

Pit 7
Summary: approximately 7 ft in diameter, located beneath the northeast corner of the enclosure wall, which is built over the pit. Date: up to end 3rd century.

Pit 7 lay beneath the north-eastern corner of the Enclosure Wall, immediately north of Pit 5. Cocks reported the foundations for the enclosure wall cutting into the pit, hence the walls post-date the pit. From his plan in the 1921 report it appears to be *c.* 7 ft in diameter.

Artefacts from Pit 7: Samian ware (one Dr38 bowl dated 140-200 AD and one Cinnamus Dr37 bowl dated 150-180 AD), one Oxford mortarium (oxidized with a red colour coat, M41, 240-400 AD), one Trajan coin 98-117 AD, and one garnet hornfels whetstone. No other finds were reported and no depths recorded. Therefore the date can only be determined as up to the end 3rd century.

Pit 8
Summary: a pit located north of the enclosure wall of the complex; bottle shaped and 17 ft deep, it is a possible underground granary or food storage area which became a refuse pit from the mid 2nd century until the end 3rd.

Pit 8 was located just north of the gravel path, north of the 3rd House (Figures 3.1 and 3.23). Similar bottle-shaped pits have been reported from other sites, e.g. Butser, Hampshire. Due to a significant proportion of Samian pottery this pit was often referred to as 'the Samian pit' by Cocks. However, the Samian appears concentrated between 12ft and 15ft depth, although not all of the finds had a depth noted.

The finds between 12 and 15 ft show a considerable amount of burning, some so burnt as to be almost melted and unrecognizable. As not all finds within these layers are burnt this is taken to represent a building fire and not a fire within the pit. If so, this would date the fire to be around the end of the 3rd century.

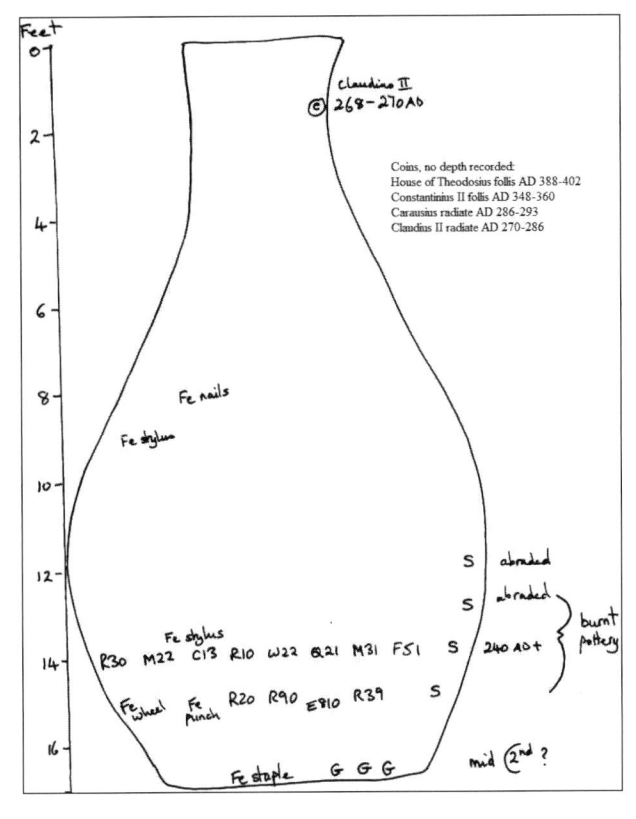

Figure 3.23 The profile of Pit 8 with finds plotted that had depth information. The profile is not known for certain, but has been estimated from Cocks' description and from the site plan, with information from the finds labels.

Artefacts from Pit 8:
Glass: the lowest recorded finds are pale green window glass and, colourless and brown vessel fragments found at 17 ft.
A pipe-clay figurine head of Venus was located at 4.5 ft depth in this pit.
Pottery: A substantial amount of Samian ware (122 sherds) was found between 12 and 15 ft depth and this consisted of all production areas (La Graufesenque, Les Martres-de-Veyre, Lezoux and East Gaul) and the residual nature also indicated by abraded pieces and burnt sherds. There is also a very wide range of oxidised and reduced wares, along with mortaria between 14 and 15 ft.
Iron objects such as a stylus, punch and wheel part were also found between 14ft and 15 ft along with a **worked bone** pin. An iron staple was located at 17 ft. A pottery **spindle whorl** was found in this pit, but no depth recorded. **Copper alloy**: a rim of a bronze pot, 2 ligulae, wire at 4 ft and a needle at 15ft.

It appears that this pit was primarily receiving household rubbish from the residential phase of the 3rd House from the mid-2nd to end 3rd century, but it may have been close to a workshop as well.

Pit 9
Summary: located within the enclosure of the main complex between two wattle and daub buildings SE of the 3rd House, 7 ft diameter and recorded to 12 ft depth, it dates from the mid-4th century to the end-4th or early 5th century.

This Pit is close to the main activities of the buildings within the north end of the Yewden enclosure. The deepest recorded finds provide good dating for the 12 ft level: **Pottery** - Samian (170-200 AD); an Oxfordshire mortarium with a red colour coat (M41; 240-410 AD) and a **coin** dated 341-348 AD. There are further occurrences of coins and Samian pottery throughout the pit, but these are younger than the base finds, some notably residual. There is a paucity of finds recorded until at 4 ft depth where there is an **iron** punch and iron fragments. This is overlain by a **quern stone** layer at 3.5 ft. The querns include vesicular basalt, quartz conglomerate and Millstone Grit types. There follows a quantity of pottery at 3 feet depth. The pottery is largely reduced ware (substantial amounts of R10 and R20, with R30, R90 and E80 grog tempered ware). There is also Oxford Colour Coated ware (240-410 AD) and a residual Oxford White ware mortarium (M22, 100-150 AD) with a Verulamium tazza (Chapter 5.2).

Not recorded with any depth, but noted as being 'Pit 9' are the following: a variety of mortaria including New Forest forms (260-370 AD) and other white wares, oxidized and black burnished wares, copper alloy finds (toiletry items, two ligulae (at 4 ft and 12 ft), furniture pins, a plate, hairpins and a brooch pin), bone knife handles, a glass vessel, and a worked bone pin.

The fill represents a household refuse pit. The date for opening can be confined to the mid-fourth century and the fill dating to the end fourth, or maybe, fifth century.

Pit 10
Summary: located within the yard of the main Yewden complex just SE of the Annexe to the 3rd House. Depth > 4 feet.

Cocks does not specifically mention Pit 10 as a description in his 1921 report and there is only one find recorded – an iron stylus at 4 ft depth.

Pit 11
Summary: located close to Pit 9 within the enclosure of the Yewden complex, 8 ft in diameter and c. 14 ft deep, mid-2nd to end 4th century, associated with the Northeast Building and the 3rd House.

Pit 11 was close to the main activities of buildings within the north end of the Yewden enclosure (Fig. 3.1). It lay between two wattle and daub buildings south of the 3rd House and would have been adjacent to the extension of this building which is associated with the 'mortar floor' (or Chalk floor as it is labelled on Cocks' 1921 plan).

The lowermost levels from *c.* 13 feet depth contain Samian pottery from La Graufesenque, Les Martres-de-Veyre and Lezoux (date range of 60-200 AD). There is a mortarium and a flagon and one Antoninus Pius coin dated 138-161 AD. There are also worked bone knife handles, a bone counter and bone pin at 7, 3.5 and 3 ft respectively. Another bone pin occurred at 2 ft along with several iron objects: a stylus, hook, cramp, saw and a nail, with more iron in the form of another cramp, a hinge and a spear shaft socket at 1.5 ft. An iron bracelet occurred at 1 ft depth with a follis of Constantinopolis dated to 330-335 AD.
The pit appears to be a mix of household and workshop waste and dates from the mid-2nd century to approximately the end 4th century.

Pit 12
Summary: a shallow pit, in the remains of a wall adjoining the Annexe, c. late 3rd century

Pit 12 was located in the remains of a wall that ran west from the south-west corner of the Annexe of the 3rd House. Cocks (1921) did not describe this pit and the only finds recorded were from 1.5 ft: 1 glass vessel fragment, 1 chunk of cullet, 2 iron nails and iron 1 iron ring headed staple, along with a coin. The coin (a Tetricus II radiate) dates this level to post 270-274 AD.

Pit 13

Summary: a shallow pit located north of the main Yewden enclosure wall; contained a fragment of adult human skull, end 3rd-early 4th century?

There are a number of pits in this area and it is close to the wattle and daub building containing the 'tuning fork' furnace. On finds labels Cocks often describes this pit as shallow and 'to the east of the Samian Pit' (Pit 8). Finds of this description are thus interpreted as Pit 13. There were very few finds from this pit which were: a ligula, 2 bronze rivets, one fragment of worked bone pin at 1 ft, a reduced ware beaker (R30), an early Abingdon butt beaker (AD 50-80) and one fragment of an Oxford white ware mortarium (M18.1 of Young 1977, dating 240-300 AD). The date for the fill is not well defined, but includes the period from the end 3rd century and possibly early 4th.

Pit 14

Summary: located north of the main enclosure wall of the Yewden complex; 14ft deep; 2nd to 3rd century.

There were a number of pits in this southern area of the 'yard' as Cocks called it (Figure 3.1) and Pit 14 lay north of the track and north enclosure wall of the Yewden villa complex. It was also located between two wattle and daub buildings containing furnaces (the tuning fork furnace and the hybrid furnace). The finds include 1 sherd of Les Martres-de-Veyre Samian **pottery** (a Dr18/31 plate) dated to 100-120 AD at the lowermost depth of 14ft and an Oxford Colour Coat bowl base with an illerate stamp dating from AD 240. Also recorded with depths are: an **iron** stylus (3 ft), iron buckle (2 ft) and a **copper alloy** brooch pin at 1 ft. Datable items are unfortunately not given find horizons, but include a Claudius II radiate **coin** (268-270 AD) and an Oxford Colour Coated vessel (240-410 AD). Other finds include reduced ware and black burnished ware dishes and a coarse ware jar, and a **worked bone** knife handle. Dating is therefore very loose, but is indicated to be 2nd to 3rd century, which could include material from the 3rd House, the Northeast Building and the Hybrid Furnace building.

Pit 15

Summary: located north of the main enclosure wall of the Yewden complex; ?6 ft deep, end 1st to 3rd century.

There were a number of pits in this area (Figure 3.1) and it lay north of the track and north enclosure wall of the Yewden villa complex. Pit 15 lay between two wattle and daub buildings containing furnaces (the tuning fork furnace and the hybrid furnace). It lay close to (just east of) Pit 14.

The deepest recorded find was at 6 ft. Finds between 3 ft and 6 ft in depth include Samian ware dishes, plates and cups from La Graufesenque and Lezoux (70-100 and 170-200 AD respectively). There are no coins that can be used for dating purposes. Pottery such as an Oxford Colour Coated vessel and an Oxford red-slipped mortarium (M41) can both be dated to AD 240-410, although no depths were given for these objects. One of the newborn infant burials occurred in this pit at 1 ft depth along with an iron spear (a shaft socket is recorded as being 'with the baby'). Also at this level was a 1st century Colchester brooch. Other finds included a blue-green glass vessel fragment, pale green window glass, 12 iron nails, a pottery spindle whorl and a worked bone needle at 3.5 ft. The datable objects indicate the fill is end 1st to 2nd century.

Pit 16
Summary: located within the northeast corner of the main Yewden complex immediately north of a wattle and daub building, 11 to 12 ft in diameter and 17 ft deep; 3rd to 4th century, household waste with minor workshop material.

Pit 16 was in the north end of the Yewden enclosure (Figure 3.1). There was only one datable item from the base of the pit and this was an Oxfordshire white slipped flagon (Q21, 200-250 AD). Residual Samian ware occurred above this level (from La Graufesenque, Les Martres and Lezoux, dating from 60 to 200 AD). Bone pins were found at this level as well. Other than an iron clamp at 10 ft there were few recorded finds at depth, most finds are between 1 and 4 feet depth. These layers contained many iron items (nails, staples, a clamp, knife blade, ox goad, stylus, hooks, hinges and various strips and fragments). There were also personal objects such as a necklace, a brooch and toiletry items. There were 3 glass vessels fragments and a chunk of cullet, with some slag with greenish copper alloy patches. There was a collection of pottery with no depths defined which includes reduce, oxidized and black burnished ware, along with Oxfordshire mortaria datable to 240-410 AD and 240-300 AD. The pit was therefore open and receiving waste from household and lesser workshop material during the 3rd and 4th centuries.

Pit 17
Summary: located north of the north enclosure wall, within an older enclosure area, c. 5 ft diameter, 17 ft deep, 1st to mid-3rd century.

There was a cluster of pits in the far NE part of the site excavations: Pit 17, 18, 19, 21 and 22 were all closely sited. There is good dating evidence in the form of Samian pottery and Verulamium ware. The Samian provided dates at 15 ft of 40-100 AD, 10 ft of 150-200 AD, and 4 ft of 160-250 AD. Iron finds included a stylus at 10 ft, a saw blade and nail. There were two pottery spindle whorls in the base at 17 ft along with a piece of copper wire adhering to an ox jaw. There are only three sherds of pottery other than Samian and these are a Verulamium mortarium (50-160 AD), a Verulamium jar (50-160 AD) and a fine oxidized ware jar. This pottery was not recorded with a depth. No coins, glass or other finds were reported.
The date for the fill of this pit can therefore be confined as the 1st to the mid 3rd century.

Pit 18
Summary: located north of the north enclosure wall, within an older enclosure area, c. 6 ft in diameter and c. 17 ft deep, 1st to 3rd century.

There was a cluster of pits in the far NE part of the site excavations: Pits 17, 18, 19, 21 and 22 were all closely sited. Datable finds included Samian pottery from La Graufesenque only and these occurred at 17 ft and 8ft (40-100 AD). The Samian assemblage comprised cups and a Dr30 bowl. A grog tempered dish and Oxford Colour Coated vessels (240-410 AD) occurred 5 ft, and a Gallienus radiate coin was found at 2ft (260-268 AD). There were no copper alloy, stone or glass objects and the only iron object (a hook) was found at 1.5 ft. An Oxford white ware mortarium (140-200 AD) was obtained from this pit, but the depth was not recorded. A further reduced ware dish was also found (R30) again with no depth. This is a household assemblage, but with a limited variety of vessels.

Pit 19
Summary: located north of the north enclosure wall, within an older enclosure area, c. 18 ft in diameter and 8 ft deep, mid-2nd to end 4th century.

This was a very large pit (Figure 3.1). By measuring the pit on Cocks's original 1921 plan, it would seem that it was approximately 18 feet in diameter. It was surrounded by four smaller pits: Pits 17, 18, 21 and 22. Although the deepest find recorded was at 8 ft, there were a large number of finds from this pit with no depths reported. The size and location may indicate this was initially for gravel extraction.

Finds from Pit 19: Four infant burials occurred in this pit, but no depths were given with their accompanying labels. There were 19 **coins** recorded from depths between 4 ft and 1.5 ft. The bulk of these coins were found at 3 ft and range in date from 260 to 341 AD. Those coins obtained from higher levels also date to within this date range.
Pottery: Oxford Colour Coated vessels found with the coins supports the date range (AD 240-410). The lowest recorded level at 8 ft is dated by Samian pottery (Lezoux and East Gaulish vessels) providing dates between 150 and 250 AD. A large range of other pottery occurs in this pit with no depths – for instance large quantities of Oxford Colour Coat and sandy reduced wares, along with other reduced and grog tempered kitchen wares, black burnished ware, Alice Holt pottery, white slipped wares, sandy oxidized ware and Oxford white ware mortaria (240-410 AD). A Samian **gaming counter** was recorded from 3 ft depth, and although this Les Martres vessel was made 100-120 AD, it is not clear what time elapsed before it was trimmed and used in a game.
Copper alloy comprised personal items such as an early forms of bracelet (8 ft and 3 ft), a brooch (4 ft), along with wire at 3 ft and 1.5 ft. Household items occur amongst the **iron** objects: latches, hooks, skewers, needle, staple and a ring, and also with **bone objects**: pins, needle and gaming counter.
Pit 19 represents household refuse dating from the mid-2nd to end 4th century.

Pit 20
Summary: located at the north end of the enclosure, c. 5 ft diameter, 19 ft deep, a well?, filled with household waste, 1st to mid-4th century.

Pit 20 lay east of the 3rd House. The narrow diameter (5 ft) yet considerable depth (19 ft) indicates that, as for Pit 6, this must have been a well. In his report Cocks did not report encountering the water table (which might be expected for the excavation date of October to December).

Datable finds included Samian **pottery** from La Graufesenque, Les Martres and Lezoux from all levels between 19 ft and 2 ft recorded. There is one **coin** – a House of Constantine follis at 3 ft dated 341-348 AD. Amongst the other (non-Samian) pottery there was datable Verulamium ware at the bottom of the pit (50-160 AD) as well as grog and sand tempered wares (E80, E810, E30), black burnished ware, sandy reduced ware (R20), fine white ware (W10) and sandy white ware (W22, 100-410 AD) and coarse grog tempered ware R90 giving this a likely first century date.
Copper alloy was present as various personal items such as two bracelets (one is 1st century), a brooch, nail cleaner and a needle. **Iron** finds include a knife handle and blade, a stylus, a hook, nails and an ox goad. There is window **glass** and a grey-green glass vessel at 1.5 ft. Taking all the finds into account, notably the coin as a *terminus post quem*, the date can be defined as 1st to mid-fourth century.

Pit 21
Summary: a household pit located north of the north enclosure wall, within the yard, 5 ft diameter, depth not recorded, 1st to mid 4th century.

There was a cluster of pits in the far NE part of the site excavations: Pit 17, 18, 19, 21 and 22 are all closely sited. Most of the finds had no depth information on the label, a few noted depths of 1.5 ft and 2 ft. A *terminus post quem* of 320-325 AD is given to the horizon at 1.5 ft due to 3 coins a Gallic Empire radiate and two Constantine I follis. Datable finds included cups and plates of Samian ware from La Graufesenque and Lezoux with dates ranging from 40 to 200 AD. Other pottery included Oxford white ware mortaria (180-300 AD) and Verulamium mortaria (50-160 AD) with undatable reduced and grog tempered wares (fabrics R10, R20, R90, E80), sandy white ware (W20), oxidized wares (O20) and shell tempered ware (C13). Only one copper alloy household item was found at 1.5 ft, and there were iron fragments at 2ft. There was one infant burial in this pit and bones of hare and rabbit.

Pit 22
Summary: a household pit located north of the north enclosure wall, within the yard, 8 ft in diameter, 6 ft or more in depth, dating from the end 1st to end 3rd century.

There was a cluster of pits in the far NE part of the site excavations: Pit 17, 18, 19, 21 and 22 were all closely sited. Samian **pottery** was represented by one sherd from La Montans, and several from Les Martres and Lezoux. The forms included cups, decorated bowls, mortaria and one plate. Other pottery comprised a large quantity of reduced wares, white ware and grog tempered pottery – all kitchen wares and a large proportion of jars and dishes, with minor bowls. There were also some Oxford Colour Coated vessels (dishes and bowls) (240-410 AD). There was one **copper alloy** hairpin at 6 ft (1st or 2nd century), a light-blue **glass** vessel and an **iron** handle at 2 ft. A **quern** fragment (quartz conglomerate from the Forest of Dean) was found at 1.5 ft.

Pit 23
Summary: a household pit, located just east of the Annexe to the 3rd House and close to Pit 10, c. 6 ft in diameter, 4 ft deep. Date: 4th century.

Much of the **pottery** was in small and highly abraded sherds. The Samian contained no South Gaulish wares, but several abraded sherds of Les Martres and Lezoux vessels, and a small amount of East Gaulish ware. The abrasion indicates these are residual. The bulk of the pottery is mostly undatable reduced wares for kitchen use (R10, R20, R30, R90, R39, E30) with Oxfordshire white ware mortaria dating to 180-300 AD. Other household and personal items included **copper alloy** hair pins, a brooch pin and a nail cleaner, with three **carved bone** pins and a needle – all located between 2 and 4 ft depth. **Iron** objects include a latch lifter, ring and washer, a hook and a knife blade. Two fragments of colourless glass vessels occurred at 1.5 ft. **Coins** of Constantinopolis I and Constantinus II give a *terminus post quem* of 348 AD at 1.5 ft.

Dating can be defined therefore as 4th century, which is supported by dates of the adjacent 3rd House and the mortar floor (the floor represents a southerly extension to the 3rd House). It appears that the area of this pit was covered by a 1st century floor for the southerly extension to the 3rd House. Following a fire, a mortar floor (a possible threshing area?) was emplaced. The mortar floor, which was seen in fragmentary condition during the 1912 excavations, was laid at the end of the 3rd century (defined by coins and Samian wares below, within and above the floor). The building extension associated with the mortar floor was demolished by the early 4th century, opening up this area as part of the inner enclosure, with the pit open throughout the 4th century.

Pit 24
Summary: immediately outside the 3rd House by the north enclosure wall, c. 8 ft in diameter and 15 ft deep. It was in use during the last part of the residential phase of this building (mid-3rd century) through to the corn drying and processing phase from the end 3rd to 4th century.

Pit 24 was adjacent to the west wall of the 3rd House (Figure 3.1). This pit contained a very large quantity of **pottery**. The Samian ware showed a great variety of forms from all regions: La Graufesenque, Les Martres-de-Veyre, Lezoux and East Gaul. Other pottery types showed a great quantity of reduced and grog tempered wares than white or fine wares including vessel fabrics E30, R10, R20, R30, R90, R91, B11, W20, W21, O10, O20, O80. Dating was provided by quantities of Oxford Colour coat (F51, 240-410 AD) at 7 ft depth. **Copper alloy** brooches (one 1st century), a boss, a chain and bronze plate, a nail cleaner, needles and a pin were residual items or not datable. **Carved bone** pins were found at 3.5, 7 and 11 ft, with a bone knife handle at 3 ft and needle at 1.5 ft. **Iron** items were found between 1.5 and 3 ft: a hook, two knife blades, an axe blade and a finger ring.

A number of **querns** were located within this pit (two Lodsworth Stone, one Lower Greensand, one Hertfordshire Puddingstone and one Millstone Grit). The pit is closely associated with the 3rd House. Further quernstones, whetstones, two furnaces and charred grain of wheat and barley occur in this building. Both lines of evidence point to the drying and processing of grain in this area of the site.

All these items show the change in use of the 3rd House from residential to workshop. The transition seems to have been during the mid- or end-3rd century.

Pit 25
Summary: located just outside and to the east of the enclosure wall of the main Yewden complex and close to Pit 5, c. 7ft in diameter and c. 2 ft deep? Date: mid- end 2nd century

This pit yielded very few finds and the deepest recorded was at a depth of 2 feet. There is only Samian **pottery** from Lezoux (120-200 AD at 2 ft and 150-200 AD at 1.5 and 1 ft). These are cups and bowls. Other pottery is only represented by sandy reduced ware dishes and jars (R20) and 1 sherd of sand & grog tempered ware. Two **copper alloy** items were present – a pair of tweezers and one ligula. The only other remaining find was one sherd of pale green window **glass** at 1.5 ft. There were no coins and no iron. This is a shallow pit with a limited selection of finds dating to the mid to end of the 2nd century.

Pit 26
Summary: a household pit, located in the far NW of the site excavations, west of the NW wall, c. 6 ft in diameter and more than 4 ft in depth, end 1st to end 3rd century.

Pit 26 was relatively isolated and located approximately 15 ft. west of the north-west wall (Figure 3.1). This area contained disconnected remains of works "whose use had ceased during the time of occupation" according to Cocks (1921, p.144).

From some finds labels he described this pit as having a 'burnt flint floor', but burnt pottery (or other burnt finds) was not a feature of this pit. There was a great quantity and range of **pottery** forms including many types of jar, dish, bowl, mortaria and flagons. The pottery was dominated by sandy reduced wares (fabrics R20 and R30), but other reduced and grog tempered wares were also numerous (such as R10, R90, R39, E80, E810 and black burnished wares). Unfortunately only a few items had depths recorded. Mortaria include Oxford white ware forms (180 and 240-410 AD), but no depths were given. Samian pottery included only one sherd of La Graufesenque (40-100 AD), the remainder all from Lezoux (120 to 200 AD to a depth of 4 ft recorded). The fine wares included datable forms such as a Gallo-Belgic imported beaker (F11, pre-conquest to 70 AD), Nene Valley wares (150-400 AD), again no depths given.

Other finds include one **copper alloy** fibula brooch at 3.5 ft and Millstone Grit **quern** fragments.

3.4 The furnaces

There were 15 structures which Cocks (1921) termed 'furnaces'. He gave them names based on their shape (e.g. the Double-T furnace) or objects that they resembled (e.g. the Horse Shoe Furnace and the Tuning Fork Furnace). These were also numbered on his site plan and the numbers will be used here, alongside Cocks' names. If furnaces were not measured by Cocks and entered in his report, then the dimensions were measured from the Cocks 1921 site plan, but checked with photographic evidence, where this was available. As some of this information derives from the current project measurements, the metric system was used.

Furnace I (Double-T)
Location: east end of 2nd House.
Form: chalk-mortar build (for the T ends) and flint-mortar build for the body section (western end) *c.* 6 m long with a stoke hole in the top of the structure, not the side. The body had a bulbous shape.
Finds: a large quantity of white wood ash, two coins dated 293-296 AD with furnace and 330-335 AD (side of furnace).
Date: 4th century.
Function: most likely a drier for grain, flax or other materials; possibly for malting barley. See the discussion of the 2nd House.

Furnace II (Multiple-T) and Furnace III (Grid-iron)
Location: in the Well Shed, a wattle and daub building south of the entrance gate.
Form: chalk-mortar build with a mortared flint end to fIII. They were well-made and contained shaped and squared blocks of chalk, lain in courses, in contrast to the rough-hewn blocks of other furnaces. Steps led down to the stoke hole end of fII. Both are c. 4.3 m in length. Figures 3.24 and 3.25.
Finds: there are no finds associated directly with the furnaces, but the finds around them within the Well shed would indicate that these were in operation from the $C2^{nd}$ to $C3^{rd}$.
Function: malting barley (as there is an associated water source), but the structure may have had other functions in addition to this use.

Figure 3.24 The Multiple T (a) looking south and (b) showing flues, looking W

Figure 3.25 The well and the Gridiron Furnace, looking *c.* **southeast.**

Furnace IV (Single-T)
Location: 8.5 m east of the 1st House, within the enclosure. No building was recognised around this feature (Figure 3.26).
Form: flint, mud build, *c.* 3 m long, the stoke hole was in the east end, the long length required to build the required draught and the top of the 'T' was built slightly higher and formed two flues. The structure was 'arched over' and then covered by rammed chalk.
Finds: white wood ash. Half a lower rotary quern and a complete, but broken, Samian DR36 dish in the stoke hole. This indicates a date prior to mid-end 2nd century when this form became common. **Date**: 1st to earliest 2nd century.
Function: most likely a drier for grain, flax or other materials; possibly for malting barley.

Figure 3.26 The Single T furnace, east of the 1st House, looking north

Furnace V (South Cream Pan) and Furnace Va (Small Horse Shoe)

Location: south end of the wattle and daub building in the north part of the enclosure. A wall division separates fV and fVa from fVI (Figure 3.27).

Form: fV: Brick and tile build for the South Cream Pan (fV) which is 3.4 m in length. A simple structure with the stoke hole in the west end.

fVa: chalk-mortar build, 1.5 m in length. Similar forms and show a similarity to fX the East Cream Pan. No trace of a floor. Burnt (reddened) internal surfaces.

Finds: the only finds directly associated with the structures were an iron cramp and a fragment of an iron ring which were found in the fill. In the surrounding floor area there is some Samian pottery from La Graufesenque and a 1st century copper alloy brooch, likely to be residual. A *terminus post quem* is provided by a denarius of 138-161 AD within the building.

Date: this appears to be a 2nd to 3rd century structure, but the end of use is not defined from finds. There is a division between these furnaces and the North Cream Pan furnace, but they are within the same building, hence the dates are estimated as similar.

Function: not certain. For fV it is likely to be workshop activity requiring quenching (in water filled 'cream pan'). The Small Horseshoe furnace (fVa) is likely to be an earlier structure functioning as a hearth.

Figure 3.27 The South Cream Pan Furnace, looking *c.* NW. A small furnace constructed of tile with an adjacent pottery vessel embedded in mortar (resembling a Victorian 'cream pan').

Furnace VI (North Cream Pan)

Location: north end of the wattle and daub building within the NE corner of the enclosure. Separated by a wall partition from fV and fVa in the same building (Fig 3.28).

Form: Chalk-mortar build, 2.2 m length, inside surfaces burnt and reddened. Two stoke holes at south end with double rounded 'apse-like' north end. Close by outside the west wall was a large, black, coarse ware vessel embedded in mortar in the ground (quenching vessel?). This is the remnant of a more complex drier (similar to the Chorleywood malting kiln).

Figure 3.28 The North Cream Pan Furnace, looking north. A double arched shape with a pottery vessel embedded in mortar alongside (resembling a Victorian 'cream pan').

Finds: dating is provided only by finds within the surrounding building, namely: a Hadrian denarius (117-138 AD), another coin of Antonius Pius (138-161 AD) and Gallianus (260-268 AD), as well as a coin with the wall partition of the House of Constantine (AD 341-348). Samian pottery associated with the floor and partition of the surrounding building include only 1 sherd of La Graufesenque, but 12 sherds of Lezoux – a combined date range of 43-200 AD. There are also reduced ware jars (R20, R30, R90, E810) and minor black burnished ware dishes, along with fragments of blue and blue-green glass vessels. The iron indicates a workshop use: knife handles, an awl, a saw, an ox goad and other fragments.

Date: 2nd- 3rd century, with modifications to the structure.

Function: drier, most likely for malting barley (with the water quencher – the 'cream pan' adjacent).

Furnace VII (Heart Shaped)

Location: S of the Annexe within the enclosure, near a remnant of rammed chalk floor.

Form: chalk-mortar build, *c.* 1.5 m diameter; a stoke hole was not visible.

Finds: no finds recorded from this feature.

Function: possibly a hearth.

Date: 2nd to early 3rd, based on finds within the general area.

Furnace VIII (East Twin) and Furnace IX (West Twin)

Location: centrally placed within the 3rd House (Figure 3.29).

Form: Chalk blocks, mortared, *c.* 6.4 x 3.2 m (fVIII with flues projecting out from this central area); *c.* 3 x 3.6 m (fIX). Covered by a rammed chalk floor.

Finds: a quantity of charred grain (wheat and barley, see Chapter 7.2) and fuel ash slag. There is also Samian ware, coins and a wealth of other finds from on and in the floor areas surrounding these furnaces (as part of the 3rd House).
Date: end 3rd to 4th century (early 5th?)
Function: most likely a drier for grain, flax or other materials, and for malting barley.

Figure 3.29 The East Twin furnace looking north.

Furnace X (East Cream Pan)
Location: far east side of the Yard, *c.* 21.5 m from the NE corner of the enclosure wall.
Form: flint-mud build, 1.5 m in length, but badly damaged. It is associated with a mortar embedded, large circular vessel similar to the North Cream Pan furnace (fV), *c.* 1 m south of the furnace.
Finds: there are no finds recorded from within this feature, but several are noted around it. The only datable find is a coin labelled as 'by east cream pan' which is a House of Constantine follis 330-348 AD. However, it is uncertain whether this relates to the structure or if it is simply a loose item in the yard next to it. This structure therefore remains undated.
Function: not certain. **Date**: not certain.

Furnace XI & Furnace XII (Hybrid Furnace)
Location: east Yard c. 15 m north of the enclosure wall, within a building ("vestiges of walls" were found by Cocks, p.155), Figure 3.30.
Form: chalk-mortar build, 6 x 6 m (widest dimensions),
Finds: there are lots of finds surrounding the Hybrid Furnace showing this was sited in an area that was residential during the 1st century. However, all finds recorded as directly associated with the furnace itself have an earliest date of 120 AD (Samian ware) and the oldest unburnt item in the flues is East Gaulish Samian dating to 160-250 AD. The date indicated is, therefore, 2nd up to mid-3rd century. The area is left open within the east side of the Yard and hence has several later coins and other finds in the general area. An infant burial is close by the furnace and the only other finds are a whetstone and a rubbing stone.
Function: a drying furnace for wheat or malting barley.
Date: 2nd to early 3rd century.

Figure 3.30 The Hybrid Furnace in the east side of the yard, looking NNE. (right)

Figure 3.31 The Tuning Fork furnace, north of the 3rd House, looking approximately east (below)

Furnace XIII (Tuning Fork)
Location: in the Yard north of the 3rd House (Figure 3.31).
Form: Chalk-mortar build; 5.0 x 5.5 m (widest dimensions), a stoke hole in the westerly 'stem', dividing into two sections, each ending in a flue. Steps led down to the furnace.
Function: most likely a drier for grain, flax or other materials, and possibly for malting barley. **Date:** 1st century.

Furnace XIV (Shears)
Location: in the far west of the Yard, south of the Northwest Wall (Figure 3.32).
Form: chalk-mortar build, **c**. 2.4 m in length, stoke hole at the eastern 'open' end.
Finds: dating is from Samian ware only as there are no coins, copper alloy or other datable finds associated with the structure. The Samian is predominantly La Graufesenque, with 2 sherds of Les Martres and 2 of Lezoux (125-200 AD). One of the unburnt Les Martres sherds lies in the stoke hole indicating a date of operation during the 1st century.
Function: an early form of drier for grain, flax, or malting barley.
Date: 1st century.

Figure 3.32 Shears Furnace, looking northwest.

The furnaces – a summary
There are three groupings of furnaces by date:

1st Century	2nd-early 3rd Century	4th Century
Single T (fIV)	N&S Cream Pans (fV, fVa & fVI)	E & W Twin (fIX & fVIII)
Shears (fXIV)	Hybrid (FXI & fXII)	Double T (fI)
Tuning Fork (fXIII)	Heart	
	Multiple T/Gridiron (fII & fIII)	

The majority of furnaces at Hambleden are T shaped or tuning fork shaped, or a complex adaptation of the T shape (e.g. furnaces I, II, III, IV, VIII, IX, XI, XII, XIII of Cocks, 1921). The T forms tend to be larger than other types of furnace. It seems that these larger furnaces had chalk floors above them - as could be seen remaining in the 3rd House around the 'Twin furnaces' fVIII and fIX. Cocks states (ibid. p. 153) that furnaces such as the Hybrid (fXI and fXII) were probably built together in order to make as square a drying floor as possible and the same probably applies to Furnaces IX and VIII. The floors over these furnaces would have been quite large, about 8.5 m x 3.5 m. The nature of the floor covering is important for interpreting their function - chalk floors would be suitable to parch the spelt before threshing or prepare barley for beer making. The T shaped furnaces have always been assumed by archaeologists to be corn drying ovens. Hambleden is commonly put forward as an example of this process. However, a T shaped corn drying oven was reconstructed in the Butser project, Hampshire by Reynolds and Langley (1979). It proved not to be suitable for corn drying, but was suitable for sprouting grain for malting and brewing. It is debatable whether drying corn for flour was necessary as experiments such as those by Reynolds show that it takes about the same time as allowing the grain to dry naturally. The only advantage would be in drying corn during an unusually wet summer.

Another common assumption of authors using Hambleden as an example of corn drying is that, with 14 driers, it must be working as an imperial estate and exporting to the continent. Even Cocks himself says that "the exceptional level of food processing at the site meant that the villa was under government control". This is assuming that all 14 of the furnaces were driers and that all of them were in use simultaneously. As demonstrated above, this is not the case. The structures are spread throughout the 1st to 4th centuries, with the most numerous being during the 2nd to early 3rd century, when 3 buildings were potentially driers or malting areas. Even so, these were not necessarily all functioning at exactly the same time, and dating cannot be refined any closer. For instance the Hybrid Furnace is likely to slightly pre-date the North and South Cream Pan furnace building, the latter of which was probably residential during its first phase. As the Heart Furnace and the Small Horseshoe Furnace are both interpreted as hearths, this indicates that at any one time there were only 2 buildings (or 3 at the most during the 2nd to 3rd centuries) functioning as drying or malting areas. The drying process is likely to have been of more value for other crops than for grain intended for flour (such as flax). The heated floor would have been an essential part of the malting process for beer-making.

3.5 Walls, the Yard and enclosure, and remaining buildings
The North Wall

Summary: an earlier wall to the main Yewden complex which defines the north end of Cocks' 'Yard'. It is not clear whether this represents a wall of a building or an enclosure. Date: mid-1st century to end 2nd.

The north wall encloses an area to the south of it that Cocks (1921) terms 'the Yard', Figures 3.1 and 3.33. There are many small finds in this location. Pits 3 and 4 are close by parts of the remaining structure. Immediately to the northwest lies another wall, at a different orientation, called the Northwest wall.

Figure 3.33 Middle of the North Wall looking west. Building foundations or enclosure wall?

The **pottery** assemblage consists of 17 pieces of Iron Age pottery in close association in the area surrounding the wall. There is no 'Belgic' transition seen as for the NW wall, but early Samian pottery is present. The Samian is from La Graufesenque (plates dating to 40+ AD) and Lezoux DR 31 and Dr18/31 plates (120-150 or 180 AD). There is one East Gaulish decorated bowl dating 130-250 AD. Other pottery types include: reduced wares (R30, R90 and R91): oxidized grog ware (O80); shell tempered ware (C13); some fine wares from Nene Valley (F52, 200-370 AD) and Oxford Colour Coated ware (F51, 240+ AD); Cocks does not label these with depths and they may be residual yard debris.

A coin found just east of the wall dates to 98-117 AD (a Trajan sestertius). There is no glass with the wall, but a scatter lies just south of it. Iron finds include a perforated strip and a tool built into the wall, with another tool, iron rod, staple and slag nearby. Four quern stones are associated with the wall (one of vesicular basalt, two Lower Greensand and one Millstone Grit) plus one whetstone and a rubbing stone.

The wall is very fragmentary and it is not clear whether this is the foundation layer for a wooden building structure (with wattle and daub walls) or if it is a wall to an enclosure as Mr Cocks suggests. Due to the relationship and angles of the North Wall with the NW wall, plus the dates, the scatter and type of artefacts associated with it, this wall is interpreted as the edge of a demolished structure dating from mid-1st to end 2nd century only. After this time Pits 3 and 4 are opened and buildings to the south are extended and improved.

The Northwest Wall

Summary: an earlier enclosure wall outside the main Yewden complex. It lay to the NW of the North wall and Yard. It was not in alignment with any other feature on site. Date: earliest Roman to end 3rd century.

There were many small finds from this location. Pit 26 lies just to the west of this collapsed feature, which is visible as a highly fragmented wall base only (Figure 3.34). There were 2 infant burials in the fill of this wall and 3 more closely associated with it.

Figure 3.34 The Northwest Wall looking approx. northeast.

Much of the **pottery** is in small and highly abraded sherds. The overall character is of a very early Roman kitchen assemblage. The bulk of the forms are jars and dishes (some with lids) composed of sandy reduced wares (fabrics R20 and R30) and grog tempered or sandy 'Belgic' wares (E80, E810 and E30) which are wheel thrown and hence very early Roman. Only one piece of Iron Age pottery was recorded here, although it is immediately adjacent to the Iron Age settlement. Other forms of pottery included sandy white wares (Verulamium 50-160 AD, and Oxford 100+ AD), and oxidized, shell tempered, and coarse tempered wares (R90 and R91). Also present are poppyhead beakers (50-160 AD) and a minor amount of Oxford Colour Coat (240-410 AD), a white slipped flagon (Q21) and a white slipped mortaria (M31, 240-410 AD).

The **Samian** assemblage consists of a large proportion of cups and plates with lesser dishes and decorated bowls. The range is dominated by La Graufesenque and Lezoux forms with a combined date of 50 to 200 AD. Minor amounts of East Gaul give a date to 250 AD. Only two **coins** were located in this area: a Domitian as (81-96 AD) and an illegible follis (300-400 AD).

The only **iron** finds are a drill bit and a brooch, along with one **bone** pin. Six fragmentary **querns**, some built into the wall, were sourced from the Forest of Dean (Quartz Conglomerate), the Pennines (Millstone Grit) and Sussex (Lower Greensand). There was also one whetstone of possibly local sarsen. There were 19 records of **glass** (17 vessels, 1 window sherd and 1 'cullet') and the predominant colour was greyish green with a small amount of blue-green.

The conclusion from the finds and character of the remaining wall is that this represents an earlier enclosure spanning the Iron Age to Roman transition and an area of habitation throughout the 1st century. A grain processing area was close by, parts of querns being utilized in the building of the wall. The pottery assemblage indicates continued habitation up to the end of the 3rd century. Finds that could potentially span older dates (Oxford Colour Coated and mortarium, and the illegible follis) are highly abraded and represent part of the general rubbish being dropped and reworked in a 4th century yard area.

Figure 3.35 The eastern enclosure wall from the SE corner. On the left of the foreground is a concrete block, possibly a pedestal.

The enclosure wall to the villa complex
The enclosure to the new complex built post end-3rd century.

The enclosure wall is only preserved on the east side of the site (Figures 3.35 and 3.36). Both north and south walls die out westwards. The complete dimensions can, therefore, only be estimated as 140 m (E-W dimension) by 110 m (at the narrowest point N-S) to *c.* 180-200 m potentially at the widest point, if the walls continue diverging.

Figure 3.36 The piers for entrance gates to the enclosure through the east wall, looking northeast

Enclosure wall dimensions:
East wall – 110 m in length.
South wall: *c.* 120 m in length?
North wall: *c.* 120 m?
The 1912 excavation did not extend to trace any remaining return wall at the western end of the complex.

Dates for the enclosure wall can be defined by cross-cutting relationships and by finds.

(1) As the wall cuts across the top of Pit 7 this dates the wall to post end-3rd century

(2) Finds associated with the wall are very few, but two coins provide TPQ dates of post end 3rd century (one illegible As or Dupondius, highly abraded 200-300 AD and one Gallic Empire radiate 268-274 AD)

(3) A little reduced and white ware gives date definition. Two mortaria – both Oxfordshire, one a white ware and the other a white slip, both dated 240-410 AD.

The 'curved wall' which is a fragmented section within the enclosure, near the gate and V ditch, can be dated to post 2nd century due to an F59 Oxfordshire beaker built into it.

Quern hole

A shallow pit north of the NW wall, diameter and depth not known, but depths of 2 ft reported. Date: 2nd and 3rd century fill.

This pit is not described well in Cocks' 1921 report and the finds labels give little depth information. It is clear that this hole is in the furthest northerly end of the NW wall and it appears to be shallow (depths only reported to 2 ft). Despite its name there is only one quern fragment in the collections seen (Millstone Grit) and one whetstone (calcareous sandstone).

Datable finds include a Gallienus radiate **coin** giving an aproximate *terminus post quem* of 260-268 AD (no precise depth reported) and also an As or a Dupondius dating 0-200 AD (illegible coin, located at 1 ft). Samian occurs in the **pottery** assemblage from La Graufesenque, Les Martres and Lezoux (collectively 40-200 AD). All but one sherd of the Samian is burnt. Other pottery also shows a substantial quantity of burnt sherds. The forms include predominantly jars, dishes and bowls, with some beakers. The bulk is reduced wares: R90, R10, R20, R30, and grog tempered E80, E810 and O80. There is a white slipped reduced fabric and mica dusted fabric F30 as well as Oxford Colour Coated ware (F51 dated to 240-410 AD). Other finds include one **copper alloy** nail cleaner, two fragments of green **glass** vessels and one blue-green bottle fragment, all at 1 ft depth.

The Well Shed

Summary: contained the well and two furnaces (fII and fIII). It is located close to and inside the eastern enclosure wall to the Yewden complex and is close to the entrance gate. Date: 2nd to end 3rd century.

The small building was located immediately on the south side of the main entrance gate. It was a wattle and daub structure (Cocks 1921, p. 142) with a thatched roof (as no tile or other CBM was found here). This building also contained two furnaces – fII and fIII which Cocks called the Multiple T and the Gridiron furnaces (Figs. 5.1). The well was inside the building and was stone-lined. The finds included a reasonable range of reduced ware pottery (R10, R20, R30 and R90) which were mostly beakers and jars with 1 dish. There is a small amount of white ware including Verulamium vessels (50-160 AD). Oxford Colour Coated ware is also present providing a date of 240-410 AD. There was only one coin found, which was located at less than 1 ft depth – a Sabina as or dupondius 117-138 AD. A copper alloy disc brooch was found (.133, Chapter 4.4) at 3 ft and this is dated 100-200 AD. Another brooch pin and a worked bone pin were not datable. Iron finds include a stylus, a door fastening and a perforated plate. It is uncertain if Samian was located in this area as each find was marked '?well shed' and hence the location could not be certain. If this Samian was located from this building then it dated from 40-80 AD for one La Graufesenque plate, to 120-200 AD for a plate, a decorated Dr37 bowl and Dr33 cups from Lezoux. In conclusion, there seem to be some items with longevity associated with this building, but this is normal for items such as brooches and Samian vessels. The *terminus post quem* from coins and datable local pottery would indicate a date of 2nd to the end 3rd century for the Well Shed.

The Northeast building
A wattle and daub structure in the northeast part of the enclosure, containing furnaces fV, fVa and fVI. Date: 2nd to 3rd century.

A wattle and daub building lies immediately north of the main entrance gates, in the northeast section of the enclosure. Cocks described it as a 'hovel' and possibly as the workers' quarters (1921, p.142). There are three furnaces (fV, fVa and fVI) described as 'domestic hearths' (ibid. p.142; p.153).
Finds: An assemblage of coins, Samian and other pottery, indicates an earlier residential area. The Small Horseshoe Furnace (fVa) is interpreted as being a hearth related to this residential phase. Other finds such as an iron saw, awl, knife, ox goad and four rubbing stones, along with the emplacement of 2 furnaces (the 'South and North Cream Pan furnaces) indicate a second phase as a workshop and possibly used for grain drying as well. See the furnace discussion of finds in this area.

The Yard and the 'Black soil' area
Summary: the Yard is a large open area outside the main Yewden complex north of the enclosure wall and track of Yewden, but within an older walled enclosure. There are 11 pits and 2 furnaces (the hybrid and the tuning fork) in this area, along with the majority of the infant burials. The 'black soil' occurs within this area and may be an organic build-up such as manure. Date: Iron Age to end of Roman occupation.

The 'Yard' is Cocks' (1921) terminology and he applies this name to the large area at the north end of the excavation. It is defined as the area north of the main Yewden complex enclosure wall terminating at what he calls the 'North Wall' which is a very fragmented wall defining an older enclosure or a building foundation. The Yard area encompasses the entire east-west exposure of this most northerly end of the excavation, up to a further enclosure wall that he calls the 'North West wall'. Artefacts found associated with both the North and the North West walls are listed separately. Cocks is not consistent in labelling his finds. This area is sometimes divided as Yard East or Yard West, occasionally North, but on numerous occasions the label just says 'Yard'.

The 'Black soil' area is Cocks' description of the part of the yard on the immediate north side of the 3rd House and enclosure wall up to the north wall which he says:

> *"must have been, during at least the latter part of its occupation, ankle deep in filthy black mud. If this were a cattle yard then the manure was obviously* not regularly utilized, *but it seemed more like dirt resulting from some sort of factory"*.

The artefacts specifically labelled as being associated with this **'black soil'** area are: 43 records of Samian pottery nearly all of which is from Lezoux 120-200 AD. There is a little Les Martres and very minor La Graufesenque. No other pottery is recorded as being found associated with this horizon. There are no copper alloy items. Coins: only 1 coin was recorded from this horizon and this is dated to the Gallic Empire 286-293 AD. The black soil horizon may only have been accumulating during the 2nd to 3rd century, in which case it is likely to have only been an enclosed part in the west yard, as Pits 8, 13, 14 and 15 were open at this time.

Artefacts and features described and recorded from the **Yard (E and W)** are as follows:

Pits: Pits 3, 4, 8, 13, 14, 15, 17, 18, 19, 21, and 22 are located in the Yard. These cover the whole Romano-British period from the 1st century to the end 4th. The 1st century pits are concentrated in the east yard, the 2nd century to the central and northeast, the 3rd century pits are in the north yard and 4th century only northeast.

Furnaces: Shears, the Tuning Fork and the Hybrid furnaces are all located in the yard. The former are 1st century and the Hybird Furnace is 2nd to 3rd century. Their location in this area, along with a good number of finds indicates the northern part of the Yewden excavation was an area of intense activity during the earliest Roman times through to the 3rd Century.

Pottery: there are 285 records of Samian ware from the yard, representing all source areas and a wide range of forms. There are also 274 records of other pottery (reduced, grog tempered, white. black burnished, fine and oxidized ware, flagons and mortaria). The dates span from the Iron Age throughout the Romano-British period.

Coins: 124 coins were found in the yard area spanning dates from a Claudius I AD 41-54 to House of Theodosius AD 378-383.

Copper alloy: a good range of toiletry items and sets, brooches, ligulae and other items were found in the yard.

Iron: 127 objects ranging from personal items such as toiletry sets and needles to household and workshop items such as keys, cleavers, knives, hinges, hooks and slag.

Worked stone: The northern yard contains 14 querns and whetstones which indicate grain preparation in this area over a sustained period of time. Some querns were built into the North and the NW walls which bound the Yard.

Spindle whorls: nearly all the spindle whorls were found in the yard (with 2 in the NW wall area adjacent) indicating that spinning occurred in this area.

Glass: 12 fragments of window and vessel glass.
Worked bone: 29 bone items, such as pins and knife handles, occur in various parts of the yard.

Infant burials: the bulk of the newborn infant burials are located in the yard. Those infants that have labels attached giving find spot information are found throughout the east and west yard, including the NW wall and pit locations.

In conclusion, the yard seems to have been a workshop, an agricultural and a residential area for the Romano-British community. At various times it was the location of houses and workshops with waste pits spanning the whole era, as well as the location of grain driers or malting areas, and an infant burial area, becoming potentially an animal enclosure in the western part during the 2nd and 3rd century.

V-Ditch (often called the V-drain)
Summary: an enclosure ditch, cut in the Iron Age and filled with Iron age deposits and throughout the Roman period to the 4th century The ditch is 8.5 to 9 ft in depth, 12 ft wide at the top tapering in to less than 1 ft at the rounded base.

Cocks' description (1921, p.142) describes the following:
"*The gravel pit is one hundred and fifty yards north of Hog-Pit Close's south-east corner. It adjoins the Hambleden road. It shows on its east and west faces a section*

of a V shaped ditch, completely filled with Roman and Late Celtic debris. In its day the ditch flowed eastwards, evidently crossing the Hambleden road (which doubtlessly already existed at least as a track) by a water splash, and eventually turned a little south into the river".

The ditch is a part of a rectangular enclosure, partly cut out by the modern car park, and which is very likely to have been an Iron Age animal enclosure. The hollow way which is the Rotten Row road today would have led directly into this enclosure; today the road bends southwards and continues as the public footpath adjacent to the site.

Finds: Iron Age **pottery** from the Early and Late Iron Age are located in the fill of this ditch (Chapter 5.1). Another early find is a **copper alloy** brooch which dates from the Iron Age to *c*. 69 AD. There is only one other copper alloy item – a 2nd century hairpin and two other **bone** hairpins were also found in the ditch (no depths given). Three **coins** indicate some of the time span for the fill to accumulate: a Trajan sestertius 98-117 AD, a Faustina II sestertius 161-180 AD and a House of Constantine follis 335-341 AD.

Some of the Romano-British **pottery** is also datable such as Oxford Colour Coated wares 240-410 AD, a Central Gaulish beaker (F43, 150-200 AD), and Oxford white ware mortaria (180-240 AD). However, most of the pottery is reduced or grog tempered wares which are particularly dominated by sandy grey wares (R20 and R30), grog tempered E80 and E810, and large coarse tempered jars (R90). White wares, oxidized wares and shell tempered wares are of lesser amounts and there is a minor amount of other colour coated wares, white slipped flagons with some black burnished wares.

There is a substantial quantity of **iron** objects which include: a key, a drop handle, three styli at 2.5 ft, a brooch at 1.5 ft, a hook and spring hook, a knife blade at 2 ft, a needle, a bracket, 17 nails, an agricultural (digging) tool, a clamp, staple and lynch pin, a pig? of iron, wire and many fragments.

There are also 3 **quern** fragments: vesicular basalt, Lower Greensand and Lower Greensand (Lodsworth) stone. Fragments of adult **skull** were reported by Cocks (but not seen in this study).

Therefore, the V ditch was open during most of the era up to the enclosure wall being built for the 4th century enhancements to the complex, including the addition of the 1st House. The location is also reasonably close to workshops or agricultural areas or path routes to and from them. The phasing from the site can therefore be assessed using all the information from buildings and structures, along with the finds associated with each. Four main phases for the Romano-British period at Yewden is displayed as Figures 3.37 to 3.40 below.

Bibliography
Cocks, A. H. 1921. *A Romano-British homestead in the Hambleden Valley, Bucks*. Society of Antiquaries, London.

Hartley, B. R. 1959. A Romano-British villa at High Wycombe. *Records of Buckinghamshire* Vol. XVI (4), 227-257.

Payne, E. J. 1870. Roman villa at Wycombe. *Records of Buckinghamshire* Vol. III, 160-164.

Acknowledgements: thanks to Allen Levy for advising on building structure and providing an architectural sketch of the 1st House, and also to John Clutterbuck for proof-reading.

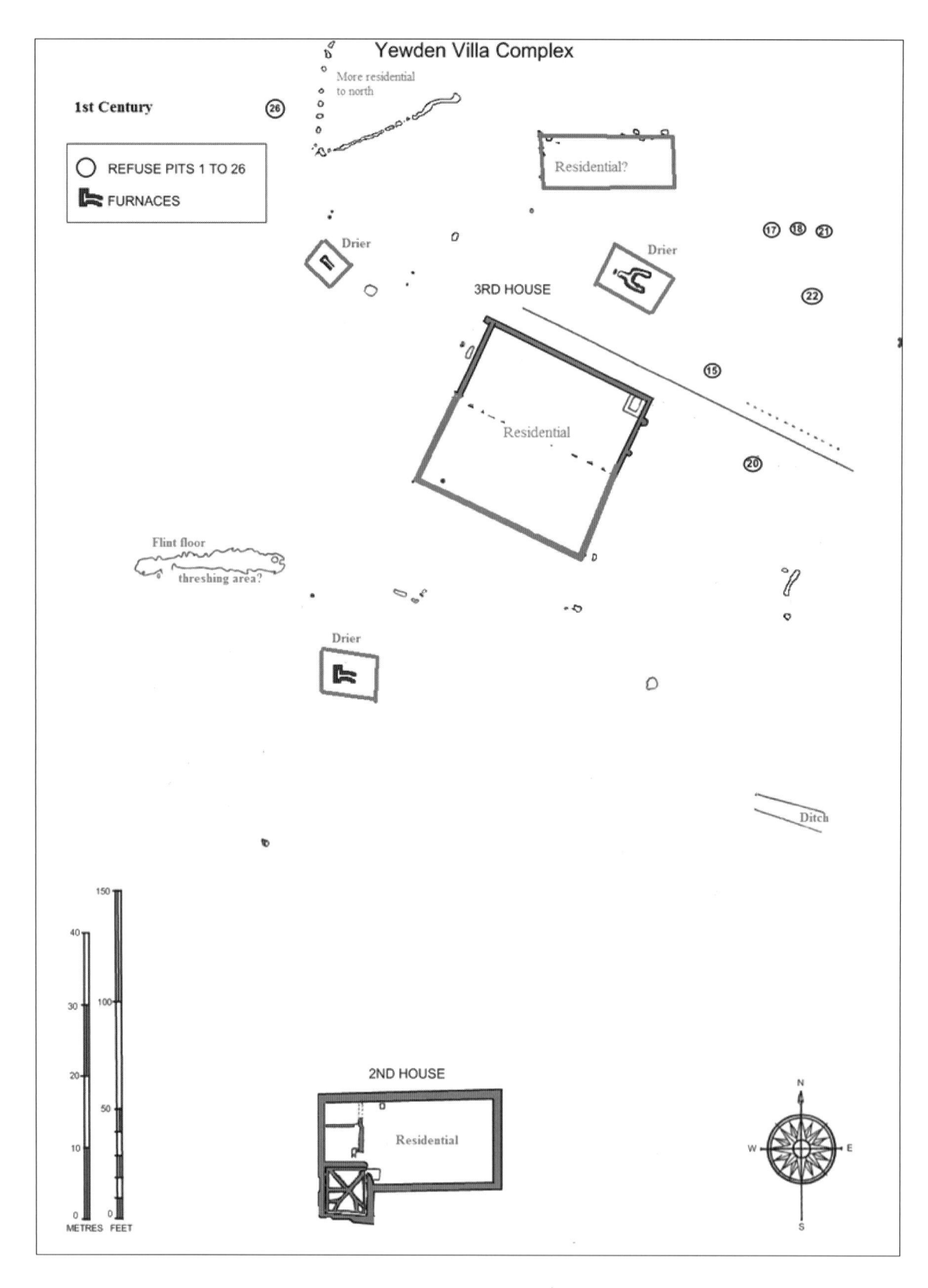

Figure 3.37 Yewden during the 1st century AD

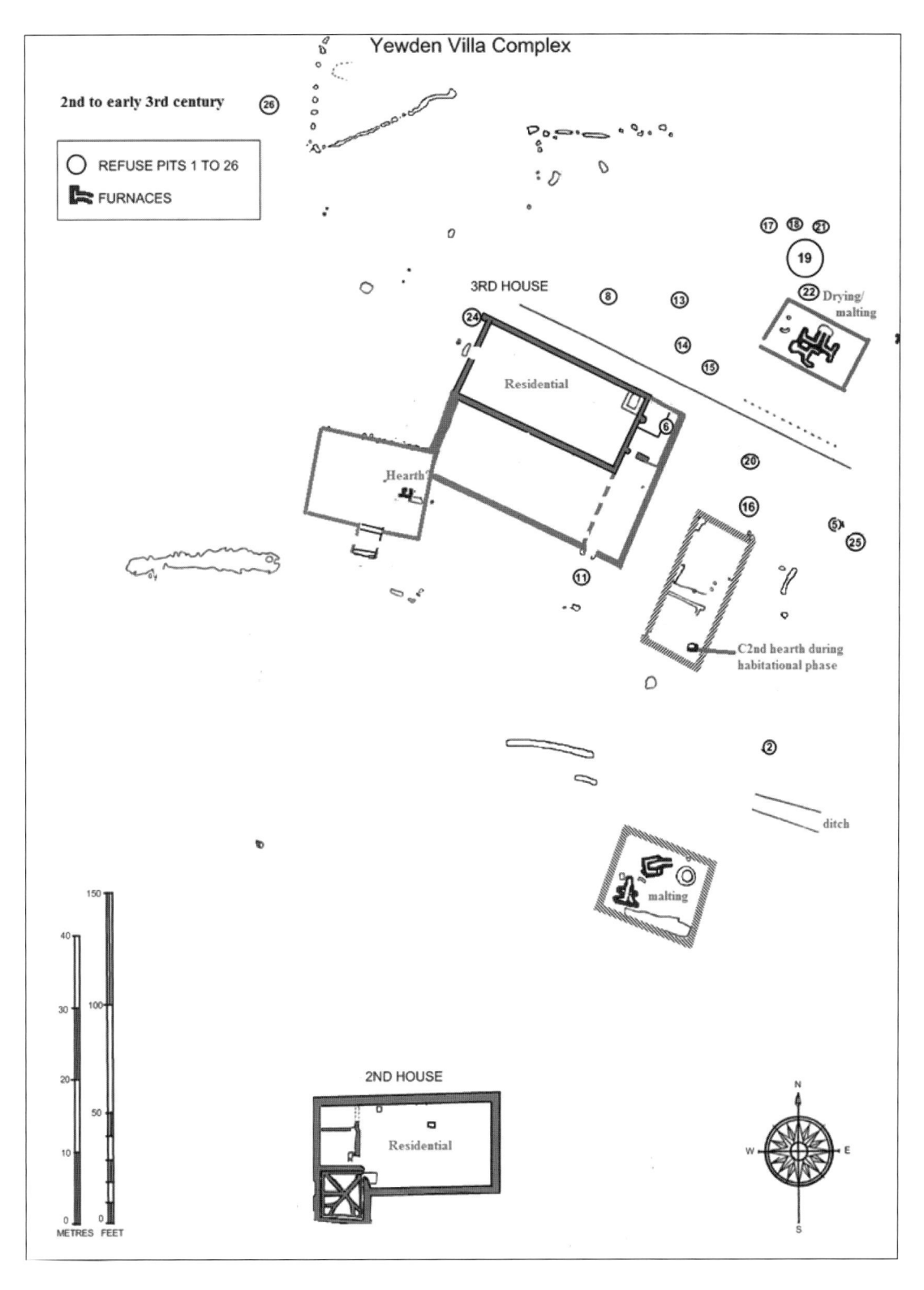

Figure 3.38 Yewden during the 2nd to early 3rd century.

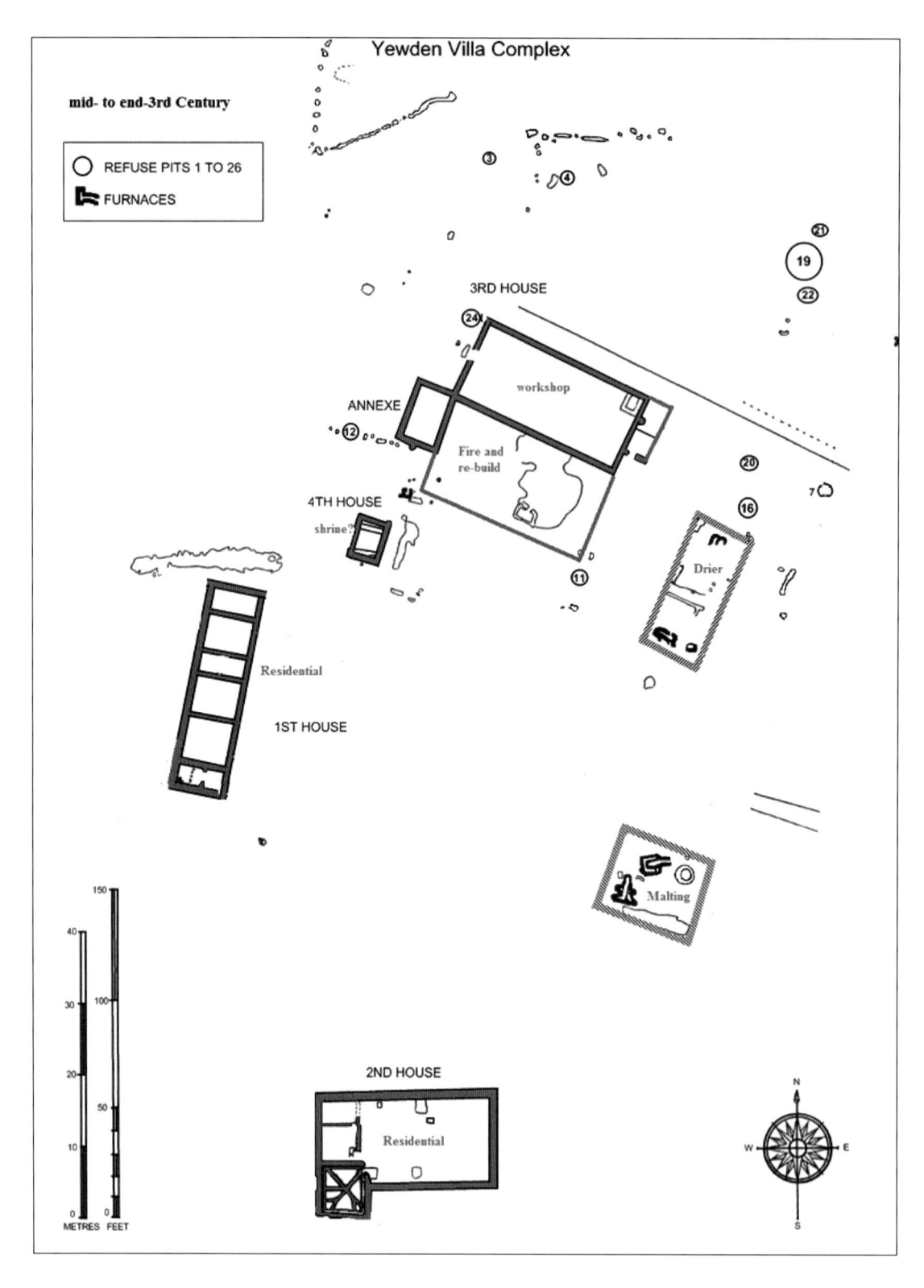

Figure 3.39 Yewden during the mid to end 3rd century

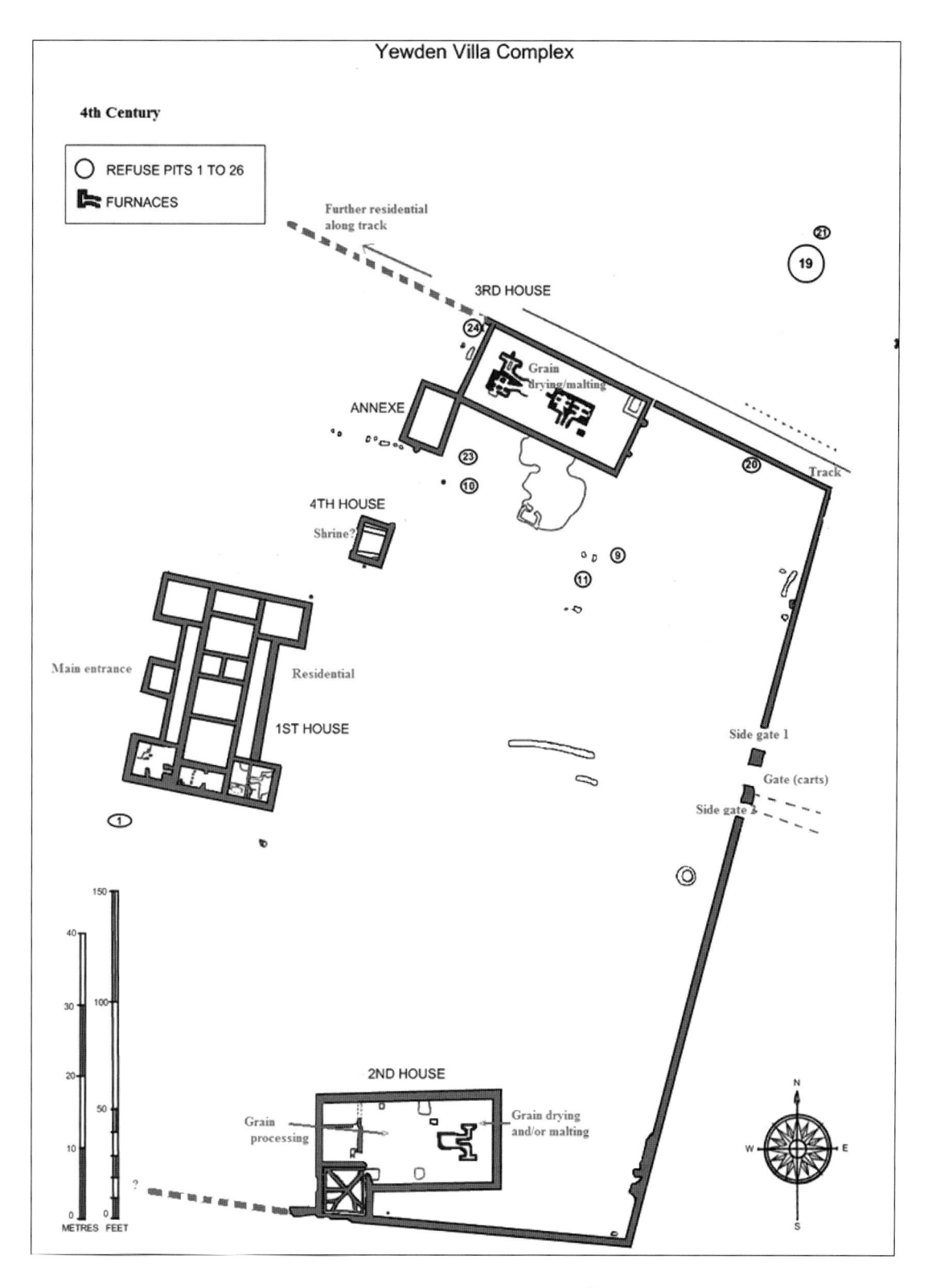

Figure 3.40 Yewden during the 4th century

Chapter 4 The artefacts (except pottery and bone)

Chapter 4.1 The 1912 excavation coins

Brett Thorn

This report is intended as a brief update on the coins found in the original villa excavation. Unlike much of the material from the 1912 excavation at Yewden, the coins have been the subject of more modern re-appraisal. In the late 1970s most of the Roman coin collection of Buckinghamshire County Museum was catalogued by Dr C.E. King, including the Yewden coins. This report is based on the existing information in the museum's database, a re-examination of the original coins not being possible within the time constraints or resources of the project.

There is further research underway which will combine recent data from the Portable Antiquities Scheme, of metal detected finds in the area, with a new examination of the original excavation coins, but the work had not been completed in time for inclusion in the current volume.

A.H. Cocks reported 818 coins in the original publication, but unfortunately, not all were deposited at the Museum in the 1950s. Currently 749 are known.

The hoard
A single hoard of 294 bronze coins, deposited around 320, was found buried in a ceramic pot, on the inside of the 2nd house, the find spot being marked on Cocks' original excavation plan. The hoard is unusual in consisting of coins spanning at least 2 major re-coinages, in 295 and 317, suggesting that these coins may have been in circulation together, despite the official demonetization of the earlier pieces. The hoard has already been published in detail (King, 1980), and will not be further considered here.

The site finds
The surviving site finds, not including 2 Post Medieval and 1 Iron Age coin, total 452 Roman coins. The original report on the coins long pre-dates the practice of grouping coins into periods of coin use, known as Reece Periods (Reece, 1972), to enable statistical comparison between sites. The assumptions that many coins from a particular Emperor, or period, means that a site was prosperous, or busy, at that time, can only be made when comparing the site against the background of other similar sites.

Thirty-nine of the Roman coins were too badly corroded or worn to enable assignation to a Reece Period. Sixteen more were only able to be assigned to the Gallic Empire, and so were split proportionally according to the British Mean, between Periods 13 and 14.

The coins themselves range in date from a single Iron Age bronze coin of Tasciovanus, to those of Arcadius (388-402 AD). There are no later Roman coins recorded.

Table 4.1.1 Number of coins per Reece period from Yewden villa

Date	Title	Reece Period	No of Yewden coins (excluding hoard)
pre 41	Iron Age & Pre-Claudian	1	1
41-54	Claudian	2	7
54-69	Neronian	3	1
69-96	Flavian	4	7
96-117	Trajanic	5	10
117-138	Hadrianic	6	11
138-161	Antonine I	7	10
161-180	Antonine II	8	4
180-192	Antonine III	9	1
193-222	Severus to Elagabalus	10	2
222-238	Later Severan	11	1
238-260	Gordian III toValerian	12	0
260-275	Gallienus sole reign to Aurelian	13	130
275-296	Tacitus to Allectus	14	39
296-317	Tetrarchy	15	7
317-330	Constantinian I	16	5
330-348	Constantinian II	17	103
348-364	Constantinian III	18	27
364-378	Valentinian	19	0
378-388	Theodosian I	20	1
388-402	Theodosian II	21	51

To make comparisons with other sites possible, the numbers are converted to a relative amount of coins per 1000 (which means what number there would have been, from that period, if exactly 1000 coins were found). Figure 4.1.1 compares the Yewden finds to other published villa sites and to Reece's 'British Mean' (an overall statistic from a variety of other Roman sites).

What is immediately apparent is that the small number of coins found before Period 13 is entirely normal for British sites, although Yewden has more coins than any of the other villas considered, it is not outstanding when compared to the British Mean. The Mean is significantly higher than the other villas because early coinage tends to be concentrated in military or urban sites, rather than rural ones. The Yewden coins are more numerous than the other villas considered from the start of the Roman period, through to the late 2nd century (Period 9). This may, as Cocks suggested, imply significant early activity at Yewden, but care needs to be taken when making interpretations based on any numerically small sample.

Table 4.1.2 Number of coins per 1000 from comparative sites

Reece Period	Yewden	Bancroft	Chedworth	Lullingstone	British Mean
1	2	0	0	0	6
2	17	0	0	3	12
3	2	0	3	0	6
4	17	3	6	3	31
5	24	2	0	12	20
6	26	0	0	12	16
7	24	1	3	9	19
8	10	3	0	3	12
9	2	0	0	0	5
10	5	0	9	6	15
11	2	1	3	0	7
12	0	2	0	9	8
13	311	35	150	45	144
14	93	46	68	51	121
15	17	3	10	6	17
16	12	93	16	100	44
17	246	552	240	320	246
18	65	105	120	210	98
19	0	126	340	110	118
20	2	3	10	3	5
21	122	25	3	60	50

The coin loss over periods 10-12 is comparable to that of the other sites considered, and is uniformly low, but in period 13 (260-275), there is a significant leap in coin loss across many British sites, including Chedworth, and the overall British Mean. This may reflect various factors, including the continual devaluing of the radiate coin throughout the 3rd century, and the occurrence of the Gallic Empire, and its focus on coin production to meet local, rather than Empire-wide, needs. Even considering this, Yewden has a remarkable peak. A look at the other sites shows that all of them have exceptional coin loss, at various other times (Bancroft in period 17, Lullingstone 18, and Chedworth 19). This is the value of the comparative data, and it offers the possibility of detecting significant periods of coin use, and subsequent coin loss, on a site.

Figure 4.1.1 Number of coins per 1000 from Yewden and comparative sites (over page)

Number of coins per 1000 from Yewden and comparative sites

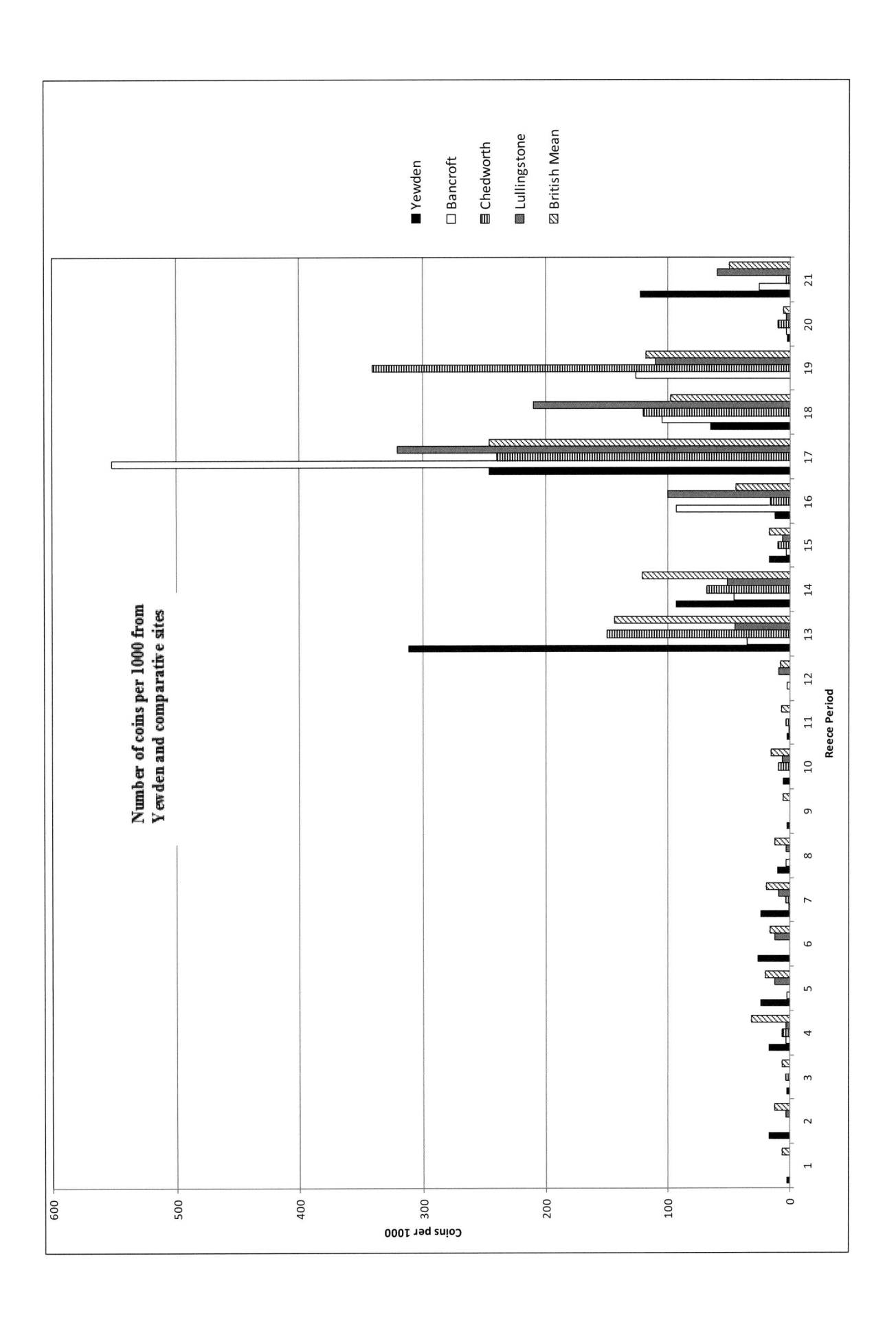

Chart showing coins per 1000 (y-axis, 0–600) by Reece Period (x-axis, 1–21) for: Yewden, Bancroft, Chedworth, Lullingstone, British Mean.

Despite an overall reduction in coin loss across all British sites, Yewden stays comparatively higher than the other villas throughout periods 14-15 (275-317). However, by Period 16, Bancroft and Lullingstone are showing a significant increase, whilst the number of coins at Yewden continues to decline, on a par with Chedworth. Period 17 (330-348) sees another huge increase, across all the sites, but Bancroft and Lullingstone, which were already increasing in the previous period, continue their rise, and further outstrip Yewden and Chedworth (Bancroft massively so).

Yewden then appears to have a very swift decrease in coin use and loss on site, dropping significantly below the other sites in Period 18 (348-364), down to no coins at all recovered from period 19 (364-378). In some ways, Yewden appears to be pre-empting the trend towards almost no coins that occurs in period 20 across the entire province. Period 21 (388-402) sees a brief, but significant, return to major coin loss on the site. Whilst the increase also occurs at Lullingstone, and to a lesser extent Bancroft, Yewden is again significantly above the numbers found on the other sites, and the British Mean. In common with many Romano-British sites, there no coins more recent than those of Period 21.

Conclusions

It is difficult to draw any conclusions about the early activity at Roman rural sites based purely on coinage, as the sample is too small to be reliable. However, a definite indication of remarkable activity can be seen at Yewden around 260-275, above and beyond other similar sites. The trend is then downwards towards a more 'normal' picture, and unlike some sites, which begin to see increased coin use 317-330 does not begin to pick up again until the 330-348 period. Again the drop in activity appears to be quite rapid, with the complete absence of coins of 364-378, at a time when many other sites are still producing large numbers, being perhaps indicative of a major change on the site with a final, substantial and significant burst of coin loss from 388-402. Lack of coins beyond this date is not uncommon, as the supplies of new coins from the Roman mints had ceased, and is by no means indicative of abandonment of the site.

Bibliography

Davies, J.A, 1994, *The Coins*, in Williams & Zeepvat, *Bancroft*.

King, C.E., 1980, The Hambleden (Bucks) Hoard of Folles, *The Numismatic Chronicle,* Series 7, Vol 20, 48-63.

Reece, Richard, 1972, A short survey of the Roman Coins found on Fourteen sites in Britain, *Britannia* III, p.269-277.

Reece, Richard, 2002, *The Coinage of Roman Britain*, The History Press

Williams, R.J. & Zeepvat R.J., 1994, *Bancroft*, Buckinghamshire Archaeological Society Monograph 7.

4.2 Worked stone objects

Jill Eyers

Identification of the stone was by macroscopic methods only (no thin sections were taken). The hand lens (x20) examination was sometimes complimented by a x40 binocular microscope. The objects were mostly rotary querns, rubbers and whetstones, with a little oolithic limestone as architectural fragments, and one limestone mortar (Table 4.2.1).

Table 4.2.1 Fragment count and lithology of worked stone objects from Yewden Villa

Lithology	Whetstones	Querns	Rubbers	Building stone	Mortar	Unclassified
Millstone Grit		25		1*		
Lower Greensand		8				
LGS Lodsworth Stone	1	9				
Quartz conglomerate		21				
Upper Greensand		1				
Lava (vesicular basalt)		10				
Sandstone, fine	2		4			
Sandstone, medium	1	1	12			2
Sandstone, micaceous calcareous	9					1
Sandstone quartz arenite	2					
Sandstone, calcareous	1					
Sandstone, ferrugenous		2				
Limestone, sandy	1					
Limestone, Burr stone					1	
Limestone, Oolitic, Cotswolds				12		
Chert			2			
Quartzite			1			
Sarsen (sandy)			1			
Hertfordshire Pudding Stone		4				
Garnet hornfels	1					
Total	**18**	**81**	**20**	**13**	**1**	**3**

(*ex-quern)

The stone object descriptions follow and the number displayed (as ST.*) is part of the BCM number and each is preceded with 1994.57. The Yewden site location names appear as Cocks described them on the labels and in the 1921 report, and these locations appear in italics with the object descriptions. For the finds plot see Figure 4.2.11.

Whetstones and hones

There were 18 whetstones and hones (Table 4.2.1). These included a variety of styles comprising 5 lithological types. The rock types consisted of: micaceous and calcareous sandstones, siltstones, a sandy limestone, and a garnet-rich hornfels. A full petrographic description is held in the archive (BCM) of which some are illustrated and described below.

ST1 **Whetstone?.** Fine sandstone. A reddened (burnt?) grey sandstone which shows recrystallisation of the fabric. It is a common pebble type within the Thames Gravels (with an original Midlands source) and it is uncertain if this is a natural object or is a whetstone. Dimensions: length 63 mm; width 60 mm; thickness 25 mm. Not illustrated. *Pit 1 at 16ft*

ST2 **Whetstone.** A grey, micaceous fine sandstone (Figure 4.2.1b). A very fine lithology with *c*. 20% mica; a finer version of ST10. Dimensions: length 47 mm; width 31 mm; thickness 13 mm wedging to 1 mm at the edge. *North of 3rd House.*

ST4 **Whetstone.** A grey, calcareous sandstone. Fine sandstone with dark flecks. Dimensions: length 60 mm; width 30 mm; thickness 25 mm.
2nd House, cross wall S of railing.

ST5 **Whetstone.** A grey, calcareous sandstone. As ST4. Fine sandstone, 3 specimens:
1. L 58 mm W 25 mm Th 15 mm, oval section. *Yard.*
2. L 37 mm W 29 mm Th 10 mm, oval section. Fig. 4.2.1. *Quern hole at 1ft deep.*
3. L 34 mm W 12 mm Th 12 mm, rounded square section. *North wall of Yard.*

ST6 **Cylinder, unknown function.** Lower Greensand, Lodsworth Stone. Fig. 4.2.1a. Length 86 mm, one end diameter 40 mm, other end diameter 35 mm. *Pit 1 or Pit 13?*

ST7 **Whetstone.** Hornfels (with garnets). High/prolonged temperature contact metamorphic rock. A greenish-grey, fine micaceous lithology with garnet porphyroblasts (<1 mm) scattered throughout. Score marks on one side. Rectangular side profile. Not illustrated. Length 130 mm, width 43 mm, thickness 15 mm thinning to 4 mm. *Pit 7.*

ST8 **Whetstone.** Bioclastic sandy limestone. Similar to ST 4 & 5. Grey weathering to light yellowish brown. Rounded square section tapering to one end. Figure 4.2.1. Length 90 mm, width 22 mm, thickness 23 mm tapering to an end profile of 21 x 18 mm.
North wall of the Annexe 3rd House.

ST9 **Whetstone.** A grey, medium sandstone (quartz arenite, sarsen?). Round edged rectangular section. Not illustrated. Length 76 mm, width 30 mm, thickness 18 mm. *Fill in NW wall.*

ST11 **Whetstone.** A grey, micaceous calcareous sandstone. As two specimens of ST10. Medium grained, highly micaceous sandstone. Figure 4.2.1b. Length 68 mm, width 36 mm, thickness 20 mm. *SW corner of 3rd House*. ST10 from *Quern hole and Hybrid Furnace*.

ST13 Whetstone (hone). A grey, micaceous, calcareous siltstone. A flat profile with rounder upper edges (Fig. 4.2.1b). Useful for small implements.
3ft E of 9th block west of the NW wall.

ST32 Whetstone (hone). Very fine sandstone. Wedge shape, broken, very smooth and mid-grey in colour. Width: 19 mm, length broken; thickness: 9 mm to 13 mm. Not illustrated.
S. end of wall E. End of Little House.

ST.47 Whetstone fragment of red-brown medium grained sandstone. Rounded profile with one flat edge. Stone source: local river gravels. Thickness 30 mm. Not illustrated.
Top of Pit 5

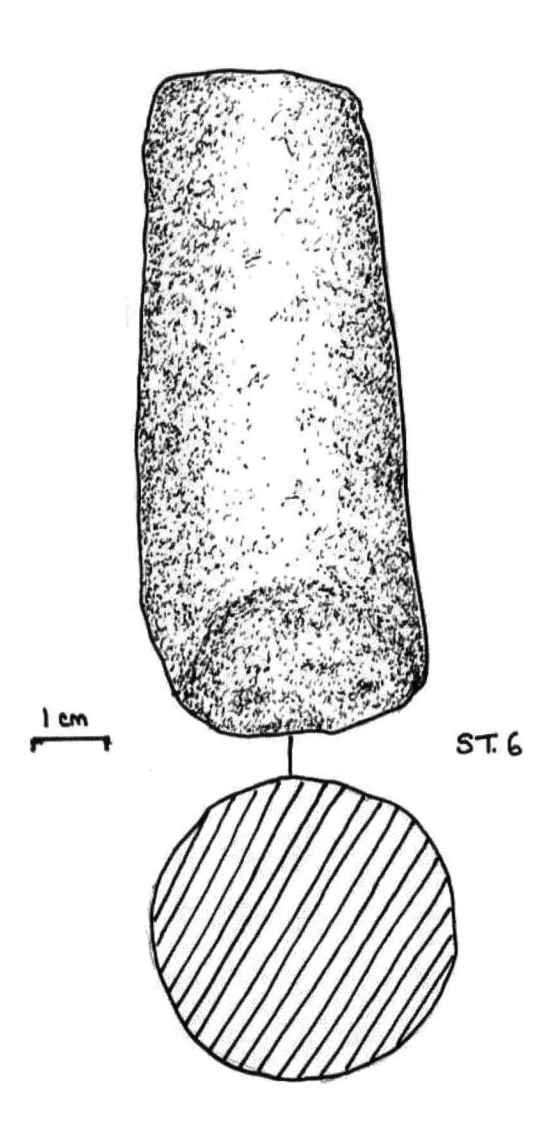

Figure 4.2.1a Whetstone ST6 from Yewden villa.
(For ST2, 5, 8 11 and 13 see below.)

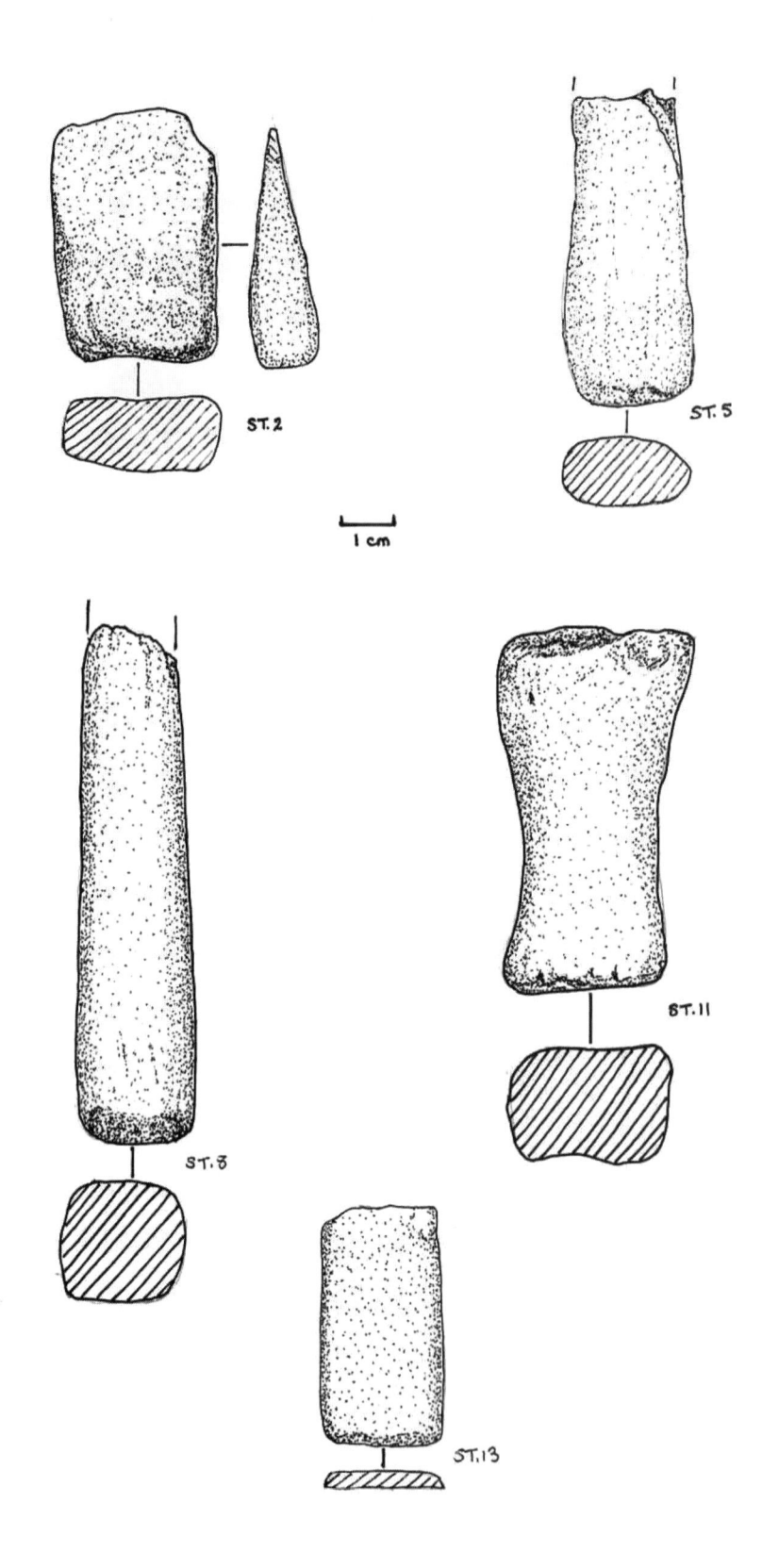

Figure 4.2.1b Whetstones from Yewden: ST2, ST5, ST8, ST 11, and ST13, with ST6 above

Querns

There were 81 quern fragments found and, where these could be determined, they were mostly from rotary querns with 1 beehive and 4 domed Hertfordshire Pudding stone types.

ST14 Quern fragment. Millstone Grit. Thickness 150 mm.

ST22 Quern fragment. Vesicular basalt. Mostly very fine grained, without visible minerals. There are no amygdales, but there are occasional phenocrysts of feldspar up to 8 mm (transparent, not weathered and showing cleavage), but the majority of phenocrysts are *c*. 1mm (plagioclase) and some are degrading to clay. Mr Cocks labelled this find as 'from Mt Etna' but this was probably a guess. Source: Europe, not Niedermendig lava.
V drain

ST36 Quern fragment. Millstone Grit. Coarse sandstone, with minor feldspar. Highly weathered. Diameter *c*. 420 mm; thickness 32 mm +.
2nd House flint floor between stoke hole and rail

ST.40 Rotary quern fragment. Millstone grit. A very coarse sandstone (average grain size c. 1 to 1.5 mm) with scattered pebbles up to 15 mm. Mostly quartz sand (glassy) with milky quartz pebbles, with feldspar (some pink) and a clay cement with some evidence of quartz overgrowth. Fragment with one tooled surface. Length: 150 mm; Width 130 mm; thickness 90 to 130 mm. Not illustrated.*Pit 3*

ST48 Rotary quern, lower stone. Millstone Grit. One tooled surface. Broken and repaired by Cocks, with the outer edge and the central hole partially present. Source Pennines. Fig. 4.2.2. Diameter *c*. 500 mm; thickness: outer edge 40 mm; inner edge 60 mm. *Quern hole.*

Fig. 4.2.2 Rotary quern, Millstone grit ST48 (above)

ST49 Rotary quern fragment. Millstone Grit. A very coarse sandstone with pebbles up to 10 mm seen. Predominantly glassy, clear or milky quartz, with minor pink feldspar. White clay cement. Source area: Derbyshire part of the Pennines. Not illustrated. Thickness: outer edge 53 mm. No location given.

ST50 Rotary quern, upper stone. Lower Greensand, Lodsworth Stone. (Fig. 4.2.3). A fine to medium-grained, glauconitic sandstone with some patchy iron oxide staining. Dispersed glauconite imports a slight green tone to the fabric and rounded glauconite clasts (dark specks) are also present. Concentric wear grooves present. Thickness: 55 mm on outer edge to 25 mm on inner portion, but this fragment is not complete. As ST59, but more weathered. Estimated diameter *c.* 400 mm. Source area Sussex or the Weald. *Pit 2*

Figure 4.2.3 ST50 Rotary quern, upper stone. Lodsworth Stone.

ST51 Rotary quern, lower stone. Lower Greensand. Highly weathered surfaces, but looks identical to ST50. Surviving thicknesses: 60 mm to 30 mm. Not illustrated. Three pieces found on the *Mortar floor between Annexe and the clay construction; N of Yard; 1st House.*

ST52 Rotary quern (lower stone?). Quartz conglomerate. Five fragments of similar lithology, although not all are the same quern stone. A poorly sorted quartz sandstone with pebbles (quartz) up to 15 mm, although most pebbles are smaller. Some pebbles are polycrystalline quartz and some are a reddened, iron-rich sandstone. Not illustrated. Thickness: outer edge of stone 40 mm; inner edge 20 mm. Fragments occur in: *Pit 2; Pit 9 at 3.5ft deep; NW wall of Yard; 3rd House; and 3rd House between W. furnace and N. wall.*

ST53 Quern fragments. Ferruginous sandstone. Two stones of dark red-brown, medium grained sandstone. Well sorted quartz grains vary in colour from colourless/transparent to pale orange to deep red-brown due to variability of iron-staining. There are also some iron oxide clasts in the fabric and the cement may well be iron oxide, but some quartz overgrowth is present. The source area is not known, although this could be Oxfordshire (for instance some of the Banbury area sandstones). Not illustrated. Thickness: between 35 mm and 20 mm. Found by the *curved wall between the entrance and the 1st House.*

ST54 Quern fragments. Quartz conglomerate. As ST 52. Diameter *c.* 440 mm; thickness 30-38 mm. *Pit 22 at 1.5ft.*

ST59 Rotary quern fragment. Lower Greensand (Lodsworth Stone). Sussex. As ST50, but with dark chert 'swirls' due to burrows and other features visible. Broken, but at least 420 mm diameter; thickness 11 to 40 mm (inner to outer dimensions). *Pit 24 at 11ft.*

ST60 Rotary quern fragments. Quartz conglomerate. Six fragments:
1. Tool marked. Thickness: 42 mm. *Pit 1*
2. Circular groove mark. Thickness: 70 mm. *Yard E of Pits 3 & 4.*
3. Diameter 320 mm; Thickness: 47 mm. *3rd House E side of E furnace.*
4. Thickness 44 mm. *Box R*
5. Diameter c. 420 mm; thickness 25 to 35 mm. *Outside enclosure wall E of north cream pan, south of Pit 5*

ST61 Rotary quern fragments. Millstone Grit. Pinkish-beige, coarse sandstone, heavily weathered. Glassy quartz with white clay cement. Tooled surface. Two fragments from different querns:
1. Diameter *c.* 450 mm. Thickness 25 mm. *2nd House N. Wall*
2. Broken, no outer edge. Thickness 60 mm. *Yard E of Pits 3 & 4.*

ST62 Quern fragment. Hertfordshire Puddingstone. Very rounded flint pebbles (up to 35 mm seen) in a fine sand matrix and quartz cement. Flint pebbles have grey, white, beige, brown and reddish centres with a dark grey to black weathered cortex visible as an outer ring. *Pit 24.*

ST63 Rotary quern. Lower Greensand, Lodsworth stone. Four fragments from:
1. Diameter 450 mm; thickness 35 mm. *Pit 24 at 11ft.*
2. Diameter 400 mm; thickness 22-45 mm. Concentric grooves. From *9th block N of W end of NW wall at 3ft deep.*
3. Diameter: 400 mm; thickness 45 mm. *V drain.*
4. Diameter 400 mm; thickness 45 mm. Concentric rings. *N wall of Yard.*

ST64 Rotary quern fragments. Quartz Conglomerate. Five fragments from:
1. Very worn, broken. *2nd House.*
2. Thickness 26-33 mm. Worn. *3rd House S wall.*
3. Diameter 410 mm; thickness 37 mm. *Built into the E end of NW wall.*
4. Diameter 400 mm; thickness 23-39 mm. No location given.
5. Broken, no location given.

ST68 Quern fragment. Lower Greensand. Concentric deep grooves (4). Thickness: 25 mm. *Yard N of E end of N wall.*

ST69 Rotary quern fragment. Millstone Grit. (Fig. 4.2.4). Three fragments:
(1) Broken. *N wall of Yard.*
(2) Tooled surface, several concentric grooves. Thickness 120 mm. No location.
(3) Very worn. *3rd House.*

Figure 4.2.4 ST69 Rotary quern, MSG (left)

ST70 Rotary quern fragment. Quartz conglomerate. Figure 4.2.5. Two fragments:
1. No location. Large piece with central perforation for spindle and outer edge with tooled markings. Diameter 440 mm minimum; Thickness 75 to 90 mm. No location given.
2. Broken fragment. *Pit 1.*

Figure 4.2.5 Rotary quern ST 70 base and profile views (left)

ST71 Quern fragment. Lava: vesicular basalt. Not illustrated. Three fragments:
Vesicles up to 4 mm with sparse feldspar phenocrysts. Thickness 65 mm.
3rd House W. wall.

Fine vesicles up to 1 mm with no phenocrysts. *S of SW corner of mortar floor.*

Vesicles up to 3mm and feldspar phenocrysts up to 7mm. No location given. Same as ST22.

ST73 Rotary quern. Millstone Grit. Coarse sandstone with minor white clay cement. Diameter 440 mm; thickness 42 mm (outer edge) to 28 mm (inner edge). *Box aa.*

ST74 Rotary quern, upper stone. Lower Greensand, Lodsworth Stone. As ST50. Two fragments:
1. Diameter 400 mm; thickness 50 mm (outer edge). *Close to Pits 5 & 25.*
2. Broken. *3rd House N. wall*

ST75 Rotary quern fragment. Millstone Grit. Feldspathic, coarse quartz sandstone with concentric rings. Diameter: 420 mm; thickness: 27 mm (outer edge) to 43 mm+ (inner edge). *Pit 6?*

ST76 Rotary quern fragment. Millstone Grit. Tool markings on outer edge and hole for spindle just visible. Diameter 440 mm; thickness 70 mm. *3rd House W of centre trench.*

ST77 Building stone? Squared edge, but may be ex-quern. L. 100 mm x w. 95 mm remaining (broken); thickness 45 mm. *Yard W of Pit 5.*

ST78 Rotary quern. Millstone Grit. (Fig. 4.2.6). Medium-coarse sandstone with rounded quartz pebbles up to 11 mm. Diameter 400 m. Thickness 18 mm (outer rounded edge) to 46 mm (inner edge). *Pit 24.*

Figure 4.2.6 Rotary quern ST78 upper surface and profile view. Millstone Grit.

ST79 Quern fragment. Millstone Grit. Broken. Clean coarse quartz sandstone with white clay cement. Thickness 28 mm. *Pit 9 at 3.5ft deep.*

BCM archt.83 Beehive quern. Hertfordshire Puddingstone. Figure 4.2.7. 100% . Good condition, well finished. *Location uncertain, matches a Yewden HPS fragment in the collections, and Hambleden Valley source available, but no information with this specimen.*

Figure 4.2.7 Beehive Quern in Hertfordshire Puddingstone (left). BCM archt.83.

1994.57.3608 Beehive quern. Hertfordshire Puddingstone. 50% upper stone. Worn. Diameter 270 mm; height 95 mm. *In single T furnace.*

1994.57.3607. Domed rotary quern. Hertfordshire Puddingstone. 50% upper stone, well finished. Diameter 290 mm; height 105 mm. (ID by Chris Green). *By burnt layer to W of detached blocks NW wall.*

1994.57.3609. Domed rotary quern. Herfordshire Puddingstone. 100% upper stone. Well finished, but worn into the handle socket, burnt and broken. Diameter 305 mm, height 115 mm. (ID by Chris Green). *Pit 20?.*

Rubbing stones

ST.41 Rubbing stones. Riders for saddle quern? Red-brown medium grained sandstone (Thames river gravels type). Seven stones ranging from 120 to 160 mm in length and 35 to 50 mm in thickness. Not illustrated. Found: *on chalk floor between N & S cream pans (3); 3rd House (1); under mortar floor S of 3rd House (2); west of 3rd House.*

ST42 Rubbing stone or natural? Fine sandstone, round flattened sphere, c. 90 mm diameter and 30 mm thick. No site location given.

ST43 Rubbing stone? Ex-glacial river pebble. Very fine, black ?chert with intense criss-cross veining of quartz. Length 80 mm; width 55 mm; Height 30 mm tapering to 20 mm. Not illustrated. *Found 'with ACCIRIAt'.*

ST44 Rubbing stone? Ex-glacial river pebble. Quartzite (patchy cream, beige, brown and orange brown). Oxfordshire source? Flattened sphere c. 100 mm diameter, 25 mm thick. Not illustrated. *Surface of chalk floor between N & S cream pans.*

ST45 Rubbing stones. Two stones of a yellow-beige medium-grained sandstone. Glassy, well sorted quartz grains with a quartz cement. Not illustrated. 1. Flattened sphere c. 85 mm diameter, 25 mm thick; 2. Elongate wedge shape length 120 mm, width 45 mm to 80 mm, thickness c. 60 mm. *Ground N end of gravel pit.*

ST46 Small rubbing stones or natural? Three rounded river pebbles (Thames terraces type) and although surfaces have slightly rougher and smoother surfaces it is not clear if they were used at Yewden or naturally occurring. Three stones: 1. 65 mm diameter and 45 mm thick; 2. Spherical 55 mm; 3. Flat oval length 70 mm, width 60 mm, thickness c. 25 mm. All red-brown medium grained sandstone. Not illustrated. *Surface near 3rd House (2) and spherical object found 10 ft from 3rd House at 18 inches deep.*

Architectural fragments

Concrete is included in this section only where it is thought to be integral to setting building stones into a building fabric.

Figure 4.2.8 ST26 Architectural fragment - ?window surround, oolitic limestone from the Jurassic Bathonian rocks of the Cotswolds (Cirencester to Bath).

ST26 Architectural fragment - ?window surround. Figure 4.2.8 above. Weathered to a dark-grey, masking a texture characterised by alternating bands of ooid grains and light grey molluscan bioclastic debris. A freshly exposed exterior, however, revealed a white (2.5Y 8/1) to pale yellow (2.5YR 8/2) shelly oolitic grainstone. This pitted character is characteristic of samples from younger softer Bathonian freestones from the Cotswolds (Cirencester to Bath). The example is finer than above with what appear to be large 5-10mm foraminifera. Lincolnshire limestones are either extremely sparry and yellow e.g. Barnack stone or very oolitic and porous (Weldon stone and Ketton stone) and can be discounted. Furthermore, French Jurassic limestones used in Roman Britain Calcaire Grossier, Marquise oolite, Calcaires Polypiers and Caen stone are very distinctive and different to this example . ID supplied by Kevin Hayward, by comparison with a type collection.

ST27 Architectural fragment. Oolitic limestone (banded, shelly oolitic grainstone. A weathered dark-grey, masking a texture characterised by alternating bands of ooid grains and light grey molluscan bioclastic debris. A freshly exposed exterior, however, revealed a white (2.5Y 8/1) to pale yellow (2.5YR 8/2) shelly oolitic grainstone. This pitted character is characteristic of samples from younger softer Bathonian freestones from the Cotswolds (Cirencester to Bath). As ST26 above. ID supplied by Kevin Hayward, by comparison with a type collection.

ST28 Concrete moulding. For keying in a window surround? Fig. 4.2.9. Three grooves on upper surface for keying in a structure. The base was set into a wall and shows a selection of local flint and chalk river gravel. Could be used to bed in stone window surrounds such as ST27.
1st House. **Figure 4.2.9 (left)**

ST58 Concrete moulding. Corner piece? Part of the building structure, with shaped internal chevron pattern. Maximum dimensions: L. 93mm; w.45mm each external side; thickness c. 12mm. *1st House.*

Mortar

ST72 Worked stone mortar. Shelly limestone (grainstone). Burr Stone (Upper Jurassic, Portlandian) Isle of Purbeck, Dorset.
Bowl shaped, with ornamental process on rim (grip?). Base diameter 210 mm (23%); rim diameter 230 mm (19%); thickness 18 mm. A banded, hollowed, very shelly limestone. The small (5-10 mm) shell fragments (bivalves) have dissolved leaving this distinctive fabric (cf. a featherstone of quarrymen). It is very similar to Burr stone, one of a suite of Upper Jurassic limestone types quarried along the southern half of the Isle of Purbeck especially between Langton Matravers and St Aldheim's Head *Yard E between Tuning Fork furnace and 3rd House.*

Figure 4.2.10 ST72 Mortar made in Burr Stone, from the side (above figure) and the top (left).

Summary of lithologies

A variety of stone has been used on site for the querns, whetstones and other worked items found at Yewden villa Table 4.2.2). These range in source areas from as far afield as the Pennines to the Forest of Dean, the Isle of Purbeck and the Cotswolds. Some stone was available locally, but in short supply and of limited types.

Representing the local stone, the **Hertfordshire Puddingstone**, found as a beehive and domed rotary querns on site, are particularly robust and were well finished. Although 'Herts Puddingtone' as a lithological type is to be found throughout large areas of Hertfordshire, Bedfordshire and Buckinghamshire, it changes subtly in character across the area. A type almost exactly matching the Yewden querns was found during the project surveys *in situ c.* 2 km north of the site.

Millstone Grit was a popular type of worked stone sourced in the Pennines for querns used in northern England, the Midlands and parts of the southeast. Most of the querns found at Yewden were Millstone Grit or **Quartz conglomerate** (*c.* 60% of the quern assemblage), with slightly more of the former. In contrast, Oxfordshire sites tend to have more quartz conglomerate and very much less or no Millstone Grit. The extensive trade in pottery from Oxfordshire to Yewden is not mirrored by worked stone items arriving by the same route. In comparison, at Silchester there were no MSG querns, but 44 % of the assemblage were quartz conglomerate with the remainder of Lower Greensand and lava types. However, as might be expected, sites further to the north, such as Bancroft (Bucks) and Verulamium (Herts), have a higher proportion of Millstone Grit querns.

The **Greensand** (including **Lodsworth Stone**) was sourced from Sussex or the Weald (West Sussex for Lodsworth) and featured well in the Yewden assemblage (*c.* 20% of the quern fragments). The remainder of sandstone sources consists of some unidentified sources of medium to fine grained varieties and one **Upper Greensand** quern from Sussex.

Surprisingly (given the close proximity to the river Thames) **lava** querns hardly feature - the count of 10 fragments is disproportionate as these were small, abraded fragments of what appear to be from only two different quern stones.

The rubbing stones only comprised **chert, quartzite** and **sarsen** varieties, all very hard wearing. As these form part of the natural rounded pebble component of the Thames Valley gravels, they were locally available.

The use of **bath-stone** in the architecture of this site is interesting. There is no immediately local source of good building stone. The only locally used stone in the building structure was whole flint and chalk, with little or no working. However, a very small amount of oolitic limestone, from the Cotswolds, was found on site. This distinctive banded oolitic grainstone is used over a large tract of southern England from the mid first century onwards (Kevin Hayward, pers comm.). The area of use is specifically the Thames and Kennet Valley (London, Cirencester, Silchester) and Bath. Use in these areas reached a peak during the middle of the second century in London and Silchester, where demand for high quality building stone was at its greatest to embellish major public buildings. The Thames provided a major routeway for transporting this stone probably from its highest navigable part at Lechlade, which is close to a major Roman road intersection. The proximity of Hambleden to the

Thames meant that suitable stone travelling downstream from west to east was widely available. It is therefore not clear why it was not used more for building at Yewden. Finally, the **Burr Stone** mortar is unusual for the Chilterns and Thames Valley sites. It was used in mortar fragments at Shapwick Villa, Dorset, (12 mm thick) from [153] and [201] and the site of Poundbury, near Dorchester (Kevin Hayward, pers comm.). But mortars and, particularly this lithology, are not common in the Yewden area.

Table 4.2.2 Relative proportions of the various lithologies of worked stone from Yewden

Lithology	% of fragments
Millstone Grit	19
Quartz Conglomerate	13
LGS (incl. Lodsworth Stone)	15
Lava (vesicular basalt)	7
Sandstone, variety, *indet.*	25
Limestone (mostly architectural)	10
Hertfordshire Puddingstone	3
Others	8

In conclusion, the source of stone to Yewden shows no preference for any particular type. The choice for whetstones, querns and the other objects is 'fit for purpose' but comes from no preferred region. It would appear to simply reflect what was available for purchase at the time. Geographical location (adjacent to the River Thames and reasonably close to the Fairmile Roman Road leading to Dorchester) ensured a variety of goods could be supplied from parts as far apart as Dorset, Sussex, the Forest of Dean and/or South Wales, the Pennines and the continent to supplement the paucity of local sources. Their location on site reflects the use of buildings and indicates which pits were open at certain times.

Pit 1 accumulated waste from the **1st House** throughout the Roman period and received quern fragments of Lodsworth stone and Quartz Conglomerate along with a black chert rubbing stone.

Pit 24 is associated with the **3rd House** and the querns in this pit, as well as within the building, consist of Millstone Grit, Quartz Conglomerate and Lodsworth stone. The whetstones within the 3rd House are the fine micaceous variety. These finds, together with the location of two furnaces and the charred grain (see Chapter 7.2) show the 3rd House to be involved in drying, malting and grinding grain.

Figure 4.2.11 Distribution of worked stone at Yewden (whetstones, querns, rubbers, mortar and architectural stone)

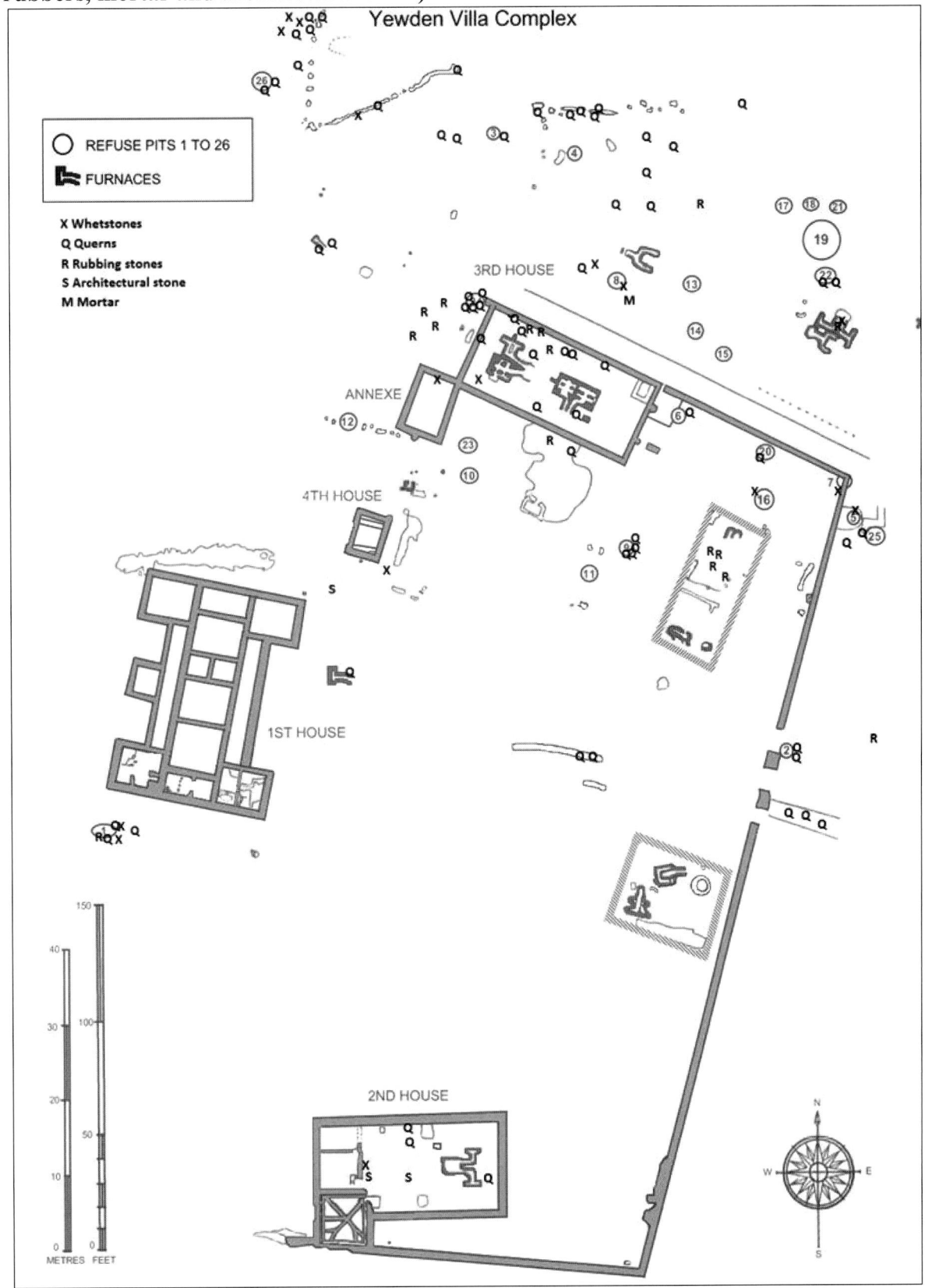

However the 3rd House follows an earlier phase (the '**mortar floor**') which may have had a similar function and **Pit 9** seems to be associated with this earlier structure (with

Quartz Conglomerate, lava, Millstone Grit and Hertfordshire Puddingstone quern fragments).

The **2nd House** shows the use of Millstone Grit and Quartz Conglomerate rotary querns during the second phase of this building (the first phase being habitational, Chapter 3.2). It also contains two of the architectural oolitic limestone fragments, perhaps window surrounds.

Pits 2 and 5 and the area around them contain Lodsworth Stone and Quartz Conglomerate only. The **V-drain** appears to be taking general waste throughout the Roman Period, from the Middle Iron Age onwards, but only contained abraded fragments of lava and lower Greensand querns.

The **Yard**, in the northern part of the Yewden complex, contained a large amount of worked stone (querns and whetstones) and confirms the process of grain preparation and grinding continued to be practised in the north area of the site throughout the Roman period (some quern fragments are built into the north and the Northwest walls). Quern types in the Yard include all the major types (MSG, LGS, QC with one HPS to the far northwest). Quartz Conglomerate, a ferruginous sandstone, and one possible local sarsen stone were built into walls.

The activities within the **wattle and daub building** (with the 'cream pan' furnaces of Cocks 1921) in the NE side of the enclosure necessitated rubbing stones (3 Thames Valley sandstone pebbles and one quartzite).

None of the worked stone objects (or sources of stone) can be used to date structures or phases of activity as these sources were exploited from the Bronze Age onwards.

Acknowledgements: thanks to Kevin Hayward for his input to some of the IDs and to Sally Munnings for proofreading.

Chapter 4.3 Worked flint

The flint assemblage comprises the 1912 assemblage with a small amount of finds obtained from the field walking programme during 2007 to 2010. The total assemblage comprises:

1912 assemblage	385	25665 g
2007-10 fieldwork	21	1064 g
Total	**406 items**	**26729 g**

The flint was in good condition, although some items were a little abraded. The colour of the flint varied enormously from small amounts of black flint, through a series of greys to the pale grey and white of those items with a secondary cortex. Development of a secondary cortex was the norm rather than the exception and this is undoubtedly due to the chalky soil.

The chronological distribution of the worked flint was from the Palaeolithic to the Bronze Age, with the largest proportion falling into the Neolithic as follows:

Chronological divisions	No of items	Percent of total
Lower Palaeolithic	1	0.3
Palaeolithic	3	0.8
Mesolithic	33	8.6
Mesolithic-Neolithic	24	6.2
Neolithic	88	22.9
Neolithic-Bronze Age	57	14.8
Mesolithic to Bronze age (undiff.)	6	1.6
No date determined	173	44.9
Total	**385**	**100.1**

The full database with descriptions of the items can be obtained from the Bucks County Museum or on DVD from Chiltern Archaeology. The summary assemblage of tool forms is shown in Table 4.3.1 below. The large number of scrapers, blades and notched flakes, along with a good variety of other tools, is indicative of a domestic area for the Neolithic to Bronze Age. The area was also near to Mesolithic activity, potentially a summer camp. There were no arrowheads.

Unworked flint is widely available from the river gravels or from the chalk hills surrounding the Hambleden Valley. The hills also provide a form of tabular flint which was used for a few items in this assemblage. Burnt flint was also seen in the fields and was collected by Mr Cocks during the 1912 excavation of the Roman villa complex, but this could be derived from any era up to and including the Roman period.

Table 4.3.1 Worked flint items for each chronological division from the Palaeolithic to the Bronze Age

	Palaeolithic	Mesolithic	Mesolithic-Neolithic	Neolithic	Neo-BA	Meso-BA
Handaxe	3					
Hafted axe			2	4		
Adze		2		2		
Fabricator			1	1		
Pick			1			
Chisel				2		
Tranchet				1		
Burin				1		
Bifacial tool				1	1	
Blade		12	2	2	3	
Bladelet		1	2			
Flake			5		3	
Scraper			1	61	12	6
Notched flake			1	12	2	
Notched blade		1				
Core tool			8	1		
Core		17	1		36	

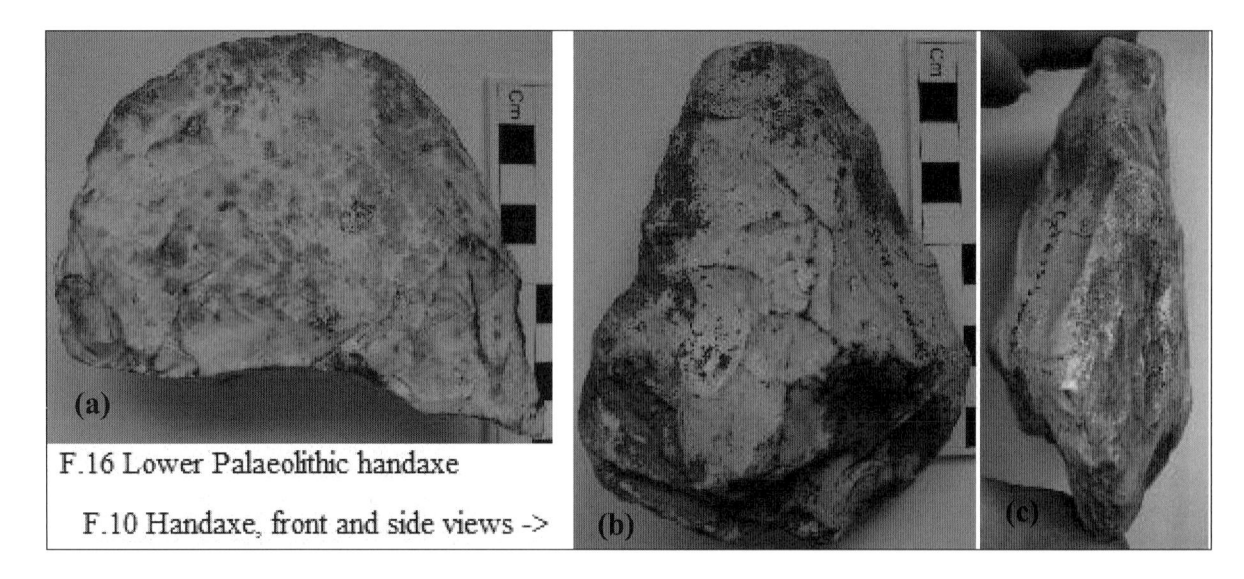

Figure 4.3.1 Palaeolithic hand axes. (a) F16 a biface broken, with a rounded end. (b) and (c) F.10 a triangular axe with invasive flaking. A secondary cortex has developed on both.

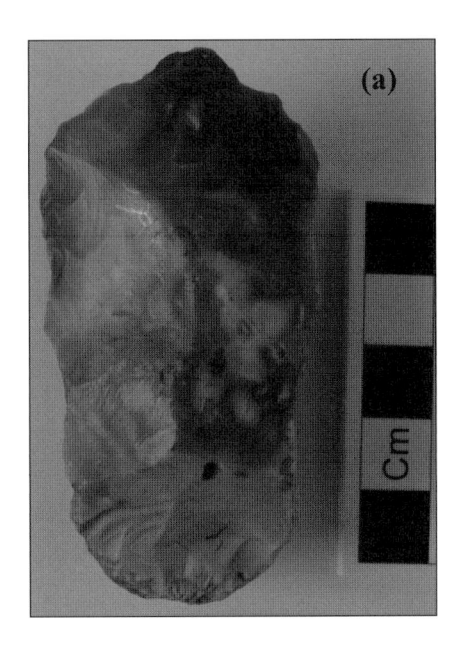

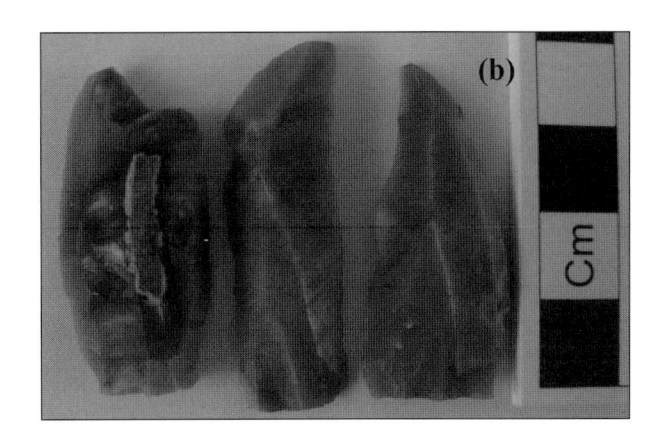

Figure 4.3.2 Mesolithic tools: (a) an adze (F.87) and (b) 3 bladelets (F.187)

Figure 4.3.3 Mesolithic-Neolithic tools: a scraper and a pick/chisel

F.15 (a) & (b) scraper on a flake

F.86 (c) pick or chisel

Figure 4.3.4 A Mesolithic-Neolithic axe, elongate and rectangular, both faces evenly flaked. BCM F.17 (*right*)

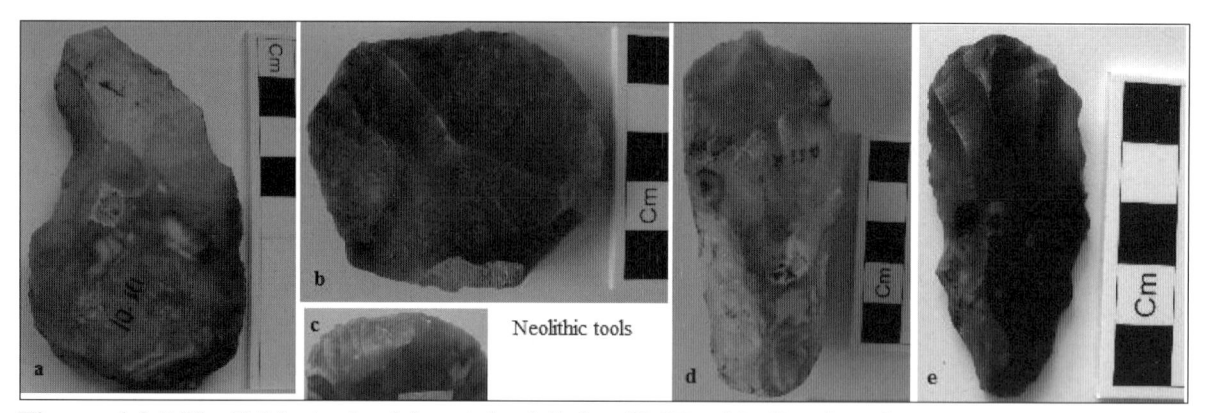

Figure 4.3.5 Neolithic tools: (a) notched flake (F.65); (b) distal end scraper (F.103); (c) close up of end of a 'duckbill' scraper (F.121); (d) an adze (F.135); (e) a fabricator (F.151)

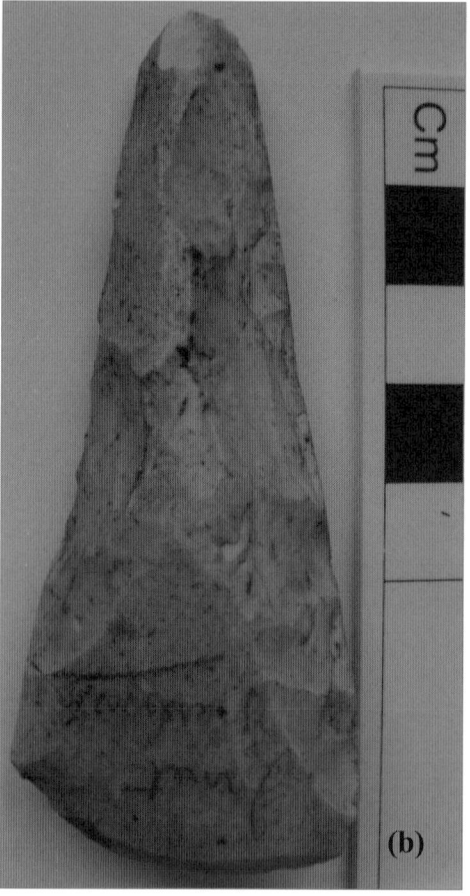

Figure 4.3.6 Neolithic: (a) a ground and polished axe (F.154) and (b) a chisel (F.160), with bilateral retouch and some ventral thinning.

Acknowledgements

The full description of the flint objects was undertaken by Doug Connor and can be requested from the BCM or Chiltern Archaeology who can provide a DVD. A subset of the collection was verified by Jon Cotton (Museum of London). This subset formed the type collection from which Jill Eyers continued to identify and add chronological information to the assemblage. The type series is labelled and held with the collections at the BCM. Thanks to Fred and Jean Reed for proof-reading and Judy Barber for assisting with the logistics of flint work identification.

Chapter 4.4 The Copper Alloy

Sandie Williams

This report is an evaluation of the copper alloy small finds from the Roman Villa complex at Yewden (Hambleden), Bucks, of which there are over 500. A select number of objects have been looked at in detail for the purposes of efficiency and in view of time constraints. These objects will be broken down into functional categories. Hopefully, at a later date, more of them will be placed contextually in their original find spot. The small finds in Cocks' 1920 report formed Appendix VII (Cocks, 1920, 195-198). However, he was unable to provide a complete catalogue of the finds from the excavation, which makes it imperative that a more comprehensive catalogue of all the finds from the Yewden Villa complex is completed at a later date. Nevertheless, in the absence of a full and comprehensive catalogue, there is insufficient information on the distribution of some of the copper object finds at Yewden for conclusions to be reached on some of the objects.

In order to create this report, the majority of complete and dateable copper alloy objects were studied, recorded and photographed at the Bucks County Museum. Thanks have to go to Brett Thorn, the curator, for allowing access to the collection, and special thanks to Nina Crummy for helping me to identify some of the more complicated objects.

The original report by Cocks was studied in an attempt to match the finds he recorded to the objects in the museum. Some of the objects are currently on display at the County Museum at Aylesbury, and therefore not available for study. In this case, the objects were photographed and identification had to be made through the photographs alone. A few of the objects on display still had their BCM (Bucks County Museum) accession number on the display and this allowed me to locate the find on the BCM database.

A large number of the finds are incomplete (e.g. brooch pins), and these have not been included in this report as they have no dateable or aesthetic value to add. However, they will be included in the complete catalogue.

The second section of this report will look at the distribution of some of the artefacts within the villa complex itself. Alfred Heneage Cocks was very forward thinking for his era and left detailed (although at times confusing) labels with the finds on the exact location of the artefacts within the complex. It is hoped that, as with the proposed work on the catalogue, a fuller evaluation of the finds including their original context might occur. This section of the report will make a start by providing distribution maps of certain groups of objects, namely, the brooches, the ligulae and the styli.

Although the majority of the styli are of iron, their importance cannot be stressed enough, and the third and final section of this report will concentrate on the large number (over 70) of styli found in the complex. As well as a large quantity of styli (never before known in that quantity from any villa complex) the final section will also look at the large number of ligulae found at Yewden and attempt to discover why so many were found in one location.

The Yewden objects all have an accession number which starts 1994.57. ###. For this report, the objects will be identified by the last digits of the accession number, for example, find 1994.57.303 will only be known as 303. The objects are briefly catalogued below. A summary description with dimensions follows. Where possible, dates have been included at the end of the description. Also included in the description (in *italics*) is Cocks' contextual information as to where the object was discovered, where this has been included in his notes.

Personal adornment

The Brooches

In his report, Cocks quoted 90 brooches had been found at Yewden, not including fragments. Re-assessment has revealed a total of over 100 complete and incomplete brooch fragments. The brooches are all of copper alloy except where indicated. Due to the lack of precisely dated contexts on the site, the majority of dates for the brooches use the dating timeline compiled by Sally Worrell of the Portable Antiquity Scheme (PAS).

21: Plate Brooch. L: c.43mm. Hexagonal copper alloy plate brooch with enamel fields in the centre. Each of the six corners has a circular lug incised with concentric rings in the centre, separated by a crenelated border. The raised enamelled centre of the brooch has four circles originally filled with red enamel, four cells forming the triangular ends were filled with yellow enamel, and the central two rectangular cells were filled with blue enamel. The brooch is currently on display at the County Museum. Date: c.2nd century. (Cocks 1921, p. 192, fig.25). *4 feet west of Urn burial.*

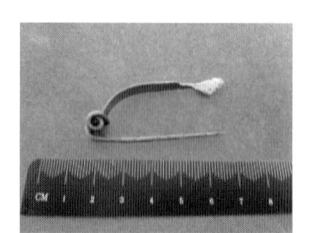

23: Nauheim derivative. L: 158mm. Incomplete Nauheim derivative brooch, one piece, 4-turn bilateral spring. The strip bow is slightly curved with knurled bilateral marginal grooves. Date: AD 25-100. *4 feet west of the west end of the curved wall, near the Single-T furnace.*

29: Headloop. L: 55mm. The top section of this cruciform shaped brooch is decorated with three impressed leaf-shaped cells of white enamel surrounded by traces of green enamel down the central bow. The side wings are flat, the bow is curved and the attachment loop is broken. The centre of the bow is decorated with a knurled moulding and a ridged bow which tapers down to a knobbed foot. Catchplate is solid. This brooch is currently on display in the County museum and is therefore unavailable for full study. Date: AD 69-200.

35: Nauheim derivative. L: 42mm. One piece Nauheim derivative brooch, good condition but incomplete. The pin is broken half way down, but catchplate is complete. Plain bow – no decoration. 4 coils of the spring. Excellent patina. AD 25-100.

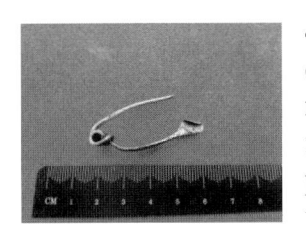

41: Nauheim derivative. L: 44mm. One piece Nauheim derivative brooch. Almost complete, with only tip of pin missing. Almost identical to 1994.57.33 in the pattern down the front of the bow, but almost twice the size. Heavy gilding present on entire bow. Date: AD 25-100. *15 feet north of the west end of the north-west wall.*

51: Hod Hill. L: 48.3mm. Almost complete Hod Hill brooch. Upper bow decorated with three transverse flutings and four beaded ridges. Lateral wings are both present at the lower end of the bow. The top and bottom elements of the bow are separated by a cross-moulding. The lower element of the bow is decorated with punch marks forming three 'arrow' patterns, and tapering down to the knurled footknob. The triangular catchplate is un-perforated. The bow has only a slight curve to it. Both the axial bar and the hinged pin which would have been housed in the rolled-over head of the bow are missing. Date: 43-75AD.

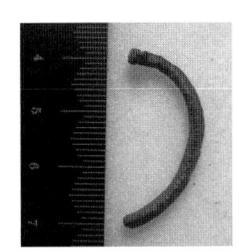

56: Penannular. L: 32mm. Broken section of penannular brooch which retains one terminal. The edge is decorated with transversal notches, and the terminal is turned over on itself, with the end being brought back, forming a lip. Fowler Type D5. Date: AD 25-250. *West end of the north wall, due north of Shears Furnace.*

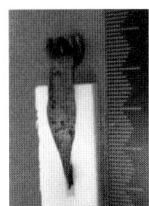

59: Nauheim derivative. L: 40mm. One-piece, Nauheim derivative brooch. 4-turn bilateral spring. Damaged solid catchplate. Pin is missing. Knurled marginal grooves on both edges of the bow. Date: AD 25-100. *3rd House, centre of west flue.*

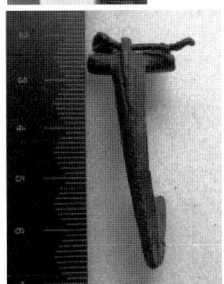

65: Colchester derivative. L: 47 mm. Two-piece cast Colchester derivative brooch. The complete catchplate is perforated with two circular holes. The spring retains six coils, with the axis bar passing through the complete plate at the head of the bow. The springs rest in the semi-cylindrical side wings. At the front of the bow, the plate behind the head which holds the exterior chord is carried over to form a crest, which ends at a central ridge decorated with a zigzag pattern. Date: *c.*AD 43-100. *South of Pit 8 on road, north of 3rd House.*

71: Nauheim derivative. (left) L: 60mm. Almost complete Nauheim Derivative brooch. Five turns of the spring. Pin missing. Solid catchplate in good condition and the brooch has a good patina. Date: AD 25-100.

76: Nauheim derivative. L: 40mm (right). Tiny one piece Nauheim derivative brooch: Complete. Solid catchplate and pin complete. Very thin bow is undecorated. Good patina. Date: AD 25-100. *East of Yard, 60 feet west of Enclosure Wall.*

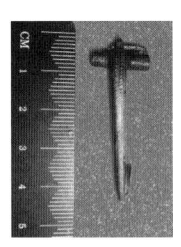

84: Colchester B. L: 40mm. Incomplete, no pin. Partial axial bar and two coils of the spring are retained. The catchplate is pierced. Semi-cylindrical side wings. Bow is undecorated apart from a double row of beaded mouldings at the crest of the bow. Date: *c.*AD 43-100, possibly pre-AD 75.

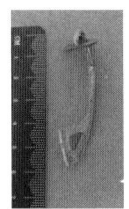

85: Colchester derivative. L: 55mm. Damaged 2 piece bow brooch. Pin missing. Pierced catchplate. Although no spring or pin remains, this gives us a good example of the two pierced holes that the axis bar and pin go through. Date: AD 43-100.

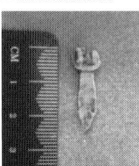

86: Nauheim derivative. L: 24mm. Small corroded bow brooch. No pin or catchplate visible. Knurled marginal grooves down the edge of the bow. Due to size this may possibly be classed as a child's brooch. Date: AD 25-100. *North end 3rd House.*

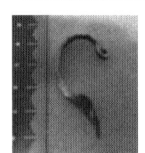

87: Nauheim derivative. L: c.50mm. Badly damaged one piece brooch. Very thin bow, no coils of the spring, only retains partial hook at the top. Date: AD 25-100. *East side of Yard, 46 feet north of Enclosure Wall.*

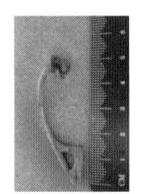

89: Colchester derivative. L: 52mm. Cast two-piece Colchester derivative brooch. Undecorated bow is almost round in section and narrows gently down to the catchplate which has a single triangular perforation. No pin is retained. Part of axial bar still present. Short side wings. Good condition. Crummy type 92. From the 2nd House. Date: AD 43-100. *2nd House, 8 feet from north wall.*

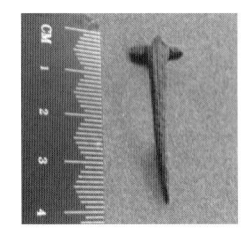

94: Colchester derivative. L: 42mm. Colchester BB brooch. There is a deep groove running bilaterally down the front of the bow with oblique strokes incised off the edge of the groove. The groove has been incised off-centre. No external chord present. Plain side wings. Both lug holes are complete. The catchplate is damaged, but does not appear to be perforated. Pit 24. Date: *c.*AD 65-80. *Pit 24.*

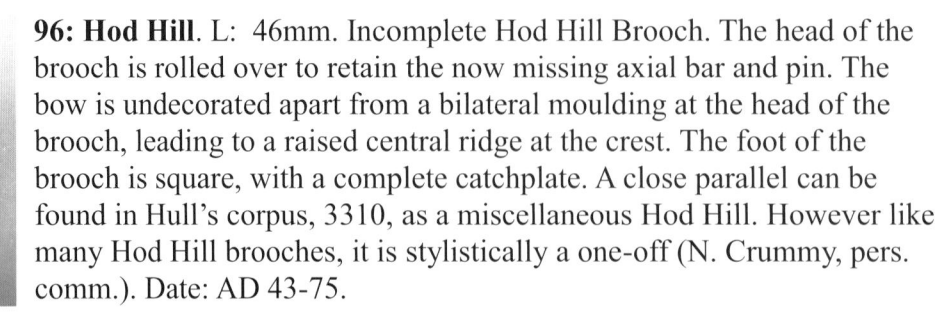

96: Hod Hill. L: 46mm. Incomplete Hod Hill Brooch. The head of the brooch is rolled over to retain the now missing axial bar and pin. The bow is undecorated apart from a bilateral moulding at the head of the brooch, leading to a raised central ridge at the crest. The foot of the brooch is square, with a complete catchplate. A close parallel can be found in Hull's corpus, 3310, as a miscellaneous Hod Hill. However like many Hod Hill brooches, it is stylistically a one-off (N. Crummy, pers. comm.). Date: AD 43-75.

97: Headstud. L: 67mm. Cast copper alloy headstud brooch, largely complete apart from its sprung pin. There is a prominent diamond-shaped stud at the head of the bow. The side edges are serrated. On the bow below the stud there is a cavity which may have once contained enamel, with three raised blocks in the centre. No evidence of enamel remains. AD 75-200.

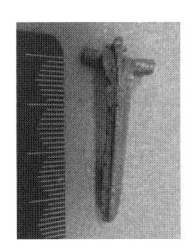

101: Colchester derivative. L: c.45mm. Incomplete cast Colchester derivative brooch. Catchplate appears perforated on one side, but not on the other. No pin remains, but there appears to be part of the chord retained in the perforations of the lug. There is a central ridge down the front of the bow, decorated with a zigzag pattern. Date: *c.*AD 43-100. *East of Yard, 40 feet north of Enclosure wall.*

102: Dolphin (Sprung). L: 52mm.(illustration below) Sprung dolphin brooch. Complete except for missing pin, but slightly bent out of original shape. No decoration on bow, but at the foot there are two lateral grooves, and at the head there is a section which appears to have been filed down to create a flatter surface. Date: *c.*AD 43-65. *East side of Yard, 35 feet north of Enclosure wall.*

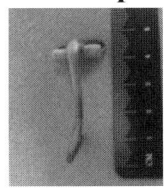

103: Nauheim derivative. L: 59mm. Th. 1mm. One piece wire Nauheim derivative brooch. 5 coils of the spring which is much distorted. No pin or catchplate. Single wide curve to the bow, possible reverse curve at the bottom. Pre-Roman – AD 69. *V-drain.*

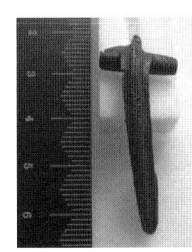

105: Colchester derivative. L: c.44mm. Almost complete Colchester derivative brooch. No pin or spring remains, double pierced lug at the head of the brooch. Catchplate complete with no piercings. There is a central ridge down the front of the bow, decorated with a zigzag pattern. Similar to (101). Date: AD 43-100. *Between Pits 6 and 20.*

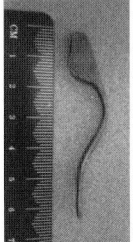

111: Nauheim derivative. L: 62mm. One piece Nauheim derivative brooch. Flat bow, pin missing. Catchplate complete. Three coils of the spring remain, one broken. The front of bow is badly decorated down the centre with off-centre punch marks. Bow is flat and wide, tapering towards the catchplate. Date: AD 25-100. *North-west of north Cream Pan.*

115: Hod Hill. L: 33mm. Almost complete simple hinged Hod Hill brooch. Ridge and groove decoration down the centre of the bow, with three ridges and two grooves. Hinge pin missing. Slight curve to the bow. Slight damage to the catchplate. Date: AD 43-75. *Trench direction of the walnut tree, 3rd House.*

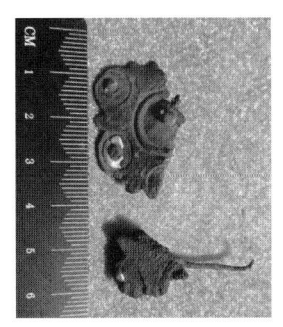

133: Disc. Incomplete cast copper alloy lugged disc brooch in two fragments. The brooch appears to take the form of a flower, decorated with enamel roundels. There is a central raised boss surrounded by smaller impressed circles, each with their own central boss. One circular indentation retains its white enamel. Another tiny fragment of white enamel adheres to a second piece. Very poor condition. Date: *c.*AD 100-200. *Well shed. 13 feet north of the base on the platform.*

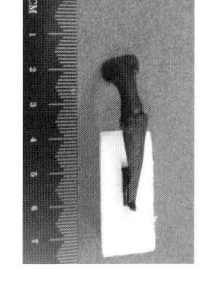

134: Trumpet brooch. Simple trumpet-headed brooch. The only decoration on the bow comes in the form of cross mouldings at the top of the brooch below the trumpet, and in the centre of the bow. There is a small protruding foot. Pin missing and no evidence of spring or chord in the two pierced lugs. One small piercing in the catchplate. Date: AD 75-175. *North of the 5th detached block north of west end of the north-west wall.*

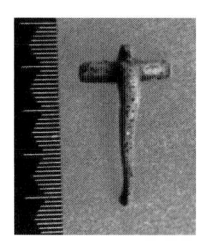

151: Dolphin (hinged). L: 38mm. Incomplete hinged Dolphin brooch. Pin missing. Semi-cylindrical cross-bar with double perforated central lug. No decoration on the bow. No catchplate. Date: *c.*AD 55-100. *Between pit and road along north wall of 3rd House.*

Discussion of the brooches

Brooches are the most common find from any Romano-British site, whether from a small villa in the countryside or from a large urban town. Their basic function was utilitarian – they were meant to fasten clothes together. However they also have other meanings: gender, ethnicity, fashion and status. At Yewden the most common form of brooch found was the Nauheim derivative. According to Reginald Smith, who wrote the brooch report for Cocks, there were approximately 37 Nauheim derivative brooches excavated in 1912, including 8 made from iron (Cocks 1921, 190). This discussion only looks at the copper alloy brooches and does not include the iron examples.

Although only approximately a quarter of the brooches from Yewden have been looked at in this report, it is clear to see that there is a much higher proportion of earlier Roman brooches compared to those from the later period. For example, there are no identifiably 4th century brooches such as Crossbows. Nauheim derivatives, which predominantly date to the second half of the first century, are extremely well represented. It should be remembered that although the brooches may have ceased production at a specific moment in time, they would not necessarily have gone out of use. Many brooches would have been kept until they broke or were lost. Some may have been family heirlooms passed down through the generations. Although we see the majority of brooches were made in the first century, many may lie in a later dated context. Some styles of brooch are known to have been found in contexts which range throughout the whole Roman occupation period.

A nice example of a Headloop brooch (29) was discovered, dating between AD 75 to 200. The design of this style of brooch indicates that they were worn as a pair, most commonly connected by a small chain (Croom, 2003). Although most commonly illustrated with the chain loop at the top, contemporary iconography shows that the loop was actually worn at the bottom, with the chain hanging between the two brooches.

The Headstud brooch (97) has a similar parallel in Smith's report on the brooches (Smith, 1920, 191, Fig. 23), however this brooch was not found during the research. Smith describes the brooch as follows:

"Solid bronze brooch with cylindrical spring-cover transversely grooved but empty, the pin having been hinged at the middle of it. At the head an animal figure facing towards the bow, its tail forming a ring for attaching chain (probably one of a pair of brooches. The bow is notched along both edges and has a row of lozenges with traces of enamel: concentric rings in relief at the end above the catch-plate."

This may well have been the twin (albeit not identical) to our example. Smith's came from "6 feet from the centre of the 3rd House", and our example contained no context information.

The Hod Hill brooch (51) originated on the Continent during the Augustan period (Corney, 2000, 322), arriving in Britain with the army. Production ceased *c*.40-50 AD and they had all virtually disappeared by AD 75 (Blockley *et al*, 1995, 975). This gives us a nice dating sequence for their existence at Yewden of mid-1st century.

The Colchester B example (84) has a general range from *c*. AD 43-100. However, Mackreth argues that brooches which have a catchplate with a large piercings indicate that the brooches were possibly made earlier than AD 75 (Mackreth 1994, 162).

There are two forms of Dolphin brooch at Yewden - the sprung type and the hinged form. Although the sprung Dolphin brooch was produced first (*c*.AD 43-65), it overlapped with the hinged Dolphin for 10 years (*c*.AD 55-100).

The hairpins

167: L: 104mm. Complete copper alloy hairpin. Very simple ovoid head above baluster moulding. The shaft is slightly curved.

168: L: 109mm. Complete cast hairpin with a bead, baluster and knurled head. (Cool Group 3, sub-group B). This type was made throughout the Roman period, so cannot be assigned a specific date. *3 feet west of the middle line of blocks, North-west wall.*

172: L: *c*.99mm (bent). Complete cast copper alloy hairpin with a slightly bent shaft. The head is barrel-shaped which is flat on the top, and sits above a double collar.

174: L: 91.5mm. Complete cast hairpin. Shaft slightly curved. Flattened bun-shaped head above a double cordon. Cool Group 2, sub-group A. Date: 1st – 4th century.

219: L: 37mm. Incomplete hairpin. Only a short section of the shaft and the spherical knob remain. Cool Group 1, sub-group C. Date: In use throughout the Roman period.

220: L: 63mm. Incomplete cast hairpin. The tip is broken and the shaft is bent in the centre. Head is conical with an incised rib pattern at the base. Cool Group 1, sub-group D. This type of pin was common throughout the Roman period. *North side of the north wall of yard.*

221: L: 37mm. Incomplete cast hairpin. Only the head and a short section of the shaft remain. Similar to Cool Group 2, sub-group C, but with no cordon beneath the head. Date: Late 1st – 4th century. *North-east corner of flue of west furnace, 3rd House.*

222: L: *c*.96mm. Incomplete hairpin, broken into two pieces and the tip is missing. Cool Group 1, sub-type C. This type of hairpin was in use throughout the Roman period. *Pit 5.*

225: L: c.50mm. Almost complete hairpin, broken at the tip. Cool Type 6. Button-shaped head with two cordons beneath. Generally this group belongs to the second half of the 1st century, to early 2nd century (Cool 1990, 157, fig. 5.3). *On mortar floor, S of 3rd House.*

227: L: 110mm. Complete copper alloy hairpin, although badly damaged and bent in the middle. The head has a complete ring and dot motif on one facet, with another incomplete one on a damaged facet. Cool Group 15. This hairpin has a parallel from Colchester which came from a 4th century grave (Crummy 1984, 29, fig. 29.490; Cool 1990, 157, fig. 5.3).

234: L: 75mm. Incomplete copper alloy hairpin, broken at the tip. The head consists of a series of nine rings, irregular in size, incised spirally around the head (Cool Group 5, sub-group A). Also commonly found in bone (Crummy 1983, 24, fig. 21.403). Although they can be found from mid-1st century to 4th century contexts, they are most popular during the 2nd century (Cool 1990, 157, fig. 4.4). *In the clay at the south-west corner of mortar floor.*

236: L: 80mm. Copper alloy hairpin, almost complete. There is damage to the top of the head and the tip of the pin. Cool Group 5, sub-group C. Mid-1st to 4th century, but most popular during the 2nd century. The broken tip of the hairpin may have had a flattened spherical head. The remainder of the head is decorated w an incised lattice pattern. Good condition. *35 feet north of Enclosure wall.*

2533: L: 82mm. Complete copper alloy hairpin in poor condition. Knob and reel head. There may possibly be some decoration further down the head, but the shaft is quite corroded. Very similar to Cool Group 8. Date: Late 1st – 2nd century. *Yard east centre, north of 3rd House.*

2545: L: 73mm. Incomplete copper alloy hairpin, broken at the tip. The head consists of a spherical knob sitting on a cordon. Cool Group 2, sub-group A. Date: Late 1st – 4th century.

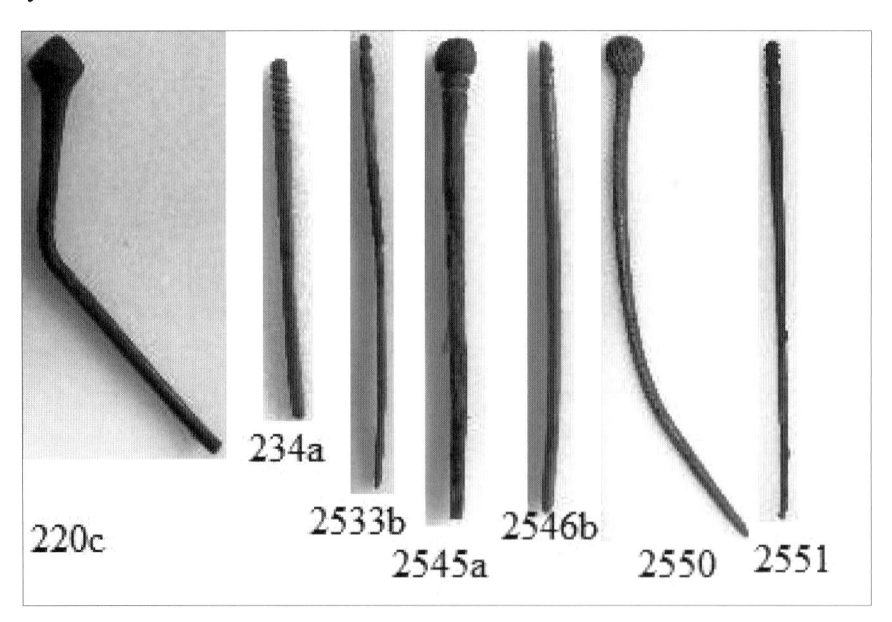

2546: L: 60mm. Incomplete copper alloy hairpin, tip and top of head missing. The end is turned. Decoration consists of a group of reels which may originally have been topped off by a knob. *Pit 24.*

2548: L: 90mm. Incomplete copper alloy hairpin. Tip missing. Cool Group 5, sub-group D, slender shaft, four grooves topped by a small knob. Date: Late 1st – 4th century, being found most commonly in the 2nd century. *10 feet west of west wall of 3rd House.*

2550: L: 90mm. Complete but bent ¾ down the shaft. Globular head covered with close-set radiating incised lines. An incised line spirals part of the way down the thick shaft from below the head. A parallel can be found in Crummy, 1983, Fig. 31.499. *Pit 23.*

2551: L: 80mm. Complete cast copper alloy hairpin. Cool Group 3, sub-group A, with a curved unit between cordons, one below and two above, and the pin is topped by a squat conical head. Date: $1^{st} - 2^{nd}$ century. *Pit 22.*

2554: L: c.120mm. Complete but bent cast copper alloy hairpin. The pin is bent ½ and ¾ the way down the shaft. The head is conical and sits on a single cordon. Cool Group 2. Date: In use throughout the Roman period. *10 feet north of Pit 11.*

2555: L: 95mm. Very similar to (2550), but this example has a collar beneath the globular head. Complete but bent slightly in the middle, and has a 90° bend *c.* 2/3 of the way down.

2556: L: 75mm. Complete, but with a broken tip. Very similar to (2554), the conical head sits on two cordons. Cool Group 2. Date: $1^{st} - 4^{th}$ century. *Yard, east side, due E of Tuning Fork.*

2561: L: 102mm. Complete but broken into two parts. Flame-shaped head sitting on a cordon beneath which is a curved unit which again sits on a cordon. Cool Group 3. Date: $1^{st} - 2^{nd}$ century. *V-ditch.*

Discussion of the hairpins
In a similar way with the brooches, hairpins were just as much functional objects, as being fashion statements. Also similar to the brooches, their style changed with the fashion, especially in relation to women's hairstyles. The study of contemporary iconography, and of those pins found as grave goods, indicates that the hairpin was either behind, or to the side, of the head. However, there is some question as to whether they were worn in the hair or used to hold clothes together (as dress pins). Only brooches were found in a position in which to hold clothes together.

Iconography throughout the Roman period shows us different styles of hair fashion. Unlike brooches, only women have been found with hairpins in their graves. In the earlier Roman period, the fashion was to wear the hair piled up on top of the head and therefore longer pins would have been required to hold the style in place. Later, a fashion was adopted where the hair was a little flatter on the top, and so a shorter pin would have been required.

The length of pins found at Yewden, as well as the style, indicate that the majority were in use during the earlier rather than the late occupation of the site. The style of hairpin is basically quite simple. No expensive 'hand' or anthropomorphic pins, were found at Yewden. We can therefore surmise that, although some may be classed as fashionable, the basic function of the hairpins found in the villa complex are purely to hold up the hair. Quite possibly they were made in small numbers on the site, or perhaps brought in by a travelling salesman who may have had some included in his wares.

Rings

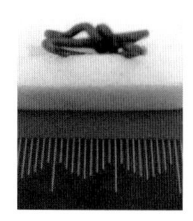

7: Ring. Diam: 18mm; Th: 1mm. A length of rectangular sectioned wire with one terminal rolled around to enclose the ring and form a simple decoration. *Fill in, north Cream Pan.*

8: Ring. Diam: 18mm. A rectangular sectioned strip with overlapping terminals. The external surface is decorated with a continual band of zig-zags. *Centre of Yard, north of 3rd House.*

10: Ring. Diam: 20mm. A very fine, thin ring of copper alloy. Broken in one section and distorted from original shape. Extreme wearing visible. Several incised grooves decorate the edges on both ends before the break. *2nd House, c.8 feet south of north wall.*

14: Finger ring. Diam: 20mm. Ornate finger ring, moulded shoulders which widen to support an empty hexagonal bezel. The bezel would originally have contained a precious stone, or perhaps an intaglio. Style suggests a male ring. The ring is currently on display at Bucks County Museum and is not available for complete study.

45: Ring. Diam: 21mm. Diamond-shaped in profile. No other decoration.
As it appears functional rather than aesthetic it is probably not a finger ring. *Pit 1.*

46: Finger Ring. Diam: 20mm. (right) Complete finger ring, showing wear on one section. The ring shows no signs of decoration and does not appear to have had any treatment. *Pit 1.*

48: Finger Ring. Diam: *c.*20mm. Copper alloy finger ring with depression for an oval stone or intaglio which is now missing. The bezel is quite wide. The base of the ring where it would have rubbed against the palm is very thin and worn. Date: 1st - 2nd century.

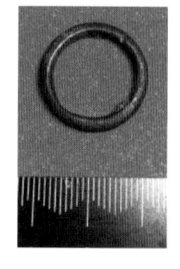

52: Finger Ring. Diam: 19mm. Quite heavily worn around the edges. Central incised groove around the circumference of the ring. Dark green patination. Slightly flattened in one area from wear on the finger where it would have rubbed against the palm of the hand. *Pit1?*

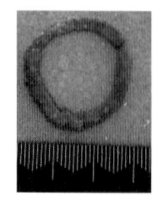

54: Ring. Diam: 28mm. Complete ring of copper alloy wrapped in copper alloy wire (c.1mm thick). The wire is tightly coiled around the internal core of wire (c.2mm thick). Poor condition although almost complete. Damage to the coils allows us to see the core. *Room C, 1st House.*

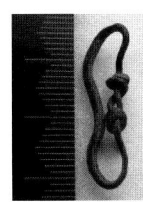

58: Finger Ring. Diam: *c.* 28mm. Thicker back wire, thinner 'decorated' front wire. Possible copper alloy finger ring. One piece of wire crudely coiled to form a finger ring with the two terminal ends coiled to create a decoration on the front. The back of the ring is approximately twice the thickness of the front. *Fill in S Cream Pan.*

Discussion of the rings

Finger rings were unknown in Britain until they were brought over by the Romans. Once here, it did not take them long to become popular and fashionable to the Romano-British population. Not only were they a stylish, decorative personal ornament, but in some cases they also defined both wealth and status for the wearer.

As well as an aesthetic value, finger rings could also double as functional objects. Ring-keys were popular between the 1st and 3rd centuries and would have been used to lock small boxes in which the wearer could keep their valuables.

One of the earliest functions of an intaglio ring was a seal. The intaglio set in the ring's bezel would be incised with the owner's device. It would be impressed into a wax seal, allowing the recipient to know who had sent the package and ensure it had not been interfered with en-route.

Rings are difficult objects to try to classify and date. Unless they are decorated or have a central setting, such as an intaglio or stone, they could easily have either been a finger ring (such as the plain wedding rings we wear today), or a functional object, perhaps to join the links of a lamp chain. In the catalogue above, only rings which are definitely identified as finger rings have been marked as such. Any ambiguity in function has them identified only as 'ring'. This does not mean to say they are not finger rings, but in the absence of decoration or other identifiers to show that they are finger rings, a functional use would have been possible.

Two rings stand out from the rest. Finger ring (14) is currently on display at the County Museum and therefore not available for a closer study, but the style indicates that it is later in date, and may have been produced around the 3rd century. Finger ring (48) is one of the commonest types of ring found in Roman Britain. It dates from the $1^{st} – 2^{nd}$ centuries, but is most commonly found in 2nd century contexts. For further information on this type of ring, the Snettisham jewellery hoard included a large quantity of them, now housed in the British Museum. As for the majority of the rings from Yewden, most are stylistically simple in design, and may have been home-made.

Earrings/Pendants

16: Earring. L: 18mm. A hollow drop earring which has been cast in two pieces with ribbing around the edges. Integral suspension loop at the top has an off-centre hole. A depression in the centre of the ring on both faces would have been used to house an oval object, possibly of stone or glass. This would have been attached by two holes at the back of the object.

57: Earring. L: 15mm. Extremely delicate and fragile single length of copper alloy wire, twisted to create an earring. *East of 3rd House.*

Bracelets/Armlets

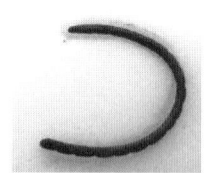

67: Bracelet. Diam: 32mm. Half-section of a copper alloy armlet/bracelet. Crenellations 1mm wide and 2mm apart decorate the circumference of the object. *Fill in south-east corner, 1st House.*

127: Bracelet. Diam: *c.*54mm. Incomplete copper alloy cable armlet/bracelet consisting of 3 strands of twisted copper alloy wire, each strand being 1mm thick. As it has been broken into two pieces which do not appear to meet, there may be a missing third piece. It is not possible to say whether or not there were terminals. One similar example from Colchester was found in a Period 2 grave deposit and had a double hook clasp (Crummy 1983, 38, 41.1628). *Pit 19.*

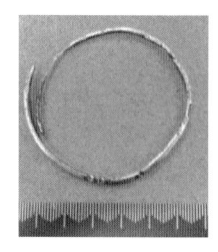

138: Bracelet. Diam: *c.*60mm. Single length of copper alloy wire curled around to form an armlet/bracelet. The two ends do not join together, but overlap to complete the circle. No decoration visible.

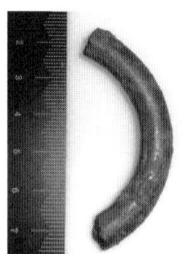

235: Bracelet. Diam: *c.*60mm. Very thick copper alloy bracelet fragment. There only remains approximately one third of the bracelet/armlet. 8mm thick. *Pit 20.*

281: Bracelet. Diam: *c.* 60mm. Crenelated bracelet fragment, bent out of shape. *West of depression across chalk floor, between Cream Pans.*

Miscellaneous Dress

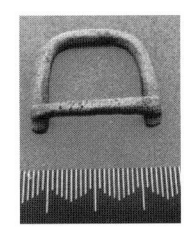

61: Buckle. L: 39mm. D-shaped Buckle loop. Pin missing, although a groove to hold the pin is clearly visible on the cross-bar. *1st House, on tessellated pavement.*

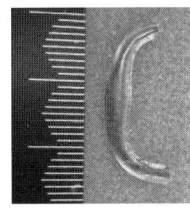

77: Buckle. L: 25mm. Fragment of a Buckle. Both ends broken, and no central cross-bar visible. Some evidence of tool marks on the rear of the fragment. *Fill in of 3rd House.*

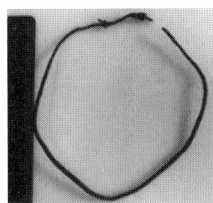

2564: Wire? Necklace. Diam: *c.*100mm. Single strand of circular sectioned copper alloy wire, broken into two sections. The smaller broken section consists of two strands of wire, knotted in two areas in order to complete the circle and possibly to move the circle in order to change its size. *Pit 16.*

Toilet and Surgical Instruments

155: Toilet Instrument, Nail Cleaner. L: 59mm. Convex sectioned strip of copper alloy nail cleaner which tapers down to the forked terminal. The head is extremely flat and large with a centrally pierced attachment hole just above the start of the shaft. *Heap from west furnace of 3rd House.*

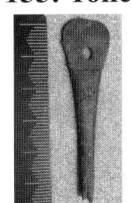

159: Toilet Instrument, Ear Scoop: L: 44mm. Slight damage, including the tip of the shaft, and slight damage to the bowl. The only decoration present is a spiralling groove just below the bowl to approximately a quarter of the way down the shaft. *West side of Yard.*

181: Toilet Instrument, Nail Cleaners x 2. L: i) 40mm. ii) 39mm. Two separate nail cleaners. The first is flat in profile and appears to be double-ended. The typical forked terminal is present, expanding into the body of the cleaner before tapering to a wedge-shape. There is a single incised line as decoration around the body. The point is incised. The suspension loop is at the side of the wedge, only visible from the side. The second nail cleaner is much simpler in design, with the forked terminal at one end and a flat suspension loop at the top. *150' north of 3rd House and c.24' east of its north wall, close to a baby.*

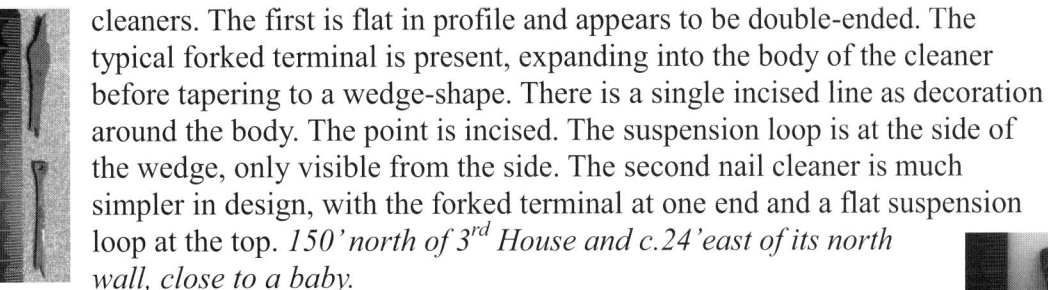

184: Toilet Instrument, Ear Scoop. L: 45mm. Flat shield-shaped attachment loop leading to a circular sectioned shaft which is slightly bent in the middle. The bowl shows some damage at the edge.

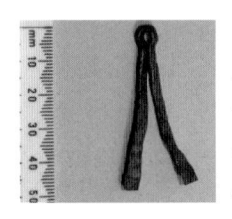

187: Toilet Instrument, Tweezers. L: 50mm. Single pair of quite crude tweezers. Created from one piece of copper alloy folded over to create the suspension look at the top and the two arms. No decoration visible on the arms. Fairly good condition. *Dug-over surface of Mortar floor, south of 3rd House.*

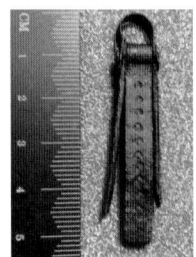

201: Toilet Instrument Set. L: 50mm. Complete toilet set comprising a pair of tweezers, nail cleaner and ear scoop held together by a bar and shackle (Eckardt & Crummy 2008, 167-9). The tweezers are decorated by a vertical row of ten crescent-shaped incisions. *Shallow pit, north of 3rd House, east of Samian pit.*

243: Toilet Instrument, Nail Cleaner. L: 54mm. Circular in section with a forked terminal one end. The head and suspension loop appear to have been formed by twisting a thin section of copper alloy wire around the top of the cleaner, finished off by creating the suspension loop. *Fill in north part of Yard, 3 feet east of Figure of 8.*

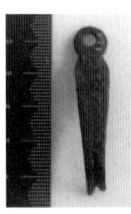

246: Toilet Instrument, Nail Cleaner. L: 52mm. Flat nail cleaner, complete. The forked terminal appears complete. The body of the cleaner has an incised groove leading from the centre of the fork to approximately one third of the way up the body. The suspension loop is flat with a central hole.

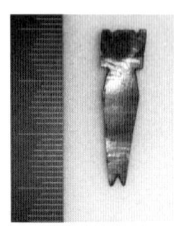

252: Toilet Instrument, Nail Cleaner. L: 30mm. Very small, flat nail cleaner. The reverse has a single rivet at the top, possibly part of a set which had been held together by a bar and shackle. The front is highly polished, but no sign of decoration is present. Evidence of the rivet is visible from the front. *East of Yard, 15' north of Enclosure wall.*

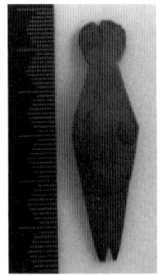

254: Toilet Instrument, Nail Cleaner. L: 54mm. Crudely made nail cleaner, appears to be unfinished. The cleaner was beaten out of a piece of copper alloy sheet with no decoration or finishing. The circular suspension end has a small v-shaped nick in the top but appears too high to have been a suspension hole. The body of the nail cleaner is lozenge shaped, with the end forming the forked terminal.

260: Toilet Instrument, Ear Scoop. L: 49mm. Almost complete ear scoop, broken at the tip. The bowl is flat and rounded and appears to have been formed by flattening the shaft at the end, then slices a section out and shaping to form the bowl. *Yard. 80 feet north of 3rd House.*

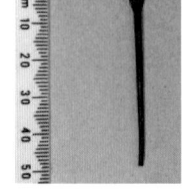

315: Spoon. Diam: (of bowl) 20mm. Long handled spoon with flat round bowl. The bowl is crumpled and the edges appear quite jagged. The handle has been bent to a

90° angle. Highly polished (possibly tinned or silvered). Roman spoons with round bowls date from the second half of the 1st century and the 2nd century (Crummy 1983, p. 69). The spoon is on display at the County Museum and so not available for closer investigation. Date: $1^{st} - 2^{nd}$ century. *North of west end of north-west wall, east of blocks.*

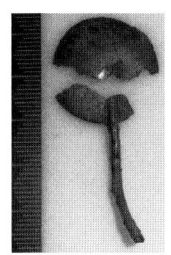

2644: Spoon. L: 82mm. Diam. (of bowl) 26mm. Long handled spoon, broken into three pieces. Tinned or silvered. The round bowl is quite shallow, and has broken into two or more pieces. One piece is still attached to the shaft, which has a shoulder where it attaches. Shaft is broken into two pieces. A third piece is missing. Date: $1^{st} - 2^{nd}$ century. *East side of Yard, north of 3rd House.*

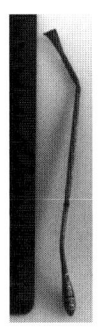

2614: Ligula. L: 100mm. (left). Incomplete ligula/spoon-probe. The spoon bowl is damaged, but the probe is complete. The shaft is circular in section. The two ends are defined by collars. The ligula is bent at both ends.

2619: Ligula. L: 101mm. (not illustrated). Heavily encrusted ligula. No decoration visible. Spoon on one end, and the circular shaft ends in a point. *Pit.*

2638: Ligula. L: 32mm. Incomplete ligula, only the leaf-shaped bowl survives, broken at the shaft. The tip is missing. Bowl is quite deep and long. *Pit 9.*

2652: mid-shaft. shaft by leading end. *Pit*

Ligula. L: 110mm. Complete ligula/spoon-probe, broken in half The spoon is long, narrow and quite deep and separates from the two collars. The circular sectioned shaft is broken in the middle, down to two more collars before ending in the bulbous probe *in Yard, 18' north of 3rd House.*

2678: Miscellaneous. L: 60mm. Large section of possible nail cleaner, broken at the bottom. Rounded section at the top with a centrally pierced attachment hole. Straight flat body which is broken before the (now missing) forked terminal. *Pit 9.*

Toilet sets

Toilet sets consisting of tweezers, nail cleaner and ear scoop are quite common finds on Roman sites. It is less common to find complete sets than it is to find individual components. Toilet sets were in use throughout the Roman period. Many of the examples from Yewden have little contextual information. Some of the examples we do have appear quite crude and 'home-made' (187), (252), (254) and may have been manufactured within the complex itself. Set (254) was apparently unfinished.

The distribution map of the toilet sets for which we do have contextual information (Figure 4.4.1) show a marked spatial distribution around the yard area or in the northern section of the complex itself. There is one example from the 2nd House and a few along the ditch outside of the main gates to the complex next to the unmetalled road.

Household Equipment

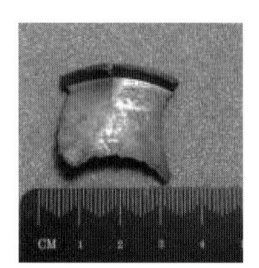

162: Vessel Rim. L: c.23mm. Small section of rim and body sherd from a vessel. There is a crack in the centre of the rim going down approximately one third of the length. Colour is very silvery, indicating tinning or silvering.

241: Vessel Rim. L: c.50mm. Rim fragment from a copper alloy vessel. Only a small section of the body of the vessel remains, corroded to such an extent that holes are visible in the material. Evidence of two circumferentially incised lines decorate the body just below the out-turned rim, with a lighter incised line just below these. Very poor condition. *Pit 8.*

304: Needle. L: 62mm. Complete copper alloy needle. Shaft is 2mm in diameter and circular in section. The head is flattened with a complete grooved thread guide above and below the longitudinal eye. Currently on display at Bucks County Museum.

305: Needle. L: 135mm. Complete copper alloy needle. Shaft is 1.5mm in diameter and circular in section. There is a slight bend in the shaft. The head is flattened and there is a complete grooved thread guide above and below the longitudinal eye. Currently on display at Bucks County Museum.

2612: Needle. L: 140mm. Complete but damaged copper alloy needle. Shaft is circular in section. Bent and almost corroded through in the middle. The head is flattened and there is a complete grooved thread guide above and below the longitudinal eye. *Trench from Tuning Fork furnace to (skeleton) pit north-east of 3rd House.*

2613: Needle. L: 101mm (right). Complete copper alloy needle. Shaft is circular in section. The head is flattened and there is a complete grooved thread guide above and below the damaged longitudinal eye. *Pit 20.*

There were a total of 25 needles found at Yewden. This is a high number of objects from one rural villa complex.

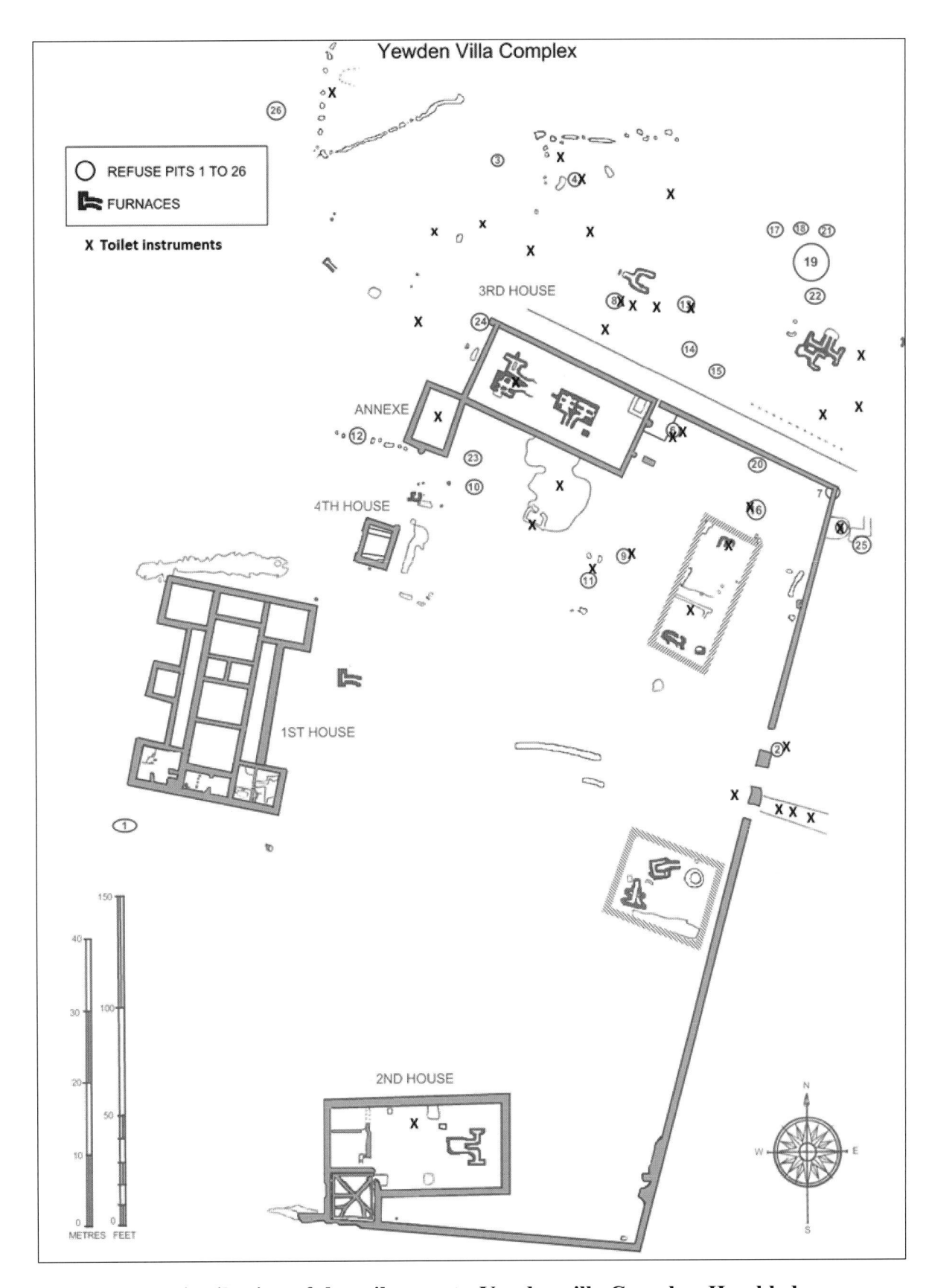

Figure 4.4.1 Distribution of the toiletry sets, Yewden villa Complex, Hambleden

Writing and Communication

158: Stylus. L: 82mm. Copper alloy stylus, wedge-shaped terminal which has incised lines. Slim shaft, triangular flattened head. The eraser end is engraved with 4 sets of 2 parallel lines and the shaft has 3 sets of 2 parallel lines: IIIII \V/ \\\II. Although generally in good condition, the point of the shaft is broken. On display at the Bucks County Museum. *Tiled drain, 1st House.*

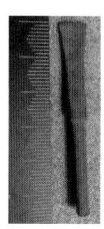

193. Stylus. L: 55mm. Copper alloy stylus fragment. Eraser end and partial shaft remain. The long erasing blade is wedge-shaped and tapers from a square section adjoining the circular shaft to a broad, flat edge. *Fill of Annexe.*

Mounts and Fittings

64: Fitting, Handle. L: 26mm. Cast copper alloy drop handle fragment. Large section of drop handle: the front is slightly grooved around the edge and the back is completely flat. The centre of the handle is hollow.

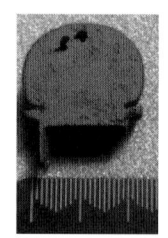

163: Fitting, Knife Handle terminal. L: 26mm. Knife handle end stop. Rounded terminal, hollow, with two straight edges which would have fitted onto the tang. Similar examples are to be found from both Newstead and the 1st century fort at Vindonissa (Curle 1911, 282, fig. 40; 283, Pl. LX, 9).

288: Fitting. Box lid/handle? L: 34mm. Oval copper alloy object, flat in profile, with a circular loop sat on a rhomboid piece of copper alloy and attached via a copper alloy rivet beneath. The object is very similar to a modern-day saucepan lid handle. Possibly lid of a small oval box. *Floor outside west end of 3rd House.*

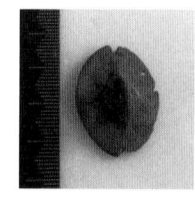

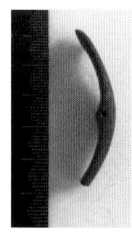

299: Fitting. L: c.55mm. Curved copper alloy fitting, thicker in centre with a circular piercing through it. Broken at both ends. Possible furniture fitting.

311: Fitting. Enamelled Stud. Diam: 14mm. Copper alloy circular stud with riveted shaft. The outer contains traces of yellow and green enamel. The inner circle contains traces of yellow and red or orange enamel.

313: Fitting. Stud. Diam: 20mm. Copper alloy domed stud with traces of silvering or tinning. No evidence of a pin on the internal surface of the stud. Possible furniture stud. *On Mortar floor, 3rd House.*

314: Fitting. Stud. Diam: 28mm. Slightly convex copper alloy stud. Square sectioned tapering shaft is complete but bent. Possible furniture stud.

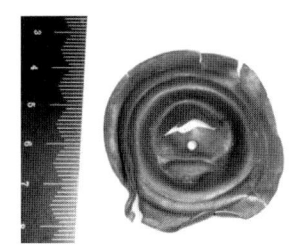

393: Fitting. Diam: 47mm. Squashed circular fitting with a high convex moulding in the middle with a pierced hole and a flanged convex rim. Cocks (1921, 195, fig. 31.5) claimed this to be similar to a tambourine 'jingle'. A parallel in Crummy (1983, 116, fig. 120.3148) has it listed as a stud with a convex head. *North of west end of north-west wall. 2 feet east of east detached block.*

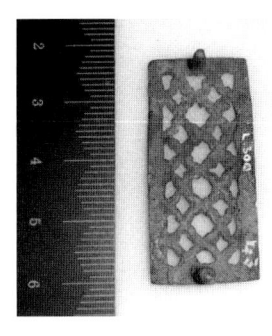

395: Mount. L: 37mm. Rectangular open-work plate mount with one rivet in the centre of each short end. There is a parallel in Crummy, 137, fig. 157.4240. Here Crummy cites two more parallels from the Rhine forts at Zugmantel and Saalburg.

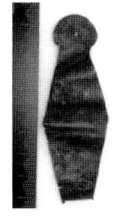

2552: Strip. L: 85mm. Thin sheet of copper alloy crudely beaten to form a possible pendant. No decoration is present on either side. The round head has a single piercing in the centre, leading to a lozenge shaped body. The base of the object is broken off. Similar in form to the nail cleaner 1994.57.254, but of thinner material. It is not possible to determine the exact function of this object in its incomplete state. *Pit in Yard, 18 feet north of 3rd House.*

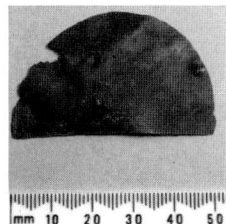

2572: Plate. L: 50mm. Semi-circular plate, slight damage to one side of the curve. No evidence of decoration on the front of the object. *Between Annexe and south-west corner of Mortar floor.*

2573: Boss. Diam: c.35mm. Boss-shaped object, broken into two pieces with another piece missing. c.20mm high, there is a protrusion both above and below the body of the object. Although it is similar in form to a bell, the end of the internal protrusion finishes beyond the rim of the object with no room for a clapper. The protrusion above the body is encrusted, with no indication of a suspension loop. *2nd House, north-west corner 5 feet south of north wall, level with wall top.*

2575: Disc. Diam: 30mm. Flat circular disc with centrally pierced hole. No evidence of decoration. *18 feet north-west of 8th block of north-west wall.*

2579: Vessel Base. L: c.65mm. Possible base from a copper alloy vessel. Shallow plate with circular central indentation and squared area. Very damaged. On the external surface, the circular indentation forms a rim (ring base) on which the vessel would have stood. Possibly base of a copper alloy platter or shallow bowl, or base of a square copper alloy jug.

2582: Boss. Diam: c.30mm. Conical boss, heavily encrusted on the external surface, with slight signs of a pattern. Internally very similar to (2573) in that there is an internal protrusion which may be mistaken for the crown staple of a bell. The length of the body of the object would not allow a clapper to hang from it. *Pit 24.*

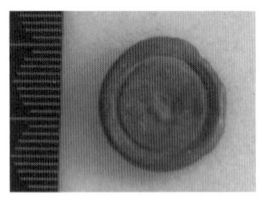

2585: Stud. Diam: 20mm. Stud with flat head with a slightly convex concentric moulding, slightly turned down head at the edge. There is a pin which is bent. Part of the moulding is coming away from the centre of the stud.

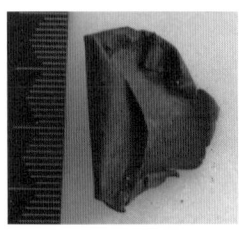

2625: Stud. Diam: c.38mm. Very damaged flat headed stud. The edges are folded over on themselves and slightly 'frayed'. A short length of pin is present. *North wall of Yard, due north of Shears Furnace.*

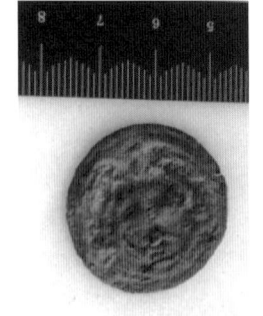

2628: Stud with Medusa Head. Diam: 30mm. Flat stud with what appears to be the head of Medusa on the front. No evidence of a pin on the reverse. Cocks believed it may have come from a bucket (Cocks 1921, 195). An alternative explanation is that it may have once had a pin and been attached to leather. *18 feet south of south-east corner of Annexe to 3rd House.*

2630: Furniture Pin. L: c.55mm. Globular headed furniture pin with square sectioned shaft. Complete. *Pit 9.*

2631: Furniture Pin. L: c. 35mm. Globular headed furniture pin with round sectioned shaft. Tip broken. *Pit 9.*

2692: Sheet Fragment. L: 33mm. Rectangular piece of copper alloy sheet. Incomplete. The front of the sheet is decorated with one row of punched decoration on the two edges, and two double rows of punched decoration running down the central length. *Yard, c.36 feet north of west stokehole of 3rd House.*

Bells

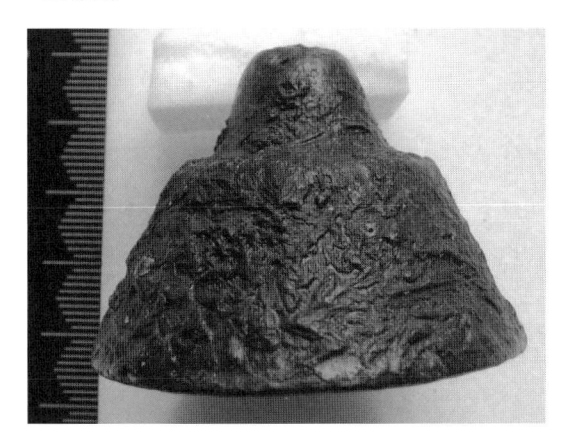

303: Shouldered Bell. L: 40mm. Diam: 52mm. Copper alloy bell and remains of an iron clapper. The suspension loop which would have been at the top of the bell is missing, leaving only three holes in the very top where it would have been attached. There is an iron residue within the apex of the bell and partially down one wall where the clapper appears to have lain before corroding. There are two small separate fragments of clapper retained with the bell. Williams Type 5: Shouldered bell. (Williams 2009). *3rd House, S of east furnace.*

2584: Shouldered Bell. L: 8mm. Diam: 21mm. Extremely damaged copper alloy shouldered bell. The bell was squashed almost flat in antiquity. The remains of four holes around the apex of the bell, with no indication of a suspension loop. An very close parallel to this bell can be found from Wroxeter (Webster 2002, 117, fig. 4.15.122) and from an unpublished bell discovered at Silchester (Williams 2009, 25). *Trench from north-west corner of House 2 to south-east corner of House 3.*

Discussion of the bells
Both the bells found at Yewden are of the Type 5 Shouldered bell (Williams, 2009). This type of bell is typically quite small in size and the majority of them have a 'step' approximately one-third the way up the length of the body which leads onto a rounded dome where the suspension loop would have been attached.

Shouldered bells have a widespread distribution – from Hadrian's Wall (Carrawburgh) south to Silchester and as far west as the Welsh border (Wroxeter). Although the bells have no definitive date, the military connection between the styles of the bells puts them at arriving in Britain with the army, around AD 43.

Security

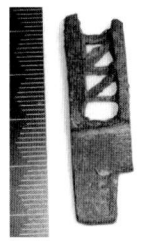

394: Lock bolt. L: 45mm. Large section of copper alloy lock plate. The bar has a stepped terminal and chevron design cut-outs.

2662: Lock plate. L: 57mm. Rectangular copper alloy lock plate. Although the plate is slightly damaged around the edges it is substantially complete. There is a square cut-out just off-centre, a smaller diamond-shaped cut-out just above this, and one rivet hole visible at the bottom of the plate. *??Constantine side of east wall of tessellated pavement?? 2nd House (under ceiling).*

It is probable that the lock plate would have belonged to a box or cupboard. As it was made of copper alloy it may not have been strong enough to be part of a main door.

Miscellaneous

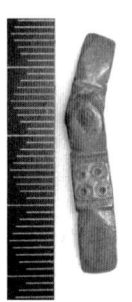

277: Strip. L: 55mm. Two copper alloy strips, decorated on the exterior surface and attached by a single rivet. The shorter length is decorated by an incised groove close to the riveted edge. The longer length is decorated by four rings and dots between two incised grooves – similar to the '4' side of a die. The reverse is undecorated. There is no curve to the object, but it does appear to swivel at the rivet. *In soil head, north of 3rd House.*

295: Miscellaneous Fitting. L: 50mm. Curved decorative strip of copper alloy, broken at the top. The bottom of the object is straight and appears complete. The central area has baluster mouldings. Possible handle or furniture decoration. *Clinker wall, east of 5th detached block, north of west end of north-west wall.*

2667: Miscellaneous. L: c.27mm. Small piece of copper alloy, two sides folded over to form a triangle. *South end of trench running between north-west corner of 2nd House to south-east corner of 3rd House.*

2668: Strip. L: 43mm. Two fragments of copper alloy. First is a strip of copper alloy, 43mm x 13mm x 1mm thick. Two halves separated by an incised line down the centre, one half plain, the other decorated with three deep grooves. The second fragment is unidentified, but appears to have the remains of a square cut-out in one section. Unknown function. *V-ditch, west of Enclosure wall.*

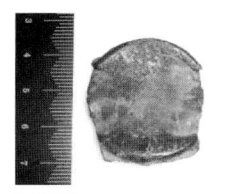

2680: Fitting. L:c.45mm (left). Circular mount fitting, possibly sword or dagger pommel. The rounded top is folded in half and has a flat top. *Little House, north of the floor (or wall) to east.*

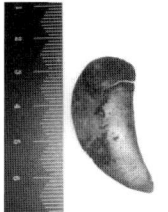

2686: Fitting. L: 40mm (right) Curved leaf-shaped fitting. Reverse has a clear shine to it. It is slightly convex in form. The underside is quite mottled, and there is no evidence of an attachment or rivet anywhere. Some damage present along one edge in the form of a crack leading from the edge to almost the centre of the fitting. *Pit 9.*

2699: Scroll. L: 22mm. Piece of copper alloy rolled up three times at each end to form a scroll. There is some evidence of iron corrosion or adhesion on the very top of a circular flattened knob. *2nd House. 6 feet south of north wall, north of west gate post.*

Distribution of brooches, toilet instruments and ligulae
Included in this report are three distribution maps showing the location of three specific types of finds from the villa complex (Figs. 4.41, 4.42 and 4.43). The first map shows the distribution of toilet instruments (above), the second shows brooches and finally the third map shows the distribution of the ligulae on the site (both below).

There are three specific areas of interest where a large number of the copper alloy finds are clustered. The first cluster can be found around the enigmatic structure at the north-west wall. The structure comprised footings of mud built flint along the wall (which runs ENE). The second wall consisted of almost equidistantly spaced footings of the same material. Within the structure (if that is what indeed it is) there is a small area of flint floor (Cocks 1921, Plate XIII). No further walls were discovered as it appears the remainder of the structure fell outside of the excavation area.

The second area of interest is around Pit 8, close to the 'Tuning Fork' furnace. This is also known as the 'Samian Pit' due to the extensive quantity of Samian ware pottery found inside it. Little is known about the structure surrounding the furnace, except that Cocks stated that steps led down to the furnace (*ibid* 153) and that it was possibly enclosed by wattle and daub walls and a thatched roof (*ibid* 151). The furnace itself was covered by a clay cap. Dr Eyers has identified this area as being of 1st century date.

The third and final area is around the area to the south of the two furnaces known by Cocks as 'The Hybrid' furnace. As with the 'Tuning Fork' furnace, this was likely to have had a wattle and daub structure built around it and a thatched roof. Dr Eyers has identified the Tuning Fork Furnace as 1st century and the Hybrid Furnace is dated to 2nd to 3rd century, although the general area of the yard was in use throughout the Roman period.

Cocks found a broken crucible and stated his belief that some of the fragmentary pieces of copper alloy '*were cast on the spot*' (Cocks 1921, 153). It may be the case that one – or more – of these areas with an abundance of copper alloy objects may have been utilised for a small scale manufacturing process.

Discussion on Ligulae and Styli

Ligulae

Ligulae are medical or toilet instruments which have several general functions. They are mainly used for the extraction of oils, ointments or powders from small narrow-necked bottles and jars (Jackson 1986, 157-8), including glass unguent bottles and bath flasks. Whether they were used at Yewden for perfumes or cosmetics, or perhaps for extracting medication, we may never know.

Within the Yewden complex, over 23 ligulae have been discovered – an extremely large number from one provincial site. To put this into perspective, some excavations of the largest urban centres in the southeast have the flowing numbers of ligulae: Canterbury 7, Chichester 11, Winchester 10, Silchester 7, and St Albans 22. Only two major Roman cities had more: Colchester 60 and London 99 (Turner-Wilson 2009, Volume 2, 10).

Further study on the contextual information of the ligulae may perhaps provide more information. Given the lack of any other medical/surgical instruments (apart from perhaps the spoon probes (2614, 2652)), we may be looking at a cosmetic rather than medical function for these objects. Alternatively, we may be seeing a small-scale production area for the ligulae.

Styli

Styli were Roman 'pens'. The pointed end was used to write on wax tablets and the usually triangular head was used as an eraser. Although styli are common on most Roman sites, the large number found at Yewden is quite unprecedented.

A total of 74 styli were found within the complex, the majority of them being made of iron and therefore not discussed further here. Cocks reported that three styli of copper alloy were found in the complex, one with an octagonal handle. This example was not found amongst the copper alloy finds in the museum store. Another copper alloy stylus is on display at the Museum (158) alongside three iron styli. The third example has an eraser end which is much thicker than the others, and wedge shaped (193).

There has been some discussion about the reason for so many styli at Yewden. One suggestion is that the number of corn driers present was sufficient to indicate that the complex was used for farming for army-supply (*anona*). The styli could have been used for 'bureaucratic checking of the produce' (Applebaum 1966, 102-3).

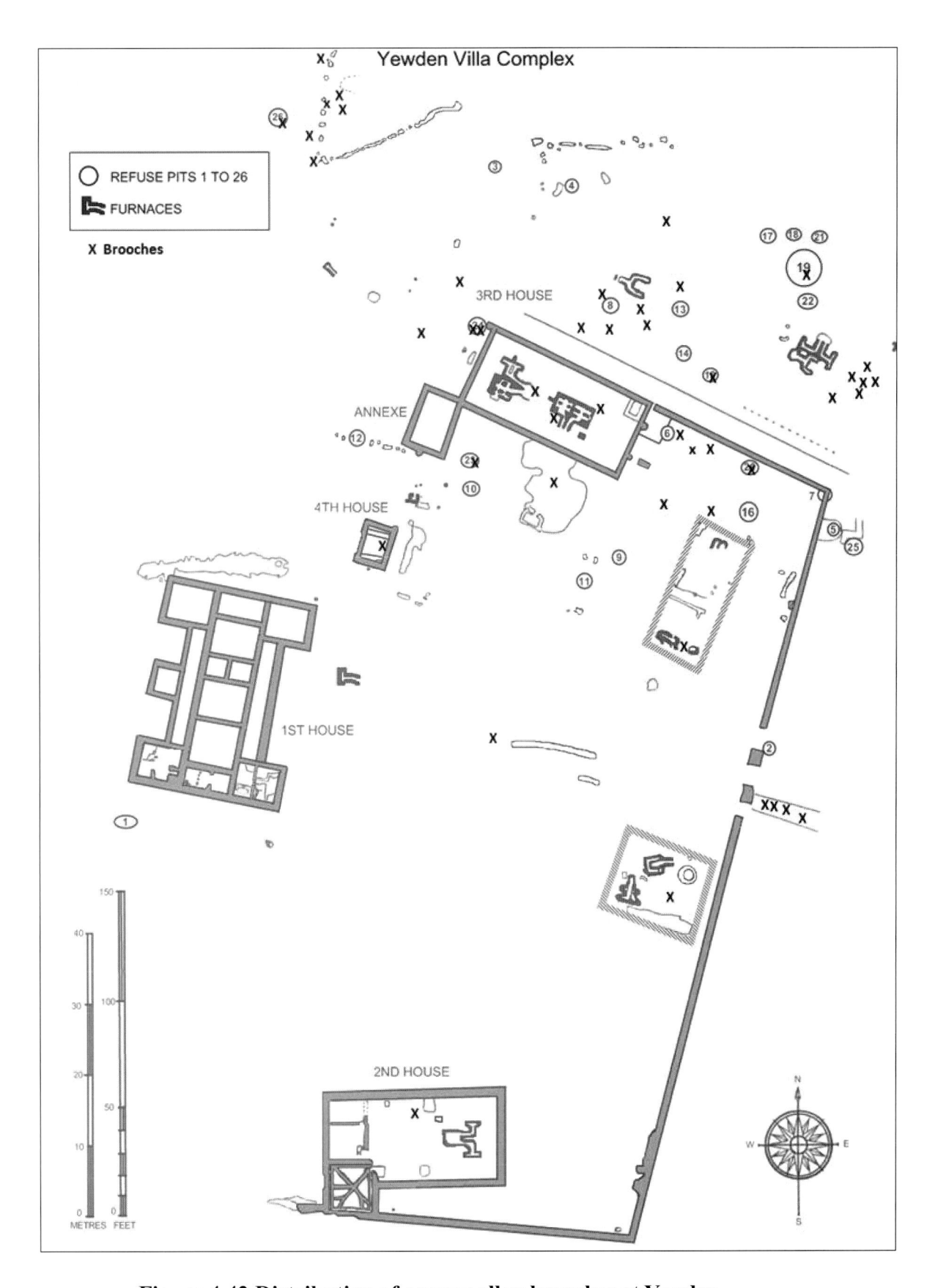

Figure 4.42 Distribution of copper alloy brooches at Yewden

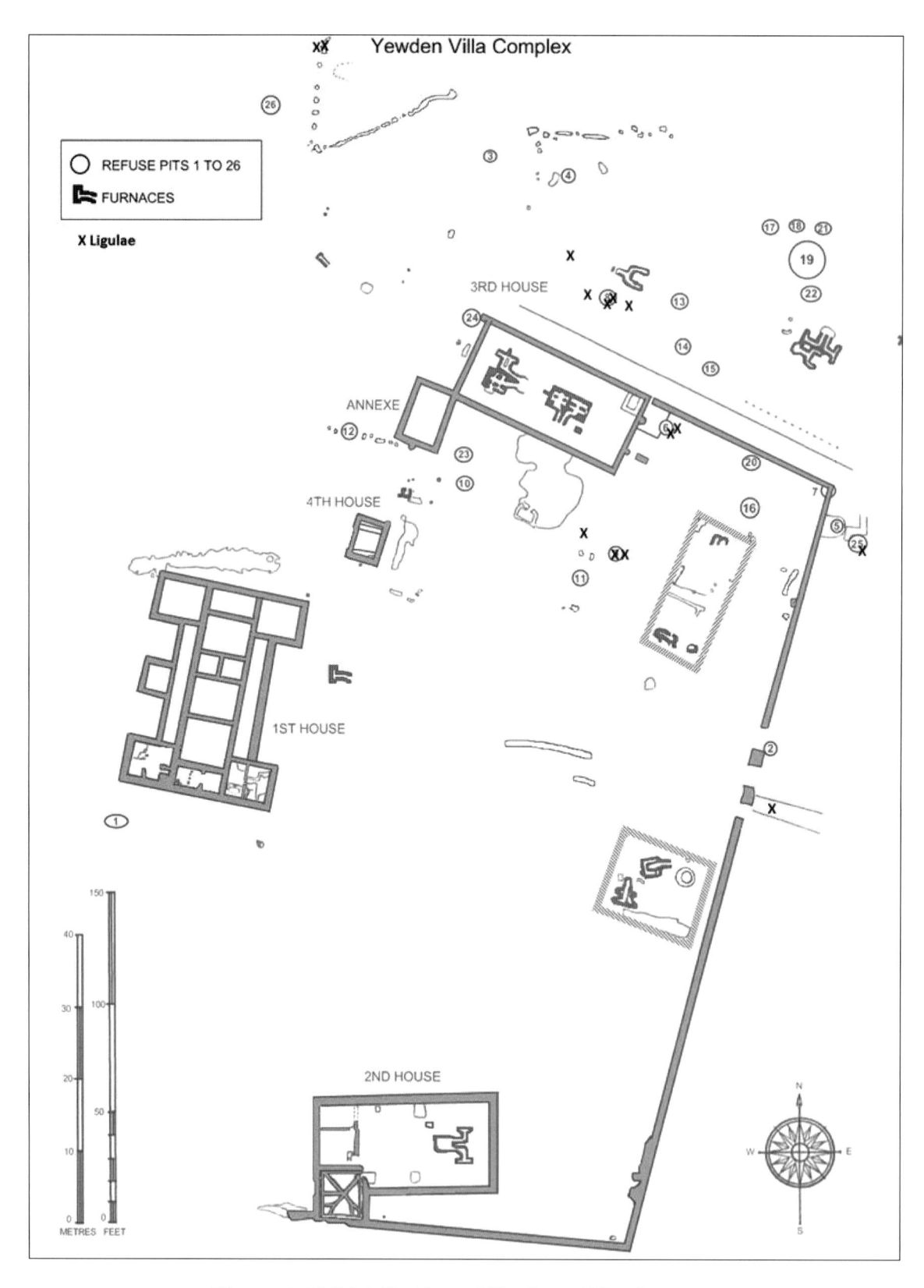

Figure 4.43 Distribution of ligulae at Yewden

Bibliography

Applebaum, S. 1966. *The Patterns of Settlement in Roman Britain.* CBA Research Report 7.

Breeze, D. J. 1972. Excavations at the Roman Fort of Carrawburgh 1967-1969. *Archaeologia Aeliana* L, 81-145. Newcastle upon Tyne: Society of Antiquaries of Newcastle Upon Tyne.

Corney, M. 2000. Objects of Copper and Iron: The Brooches, in Fulford, M. and Timby, J. *Late Iron Age and Roman Silchester: Excavations on the Site of the Forum-Basilica 1977, 1980-1986.* Britannia Monograph Series 15. London: Society for the Promotion of Roman Studies.

Croom, A. 2003. *Sexing Brooches.* Roman Finds Group Newsletter, Autumn 2003.

Curle, J. 1911. *A Roman Frontier Post and its People: The Fort of Newstead in the Parish of Melrose.* Glasgow. Society of Antiquaries of Scotland.

Eckardt, H. and Crummy, N. 2008. *Styling the Body in Late Iron Age and Roman Britain – A contextual approach to toilet instruments.* Instrumentum Monograph 36. Instrumentum, Montagnac.

Farley, M. E. 1983. The Villa at Mill End, Hambleden, Buckinghamshire, and Its Neighbour. *Britannia* 14, 256-259.

Jackson, R. 1986. A Set of Roman Medical Instruments from Italy. *Britannia* **17**, 119-167.

Johns, C. 1996. *The Jewellery of Roman Britain: Celtic and Classical Traditions.* Abingdon: Routledge.

Mackreth, D.F. 1992. Copper alloy and iron brooches. *In* Cracknell, S. and Mahany, C. *Roman Alcester: Southern Extramural Area. 1964-1966 Excavations. Part 2: Finds and Discussion.* CBA Research Report 97. London: Council for British Archaeology.

Marshall, F. H. 1907. *Catalogue of the Finger Rings, Greek, Etruscan and Roman in the Departments of Antiquities, British Museum.* London: British Museum.

Swift, E. 2003. *Roman Dress Accessories.* Oxford: Shire Publications Ltd.

Turner-Wilson, A. 2009. *Healthiness through the Material Culture of the late Iron Age and Roman Large Urban-Type Settlements of the South East of Britain.* Volumes 1 & 2. PhD Thesis. Bournemouth University.

Webster, G. 2002. *The Legionary Fortress at Wroxeter: Excavations by Graham Webster 1955-1985.* London: English Heritage Archaeological Report 19.

Williams, S. 2009. *Ritual Sounds in Britannia: Bronze Bells in Roman Britain.* Unpublished MA dissertation. University of Reading.

Chapter 4.5 Catalogue of iron objects

Brian Gilmore

Introduction/overview

The cataloguing and study and of the iron finds from Yewden Roman villa is as yet incomplete and the brief summary included here is intended as an interim assessment of 838 iron objects (either whole or partially surviving), something approaching three quarters of the total number of ferrous artefacts recovered. These are summarised below. It is planned that this study will be completed as soon as possible and the results published as a supplement to the present volume.

Construction

Most numerous of all artefacts recovered are 394 nails of various types and sizes. These would, one way or another, all appear to be associated with the construction of the villa or related buildings, or with associated furniture, containers, agricultural equipment and so on. In addition to the nails were four heavier headed items interpreted as studs for attachment to doors.

Buildings/furniture/container or miscellaneous related fittings

One lock (fragment), two keys, two hinges, 5 latch lifters, one (?) window bar (in two halves), roves (nails) plus associated plates, two iron plates, 25 fragments of strips/bars etc, one lead strip with eye hole.

Craft

This object category relates mainly to woodworking and metalworking (Figure 5.4.2). Most numerous were some 89 chisels, 11 (related) scrapers, 34 scribers, six joiners dogs (wood joining staples), two holdfasts, nine drill bits, 19 files, 30 punches, 12 gravers, nine T clamps, eight L clamps, 25 awls, one auger, one spokeshave, two jewellers stakes (small anvil-like objects), one saw, one hammer head (adze type end), 3 unidentifiable tool/fittings. It was fairly clear that some of these were found near one another and had belonged to small 'tool-kits' of small groups of similar very worn or broken items. Three of these groups have been identified so far here. The first of these consisted of 32 worn/broken items, these being a mixture of small chisels, punches, gravers, possible files and two broken hooks. A second group of similarly worn items consisted of 11 chisels and one probable key. The third group was a 'set' of six chisels.

Agricultural related

Three plough shares, one spike, two 'ox goads', one crowbar/jemmy, two hipposandals (temporary horseshoes), one lynch pin, one ring, one disc, one loop/bar/bracket, wire loop. One stout large bar.

Writing related, toilet implements and other domestic items

Most durable and hence numerous of these were 92 styli (Figure 5.4.1). There were also 11 spatulae, 22 needles, one pin, 9 knives, 14 hooks, and recognisable toilet items such as 3 tweezers, seven decorative studs (one of which was copper alloy), one spoon (part of bowl only), one ?strigil fragment, one chatelaine (part), two pieces of mesh/sieve, two fibulae/pins, and one ?ear cleaner.

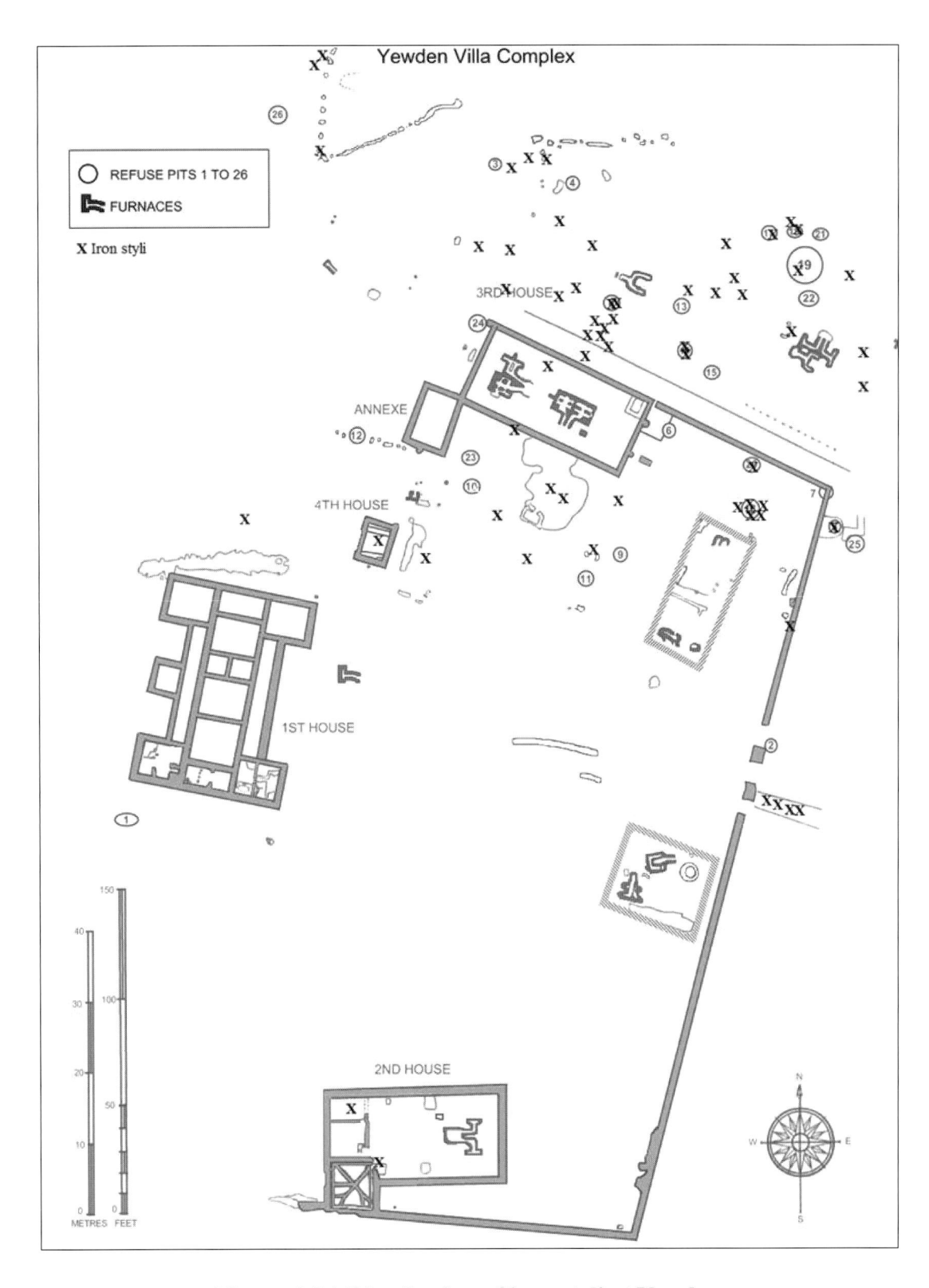

Figure 4.5.1 Distribution of iron styli at Yewden

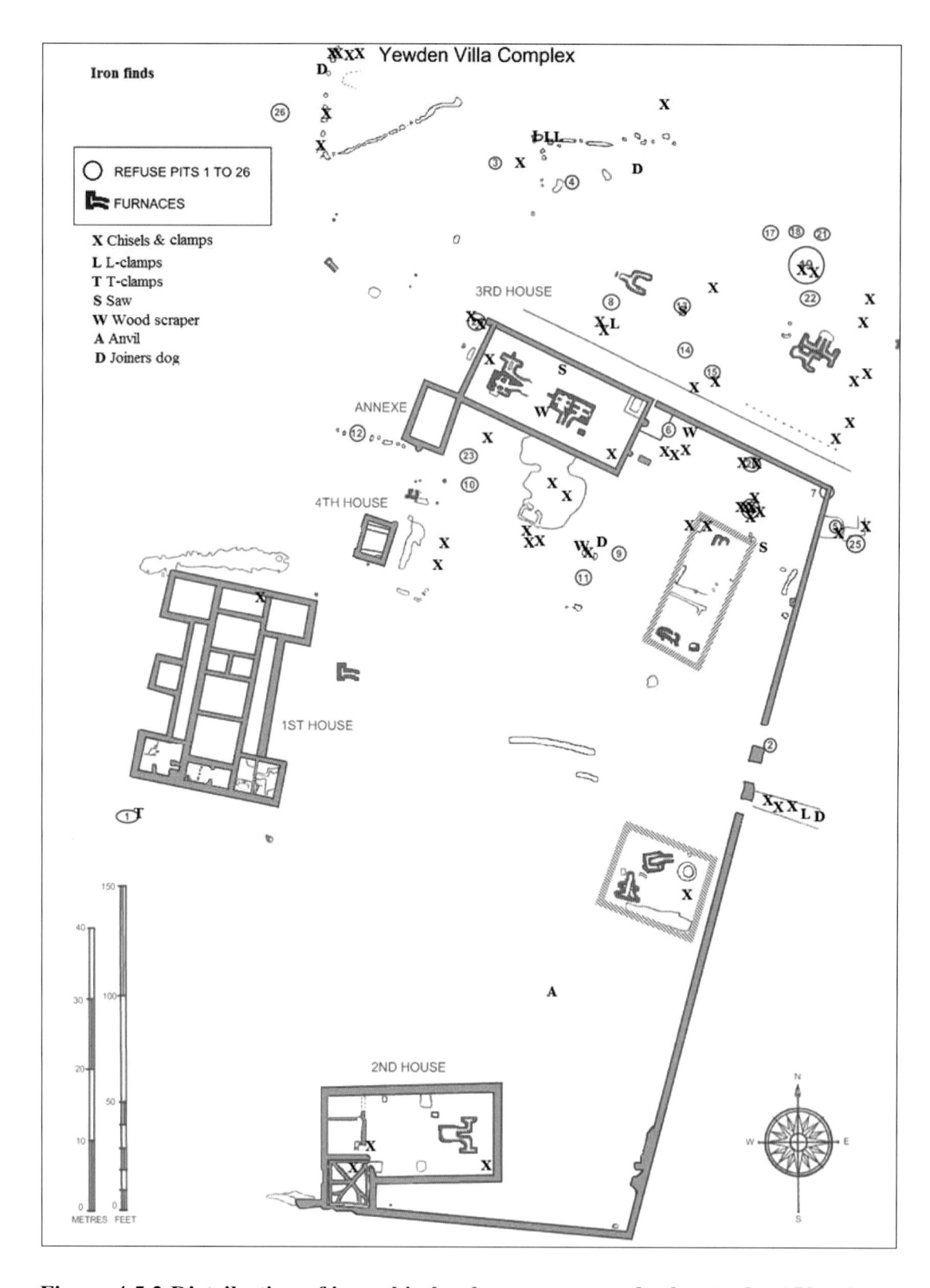

Figure 4.5.2 Distribution of iron chisels, clamps, saws and other tools at Yewden

Chapter 4.6 Glass

Jill Eyers

Glass from Yewden comprises an assortment of window fragments and vessels. There were 250 pieces recorded (Appendix 1 and Table 4.6.1) with a total weight of 1143g.

Distribution: There is a good proportion of the glass associated with two buildings – the 1st and the 3rd Houses (Figure 4.6.1). The 1st House contains vessel and window fragments. The 3rd House contains vessel fragments within the building, but window fragments occur in the pits adjacent (Pits 8, 15 and 24, as well as in the yard between the 3rd house and Pit 8. The distribution shows that the 3rd House may have contained glass windows, but the 1st house definitely had window glass and this also belonged to the earlier phase (as window glass was found beneath the floor of Room H and below the walls of the NE wing).

The remainder of the fragments of glass vessels occur scattered in the yard at the north end of the site and also along the Northwest Wall area.

Type of glass: The window glass makes up *c.* 12% of the sherds (*c.* 8% by weight) and hence is only a small part of the glass assemblage (Table 4.6.1). The vessels (*c.* 90% of the assemblage) were, as expected, very fragmentary. Identification of specific types was therefore difficult, but the assemblage clearly included a variety of bottles, cups and jugs which indicate the use of glass table ware (Figure 4.6.2). Cullet was found in Pits 12 and 16 within the villa enclosure, as well as in the yard. There were 11 pieces of 'cullet' weighing 79 g. This is not to infer there was glass manufacture on site, but molten glass occurred in these locations, potentially due to building fires.

Colour of glass: the blue-green and grey-green types make up the largest portion of the assemblage, together totalling 62% by weight (43% by sherd count). Pale green is the next significant proportion by colour totalling 13% by weight (16% by number of sherds). The remaining colour varieties of: blue, brown, green, grey-blue, olive grey, yellow and yellow-green were all less than 5% of the assemblage (Table 4.6.2).

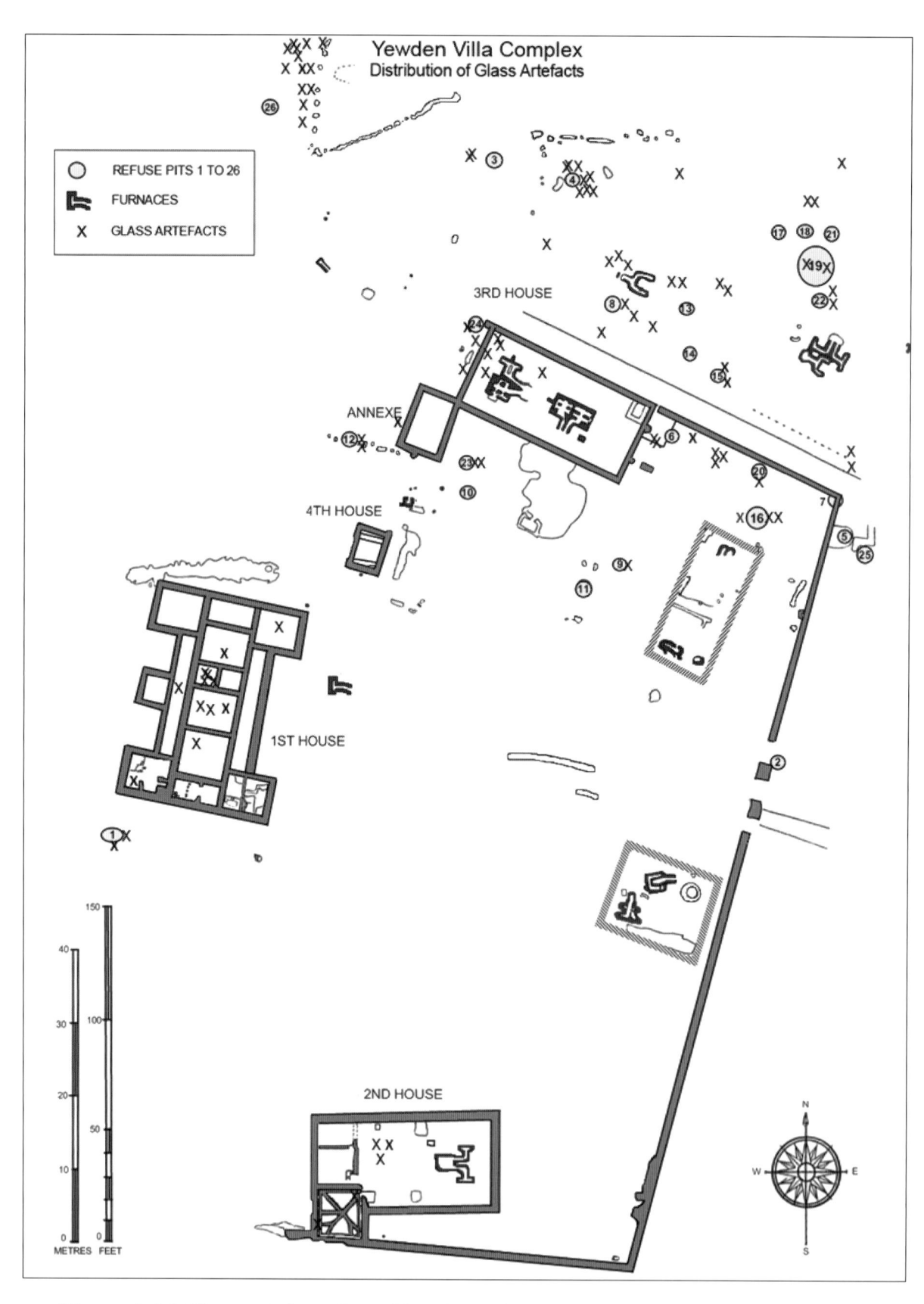

Figure 4.6.1 Glass artefacts from Yewden, window fragments and vessels

Table 4.6.1   1 . Analysis of glass by type

Category		Weight (grams)	Number of Items
Cullet	Total -	79	11
	% of Overall Total -	6.91%	4.40%
Vessel	Total -	614.5	143
	% of Overall Total -	53.76%	57.20%
Vessel & Base	Total -	30	8
	% of Overall Total -	2.62%	3.20%
Vessel & Bottle	Total -	229	32
	% of Overall Total -	20.03%	12.80%
Vessel & Bottle & Rim	Total -	1	1
	% of Overall Total -	0.09%	0.40%
Vessel & Cup	Total -	3	2
	% of Overall Total -	0.26%	0.80%
Vessel & Handle	Total -	9	1
	% of Overall Total -	0.79%	0.40%
Vessel & Neck	Total -	8	1
	% of Overall Total -	0.70%	0.40%
Vessel & Rim	Total -	50.5	17
	% of Overall Total -	4.42%	6.80%
Waste	Total -	21	2
	% of Overall Total -	1.84%	0.80%
Misc	Total -	1	1
	% of Overall Total -	0.09%	0.40%
	Total (non-Window) -	*1046*	*219*
	% of Overall Total -	*91.51%*	*87.60%*
Window	Total -	97	31
	% of Overall Total -	8.49%	12.40%
	OVERALL TOTAL -	1143	250

Table 4.6.2   2 Analysis of glass by colour

Colour		Weight (grams)	Number of Items
Blue	Total -	29	9
	% of Overall Total -	2.54%	3.60%
Blue-green	Total -	413	54
	% of Overall Total -	36.13%	21.60%
Brown	Total -	15.5	8
	% of Overall Total -	1.36%	3.20%
Colourless	Total -	66.5	49
	% of Overall Total -	5.82%	19.60%
Green	Total -	34	4
	% of Overall Total -	2.97%	1.60%
Grey-blue	Total -	53	7
	% of Overall Total -	4.64%	2.80%
Grey-green	Total -	294	54
	% of Overall Total -	25.72%	21.60%
Olive-grey	Total -	21	6
	% of Overall Total -	1.84%	2.40%
Pale Green	Total -	151	41
	% of Overall Total -	13.21%	16.40%
Pale Olive	Total -	10	3
	% of Overall Total -	0.87%	1.20%
Yellow	Total -	3	1
	% of Overall Total -	0.26%	0.40%
Yellow-green	Total -	34	8
	% of Overall Total -	2.97%	3.20%
Other (unidentified)	Total -	19	6
	% of Overall Total -	1.66%	2.40%
	OVERALL TOTAL -	**1143**	**250**

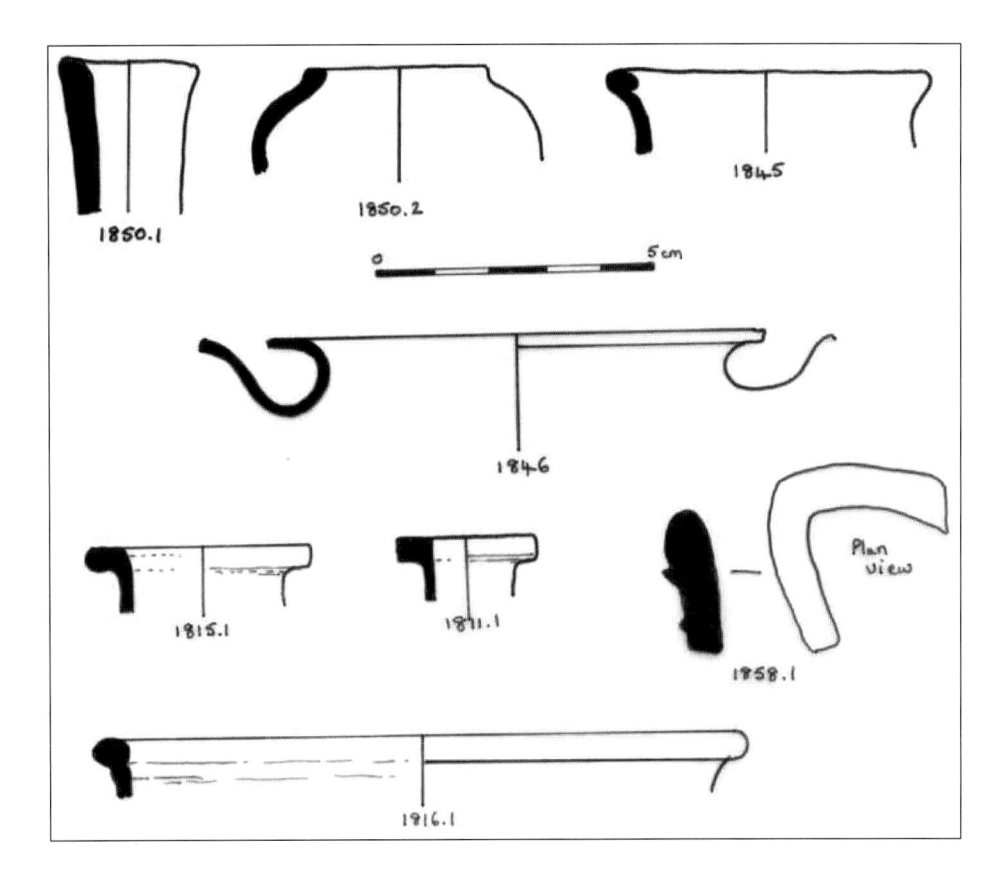

Figure 4.6.2 Glass from Yewden:

1850.1 Flask neck, greyish-green, NW wall.
1850.2 Bowl, light greenish-grey, NW wall.
1845 Cup rim, colourless, Pit 19 at 2.5 ft.
1846 Brown glass rim, Pit 8 at 15 ft.
1815.1 Bottle rim, greyish green, Yard 30 ft N of Enclosure wall.
1811.1 Bottle rim, greyish green, 3rd House above platform inside S & W walls
1858.1 Light blue-green, Quern hole at 1 ft deep.
1816.1 Bowl, yellow green, Pit 9 at 12 ft.

Acknowledgements: thanks to Alison Jewsbury for the finds distribution plot, and to Keith Spencer for preparing the statistics and tabulation of the data for the glass assemblage. Also thanks to Tony Eustace and Alan Leach for working through the finds at the BCM and making the first drawings of the items. Thanks also to Allen levy, Alan Winchcomb, Jill Hender and Roger Allen for working through the collections. Last, but not least, thanks to Fred Reed for photographing the glass objects (the full archive of which is on the DVD).

4.7 Worked bone objects

Raihana Ehsanullah

Introduction

A large quantity of bone, both animal and human, was recovered during the excavations (see the distribution map, Figure 4.7.1). The objects presented below are all of bone with the exception of one knife handle of antler. Since not all the animal bone from the site has been checked for signs of working, a few minor worked objects may have escaped notice.

By far the most numerous of the bone objects recovered were pins. The illustrated pins were the most complete examples of each of the six main types present with particular consideration being given to Type 2, the most prolific on the site. Only pins with partial or complete heads were considered for illustration. Three of the four 'heavy' points and the majority of the other bone objects present have been illustrated except where more than one example of similar type exists.

It should be noted that, although reasonably thorough by the standards at the time of the excavations, the extensive finds were incompletely described. No catalogue exists from the 1912 excavation and therefore there is no record of any losses that may have occurred since that time. A proportion of the original labels survives, enabling simple find spot maps to be prepared. The resulting locations are not necessarily archaeologically secure.

The Pins

Distribution

As the distribution map shows, all but three of the sixty pins whose find spot could be determined were found in the northern half of the site both inside and outside the boundary wall. All the other worked bone that could be plotted also followed this pattern, with the exception of two pieces of comb found inside the villa building. One possibility suggested by this distribution is that the boundary wall was a late addition and did not exist at the time of loss. The quantity as well as the distribution of the pins suggests that this may have been an area of pin manufacture. However, if they were produced in quantity on site unfinished pins would be expected, whereas none has been recognised with certainty. The area outside the boundary wall, where the majority was found, was interpreted by the excavator as 'some sort of factory' on account of the inhospitable layer of 'filthy black mud'. In the same general area were a number of furnaces interpreted as corn driers.

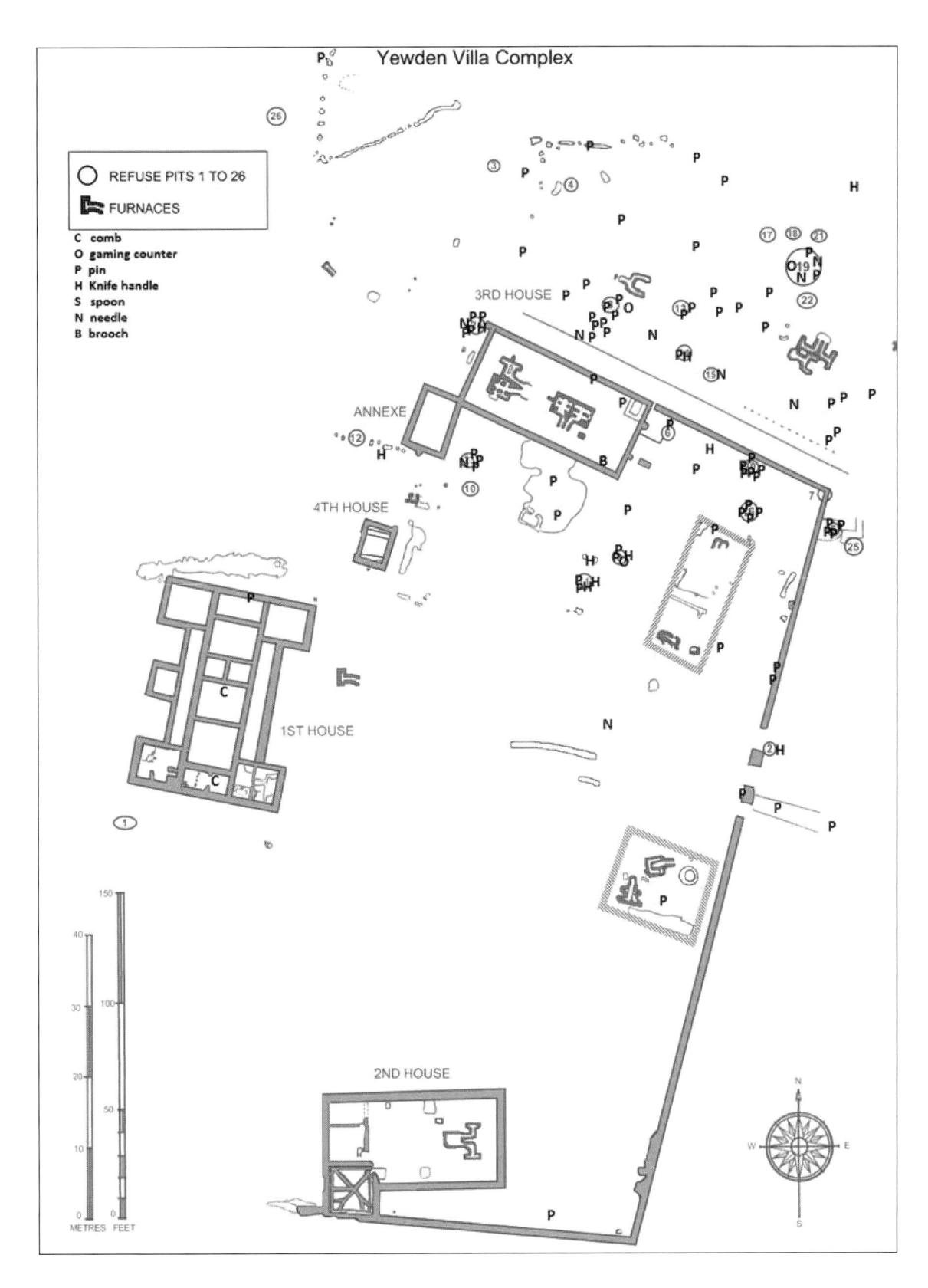

Figure 4.7.1: Finds distribution map of worked bone objects.

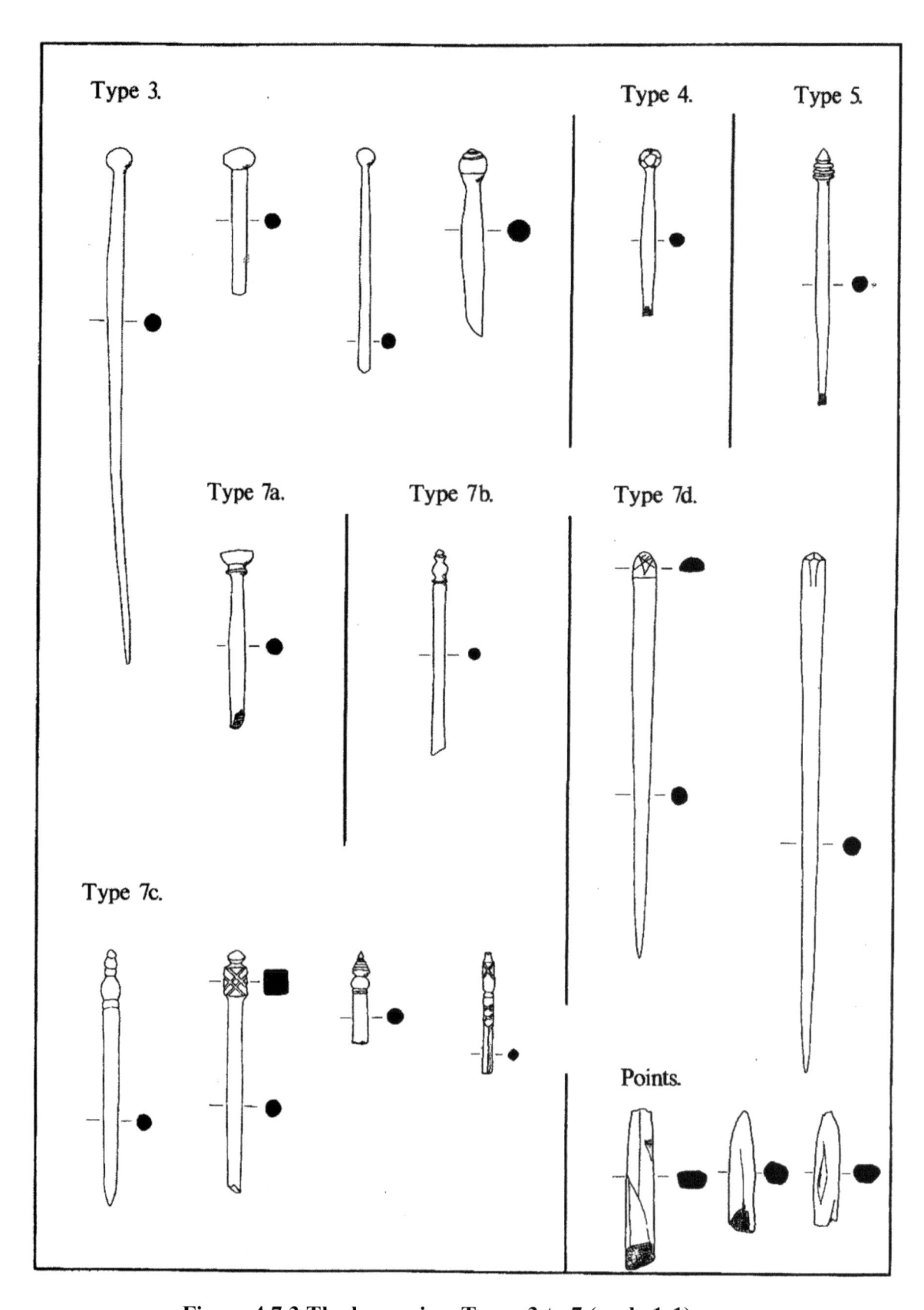

Figure 4.7.3 The bone pins. Types 3 to 7 (scale 1:1)

Parallels and Dating

Crummy (1979) considers that some pin types can be roughly dated. Types 1 and 2 (those with head equal to or less than shaft diameter) occur earlier, approximately AD 50-200/250, than Types 3-7 (head greater than shaft diameter), of late fourth-early fifth century. At Hambleden no Type 6 pins were found and only one Type 1. Crummy suggests a date range of *c.* AD 70-200/250 for Type 1 pins, and the single Hambleden example came from a V-ditch just east of the enclosure wall.

Type 2 is by far the most common form at Hambleden, as it was at the Jewry Wall, Leicester (Crummy 1979), and on the evidence of the finds from Colchester a terminal date of *c.* AD 200 has been suggested (Crummy 1983). Nearer home, Verulamium, near St Albans, has an example with a curved shaft dated AD 135-145 (Frere, 1972). Those from Hambleden generally possess straight shafts, though curved examples do occur. Although no Type 2 pins appear at the relatively close Latimer villa site near Amersham, the next largest group from Hambleden, Type 3 (of which nine have been recognised) is common there and dated mainly to the third century (Branigan, 1971). Type 3 pins do occur at Shakenoak in Oxfordshire (Brodribb, 1968, 1971 and 1972) and these are dated to the third or fourth century, but the heads are more accentuated than the Hambleden examples.

Type 4 is not a common style and seems only to be known in any quantity from Colchester (Crummy 1979). Crummy dates them from *c.* AD 250 to the late fourth/early fifth century. This style does, however, appear in jet at York (RCHM, 1962) and at Lydney (Wheeler and Wheeler, 1932), and it is worth speculating in which material the style made its debut. The angular features suggest it could have been a form originated by the jet workers, although the globular Type 3 was also found in jet at York.

There are few readily available parallels for the remaining groups. There is an example of Type 5 at Portchester dated AD 335-340 (Cunliffe, 1975), but overall the Portchester pins contrast with those at Hambleden, the former invariably having heads of a greater diameter than the shaft, which in turn is bulbous in character. The great majority of pins at Hambleden, however – namely Type 2 – have parallel-sided shafts of the same diameter as the head above. This seems to show a totally different approach to the technique of pin manufacture.

One other ?pin worthy of note is Type 7b, which at Verulamium was considered not necessarily to have been a pin at all, being described as a "tapering rod with decorative mouldings at head a flat broader end with traces of iron corrosion upon it" (Frere, 1972).

Other Bone Objects

In addition to pins, a number of other bone artefacts were recovered (Fig. 4.7.4 below). The distribution of these objects has been commented upon above (see Fig. 4.7.1). Photographic images of one of the counters, an ornament and a comb are shown below.

Counters

Five bone counters were recovered, four of which have been illustrated.

2.

Plain with centrally placed dot, 19mm diameter.
Two centrally placed concentric rings, 17mm diameter.
Single ring of decoration, 22mm diameter.
Deeply cut concentric rings, 24mm diameter.

Figure 4.7.5 Gaming counter. (BCM 1994.57.460)

Spoons

A number of circular or sub-rectangular discs are probably spoon bowls. Of the five examples recovered, one had a small length of handle attached.

5. Bowl only, roughly circular, flat section, 21mm diameter.
6. Bowl with fragment of handle, sub-rectangular shape to bowl. This was the most common shape and was represented by four examples, 16mm diameter.

Ornament

7. Part of circular ornament. Precise function unknown although a lozenge-shaped plaque with incised ring-and-dot decoration found at Portchester (Cunliffe, 1975) was considered to be a possible gaming counter, 31mm diameter.

Figure 4.7.6 Decorated ornament, with incision top right for attachment. (BCM No. 1994.57.457)

Combs

Three fragments of bone combs were recovered, two from within the house. Only one is worthy of illustration.

8. A simple double-sided comb with a decoratively cut edge to the solid zone and a small hole for ?suspension, 34 mm width.

Figure 4.7.7 Double sided bone comb (BCM No. 1994.57.456)

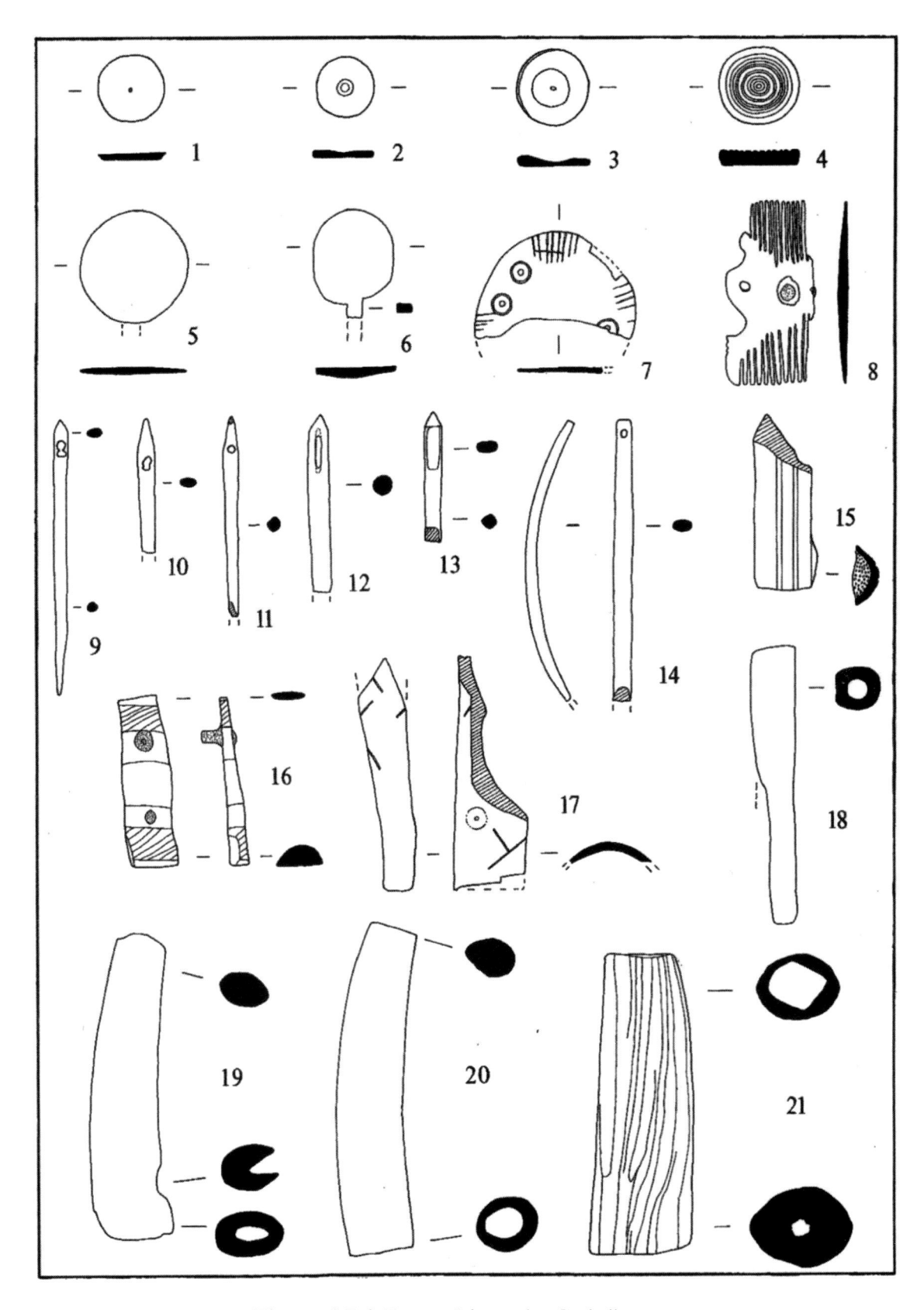

Figure 4.7.4 Bone objects (scale 1:1)

143

Needles

Twelve bone needles were recovered. One object in this section (Figure 4.7.4 no. 13) has been included as it may be a needle at an intermediate stage of manufacture.

9. The eye appears to have been made by piercing the bone with two separate but adjacent holes and then connecting them by cutting away the remaining section. Green patina, 77 mm long. This was the only complete example of a needle. Two other broken examples with a similar form of eye were much longer, being 86 mm and 90 mm.
10. Similar to 9. Three individual fragments ranged in length from 38 (illustrated) to 68mm.
11. Single eye, green patina. The length of the three fragments with this form of eye ranged from 31 to 56 mm.
12. Elongated single eye. Fragments ranged in length from 50 to 89 mm.
13. Intermediate stage of manufacture, the head being very similar to 12 but unpierced.

Bracelet

14. Fragment of dog rib with a single hole drilled in one end, length 80mm. A similar example found at Portchester (Cunliffe, 1975) was decorated and pierced with a hole at each end, and was considered to have been part of a large bracelet.

Figure 4.7.8 Carved bone knife handle (BCM No. 1994.57.465)

Knife Handles

Seven knife handles were recovered; one of antler, the rest bone. Three of the bone examples had some decoration and one of these was a rivetted form.

15. Part of a ?knife with incised linear decoration, 33 mm length.
16. Part of a decorated knife handle with two iron rivets, 32 mm length.
17. Part of a ?knife handle decorated with short straight lines and circle, 44 mm length.
18. Plain knife handle in highly polished bone, 54 mm length.
19. Bone knife handle with asymmetrically placed hole, 58 mm length.
20. Plain bone knife handle, 63 mm length.
21. Knife handle made from antler, 57 mm length.

Brooch

A pin catch of a fibula point of a bone pin, thought to be a brooch (not illustrated), was recovered in the 3rd House, inside the S wall, near the E end.

References

Branigan, K. 1971 — *Latimer.* Chess Valley Archaeological and Historical Society.

Brodribb, ACC, Hands, AR and Walker, DR. 1968 — *Excavations at Shakenoak Farm, Oxon, I.* Oxford Archaeology.

Brodribb, ACC, Hands, AR and Walker, DR. 1971 — *Excavations at Shakenoak Farm, Oxon, II.* Oxford Archaeology.

Brodribb, ACC, Hands, AR and Walker, DR. 1972 — *Excavations at Shakenoak Farm, Oxon, III.* Oxford Archaeology.

Crummy, N. 1979 — 'A Chronology of Romano-British Bone Pins', *Britannia* 10, 157-168.

Crummy, N. 1983 — *The Roman Small Finds from Excavations in Colchester 1971-9*, Colchester Archaeological Report 2.

Cunliffe, B. 1975 — *Excavations at Portchester Castle*, Vol. 1: Report of the Research Committee of the Society of Antiquaries of London XXXII, London.

Frere, S. 1972 — *Verulamium Excavations*, Vol. 1: Report of the Research Committee of the Society of Antiquaries of London XXVIII, London.

Royal Commission on Historical Monuments 1962 — *Eburacum, Roman York*, Vol.1, HMSO, London.

Wheeler, REM & TV. 1932 — *Report on the Excavation of the Prehistoric, Roman and Post-Roman site in Lydney Park, Gloucestershire*, Res.: Report of the Research Committee of the Society of Antiquaries of London XII, London.

Acknowledgements: The worked bone objects were identified and catalogued by a volunteer team at Buckinghamshire County Museum under the supervision of Michael Farley, and the above text is adapted from the 1984 report by Buckinghamshire County Museum Archaeological Group members. Thanks to Fred and Jean Reed for proof-reading.

4.8 Miscellaneous: small finds

Raihana Ehsanullah

Scarab Beetle (BCM No. *1994.57.1748*)
A dark green intact carved scarab beetle (Figure 4.8.1) was found 25 cm deep, 30 cm from the wall outside the NW corner of Room D, 1st House. It measures 33 mm long by 26 mm wide and is probably made of serpentinite. It is thought to date from the later Egyptian period (400-800BC).

In ancient Egypt, where the scarab beetle was a symbol of rebirth, carved scarab amulets were very popular. The Romans too had great faith in the scarab's protective power. It is likely that the Yewden scarab was brought to Britain by a Roman soldier.

Figure 4.8.1 Carved scarab beetle. (BCM No. 1994.57.1748)

The *Dea Nutrix* (BCM No. *1994.57.3613*)
A portion of a pipe-clay figurine (Figure 4.8.2) was found 60 cm deep in the 3rd House, 1.8 m S of the N wall, W of the stoke hole. It shows a female seated in a wickerwork armchair nursing a baby. Such figurines were cast in moulds, the majority of which fell into two categories: (i) figurines of Venus; and (ii) figurines of a seated goddess suckling either one or two infants – the *Dea Nutrix* (the nursing goddess).

The fragment of the Yewden figurine bears close resemblance to the intact *Dea Nutrix* found in an infant grave at Baldock in Hertfordshire in 1988 (Figure 4.8.3). However, it cannot be ascertained whether the Yewden figurine in its original state would have been holding one or two infants. Furthermore, unlike that at Baldock, the Yewden nutrix was not found in a grave. These figurines were common in Central Gaul where they were produced around AD120-200, but were much rarer in Roman Britain and usually imported from France. They were associated with childbirth and sometimes used as charms for domestic worship or as offerings to the gods.

Figure 4.8.2 *Dea Nutrix*. (BCM No. 1994.57.3613)

Figure 4.8.3 Baldock *Dea Nutrix*. (Courtesy of North Hertfordshire District Council Museums Service)

'Venus' Head (BCM No. *1994.57.1754*)

A pipe-clay head of a female (Fig. 4.8.4, front and back) was found 4.5 m deep in Pit 8. It is made from a mould and measures 44 mm from the top of the head to the neck (which has a pointed break point), 37 mm wide, by 26 mm

Figure 4.8.4 Venus head, front and rear view. (BCM No. 1994.57.1754)

The hair is parted in the middle and braided on either side to behind the ears. It is uncertain whether this head came from a Venus statuette or a *Dea Nutrix*; however, it appears more likely to be the former as it compares well with a photograph of a Venus (in M. Rouvier-Jeanlin, Les Figurines Gallo-Romaines en Terre Cuite au Musee des Antiquites Nationales (XXIVe Supplement a Gallia, Paris 1972) p. 138, no. 210) which also has a central hair piece, and furthermore none of the known nutrices has the same coiffure (Dr Martin E Henig, Institute of Archaeology, Oxford; *personal communication*).

Spindle Whorls (BCM Nos. *1994.57.1750, 51, 52, 55, 56, 59, 64, 65, 66, 67, 68, 70, 71, 73, 75, 84, 1800 & 1802*)

Eighteen broken spindle whorls (Figure 4.8.5, base and side view) in a huge variety of materials - reused pottery, bone, etc. - were found in various locations and pits (see distribution map, Figure 4.8.6).

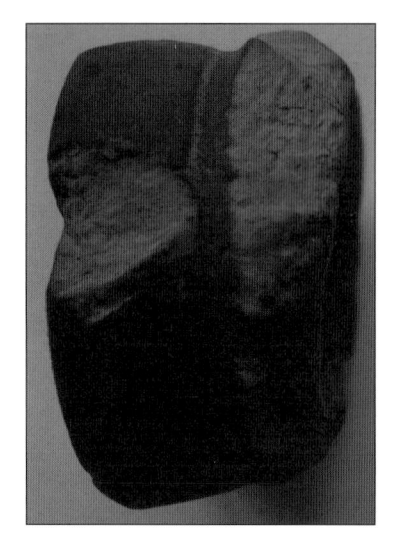

Figure 4.8.5 Spindle whorl. (BCM No. 1994.57.1751)

Figure 4.8.6 Finds distribution map of spindle whorls (next page).

Pipe-clay Arm (BCM No. *1994.57.1760*)
A broken arm-shaped pipe-clay object, which has a small bore hole running through the centre, was found in surface layers within the ploughed soil. It is not possible to identify what this fragment would have been attached to. However, it appears to be an arm or a leg, perhaps from a doll, and looks post-Medieval rather than Roman.

Samian Gaming Counters (BCM Nos. *1994.57.458 & 459*)
Two gaming counters were found, one from Pit 19 at 1 m depth and one from the 'mortar floor' in the enclosure area near the 3rd House.. Both were from vessel bases originating from Les Martres-de-Veyre (AD 100-120). At some point after this date the vessel bases had been trimmed to form the counters.

Figure 4.8.7 A samian gaming counter

Acknowledgement
The photograph of the Baldock Dea Nutrix is reproduced with kind permission of North Hertfordshire District Council Museums Service, which owns the object.

Yewden Villa Complex

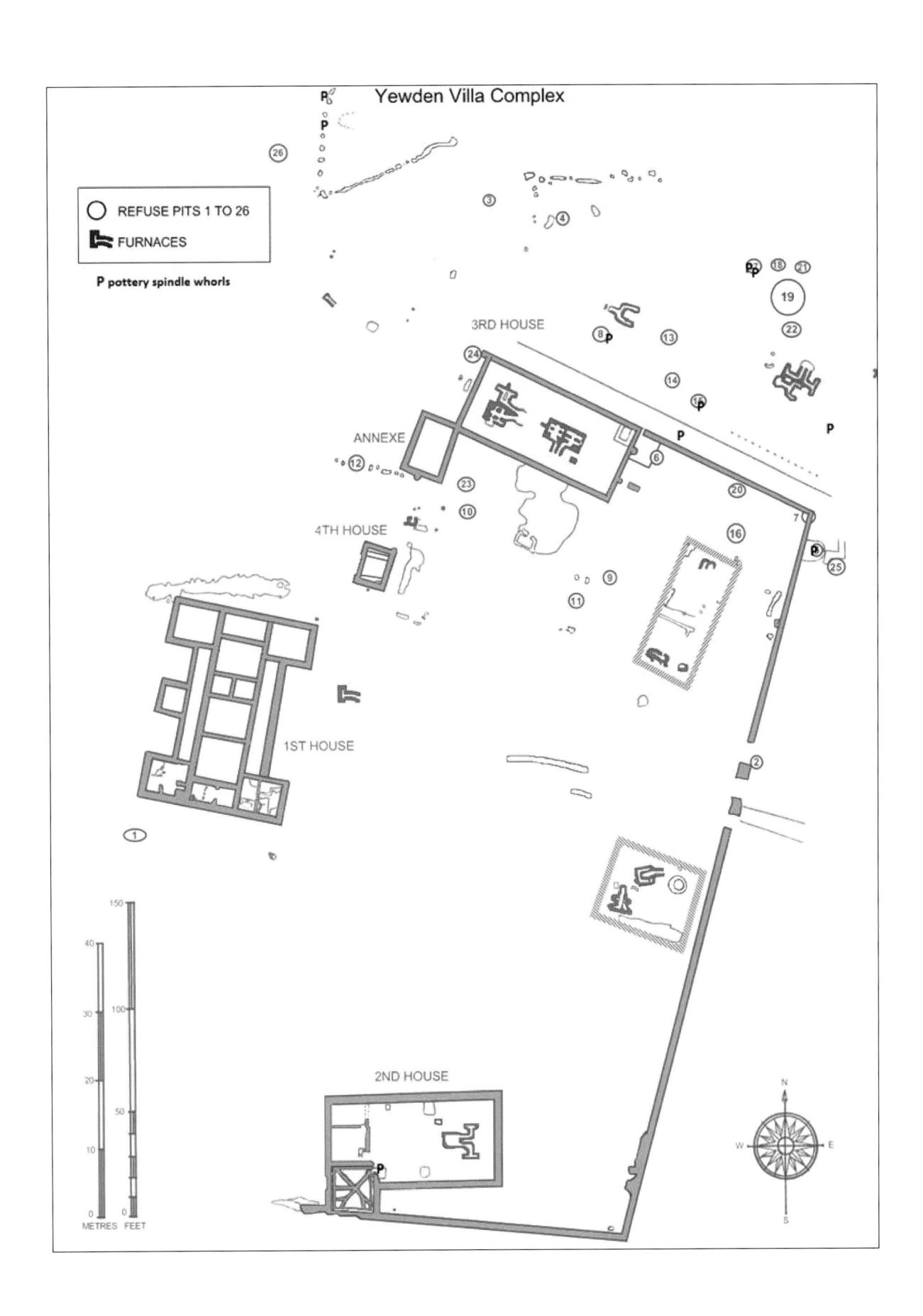

○ REFUSE PITS 1 TO 26
⌐ FURNACES

P pottery spindle whorls

Examination of residue from two sherds, Yewden Roman Villa, Hambleden, Buckinghamshire

David Dungworth

Two sherds of pottery (1994.57.P.562.1 and 1994.57.P.562.2) were recovered during the archaeological excavations at Yewden Roman Villa and were made available for scientific examination. The visual appearance of the sherds and their associated residues (see figures below) resembled the descriptions of waste materials generated during the parting (refining) of gold. The residues were sampled in order to determine their nature and any association with gold parting.

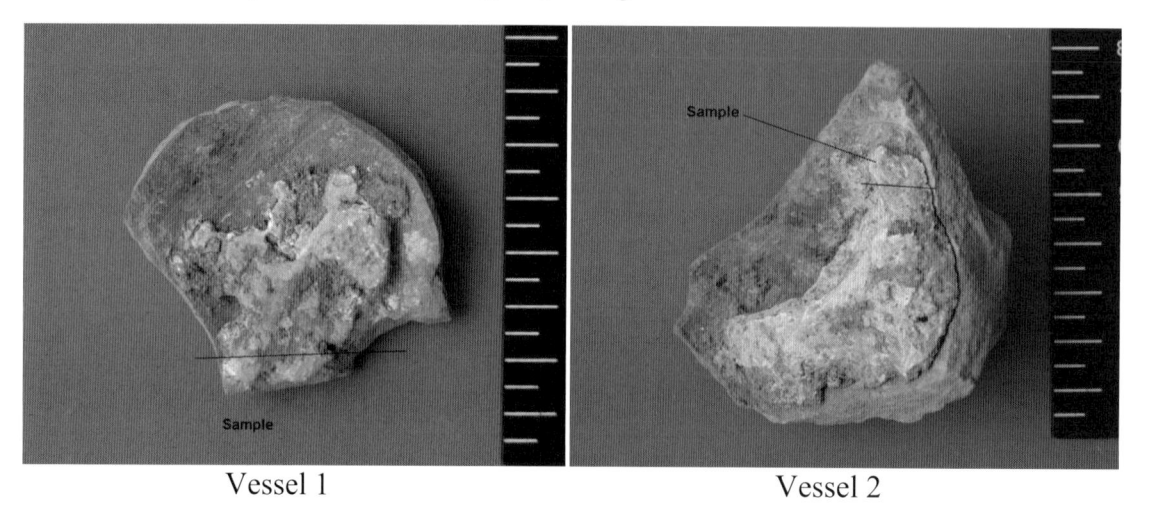

Vessel 1   Vessel 2

Both sherds and residues were analysed using Energy Dispersive X-Ray Fluorescence (EDXRF) which allowed the non-destructive determination of the elements present. This indicated that calcium was the most abundant element present. A range of other elements were also detected including silicon and iron. A small amount of phosphorus was also detected in the residue adhering to vessel 2. It was initially thought that a small amount of silver was detected in the residue adhering to vessel 1 and so further sampling was undertaken.

A small amount of material was detached from each sherd (see figures above), ground to a powder and analysed using X-Ray Diffraction (XRD). Vessel 1 is composed of quartz (SiO_2) and calcite (CaO_3) but the residue of only calcite. The residue from vessel 2 is composed of calcite, quartz and hydroxylapatite ($Ca_5(PO_4)_3(OH)$).

Small samples of the residue were also examined using a scanning electron microscope (SEM). This confirmed that the residues were rich in calcium but but was unable to confirm the presence of silver or any other metals relevant to gold parting (such as gold or copper). Further EDXRF analyses also failed to repeated the earlier identification of silver.

The scientific examination of the two sherds from Yewden Roman villa has not been able to find any evidence that these two sherds were used for parting gold. The exact nature of the processes carried out in these vessels remains uncertain. The presence of calcite suggests a process with no more than mild heating. The presence of hydroxylapatite in one may be due to the deliberate preparation of ground bone, however, traces of the mineral may have been transported by ground water during burial.

Chapter 5: The Pottery:

5.1 Iron Age Pottery

Jonathon Dicks

Introduction
This pottery report is based on material from the 1912 excavation at *Yewden Roman Villa* by Mr. A. H. Cocks. Forty-nine sherds of pottery were identified as Iron Age. The sherds were generally in a poor state and abraded as would be expected for material that has been subject to continual re-disposition over the centuries causing abrasion. Many of the co-jointing sherds had been poorly glued together after their initial recovery from the excavation by Mr Cocks' post-excavation team.

Methodology
The advent of a uniform recording system for pottery in the 1990s has enabled assemblage compositions to be compared and analysed and this approach to a standard method of recording has been adopted in this study.

Fabrics were identified by using a x10 magnifying glass and/or a x20 microscope and quantification of the assemblage was by sherd count, sherd weight, fabric and form wherever possible. Rim count and, where feasible, rim diameters and estimated vessel equivalents (EVEs) were recorded (Orton *et al.*, 1993). Sherd condition, decoration and use wear were also noted. The data was entered into an Excel spreadsheet to facilitate a full, detailed analysis of the assemblage. The vessel forms were established and classified by reference to the existing published typologies. Iron Age pottery is notoriously difficult to closely date and the following date bands have been used in this report (Cunliffe, 2005).

    Early Iron Age (EIA):   c. BC 600 – 400/300
    Middle Iron Age (MIA):   c. BC 400/300 - 100
    Late Iron Age (LIA):   c. BC 100 – AD 50

Fabrics

Flint tempered fabrics
A moderately hard black to dark grey fabric with a matrix containing a temper of calcified flints ranging in size from 1 to 4 mm. Flint-tempered fabrics are usually associated with the Early Iron Age, but do occur throughout the Iron Age period.

Sherds: *1994.57.P.29, 157, 2743, 2814, 2927, 3013, 3101, 3180.*
The catalogue of Iron Age pottery appears as Appendix 2.

Shell Tempered Fabrics
A moderately hard dark brown to dark grey fabric with a matrix containing a temper of profuse shell ranging in size from 1 to 3 mm long. It was not unusual for grog/clay

pellets to be included within the matrix. Shell tempered fabrics are usually associated with the Middle and Late Iron Age period. (Fig. 5.5.1)

Sherds: *1994.57.P. 154, 798, 2268.*

Grog Tempered Fabrics
A soft smooth fabric with a soapy feel with a matrix containing rounded and sub-rounded fragments of grog/clay pellets. This fabric occasionally contained fine quartz sand and/or fine shell fragments. Grog tempered fabrics are usually associated with the Middle and Late Iron Age period.

Sherds: *1994.57.P.15, 2094, 2573, 2576, 2743, 2936 and 3000*; the last two both with very sparse flint inclusions.

Quartz (Sand) Tempered Fabrics
A hard fired dark grey fabric with a matrix containing profuse quantities of fine quartz sand temper. A variant of this fabric was the occasional addition of sparse grog/clay pellets. Quartz sand tempered fabrics are usually also associated with the Middle to Late Iron Age period.

Sherds: *1994.57.P.494, 2115, 3066, 3168, 798* (grogged), *2147* (grogged), *2155* (grogged), *2743* (grogged) and *2592* (flint and grog).

Forms
There were no large pottery production centres during the Iron Age and most ceramic vessels were manufactured and distributed locally. This had the effect of producing of vast range of similar forms from different regions using slightly different materials. This, and the relatively small amount of stratified material recovered, has limited the ability of archaeologists to closely date and source Iron Age ceramic objects. Very few of the Iron Age sherds recovered from the excavation at *Yewden* had any decoration or features to help in assigning the material to specific groupings. Where decorations and features were present it has been possible to suggest probable associations with known regional groupings.

Early Iron Age vessels were characterised by finger-tip decorated jars and bowls with strongly marked shoulders and carinations. The *Chinnor-Wandlebury* group consisted of bowls with flared rims and shoulders frequently decorated with simple geometric patterns (Cunliffe, 2005, 101-2). Sherd *1994.57.P.154* (Fig. 5.5.1) may well be a late example of this EIA grouping. *1994.57.P.2936* is a small sherd (12 grams) which has a polished red surface that could possibly be haematite, but the sherd is too small to be certain.

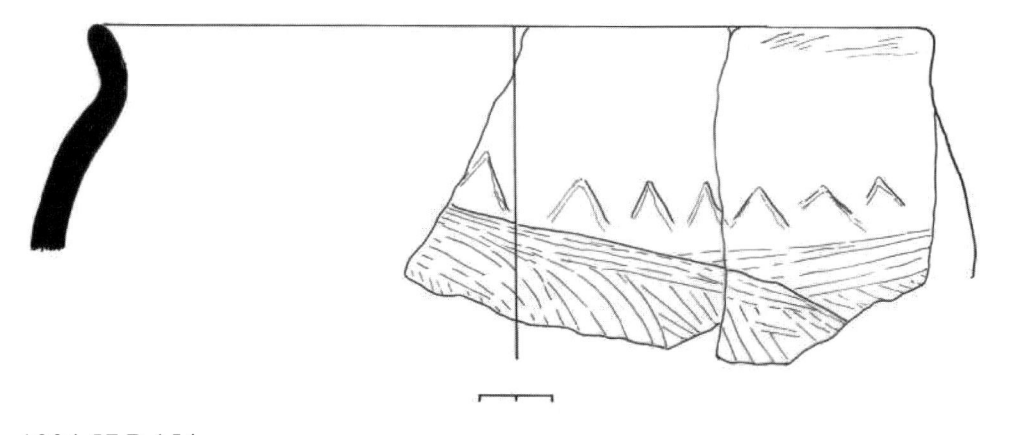

1994.57.P 154

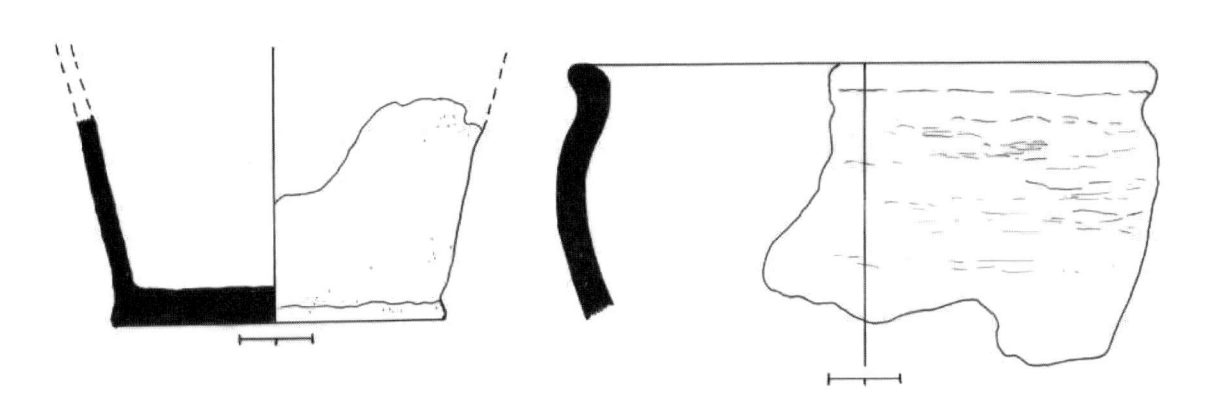

1994.57.P.157   1994.57.P.2268

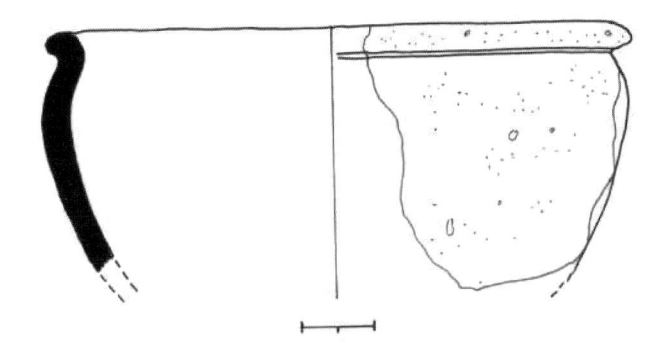

1994.57.P.3168

Figure 5.5.1 Iron Age pottery from Yewden:
P.154   Chinnor-Wendlebury group jar. Early Iron Age;
P.157   Flint tempered base. Middle Iron Age;
P.2268 Bead rimmed bulbous bowl. Late Iron Age
P.3168 Jar. Late Iron Age.

Middle Iron Age vessels were still hand-built and characterised by a range of burnished jars, bowls and saucepan pots. Saucepan pots, which had a long lived tradition, can be found over large areas of southern England. Sherds *1994.57.P.3013* and *3180* are examples of saucepan pots in a flint tempered material and *1994.57.P.2573 and 2576* are in a grog tempered fabric.

Late Iron Age vessels were dominated by bead-rimmed and necked jars. LIA pottery vessels showed an increasing tendency towards the expansion of discrete regional styles which were further developed with the introduction of the centrifugal wheel in the last century BC (Gibson, 2002). There were several examples in the assemblage of wide mouth bulbous bowls with simple beaded lips. These vessels are very characteristic of the Late Iron Age. Examples were sherds *1994.57.P.798, 2155, 2268 (Fig.5.5.1), and 2743* which were in a variety of different fabrics. Sherds *1994.57.P.798 and 2155* both have incised geometrical decoration on the neck area of the bowls which is typical of these vessels.

Sherds *1994.57.P.2147 and 3000* were examples of early wheel thrown vessels typical of the transition period between the Late Iron Age and the Roman ceramic period. *1994.57.P.2147* was a carinated bowl and *.3000* was a jar with a simple everted rim.

Date Range

The majority of the pottery can be dated to the Late Iron Age with a few examples of the transition period between the Late Iron Age and the early Roman period of the first century AD. There were, however, examples of Early and Middle Iron Age pottery which would seem to indicate that the site at *Yewden* may have been occupied for many centuries before conversion to Romanised cultural values and life styles. The variety of fabrics and different forms present amongst this pottery assemblage would support this conclusion and implies that *Yewden* had a long and varied history.

References

Cunliffe, B. 2005. *Iron Age Communities in Britain,* Abingdon, Routledge.
Gibson, A. 2002. *Prehistoric Pottery in Britain & Ireland,* Stroud, Tempus.
Orton, C., Tyers, P. and Vince, A. 1993. *Pottery in archaeology*, Cambridge University Press.

Notes:
The full catalogue of Iron Age pottery is in Appendix 2.
Since completion of the pottery report a further 8 sherds of IA pottery has emerged from the collections and these are plotted on the finds distribution plot below, but not described.

Finds plots and drawings: J. Eyers.

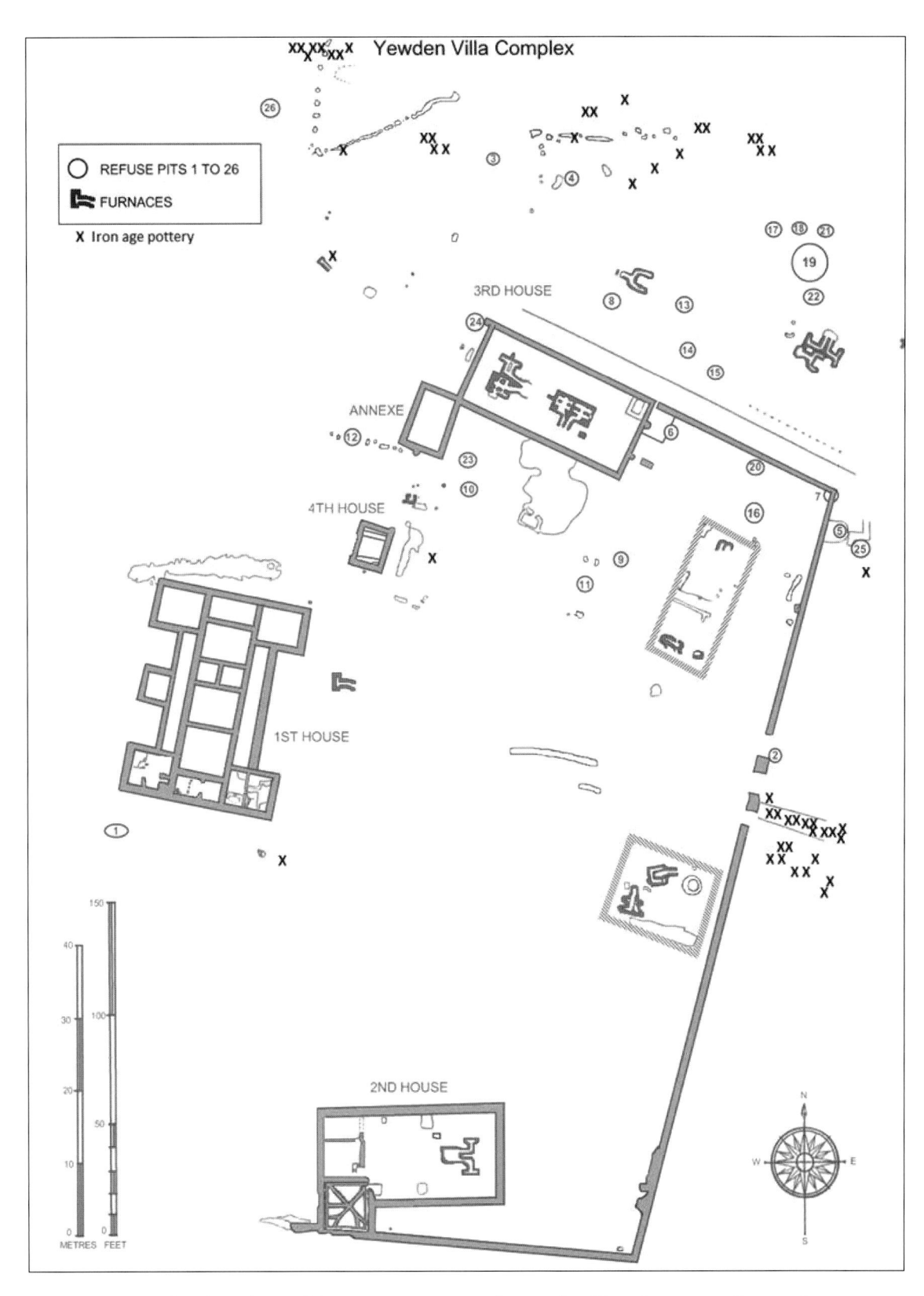

Figure 5.5.2 Distribution of Iron Age pottery from the Yewden complex and surrounds

Chapter 5.2 Roman coarse wares, fine wares and mortaria

Jill Eyers

Introduction

The pottery examined was from the 1912 excavation collection only, there being no significant finds during the 2008-10 field walk programme. The 1912 assemblage is an extensive collection. Mr Cocks employed a total retention policy and attempted to label all sherds, including small abraded samples. The pottery was in variable condition – some in extremely good condition, with many of the large pieces restored during the post-excavation work, but numerous boxes contained many hundreds of abraded sherds (which were not surprisingly from areas such as the Yard). No matter what the condition, the vast majority of sherds have a find location, and often a depth noted with them. This information was often attached to each sherd via a label with a date and other information, but occasionally the information was on a loose label inside the box. The information was carefully transferred to a card remaining with the finds and also entered onto a database before packaging the pottery. All artefacts, databases and records are archived at the Buckinghamshire County Museum. The Yewden collection thus provided a massive database which is a valuable insight into the total pottery assemblage for this rural Roman villa.

The 1912 excavations produced a total of 37707 sherds and over 935 kg of Roman pottery, with 259 sherds and almost 12 kg of Iron age pottery (discussed in Chapter 5.1). In addition there were 15 sherds (295g) of post-Medieval pottery, which is not discussed in this monograph. The Samian ware is presented separately in Chapters 5.3, 5.4 and 5.5. Due to the time and funding constraints it was not possible to work on all Roman pottery in the detail employed for the Samian. As a result the black burnished ware and amphora have not been researched, but were counted and weighed within these broad groupings. A future project could provide more detailed work on the these categories as well as some of the other pottery fabrics and forms, which were sometimes identified only to broad generic groupings such as 'sandy reduced ware (R20)' for instance. With further expertise, and more time available, a greater refinement of the fabrics and vessel types would enhance this work greatly.

Methodology

All material was recorded, and assigned a fabric grouping. The ware groupings use the Oxford Archaeological Unit's Roman Pottery Recording System, which can provide a hierarchical organisation of fabrics at several levels of precision. Dependant on the condition of the material and the fabric type, the identification of fabric was sometimes very precise, and sometimes left as a broad grouping (the latter system was used particularly for some boxes of highly abraded reduced wares). The pottery was examined box by box as this was the only practical way to deal with the large mass of material. However, each box generally contained a mix of many different fabrics and these were often from many different areas of the site, although occasionally there had been some rough sorting into similar fabric types, vessel types or site location. Adding to the sorting problems were the myriads of other objects within the 'pottery boxes' (human bone, stone, flint, iron, glass, slag, etc) all of which were exceptionally important to the site interpretation, and were sometimes linked to pottery finds, thus enhancing interpretation. Entering details of all finds methodically, and box by box, onto their relevant databases was the only way forward to researching this assemblage.

However, by using this method, some co-joining pottery sherds will certainly not have been recognised and placed together.

In addition to the fabric groupings, the pottery was also assigned a vessel form where this was clear, but this was often a broad categorisation such as 'jar, dish, flagon or bowl'. The exception was for some Oxfordshire wares where some well established typologies were available to the group (e.g. Young, 1977).

Table 5.2.1 Total quantity of pottery at Yewden Villa, Hambleden (as major categories; see the subsequent tables for a more detailed break-down

Fabric	No. sherds	%	Weight (g)	%	Rim EVEs	%
S Samian	2680	7	33549	4	79	13.2
F Fine wares	1992	5	26811	3	31	5.2
A Amphorae	253	1	31472	3	-	-
M Mortaria	925	2	55922	6	21	3.5
W White wares	1588	4	34794	4	41	6.9
Q White-slipped wares	212	1	4455	1	13	2.2
O Oxidised coarse wares	3387	8	131228	14	24	4.0
R Reduced coarse wares	24432	65	540089	58	316	52.9
B Black-burnished wares ǂ	515	1	17572	2	25	4.2
C Calcareous-tempered wares	286	1	9014	1	12	2.0
E 'Belgic' wares	1437	4	50516	5	35	5.9
Total Roman pottery	**37707**	**99%**	**935422**	**101%**	**597***	**100%**
Iron Age	259	-	11810	-	2.5	-
Post-Medieval	15	-	295	-	-	-
No ID	1321	-	16872	-	-	-
Total Yewden pottery :	**39028**	-	**952294**	-	-	-

*Base EVEs for Roman pottery = 608; EVE measurements are not complete – see the end note
ǂtotal black burnished wares, indet. Percentages are of the whole Roman pottery assemblage.

these are discussed in Chapter 5.3 (and an image is shown in Chapter 3, Figure 3.19). A decorated fragment from a New Forest vessel is also shown in Figure 3.21.
The Oxfordshire white mortaria (M22) included a great many different types including Young's 1977 forms: M2.1, M2.2, M2.3, M2.5, M2.8, M3.3, M3.4, M3.7, M5.5, M6.1, M10, M13, M14.2, M14.6, M15.1, M17.2, M17.3, M17.6, M17.8, M17.10, M18.1, <19, M20.1, M21, M21.1, M21.2, M21.3, M22.3, M22.5, M22.9, M22.16. This assemblage shows a predominance of sources from the Blackbird Leys, Cowley and Sandford kilns, with some Churchill 4a, Littlemore and Allens Pit Dorchester. However, the popular M18 and M22 forms were produced at many late kiln sites in the Oxford region. Figure 5.2.3 shows distribution of the Verulamium and Oxford white ware mortaria at Yewden.

The oxidised white slipped mortaria from Oxfordshire were Young 1977 forms WC5 and WC7.1, while the red-slipped mortaria was a C97 form.

Table 5.2.3 Mortaria fabric quantities by sherd count, weight and EVEs

Fabric	No. sherds	%	Weight (g)	%	Rim* EVEs	%
M20 white fabric (indet.)	80	9	6246	11	-	-
M21 Verulamium region	55	6	5272	9	-	-
M22 Oxfordshire, white fabric	647	70	39040	70	16.5	79
M25 New Forest	8	1	905	2	0.6	3
M30/31 Oxidised with white slip/Oxfordshire	46	5	1434	2	1.6	7.5
M36 S. England, oxidised with pale grey core	2	0.2	228	0.4	-	-
M41 Oxfordshire, oxidised with red colour coat	80	9	2339	4	1.0	5
S Samian	34		4925		3.6	

Percentages are of the mortaria assemblage, for the % of the whole Yewden assemblage see Appendix 5; Samian data are added for comparison, but discussed elsewhere.
*Pottery EVEs are not reliable with the mortaria as the final 33 boxes of pottery (containing mortaria amongst other types) could not be obtained from the museum stores and hence, although weighed and counted, had no EVEs measurements undertaken.

W White wares

The white ware assemblage is almost all sourced fairly locally. Oxfordshire dominates the assemblage with fine and sandy fabrics as well as parchment ware. The sherds confidently identified as Oxford forms amount to 37% of the total white ware sherds (58% by EVEs). However, the large categories of indeterminate sherds (W10 and W20, amounting to $c.$50% of the white ware) are most probably a large proportion of Oxfordshire forms. Verulamium white ware amounts to 10% of total white fabric sherds (11% by EVEs).

The fine white fabric vessels (fabrics W10/W11) were almost exclusively flagons (including the form W3.1 of Young 1977) and jars. Flagons (such as the form W2.3 of Young) were also a notable part of the parchment ware assemblage (fabric W12), but this category also included significant amounts of jars, dishes, bowls and beakers. Verulamium sandy white ware was predominantly jars although there was an interesting find of a tazza (see figure below, BCM P. 939), Jars also form a large component of the Oxford Sandy White ware fabric group (61% of this category) with 18% flagons, 8% dishes and 6% bowls. Also present in this category was one jug, one beaker and one lid (see figure below (BCM P.2234a and b). The W22 fabric flagons comprised Young forms W1,W2.1 and W3. The kilns associated with this production again fall into a similar area: Oxfordshire kilns of Littlemore, Blackbird Leys and Rose Hill, although the W3.3 flagon was made at all Group 3 kilns (Young 1977).

Table 5.2.4 White ware fabric quantities by sherd count, weight and EVEs.

Fabric	No. sherds	%	Weight (g)	%	Rim EVEs	%
W10 Fine white fabric, indet.	144	9	1645	5	1.2	3
W11 Oxfordshire Parchment	10	0.6	357	1	0.3	1
W12 Oxfordshire fine white	68	4	957	3	12.5	31
W20 Sandy white fabric, indet	700	44	16083	46	11.5	28
W21 Verulamium region	160	10	4979	14	4.7	11
W22 Oxfordshire sandy white ware	504	32	10446	30	10.8	26

Percentages are of the white ware assemblage, for the percent of the whole assemblage see Appendix 5

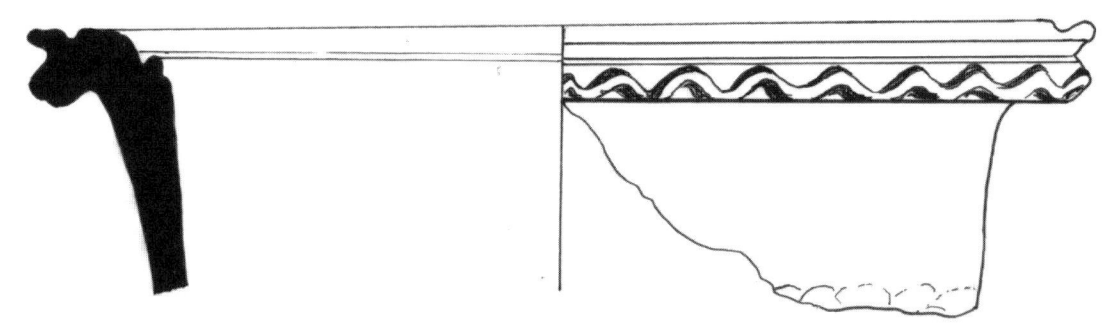

BCM No. 1994.57.P.939. Verulamium white ware (W21). Tazza. Stained exterior and interior. A fresh break shows the fabric is packed with quartz, both glassy and milky, some salmon pink. The rim has a 'crimped' edge decoration and there is a faint impressed decoration lower down the vessel. Rim 200 mm. Pit 9.

(a) BCM No.1994.57.P.2234a. Oxford sandy white ware (W22). Beaker with a white slip and a painted decoration in a red-brown slip on the lower part of the vessel. Rim 60 mm. Found under the mortar floor (S of 3rd House).
(b) BCM No. 1994.57.P.2234b. Oxford sandy white ware. Lid with a slip painted line decoration (red-brown stripes) over a cream-white non-slipped body. Lid diameter 170 mm. Under mortar floor (S of 3rd House). (*next page*)

(a)

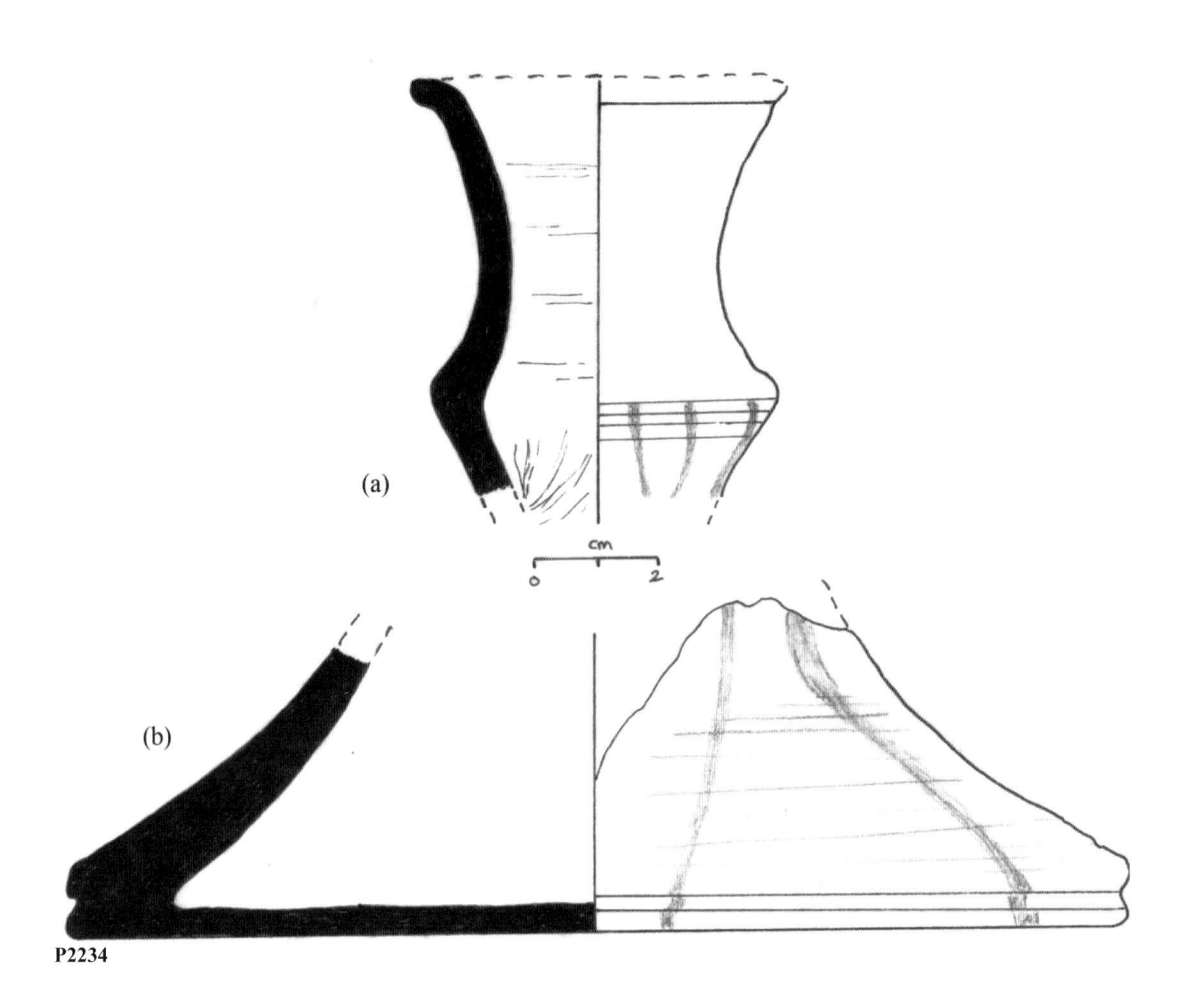

(b)

P2234

Q White slipped

The white slipped wares are most likely to be sourced from Oxfordshire, and upper Thames sources. Oxidised white slipped fabrics are more popular amounting to 84% of all white slipped wares (76% by EVEs), the remainder comprising a reduced fabric.

Flagons comprise the largest component of the oxidised fabric (Q21) which amount to 48% of the white slipped assemblage, whilst jars account for 32%, dishes 11%, bowls 5% and 1 single beaker. The flagon forms were WC1.1 of Young (1977) and sourced from the Sandford, Rose Hill, Cowley and Allen's Pit Dorchester kilns.

The reduced fabric forms (fabric Q30) were jars, dishes and beakers.

Table 5.2.5 White slipped ware (not mortaria) fabric quantities by sherd count, weight and EVEs

Fabric	No. sherds	%	Weight (g)	%	Rim EVEs	%
Q20 Oxidised white slipped, indet	73	34	1644	37	1.5	12
Q21 Oxfordshire oxidised white slipped	106	50	1892	42	8.3	64
Q30 Reduced, white slipped fabric	33	16	919	21	3.2	25

Percentages are of the white slipped (Q) assemblage, for the percent of the whole assemblage see Appendix 5

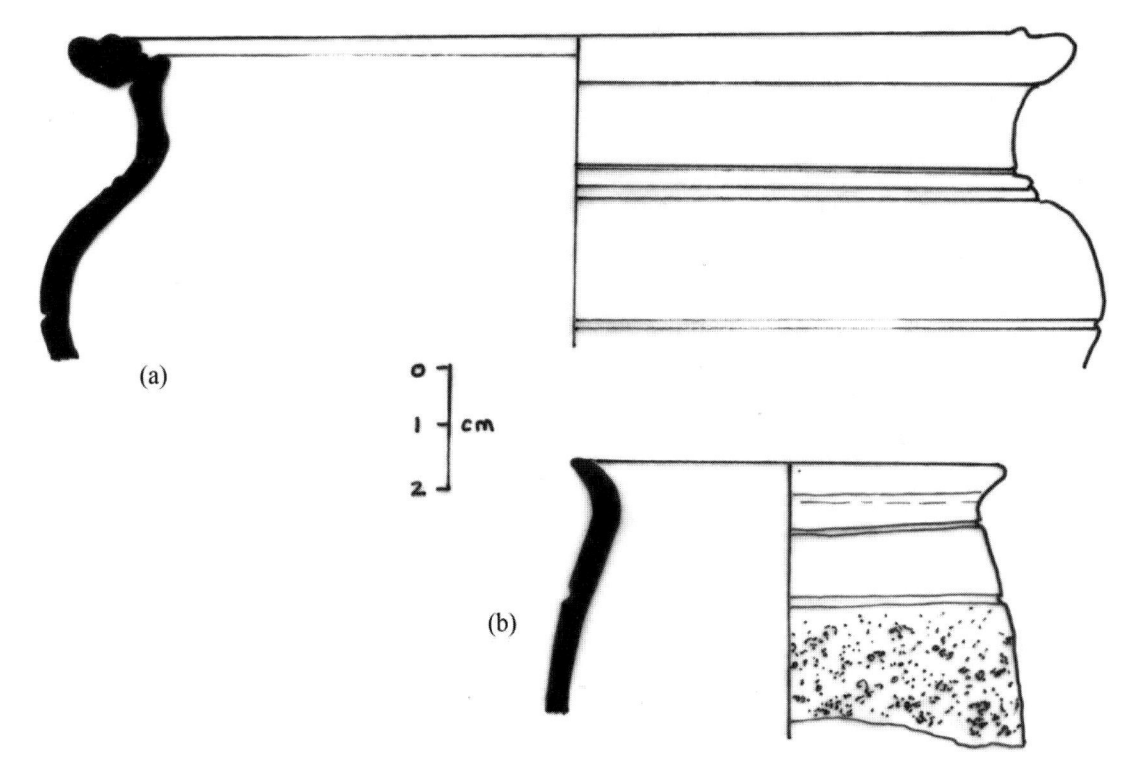

(a) BCM No. 1994.57.P.2395. White slipped reduced fabric (Q30). Blackened inner surface, cream-beige slip on outer surface. Rim 160 mm. Pit 1.
(b) BCM No. 1994.57.P.2825. White slipped reduced ware (Q30). Roughcast beaker. Rim 70 mm. Yard W.

O Oxidised

The oxidised ware was dominated by jars and dishes. The coarse grog tempered fabric O80 was entirely comprised of large jars (there was only 1 dish within the O80 fabric category). O80 makes up 6% of the total Yewden assemblage (12% by weight, but only 1,8% by EVEs – the discrepancy is no doubt due to the difficulties in measuring small segments of these large rims). The O80 fabric dominates in sherd count, weight and EVEs measurements.

Table 5.2.6 Oxidised ware fabric quantities by sherd count, weight and EVEs

Fabric	No. sherds	%	Weight (g)	%	Rim EVEs	%
O10 Fine fabric, indet.	190	6	2226	2	1.3	5
O11 Oxfordshire fine fabric	65	2	1052	1	1.4	5
O14 fine, very micaceous	3	<0.1	94	0.1	0.2	1
O20 Sandy, indet.	387	11	6591	5	6.2	26
O21 Oxfordshire sandy	42	1	1077	1	1.3	5
O24 Overwey 'Portchester D' type	119	4	2685	2	2.1	9
O80 coarse grog tempered	2429	72	114409	87	11	46

Percentages are of the oxidised ware assemblage, for the percent of the whole assemblage see Appendix 5

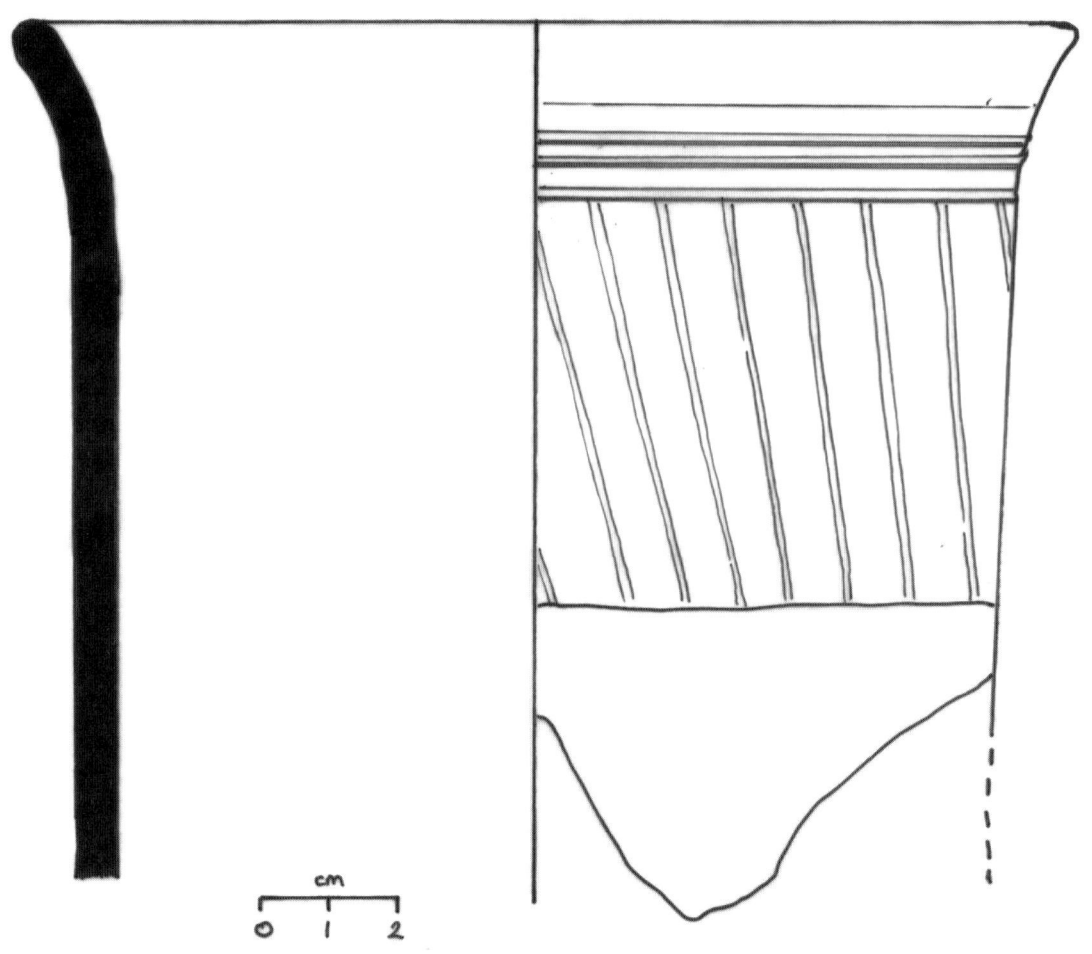

BCM No. 1994.57.P.94. Oxfordshire fine oxidised ware (O11). Straight-sided bowl with a faint burnished line pattern. Rim 150 mm. West of 1st House.

R Reduced wares

The reduced ware is a large assemblage, accounting for 65% of the sherds and 53% EVEs of the total Yewden Roman pottery assemblage. The R20 and R30 fabrics dominate the reduced wares.

The fine ware (R10/R11) fabrics are dominated by jars (62% of the fine assemblage), with beakers (many are poppyhead types) account for 17%, dishes 12%, bowls 6%, and flagons, bottles and plates are less than 1% each of the fine ware category. A crucible in fine reduced ware was found in Pit 3.

Coarse sandy reduced ware (R20) was dominated by jars (76% of the R20 assemblage), with dishes (16%), bowls (5%), lids (3%) and, beakers and strainers are less than 1%.

Medium sandy reduced ware (R30) was similarly dominated by jars (67% of the R30 assemblage), with dishes 21%, lids 6%, bowls 5% and minor beakers 2%. In addition one lamp was found within the enclosure, just southeast of the Annexe to the third house. Some of these vessels are decorated with incised line patterns of many types.

R37 and Alice Holt vessels (R39) are both dominated by jars and flat rimmed dishes, whilst the coarse R90 and R91 fabrics are all large cooking and storage jars.

Table 5.2.7 Reduced ware fabric quantities by sherd count, weight and EVEs

Fabric	No. sherds	%	Weight (g)	%	Rim EVEs	%
R10 Fine reduced ware	1854	8	23744	4	40.2	13
R11 Oxford fine reduced	86	0.4	1642	0.3	3.2	1
R20 sandy reduced ware	11301	46	256847	44	142.2	45
R30 Medium reduced ware	3257	13	64032	11	95.7	30
R37 Fine sandy, black incl.	29	0.1	807	0.1	1	0.3
R39 Alice Holt fine sandy ware	237	1	7776	1	13.9	4
R90 Coarse tempered fabric	1965	8	107547	18	18.7	6
R91 Coarse with orange & grey grog	126	0.5	6441	1	0.5	0.2

Percentages are of the reduced ware assemblage, for the percent of the whole assemblage see Appendix 5.

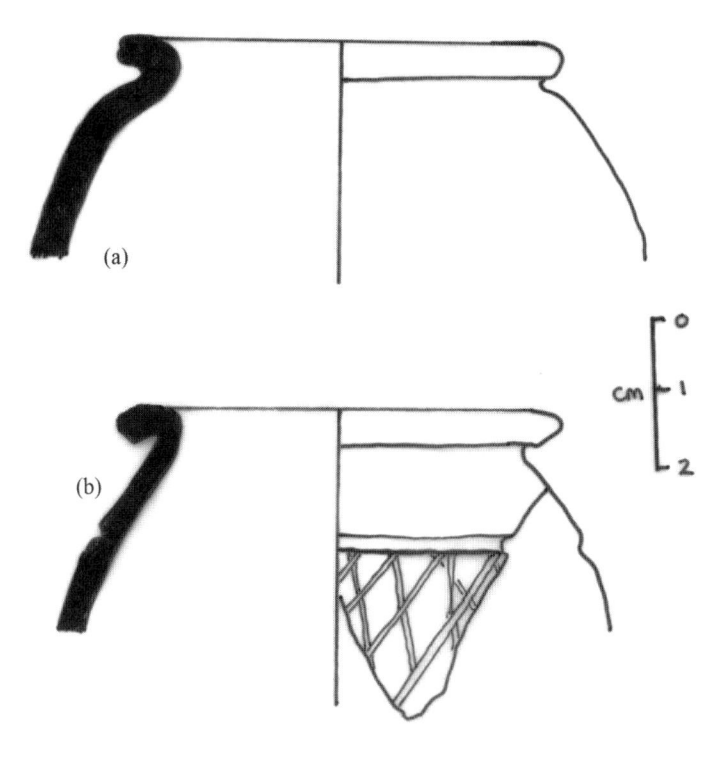

(a)
BCM No. 1994.57.P.2816a
Fine reduced ware (R10). Beaker, mid-grey, rim 60 mm. From the clay construction SW corner of the mortar floor.

(b)
CM No. 1994.57.P.2816b
Fine reduced ware (R10). Beaker, mid-grey with darker grey burnished line decoration. Rim 60 mm.

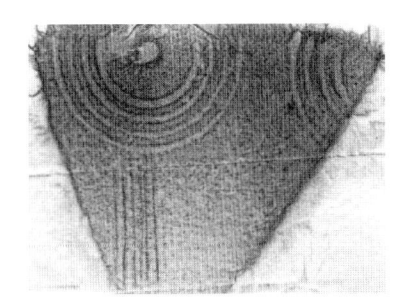

BCM No. 1994.57.P.2834b.
Oxford fine reduced ware (R11). Bowl from R68.2 (Young 1977). 'London Ware' copy of Samian form bowl Dr37. Rubbing of design. AD 100-200.
1st House centre.

P.2775 & P.996

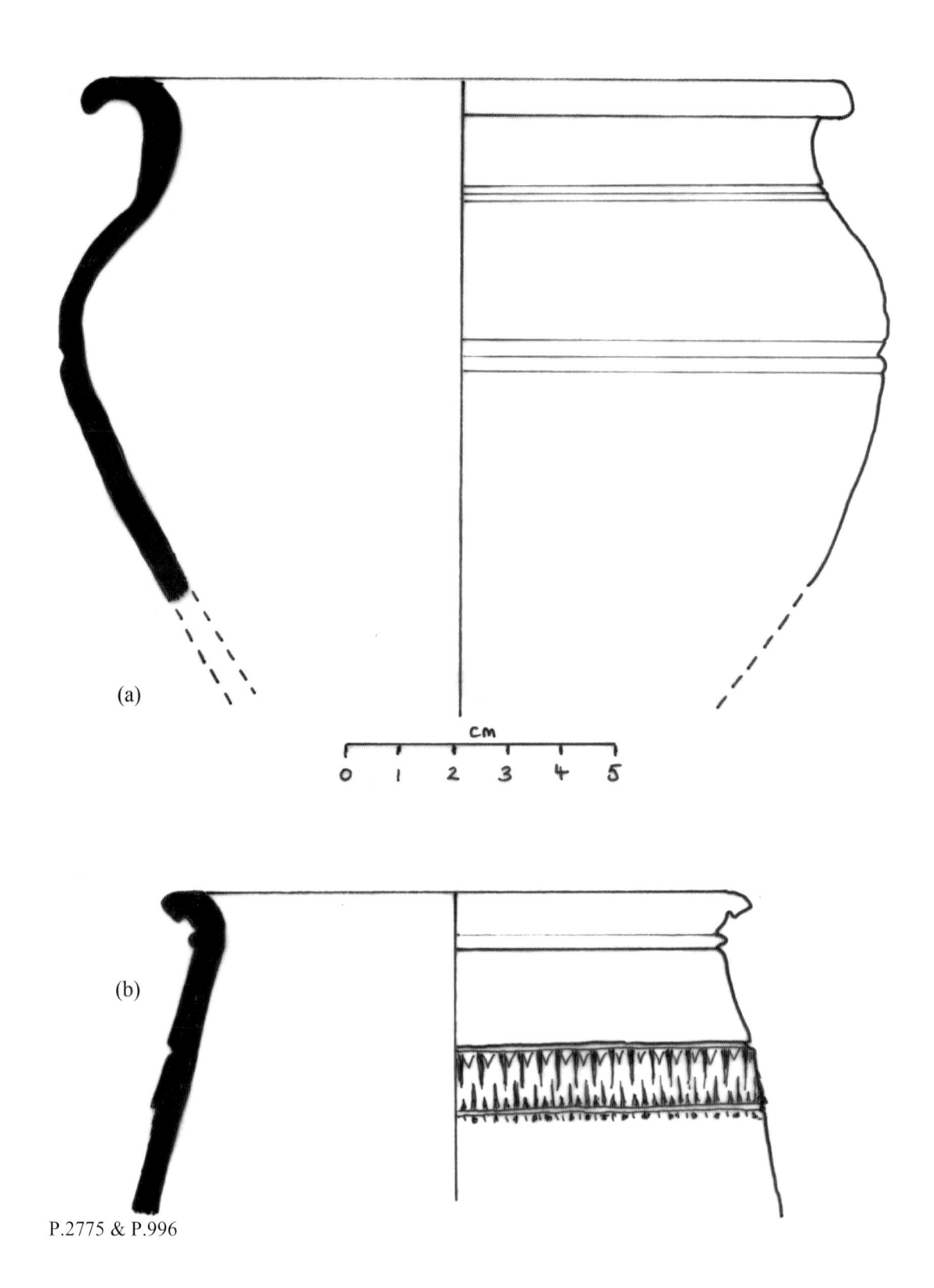

**(a) BCM No. 1994.57.P.2775. Fine reduced ware (R10). Jar, pale mid-grey and a very smooth surface.. Rim 140 mm. From the 2nd House stoke hole.
(b) BCM No. 1994.57.P.996. Fine reduced ware (R10). Beaker with roulette decoration. Rim 110 mm. Pit 9 at 3.5 ft depth.**

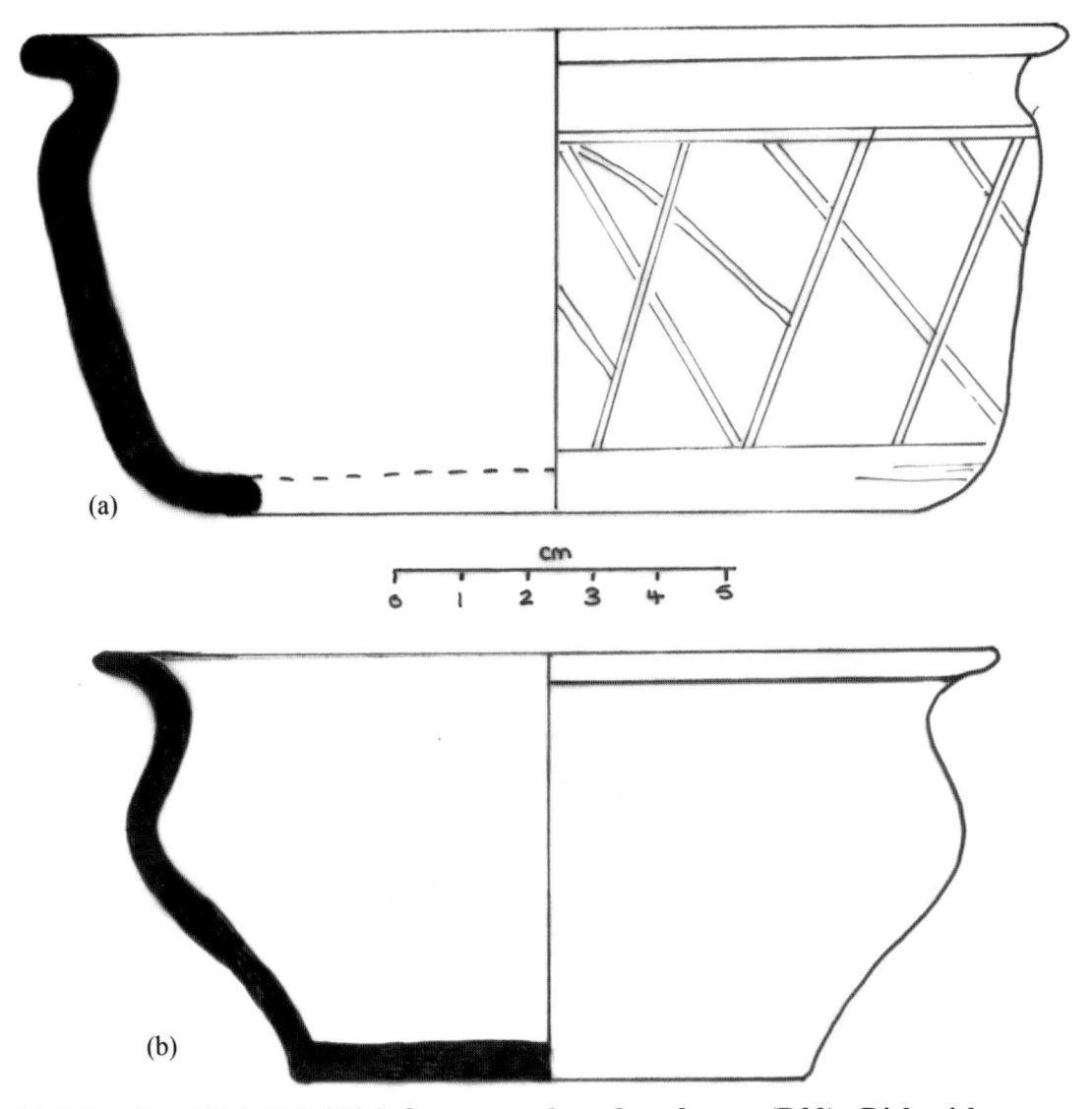

(a) BCM No. 1994.57.P.2786. Coarse sandy reduced ware (R20). Dish with burnished line decoration. Rim 160 mm, base 120 mm. Top of Pit 2.
(b) BCM No. 1994.57.P.3055.1. Coarse sandy reduced ware (R20). Dish with blackened outer surface and dark quartz-rich fabric. Rim 140 mm, base 80 mm. Pit 5.

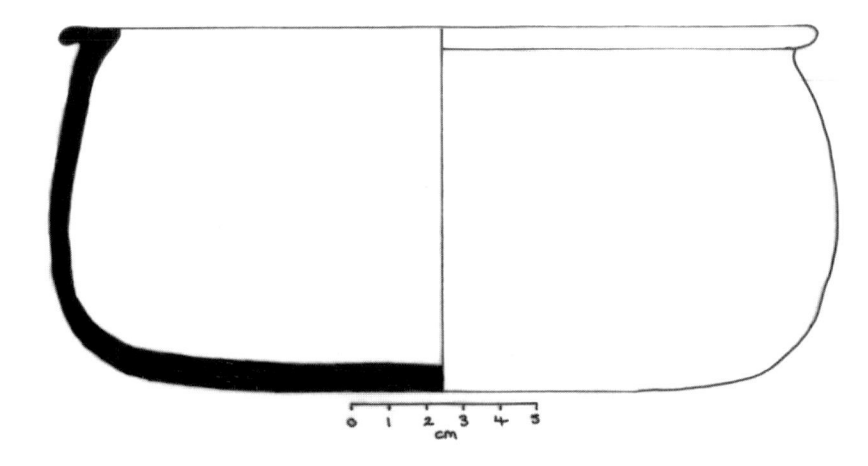

BCM No. 1994.57.P.3055.2. Coarse sandy reduced ware (R20). Blackened exterior, cooking vessel. Rim 200 mm. Yard, 1.5 yards from the wall.

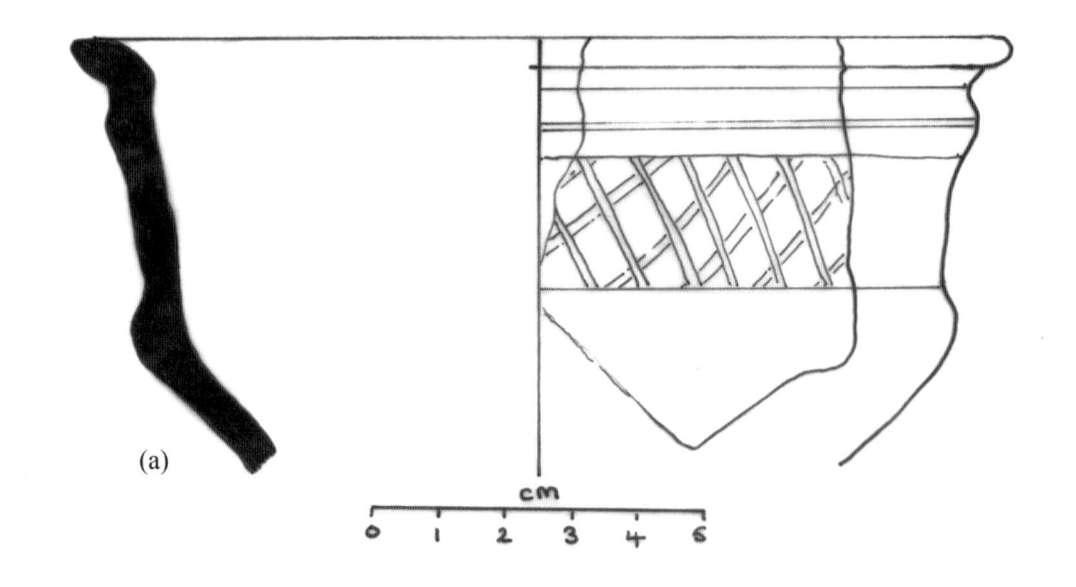

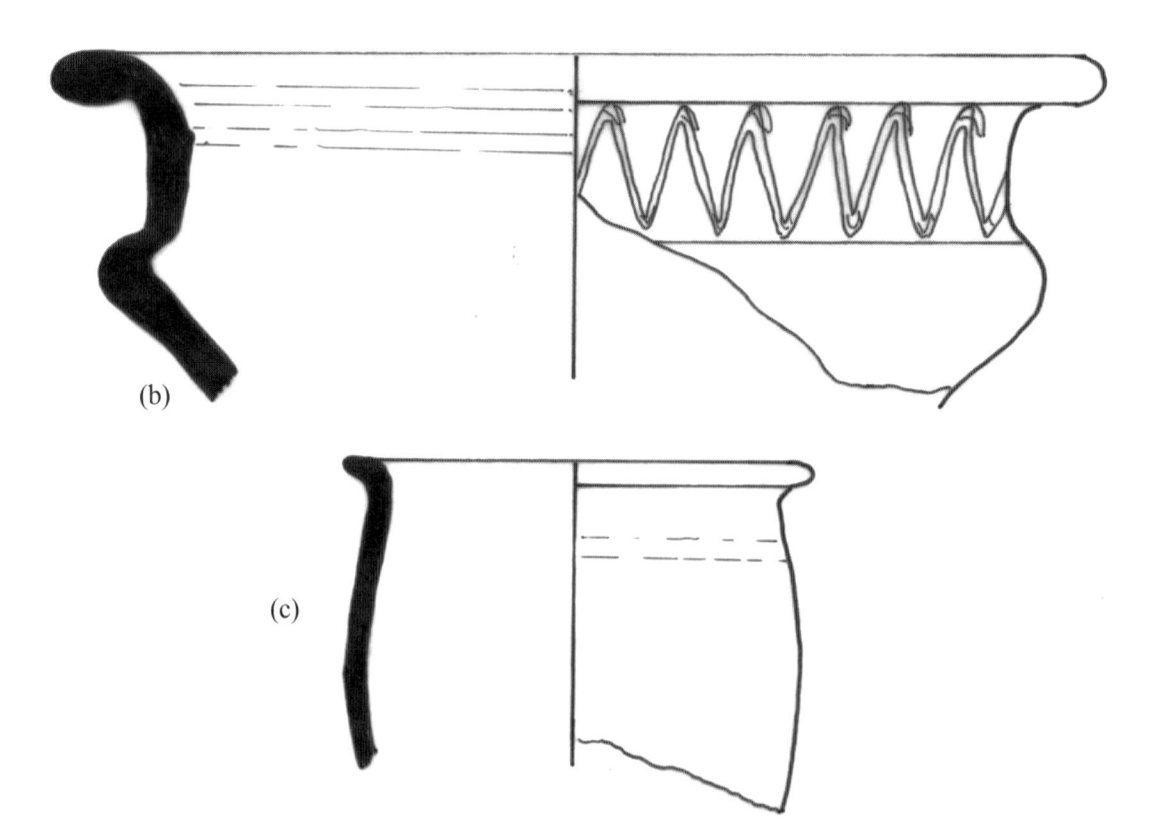

(a) BCM No. 1994.57.P.356.1. Medium reduced ware (R30). Burnished line decoration. Rim 140 mm. Yard 12-19 ft N of 3rd House.

(b) BCM No. 1994.57.P.356.2. Medium reduced ware (R30). Dish with light burnished line decoration. Rim 160 mm. V drain.

(c) BCM No. 1994.57.P.3080. Medium reduced ware (R30). Beaker, mid-grey with very fine evenly dispersed quartz temper. Faint potting marks on outer edge. Rim 70 mm. Pit 26.

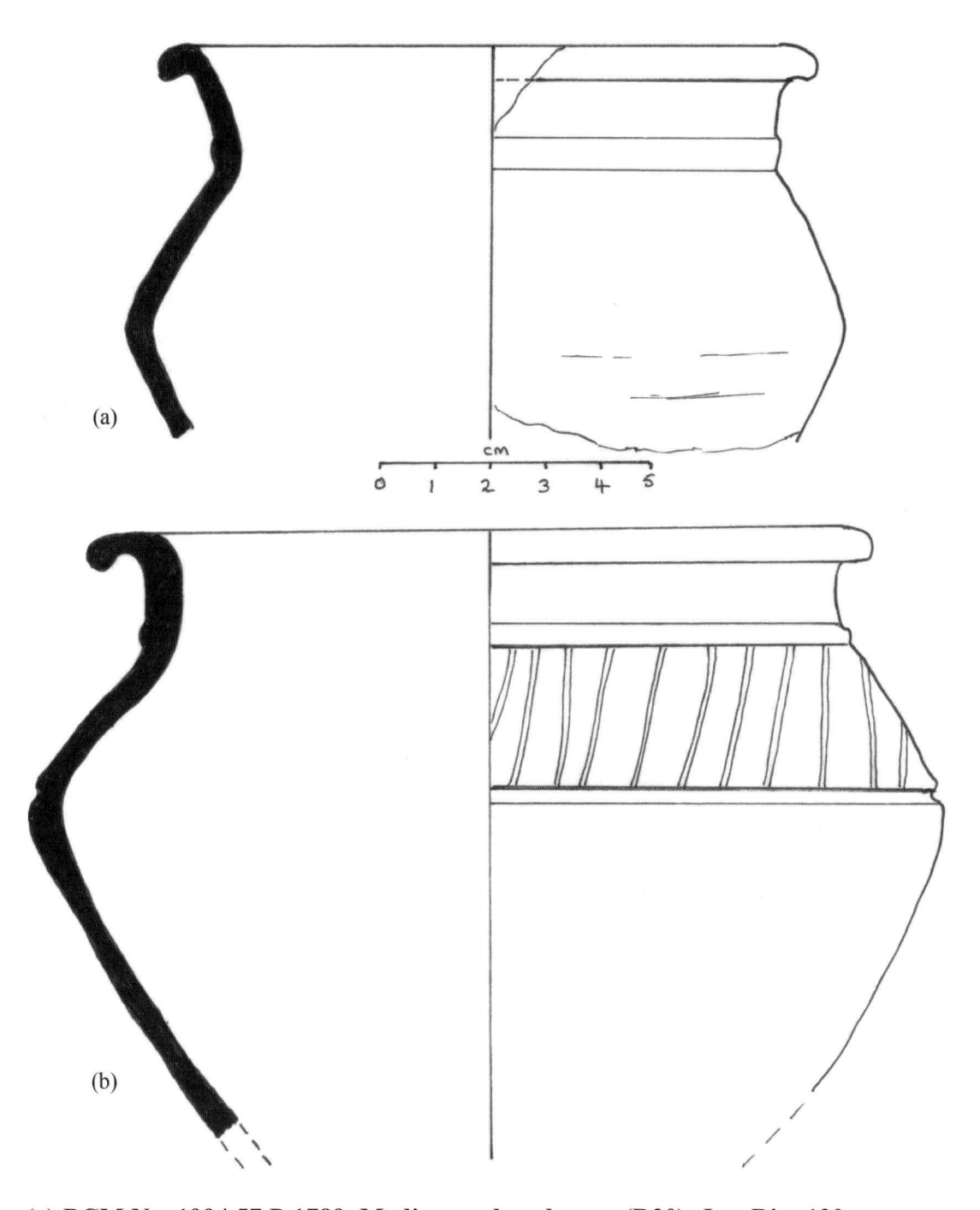

(a) BCM No. 1994.57.P.1789. Medium reduced ware (R30). Jar, Rim 120 mm. Shears Furnace.

(b) BCM No. 1994.57.P.2257. Medium reduced ware (R30). Jar with fine burnished line pattern. Rim 145 mm. Pit 25.

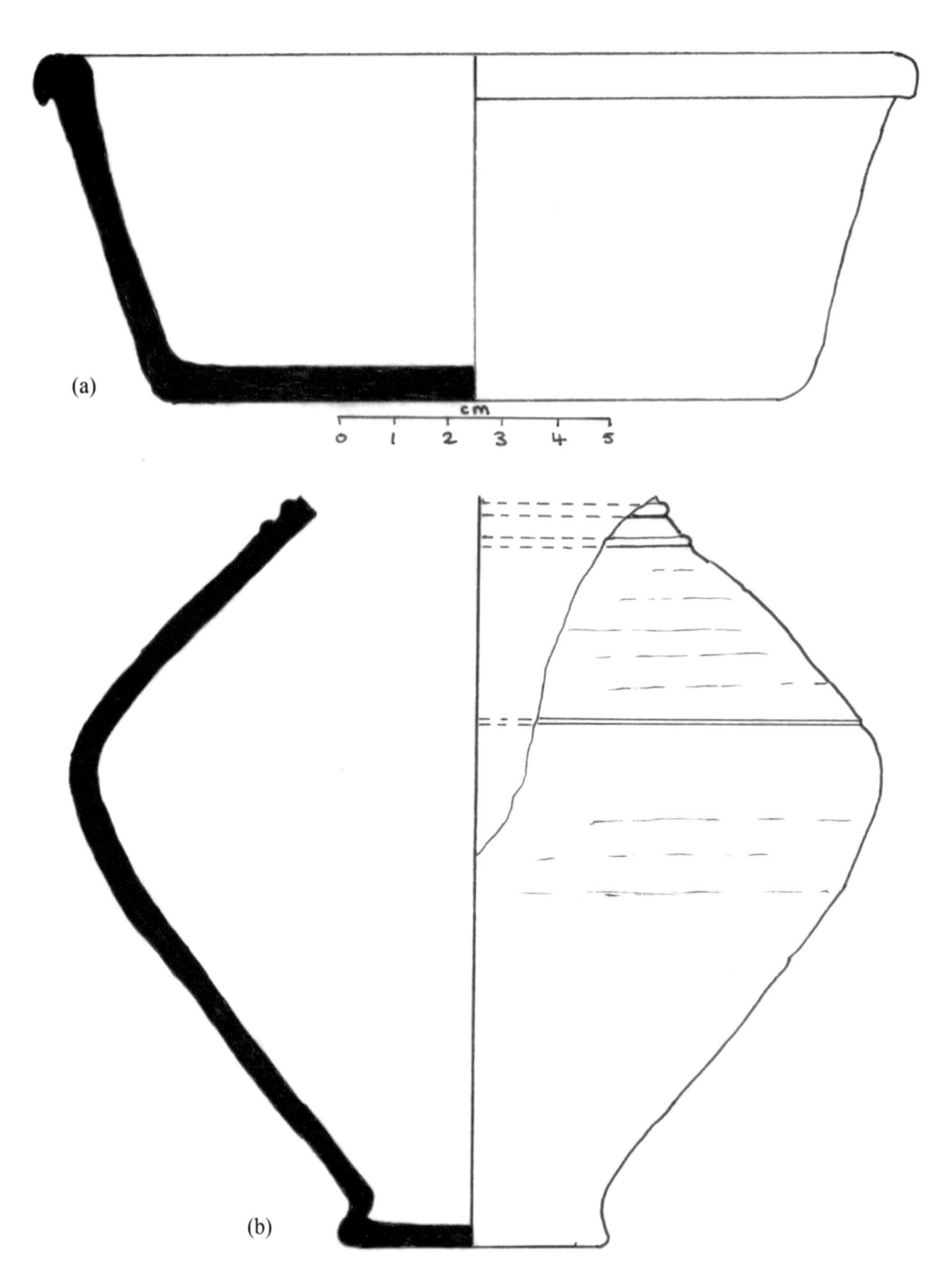

(a) BCM No. 1994.57.P.2107. Dish, mid-grey, more quartz than average R30, but not quite R20. Rim 160 mm, base 120 mm. Enclosure S of E end of 3rd House.

(b) BCM No 1994.57.P.2266. Medium reduced ware (R30). Jar with faint potting lines on outer surface. Base 50 mm. Pit 22 at 3 ft depth.

(a) CM No. 1994.57.P.3389. Medium reduced ware (R30). Jar, abraded. Rim 130 mm. Quern Hole.

(b) CM No. 1994.57.P.2254. Medium reduced ware (R30). Jar, mid-grey with a darker interior. Smooth neck with faint burnished line decoration of acute diamonds. Rim 130 mm. Pit 25.

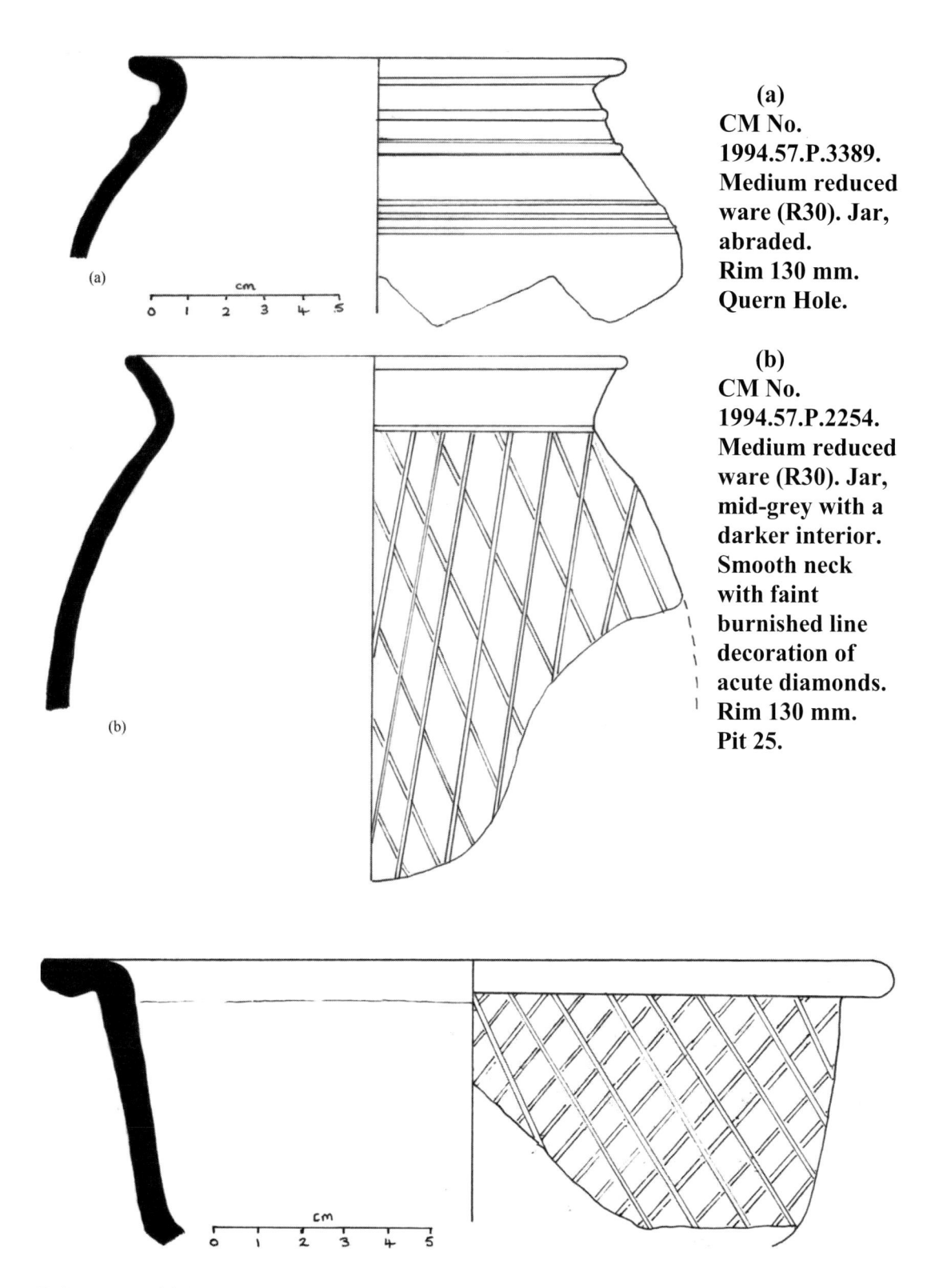

BCM No. 1994.57.P.1790. Alice Holt ware (R39). Dish with burnished line decoration of diamond pattern. Rim 200 mm. Mortar floor S of 3rd House.

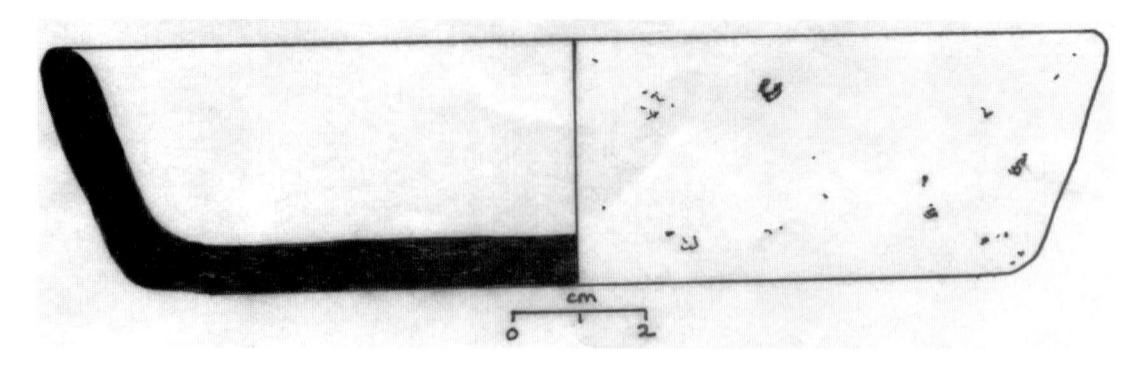

BCM No. 1994.57.P.1550. Coarse tempered fabric with orange and grey grog (R91). Dish. Rim 160 mm, base 140 mm. N side of NW wall.

B Black burnished wares

This fabric was not further divided when it became clear that there were a number of different varieties including wheel thrown and hand-made forms. Some could be identified as Black Burnished ware from Dorset (BB1) and some were clearly imitations (B30), but the research group did not have the expertise to determine the fabrics further. However, vessel forms could be defined and amounted to 78% dishes (comprising 25% of the type known as the 'dogs dish'), bowls 11%, jars 9%, lids 3%, with platters and beakers comprising less than 1%.

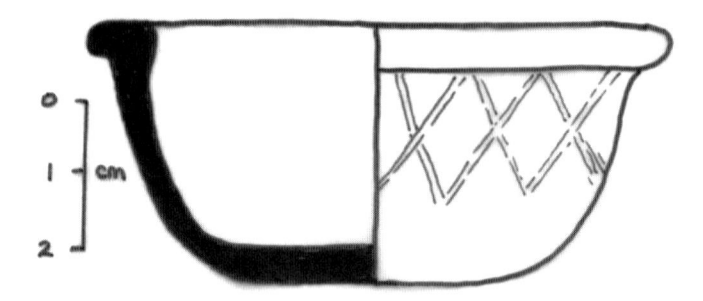

BCM No. 1994.57.P.2721 Black Burnished Ware (B11) dish found in Pit 24 at 3 ft depth. Rim 80 mm diameter with a very faint burnished line decoration.

C Calcareous tempered fabric

C13 amounts to 99% of the C fabric assemblage, with only 18 sherds of C11 present. The C11 and C13 fabrics were dominated by storage jars (96%). In addition there were 3% dishes and *c.* 2% bowls. This category only amounts to 1% (by sherd count) of the whole Yewden pottery assemblage (1.9% by EVEs). Site distribution of the shelly ware is shown in Figure 5.2.4 at the end of the chapter.

Table 5.2.8 Calcareous tempered fabric quantity by sherd count, weight & EVEs

Fabric	No. sherds	%	Weight (g)	%	Rim EVEs	%
C11 Late Roman shell tempered fabric	18	1	383	4	0.3	3
C13 abundant shell tempered fabric, reduced	268	99	8631	96	11.6	97

Percentages are of the calcareous tempered (C) assemblage, for the percent of the whole assemblage see Appendix 5.

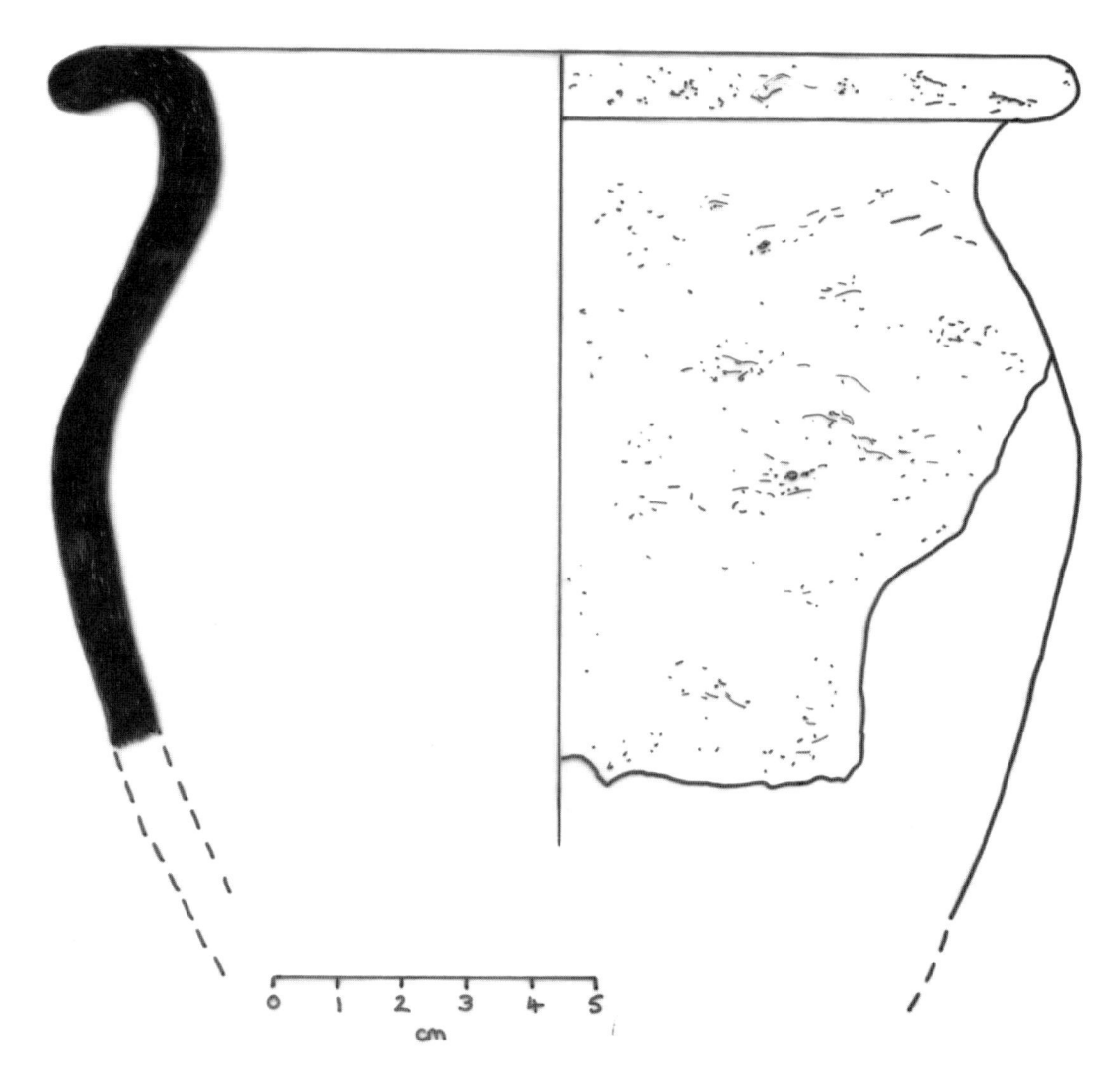

BCM No. 1994.57.P.2780. Shell tempered jar (fabric C13), rim 160 mm diameter found in the stoke hole of the 2nd House.

E Early Roman-late Iron Age 'Belgic' forms

The 'Belgic' forms make up 3.7% of the whole Yewden Roman pottery assemblage. This category is dominated by jars (67% of the E group) and dishes (22%) with minor bowls (6%), lids (4%) and beakers (1%). Some of the jars and bowls are carinated and some show incised decoration.

Table 5.2.9 Early Roman-late Iron Age 'Belgic' fabric quantities by sherd count, weight and EVEs

Fabric	No. sherds	%	Weight (g)	%	Rim EVEs	%
E20 Fine sand tempered	47	3	1370	3	0.4	1
E30 Med-coarse sand tempered ware	531	37	17606	35	11.7	33
E80 Grog tempered ware	519	36	18638	37	12.7	36
E810 Grog & sand temper	299	21	10899	22	10	29

Percentages are of the 'Belgic' (E) assemblage, for the percent of the whole assemblage see Appendix 5

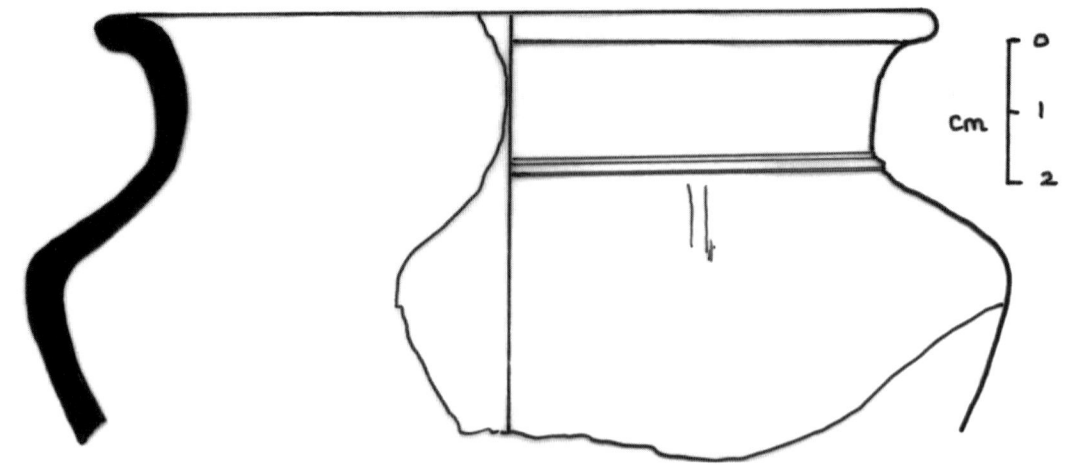

BCM No. 1994.57.P.1845. Fine sand tempered fabric (E20).

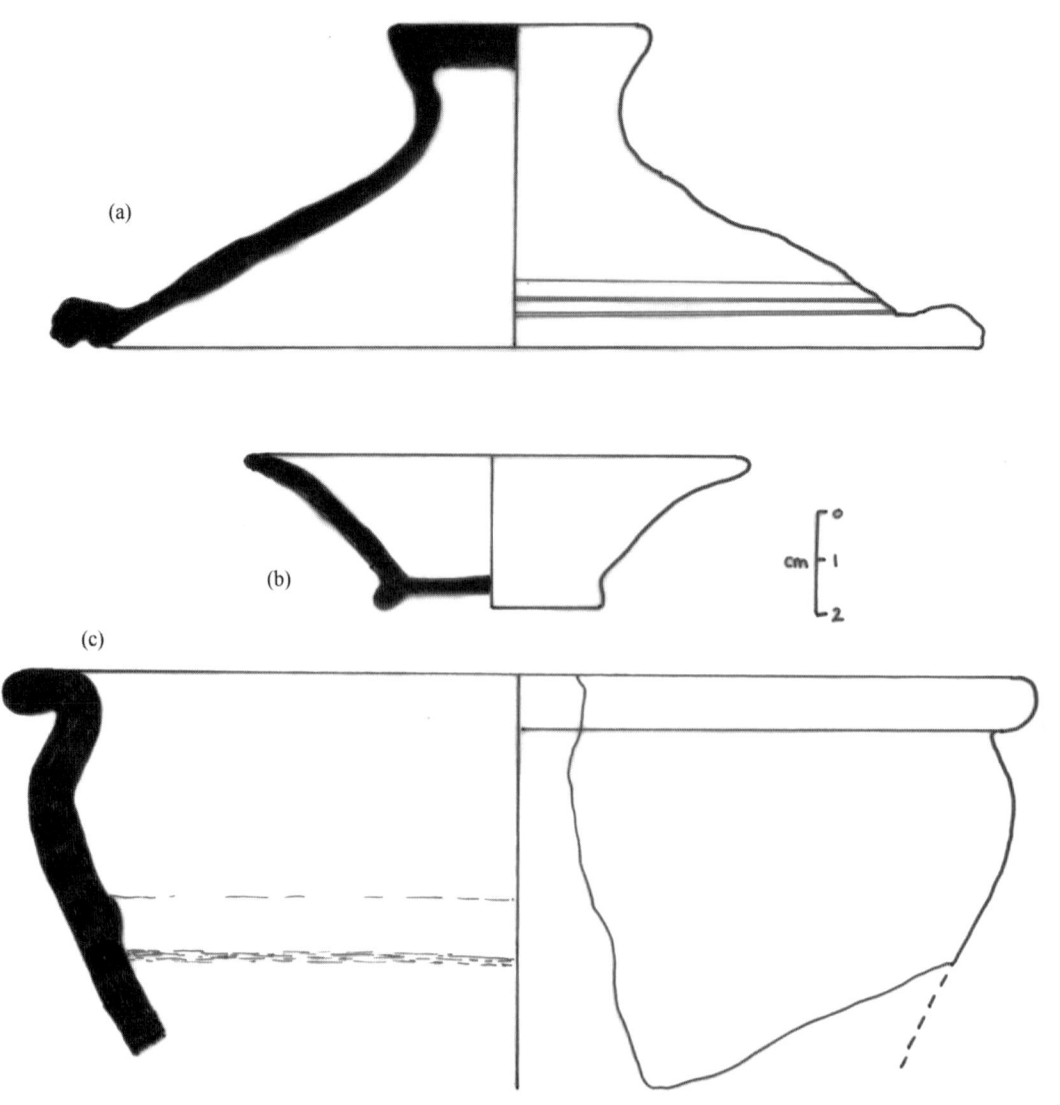

(a)

(b)

(c)

(a) BCM No. 1994.57.P.1560. Sand tempered fabric (E30). 'Belgic' lid of Thompson 1982, of type L10. Lid diameter 180 mm, found in Pit 24 at 3 ft depth.
(b) BCM No. 1994.57.P.2716. Sand tempered fabric (R30), shallow dish, Rim diameter 100 mm, base 45 mm. V drain.
(c) BCM No. 1994.57.P.2232. Sand tempered fabric (E30). Bowl, rim diameter 200 mm, found under the mortar floor south of the 3rd House.

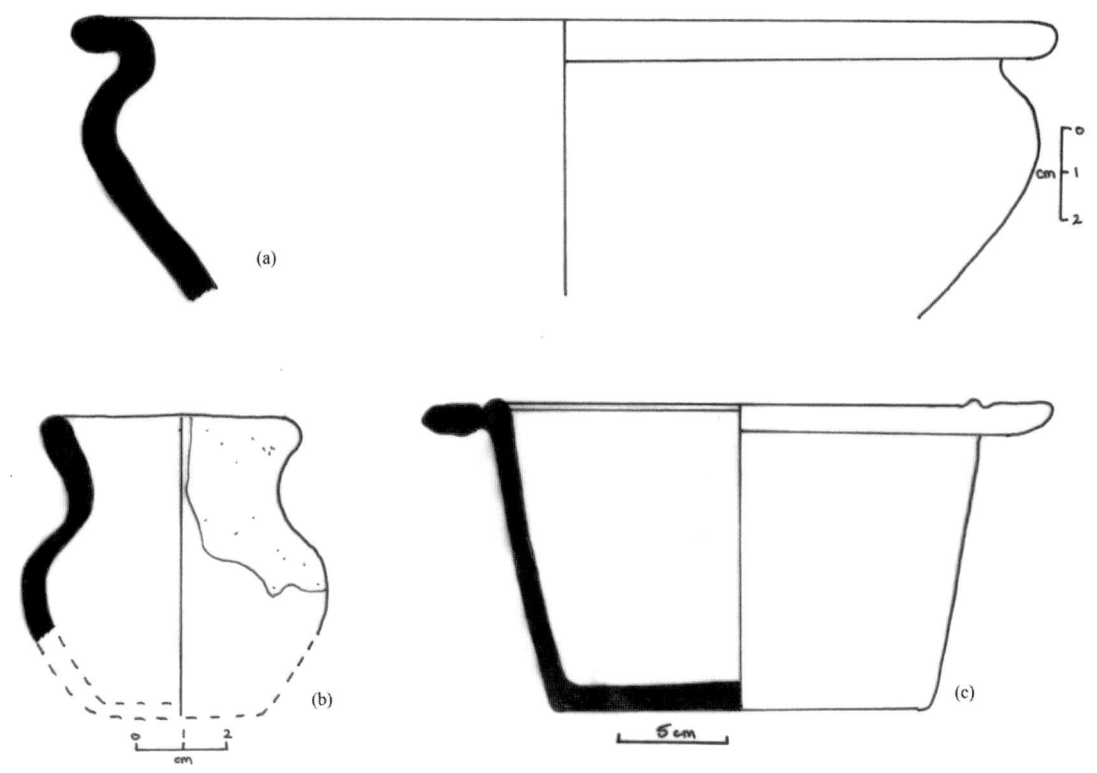

(a) BCM No. 1994.57.P. 2256. Grog tempered ware (E80). Dish with a dark grey, blackened exterior. Rim 220 mm diameter. Pit 18.
(b) BCM No. 1994.57.P.991. Grog tempered ware (E80). Beaker. Rim 60 mm. Northwest wall.
(c) BCM No. 1994.57.P.354. Grog & sand tempered ware (E810). Rim 200 m. Base 180 mm. Blackened exterior, paler interior with poorly sorted quartz up to 0.5 mm. Pit 21.

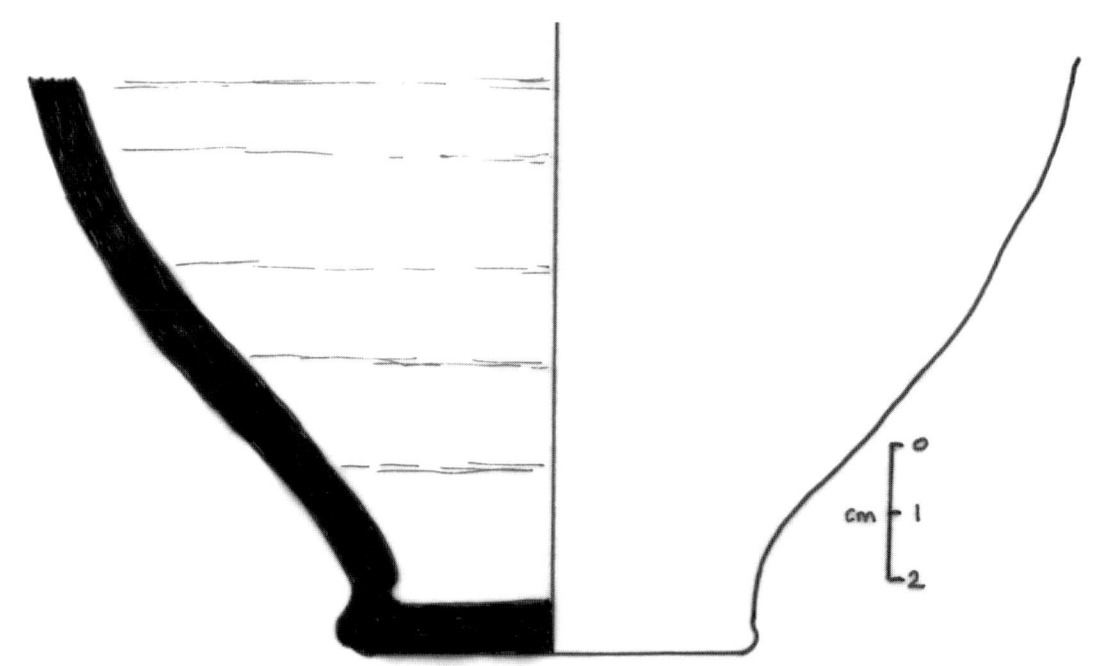

BCM No. 1994.57.P.1796. Grog & sand tempered ware (E810). Base 60 mm. Faint rill lines on inner surface. 3rd House between E and W furnace flues.

Bibliography

Thompson, I. 1982. *Grog tempered 'Belgic' pottery of southeastern England.* **BAR 108** (Oxford).

Young, C. J. 1977. *Oxfordshire Roman Pottery.* **BAR 43** (Oxford).

Acknowledgements

Thanks to Paul Booth for assisting in setting up a type series from which consistent identifications could be made throughout many hundreds of pottery box examinations. Thanks also to Nicky Metcalf of the Verulamium Museum, Suzie Tilbury at the Henley Museum, Esther Cameron at the Oxford Museums Resource centre at Standlake, and also the Hampshire Museums Service for making their Roman pottery collections accessible for study during this project.

Future work:

EVE measurements need completing. Access to the collections could not be arranged for the last 5 months of the project and hence some boxes, although previously identified, counted and weighed, had not had rim or base EVEs measurements completed. This is why sherd or weight percentages were sometimes used in place of EVEs statistics during some assessments in this monograph. The boxes invoved will need both ID checking and EVEs measurements undertaken and these are box numbers: 536, 538, 539, 541, 543, 545, 550, 554, 555, 556, 558, 2195, 2196, 2197, 2198, 2199, 2200, 2201, 2202, 2203, 2204, 2205, 2206, 2207, 2209, 2215, 2217, 2218, 2228, 2230, 2237, 2244, 2246, 2248, 2250, 2251, 2259, 2264.

Black Burnished ware – requires full ID and assessment.

Generic groupings such as F30, F50, O10, O20, O80, R10, R20, R30, W10, and W20 each need further refinement into detailed fabric types. **Reduced ware** categories R20 and R30 need further work to extract further sherds from R37 and R39 categories, amongst potential others.

Amphora – require full ID and assessment.

Further **drawing and more detailed recording** of the vessel types, for all fabric categories, would create an excellent record of the vast range of forms present in this assemblage.

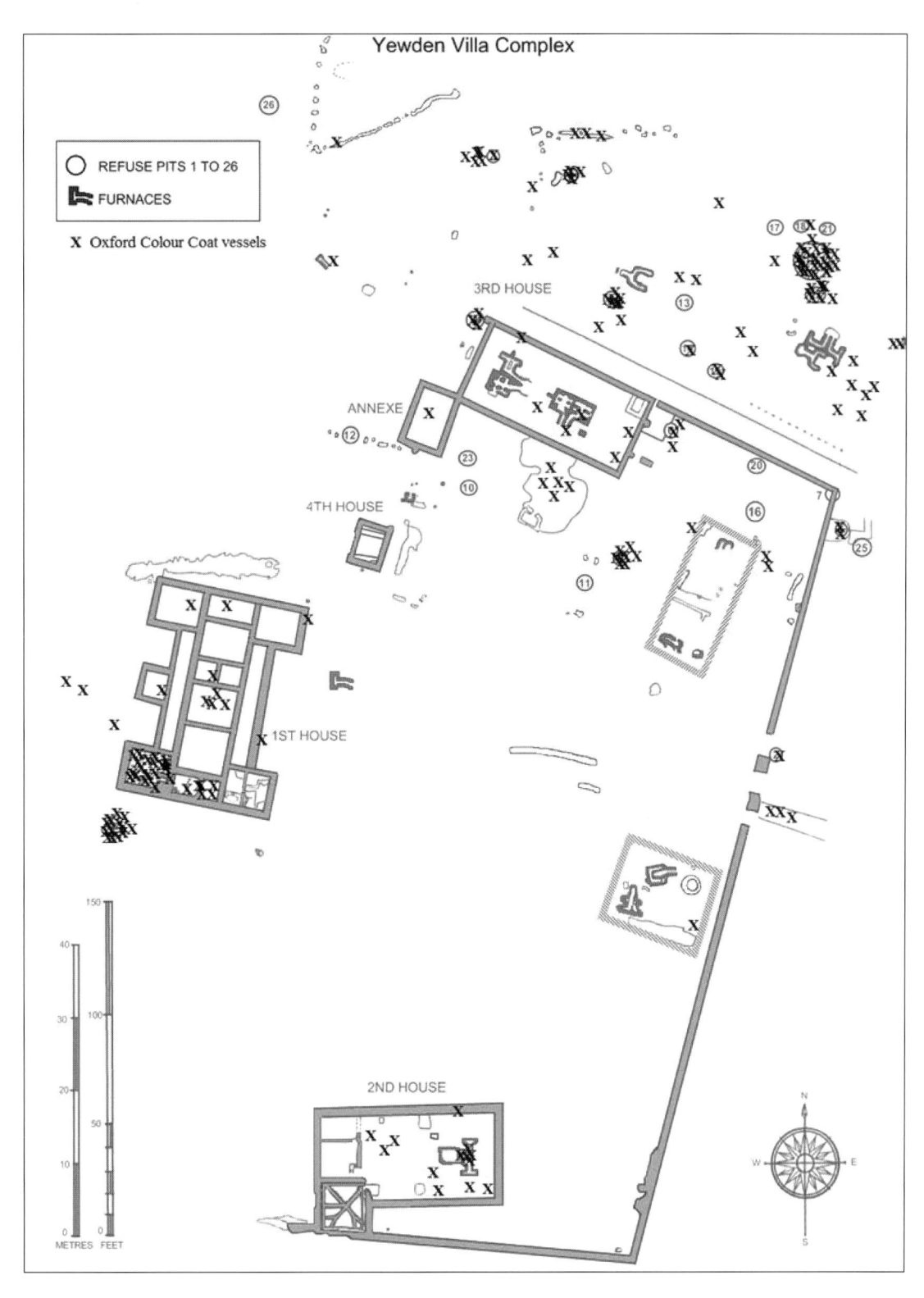

Figure 5.2.1 Distribution of the Oxford Colour coated pottery (F51) at Yewden

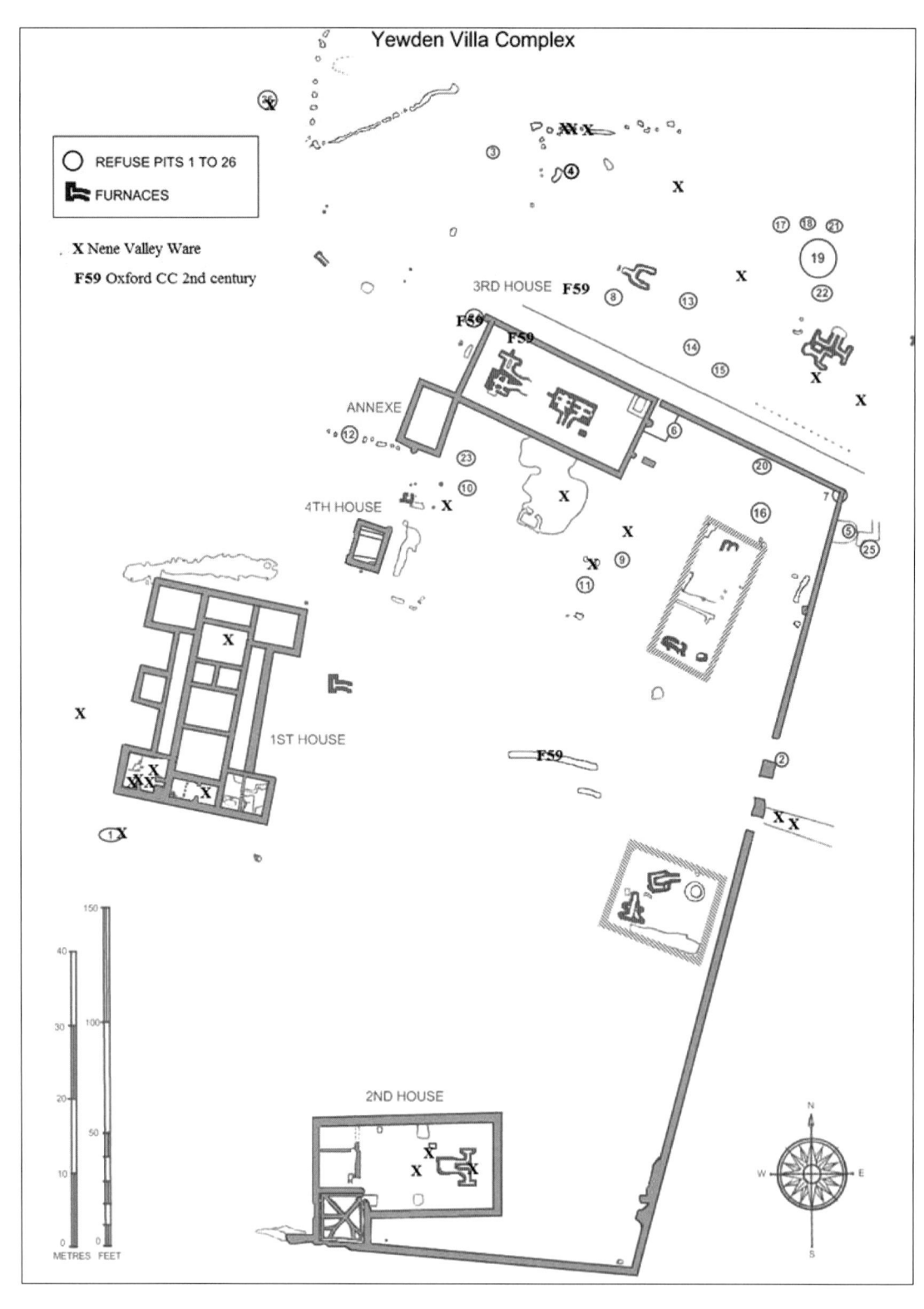

Figure 5.2.2 Distribution of the Nene Valley ware (F52) and early Oxford Colour Coated ware (F59)

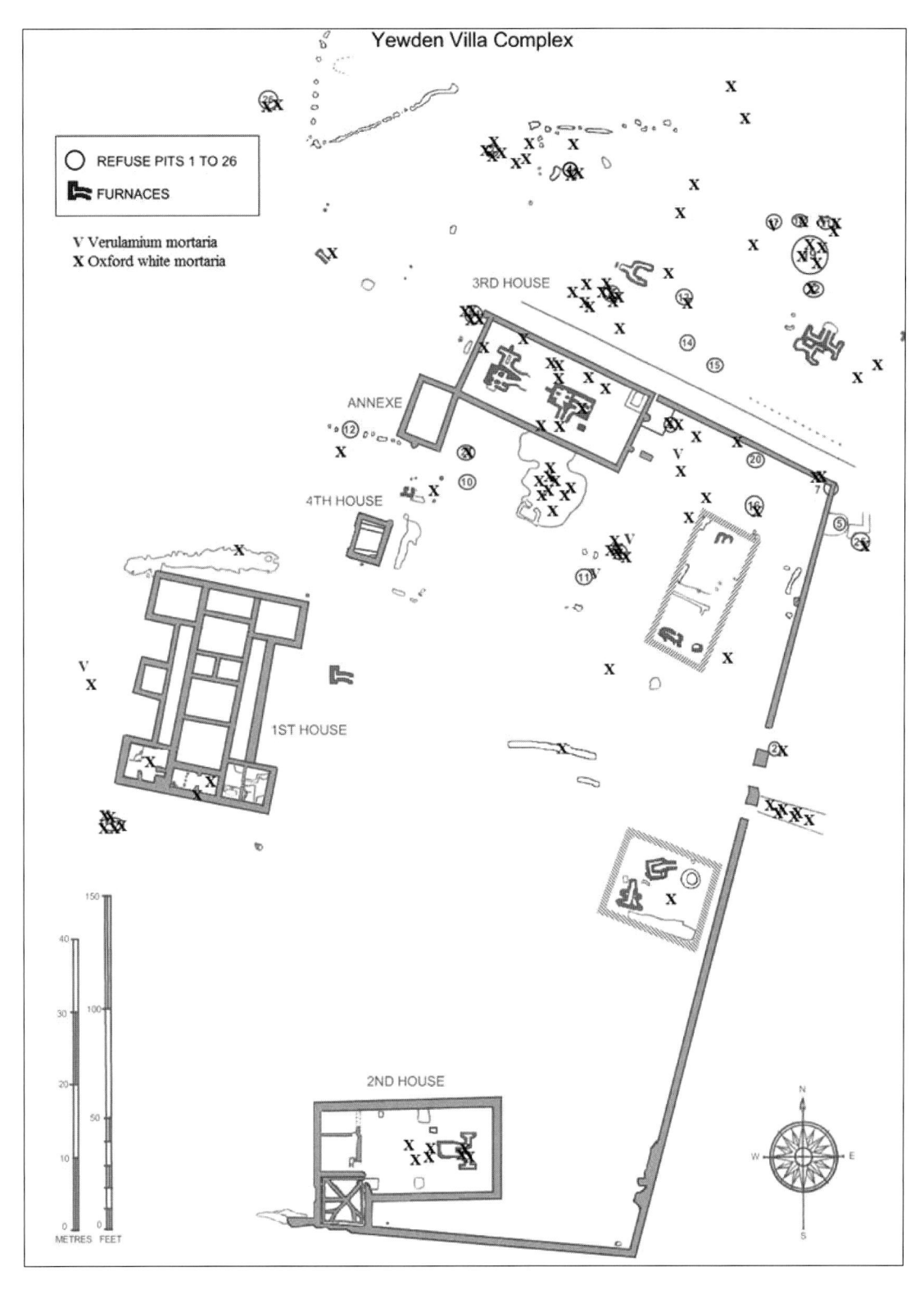

Figure 5.2.3 Distribution of Verulamium mortaria (M21) and Oxford white mortaria (M22) at Yewden

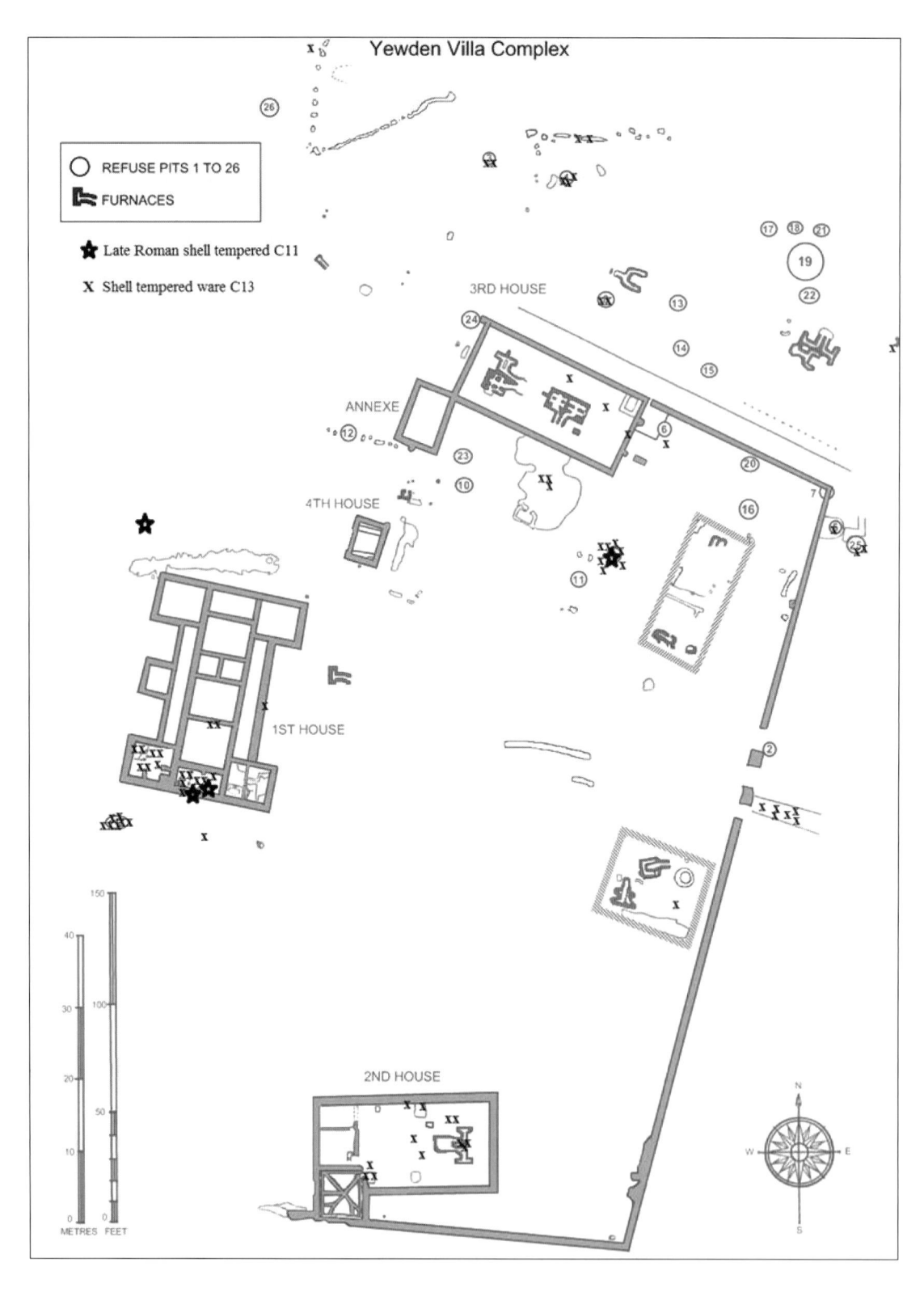

Figure 5.2.4 Distribution of shelly ware C13 and Late Roman shelly ware (C11) at Yewden

Chapter 5.3 Samian pottery

Jill Eyers

Summary and methodology

Some 2664 sherds were recorded by reassessing the Samian assemblage from the 1912 excavation at Yewden villa. They represent a total of 33.5 kg (Table 5.3.1) for a minimum of 211 vessels (which is undoubtedly an underestimate) and a rim EVE total of 79. The maximum vessel number is not reported as it is too large to be realistic and simply reflects the broken nature of pottery collected from some areas of the site, such as the yard and the waste pits. Samian accounts for 13% (by EVEs), 7% by sherd count and 4% by weight of the total pottery assemblage.

Pottery fabrics were identified using a x20 hand lens and the x40 objective on a binocular microscope. The full database is held at the Buckinghamshire County Museum. Tables 5.3.1 and 5.3.2 give summary data on sherd count, weight, minimum number of vessels, rim EVEs and base EVEs. Table 5.3.1 shows the counts and Table 2 displays these figures as percentages of the total. The minimum vessel calculations were rounded up to the nearest whole number, and adjusted by EVEs information. Percentage calculations were only rounded to give the second decimal place. Percent rim EVEs is used to present the data in graphical form, as it is the most unbiased value calculated from the assemblage. However, when comparing Yewden Samian to the assemblages from other sites this data was not always available and hence other methods have been used, such as percent by sherd count, or as published data allowed.

Table 5.3.1 Samian statistics: sherd count, weight, minimum vessels, EVEs

Source area	Sherd count	Wt (g)	Min. Vessels	Rim EVEs	Base EVEs
Montans	2	21	2	0.1	0.23
La Graufesenque	634	4620	46	16.07	14.39
Total S. Gaul	**636**	**4641**	**48**	**16.17**	**14.62**
Pre-import Lezoux	4	21	1	0	0.02
Les Martres	239	2539	37	4.52	5.31
Lezoux	1600	21376	91	52.29	52.60
Total C. Gaul	**1843**	**23936**	**129**	**56.81**	**57.93**
East Gaul	168	2359	22	4.52	3.13
Rheinzabern*	13	2567	8	1.12	3.03
Trier?	1	14	1	0	0
Total E. Gaul	**182**	**4940**	**31**	**5.64**	**6.16**
indeterminate	3	32	3	0.23	0
Total Yewden assemblage	**2664**	**33549**	**211**	**78.85**	**78.71**

LGF: La Graufesenque   MLEZ: Micaceous Lezoux   LMV: Les Martres-de-Veyre
*The total weight of Rheinzabern is increased relative to minimum vessel number due to one large, complete Dr43.

Table 5.3.2 Samian statistics as percentages of the whole Samian assemblage

Source area	% sherds	% weight	% min vessels	% Rim EVEs
Montans	0.07	0.06	0.47	0.13
La Graufesenque	23.80	13.77	22.27	20.38
Total S. Gaul	**23.87**	**13.83**	**22.74**	**20.51**
Pre-import Lezoux	0.15	0.06	0.47	0.02
Les Martres	8.97	7.57	17.54	5.73
Lezoux	60.06	63.72	43.13	66.31
Total C. Gaul	**69.18**	**71.35**	**61.14**	**72.06**
East Gaul	6.31	7.03	10.43	5.73
Rheinzabern*	0.49	7.65	3.79	1.42
Trier?	0.03	0.04	0.47	0
Total E. Gaul	**6.83**	**14.72**	**14.69**	**7.15**
indeterminate	0.11	0.10	1.42	0.29
Total assemblage	99.99	100.00	99.99	100.01

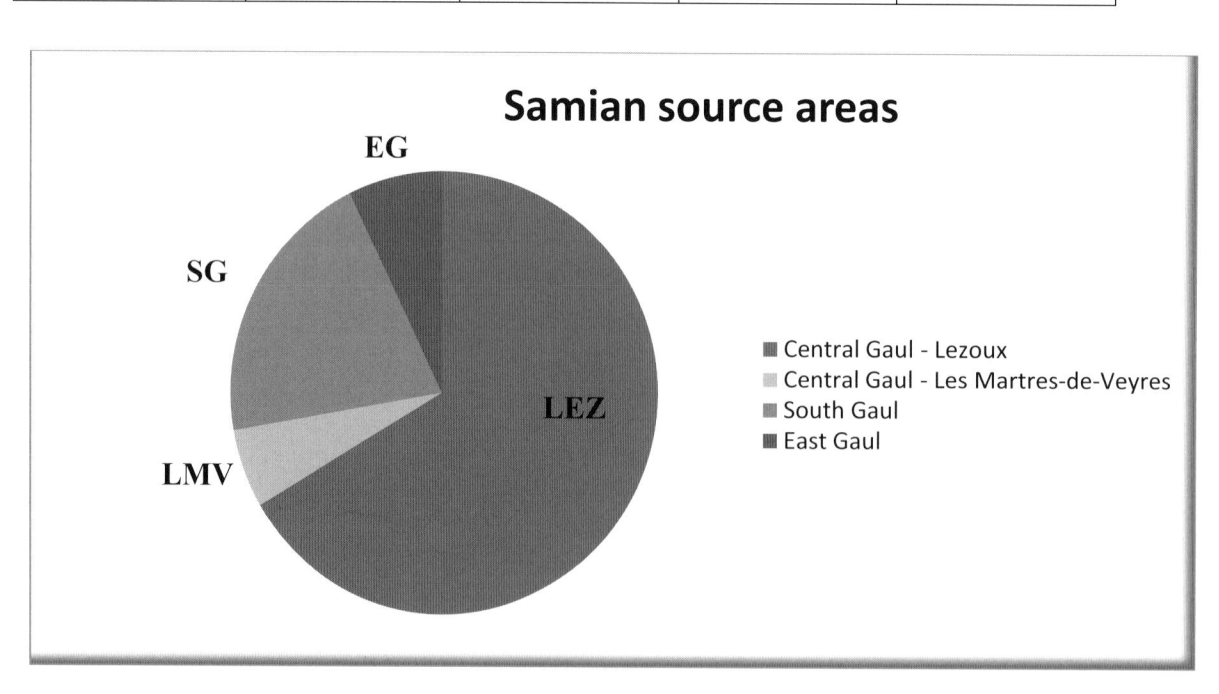

Figure 5.3.1 Proportion of each of the main Samian source areas

Provenance and dating

The earliest vessels are from South Gaul (*c*. AD 50) with only one vessel from Montans and the remainder from La Graufesenque. There are notable individual vessels within the assemblage from South Gaul (especially within the decorated DR29s and DR30s). La Graufesenque comprises 20% of the total Samian assemblage (calculated from EVEs) and is represented in the pottery assemblage throughout the 1st century until the end of its production *c*. 100 AD. The assemblage is then dominated by Central Gaulish pottery largely the mid- to late-second century Lezoux (Antonine), by also a notable earlier amount from Les Martres-de-Veyre (Trajanic-Hadrianic AD 100-130, as dated by potters). However, after the Les Martres kilns close there is minor reduction in supply, with about one-third of the Lezoux pottery arriving between AD 120-150 and the bulk (two thirds) of Lezoux arriving at Yewden between AD 150-200. The results presented in Tables 1 and 2 show the total proportion of the Samian assemblage from Central Gaul is 72%, with Lezoux providing the largest amount of the total (66%). The dating of these vessels is defined by named potters, and hence it is based on vessels with decoration or stamps. The Antonine pottery is dominated by the Cinnamus and Paternus workshops, which along with their contemporaries, are listed in Appendix 3 with the minimum vessels attributed to each. This bias of the Samian assemblage to the second half of the second century is also seen in other sites in southeast England (e.g. Northfleet, Ed Biddulph, *pers comm.*)

In contrast, East Gaulish forms are poorly represented (Table 5.3.1), and has the smallest proportion of vessels from all three regions of Gaul, amounting to only *c*. 7% of the Samian assemblage (based on EVEs or 14% based on minimum vessel estimate). This pottery arrives from East Gaul between AD 140-260.

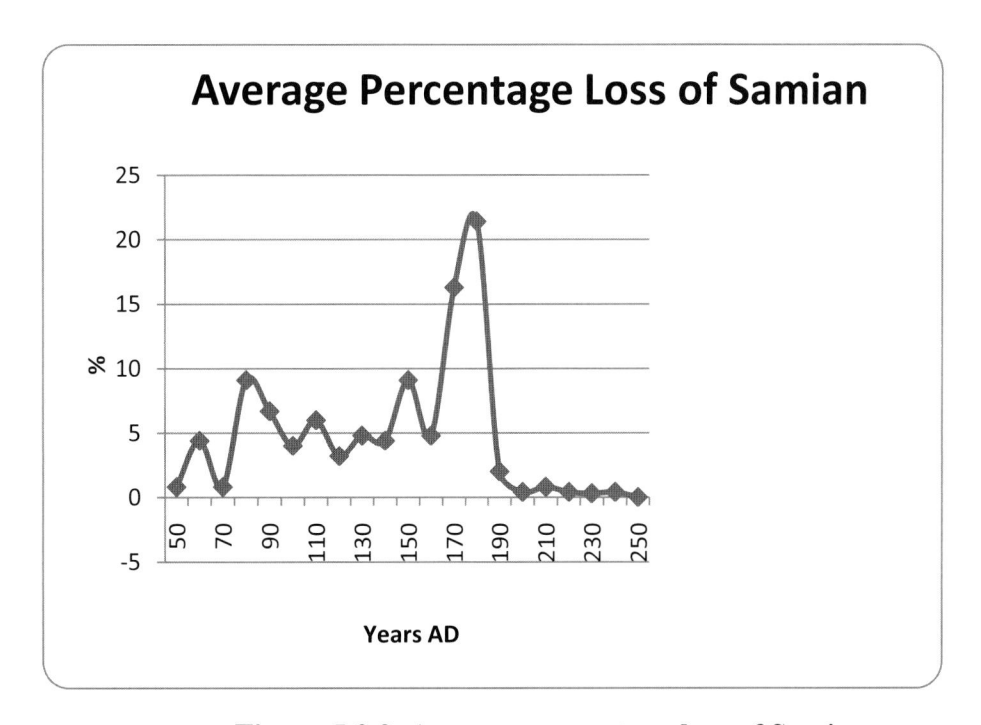

Figure 5.3.2 Average percentage loss of Samian

When the forms are presented as a percentage loss graph it highlights several increases in supply and rapid declines which can be linked to local issues and also to

wider production disruption in Gaul. Supply rises fairly rapidly from about 50 AD to fall sharply about 65
to 70 AD (possibly a reflection of disruption to river trade following the Boudican revolt from 60 AD). La Graufesenque vessels then increase fairly rapidly through AD 70 to 80, beginning to decline in the latter part of the South Gaul production period during the AD 90s. The supply is then fairly rapidly replaced from the Les Martres kilns and the substantial hiatus at this point, which is seen at some other sites, is not present at Yewden – and neither is the disruption in supply due to the production moving to Lezoux from AD 120. There is a small increase in supply from Lezoux *c.* 150 AD, followed by a greatly increased acquisition of Samian forms from the Lezoux mass production workshops between 160-180 AD. The supply chain is then broken as production shifts to East Gaul with relatively little Samian from the eastern kilns arriving at Yewden (despite some London sites such as Shadwell having a large East Gaulish assemblage).

The forms

The full list of forms from Yewden appears in Appendix 4, which is expressed as minimum numbers of vessels so as to include all forms present, including those not represented by any part of a rim or base, and therefore having no EVEs value to carry into statistical analyses.
A total of 42 forms were identified from the whole assemblage. There were 20 different forms from South Gaul, 14 from Les Martres, 28 from Lezoux and 16 from East Gaul. What East Gaul lacks in quantity, it is not lacking in variety (Figures 5.3.3 to 6, and Appendix 4).

The South Gaulish forms show only a small quantity of early forms, arriving from the mid-1st century (from *c.* AD 50-65) with potters such as Modestus adnd Masculus/Aquitanus both supplying DR29s. The majority of the South Gaulish forms are Flavian from La Graufesenque and includes vessels from potters such as Frontinus, Germanus, Tetlo and Mercator, amongst others (Appendix 3). There is a larger quantity of DR37 bowls compared to the DR29s, which are often a popular vessel from South Gaul. This further emphasises the Flavian dominance of the assemblage.

The South Gaul assemblage shows a dominance of the DR27 cups, with the DR36 dishes and the plates (DR18s and, from AD 90, the DR18/31s) almost as common. The late Flavian dishes commonly in assemblages are also present (the Curle 15 and 23, DR42 and DR23), whilst some characteristic early 1st century forms are missing (e.g. the Ritterling 8's or 9's and the DR24/25 cups). Note that some forms are missing from the graph, although present in the assemblage (Appendix 4), as they are not picked up by rim EVEs (e.g. De67, Ritterling 12 and 13).

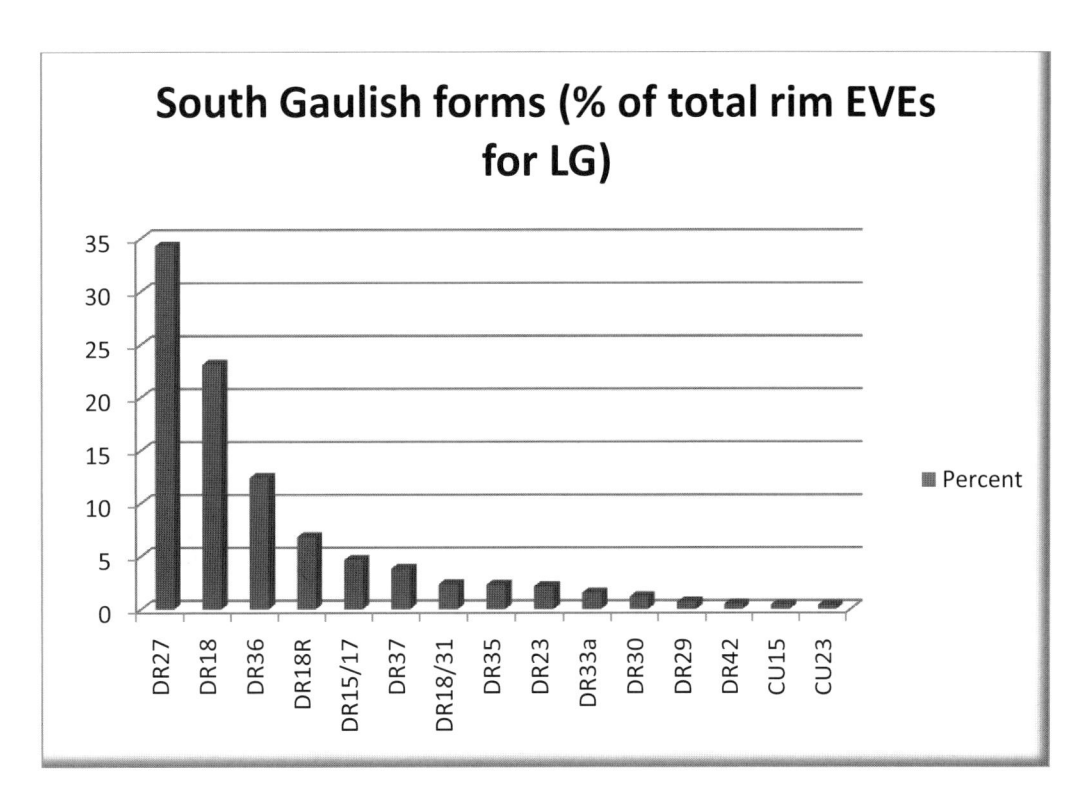

Figure 5.3.3 Forms from La Graufesenque (as percent of total rim EVEs)

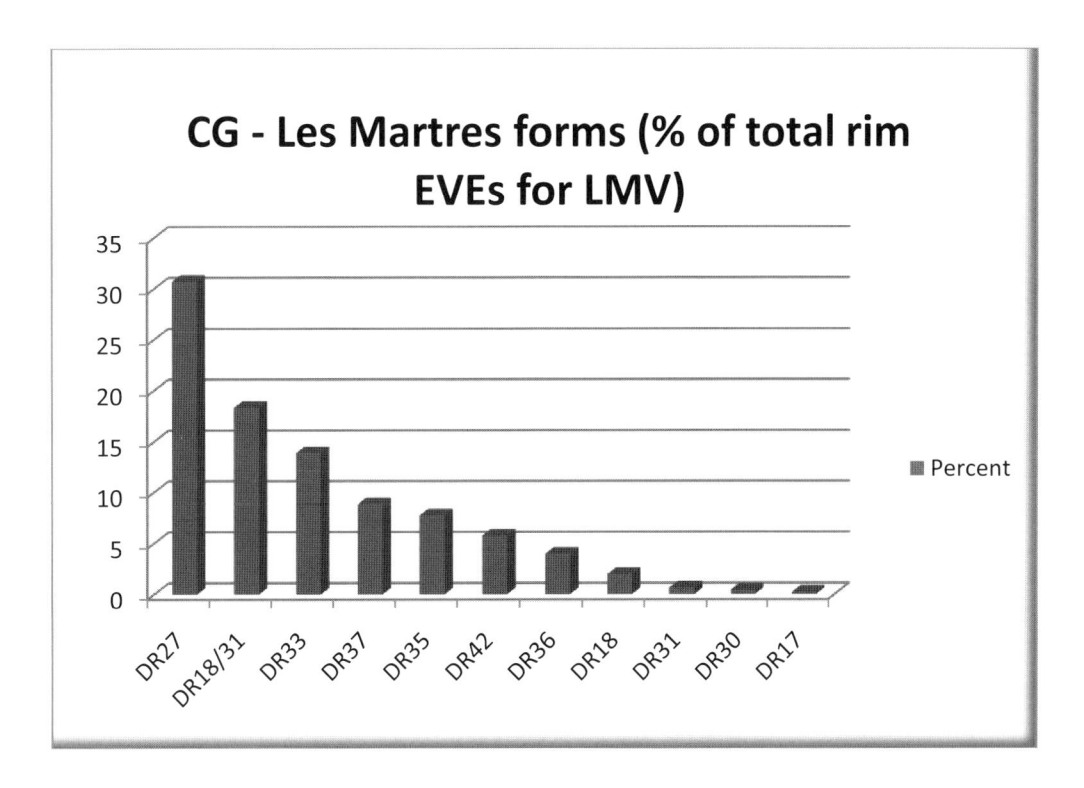

Figure 5.3.4 Forms from Les Martres-de-Veyre (as percent of total rim EVEs)

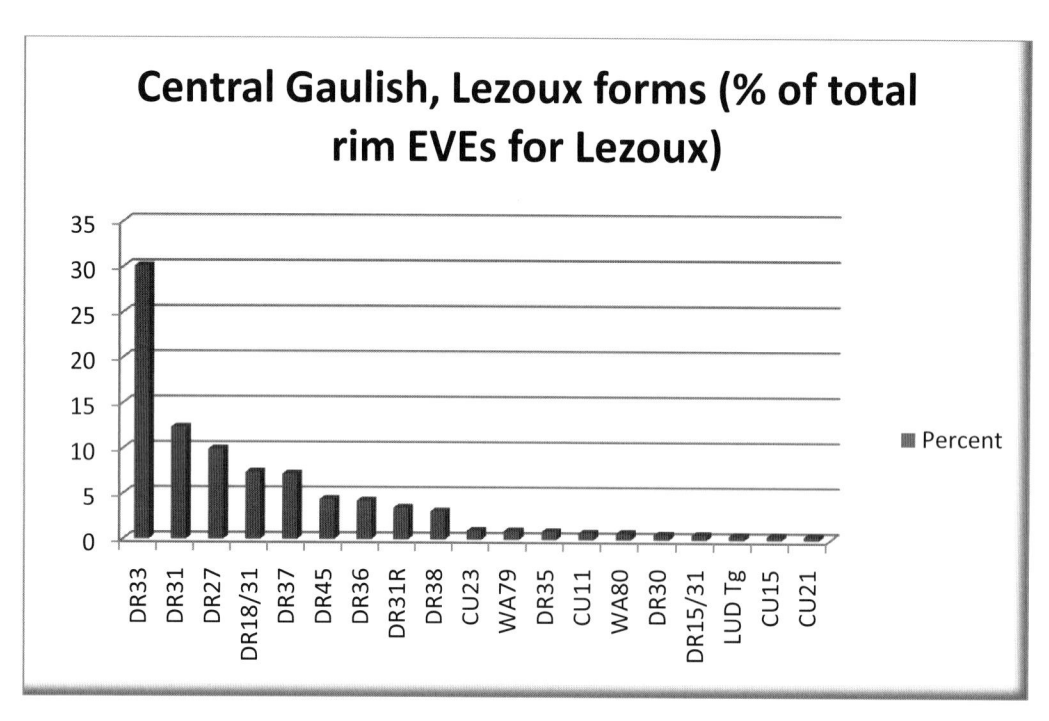

Figure 5.3.5 Forms from Lezoux (as percent of total rim EVEs)

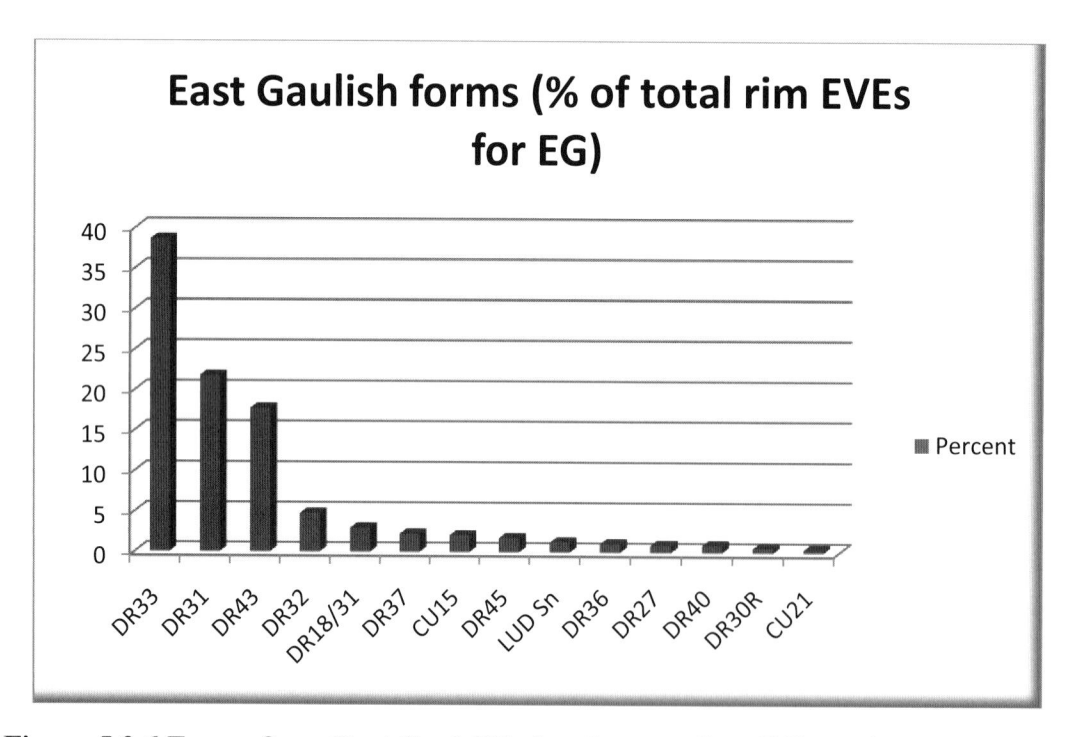

Figure 5.3.6 Forms from East Gaul (Rheinzabern and undifferentiated) as percent rim EVEs

From the Les Martres kilns it is the cups, dishes and decorated DR37 bowls that dominate the assemblage. The popular DR27 and DR33 cups make up 43% of the vessels (by EVEs), followed by the DR18/31. The DR37 bowls are very good quality from LMV and it is therefore not surprising that these proved popular (with a minimum of 14 bowls identified by potter). In fact, all the typical LMV forms are present, except for the Curle 11.

Similar forms remained popular when production switched to Lezoux. For instance, the cups (DR27 and DR33), the DR18/31 plates, and the DR31 bowls comprise more than 50% (by EVEs) of the total vessels. The LudTf and the DR40 cups are not present at Yewden, and neither is the DR81 bowl, all of which are often present in late 2nd century assemblages. It is assumed these are supply differences rather than preferred choice.

The East Gaulish assemblage is dominated by the always popular DR33 cups and the DR31 bowl. These forms, along with the Curle 21, DR43 and DR45 mortaria, as well as the DR32 dish, are all common East Gaulish forms found in southeast England. However, although the quantity of vessels sourced from East Gaul is unusually small, there is a wide variety (a further 10 forms) present in the Yewden assemblage. This includes forms such as the DR27 cup which were only made at a few kilns in East Gaul.

The most popular vessels numerically (looking at the whole Yewden Samian assemblage) are as follows:

Form	Proportion of vessels
DR37	17%
DR33	10%
DR27	8%
DR31 & DR31R	7%
DR18/31 & 18/31R	4%
DR30	4%
DR18 & DR18R	3%
DR36	3%
DR29	2%
DR38	2%
All other forms	<1%

Although some of the variations in the above numbers of vessels is due to chronology, and what was available when supply was high, there is a preference for cups, decorated bowls, and plates/dishes.

The Samian can be divided into the various functional categories (Table 5.3.3) and from this it is clear that decorated bowls and plain cups (notably the DR33s and DR27s) are the most common type of vessel at Yewden. Decorated bowls, when taken as a whole group, show a continued presence on site from the 1st century, through the hiatus of changed production to LMV during AD100-120, and continued in popularity through to the end of the second century. Finally, as production shifts to East Gaul there is a drop off in Samian pottery sourced from this area and the Oxfordshire potteries fill the gap for supply to Yewden.

Functional groupings of forms
The ratio of plain to decorated Samian for the whole assemblage can be calculated:

Decorated	Plain	Mortaria	
53	143	11	vessels
26%	69%	5%	

The data for the proportions of decorated and plain forms, displayed by source areas, is shown in Figure 5.3.7. The proportion of 26% decorated Samian within an assemblage is similar to those recorded for major civil sites in Willis (2005). As a comparison, Willis shows military sites to average at 30% and rural 20%.

Table 5.3.3 Yewden Samian ware as functional categories displayed by source area.

Functional category	South Gaul	LMV	Lezoux	East Gaul	Total
Decorated beakers/jars	1	0	3	1	**5**
Decorated bowls	14	16	17	3	**50**
Plain bowls	1	3	11	5	**20**
Indet, bowls	1	4	4	2	**11**
Dishes	7	3	9	4	**23**
Plates/platters	9	5	10	2	**26**
Cups	13	5	28	7	**53**
Mortaria	0	0	7	4	**11**
Inkwells	1	0	0	0	**1**

(This table displays proportions as minimum vessels in order to compare with the data of others in the next section, where only this data is available.)

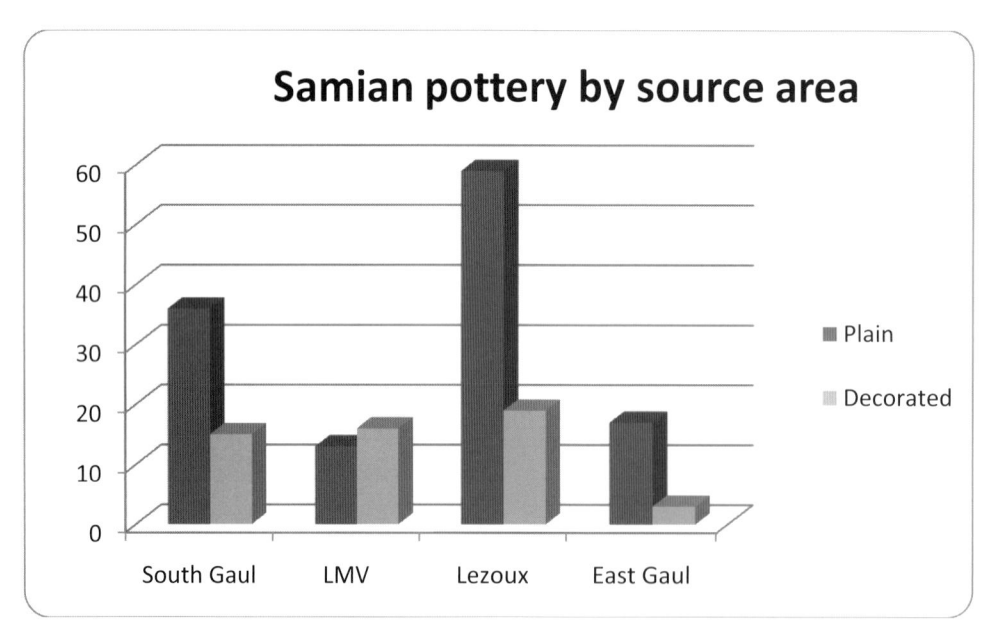

Figure 5.3.7 Percent of plain and decorated Samian for each of the three source areas of: 1. South Gaul (nearly all La Graufesenque); 2. Central Gaul: Les Martres-de-Veyre and Lezoux; and 3. East Gaul (combining all East Gaul kiln sites). The plot uses per cent of minimum vessel count.

Use-wear and repair

For repair to Samian vessels see Chapter 5.6 where a number of rivet types are shown and discussed. The majority of the Samian pottery is in good condition, and the mortaria have not been used for grinding (as the grits show no wear). There are some abraded sherds and unsurprisingly these mostly originate from the yard. Some sherds have been burnt and indicate major events in the villa buildings (as discussed in

Chapter 3). The residuality and post-depositional disturbance may be indicated by three methods (Table 5.3.4 below) which are average sherd size, brokenness and completeness. Brokenness may be calculated by sherd count/vessel equivalent; completeness by vessel equivalent/number of vessels represented.

Table 5.3.4 An assessment of post-depositional processes affecting the Yewden Samian assemblage.

	Average sherd wt (g)	**Brokenness**	**Completeness**
South Gaul (LGF)	7	39	0.34
Les Martres-de-Veyre	11	45	0.12
Lezoux	13	31	0.58
East Gaul	14	37	0.21
Rheinzabern*	197	12	0.14
Yewden, whole site	13	34	0.38

*the high average sherd weight for Rheinzabern is due to one complete and large DR43 mortarium within a relatively small East Gaul assemblage.

Les Martres-de-Veyre vessels are marginally more broken than other fabrics, but overall this assemblage shows that a good proportion show only little post-depositional disturbance. Abrasion is only common on sherds found within the yard.

Comparison of the Samian assemblage to other sites

Proportion of Samian to the whole pottery assemblage

The Samian at Yewden represents 7% of the total pottery assemblage. When compared with other Roman sites, that reveal similar information, it can be seen that this is a high proportion. Latimer and Alchester, for instance, both have pottery assemblages where Samian is *c.* 2.4% of the total pottery recovered. The proportion of Samian within the assemblage at Asthall, which is a small town site, amounts to 5.5%. The largest proportion that could be located in the literature was Colchester (15.8%) which is a busy coastal town site with a major military presence.

% Samian in whole pottery assemblage at various sites:

Site	Samian %	Reference
Yewden	7%	
Latimer	2.4%	Branigan, 1971
Alchester	2.4%	Booth *et al.*, 2001
Asthall	5.5%	Booth, 1997
Colchester	15.8%	Simmons and Wade, 1999

(calculations are % of total sherds)

The type of pottery purchased (decorated pieces, mortaria, a wide variety of cups, plates and dishes, in addition to the inkwell) indicates that, although in a rural location, Yewden villa is a notable wealthy site. In fact it compares in many ways to the vessel proportions of civil centres (Table 5.3.5).

This assemblage represents a significant Samian collection, not least due to the good preservation of the sherds, but also because of a number of almost complete vessels restored by the excavator during post-excavation work from 1912. A number of other Romano-British villa sites are listed below (Table 5.3.6) with which to compare this assemblage. It is difficult to find comparable sites to Yewden, either by virtue of a similar river location (i.e. a main arterial transport route), or within a similar rural location, or as a site with almost total excavation. However, the list of sites serves as a broad comparison of the bulk pottery in terms of the estimated vessel number, or weight, or sherd count (as variously reported in excavation reports). By comparison, the Yewden villa assemblage is rather large.

Table 5.3.5 Comparison of overall relative frequency of the different Samian functional categories at different types of Romano-British sites

Functional category	Yewden	Military*	Major civil site*	Smaller civil site*	Rural*
Decorated beakers/jars	2.4	1.2	1.1	1.0	1.0
Decorated bowls	23.7	27.1	23.3	19.4	21.0
Plain bowls	9.5	3.7	4.9	11.9	3.0
Indet, bowls	5.2	0.6	0.4	0.0	0.3
Dishes & plates/platters	23.2	41.3	38.8	40.4	47.7
Cups	25.1	25.6	30.1	23.7	25.1
Mortaria	5.2	0.1	0.2	2.2	1.0
Inkwells	0.5	0.4	0.4	0.3	0
Total	94.8	99.0	99.1	98.9	99.1

* Data from Willis (2005, Table 45).

Table 5.3.6 Comparative sites with recorded Samian assemblages

Site name (Ref)	Site type	Sherds	Vessels*	Wt (g)	Comments
Yewden, Buckinghamshire	**Villa**	**2664**	**211 (MNV) 79 (EVEs)**	**33549**	**R. Thames**
Alchester, Oxfordshire (1)	Small town	1142	585		Gaggle Brook, close to Akeman Street
Asthall, Oxfordshire (2)	Small town	621		4556	R. Windrush
Bancroft, Milton Keynes (3)	Villa		48 ǂ		Bradwell Brook, close to Watling Street
Colchester, Essex (4)	Town	27,934	915 (EVE)	425939	Major excavation
Crofton, Orpington, Kent (5)	Villa		203		R. Cray
Folly Lane, Verulamium (6)	Ceremonial		50 +		R. Ver
Northfleet (7)	Villa	273	183 (max)	4758	R.Thames
Rye, High Wycombe, Bucks (8)	Villa		16		R. Wye
Saunderton, Bucks (9)	Villa	38			R. Wye

Shakenoak, Oxfordshire (13)	Tributary Evenlode	1202			
Somerford Keynes, Cotswolds (10)	Villa	152	45	1299	
Watkins Farm, Oxfordshire (11)	Villa	35			R.Thames
Wilcote, Oxfordshire (14)	Roadside settlement	1276		11191	Akeman Street
Woughton, Milton Keynes (12)	Villa		101		R. Ouse

Notes:
* It is not always reported how the vessel numbers were estimated; it appears that maximum vessel number is usually reported, which is prone to gross over-estimation and is dependent on how intact the vessels from the assemblage have remained.

‡ Only 48 vessels were described in the excavation monograph for Bancroft, and the site archive is not available.

References: 1.Booth *et al* 2001; 2.Booth, 1977; 3.Williams & Zeepvat, 1994; 4.Symonds & Wade, 1999; 5.Philp, 1996; 6.Niblett, 1999; 7.Ed. Buddulph, pers comm.; 8.Hartley, 1959; 9.Ashcroft, 1939; 10.Brown, internet; 11.Allen, 1990; 12.Marney, 1989; 13.Brodribb *et al*. 2005; 14. Hands, 2004.

Distribution of Samian pottery at Yewden

The distribution of the Samian ware across the Yewden villa site is very informative (Figures 5.3.8 to 5.3.11). It reveals which areas were used as residential and assists in the dating and phasing of the buildings, pits and other areas of the site. The distribution clearly shows the 1st century residence to be within the 3rd House and a concentration of buildings and pits to the north end of the site. The same holds true for the Central Gaulish Samian (Les Martres and Lezoux). However, the East Gaulish pottery, although in lesser quantity, shows a broader spread across the site – occurring in the other buildings such as the 1st, 2nd and 4th Houses of Cocks' plan.

Conclusions

The Samian assemblage shows a supply source from the invasion period, but a significant decline between AD 60 to 70. Significant amounts of Samian arrived at Yewden from South Gaul during the Flavian period (between AD 70 to 80). There is a decline in South Gaulish pottery towards the end of the production period (from *c*. AD 85 to 100). A significant amount of pottery arrives from Les Martres-de-Veyre once the production starts in this part of Central Gaul between AD 100-120. There is only a small drop in supply when Les Martres pottery ceases and the kilns of Lezoux start full production (although only 4 sherds of early micaceous Lezoux occur on site). The largest input of Samian pottery arrives AD 170 to 190 with significant proportions from the large workshops of Cinnamus, Paternus and contemporaries. The pattern of supply at Yewden (in terms of increases and decreases) is comparable to other southeast villas (including urban locations as well). These can be linked to events in broader terms such as changes in the manufacturing areas in Gaul, or more local events such as the Boudican revolt (AD 60). However in terms of the variety and quantity of forms, as well as the high quality of the vessels present within the Yewden assemblage, this site is shown to be rather more than simply a rural villa. The ratio of decorated to plain forms is high and is similar to major civil sites. In addition, the proportion of forms differs to other villa sites - such as the smaller quantity of plates and dishes, but larger amount of bowls, along with the presence of an inkwell and Samian mortaria (which were not used for grinding in a kitchen). This assemblage separates Yewden villa out as being a major site, and a site that is very different to neighbouring Buckinghamshire and Oxfordshire villas.

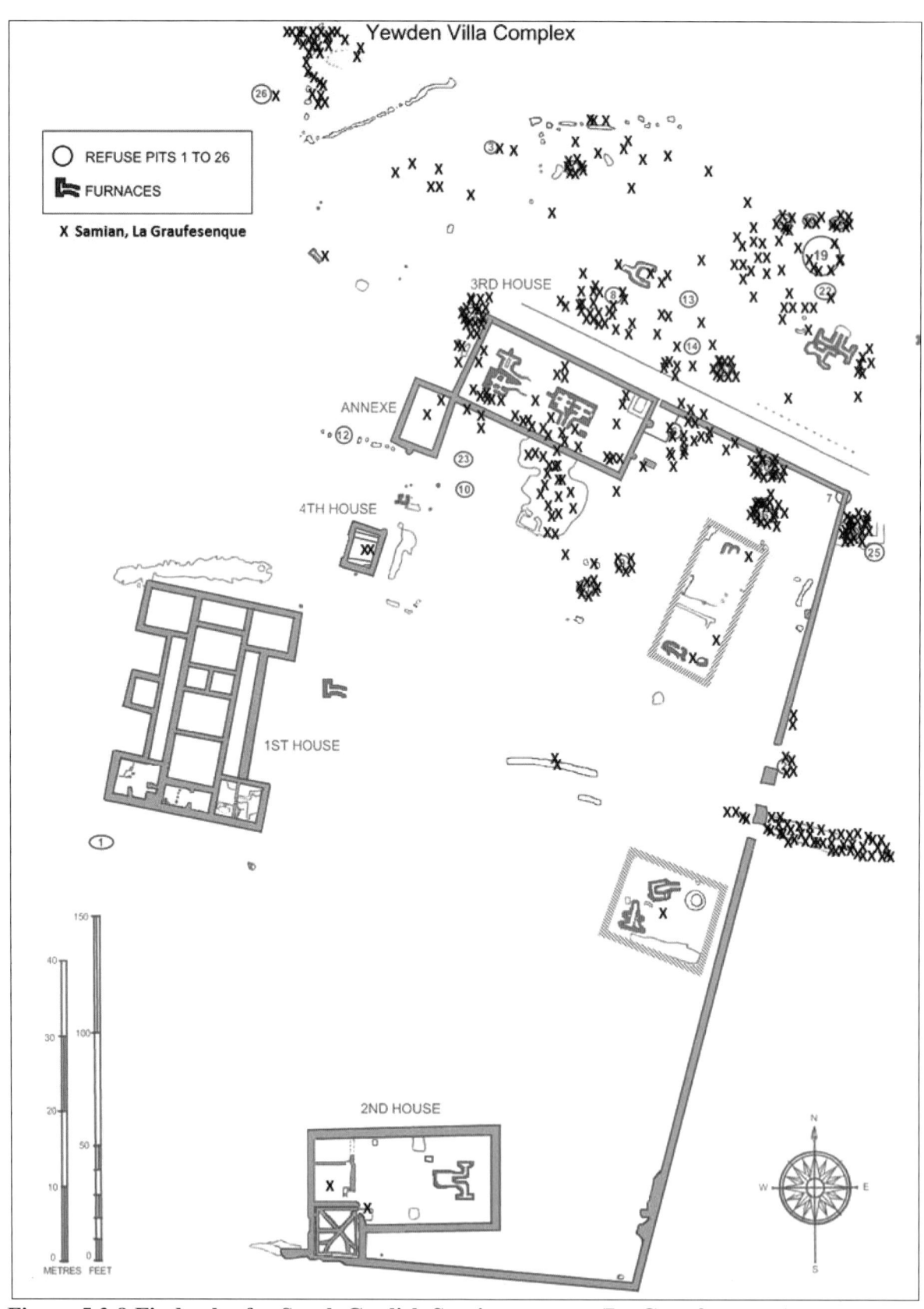

Figure 5.3.8 Finds plot for South Gaulish Samian pottery (La Graufesenque) across the Yewden villa complex

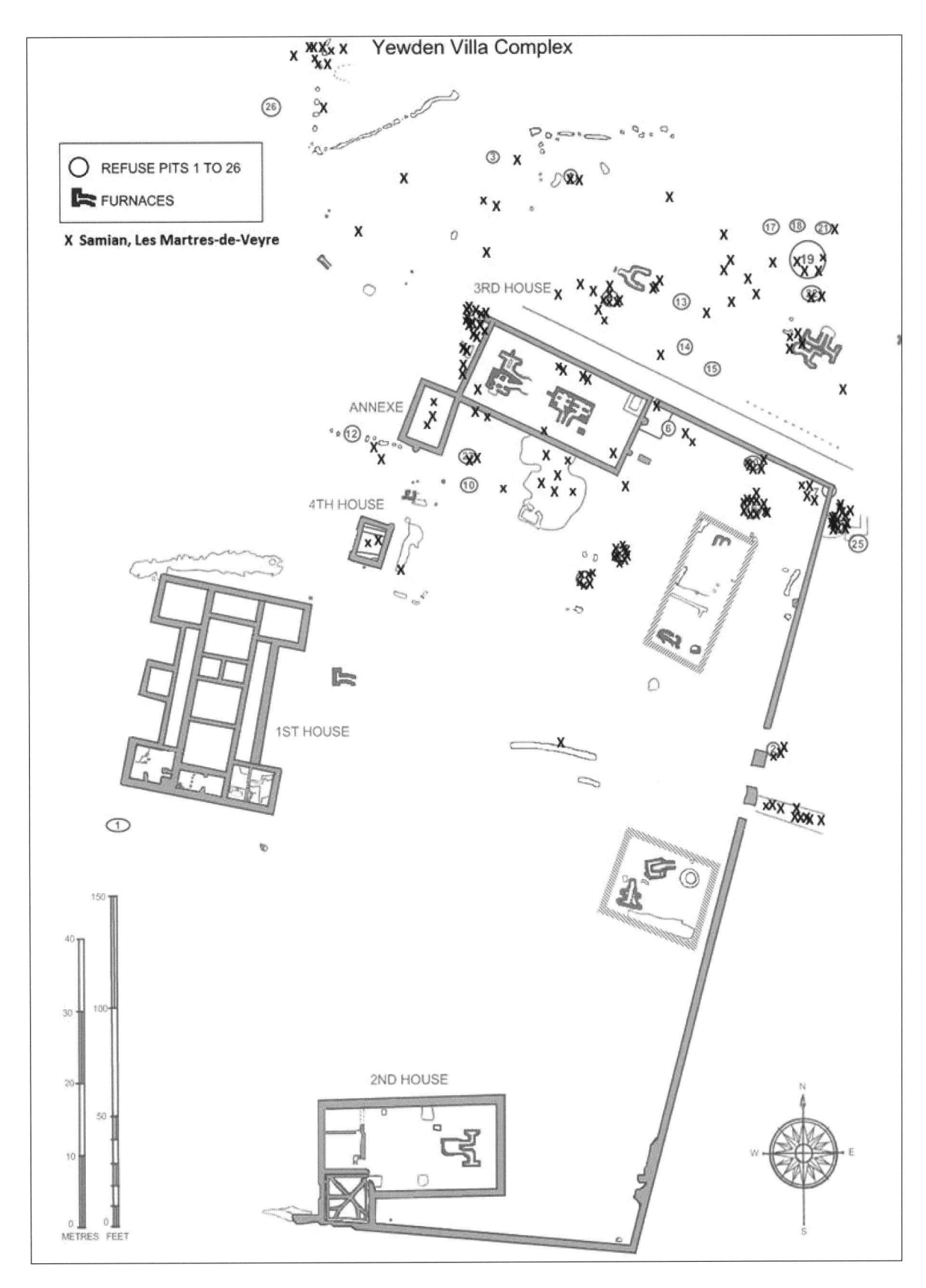

Figure 5.3.9 Finds plot for Les Martres-de-Veyre Samian pottery across Yewden

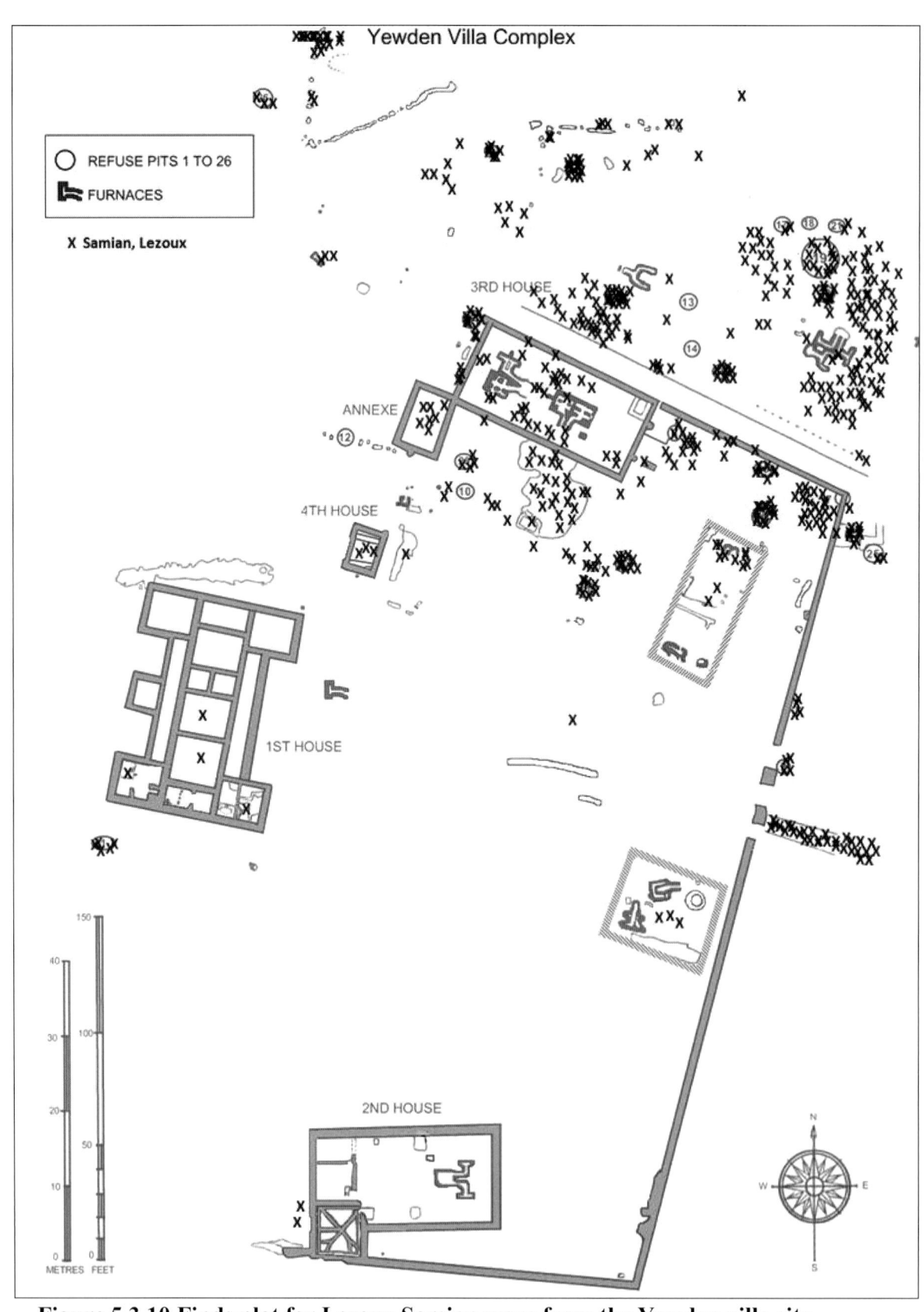

Figure 5.3.10 Finds plot for Lezoux Samian ware from the Yewden villa site

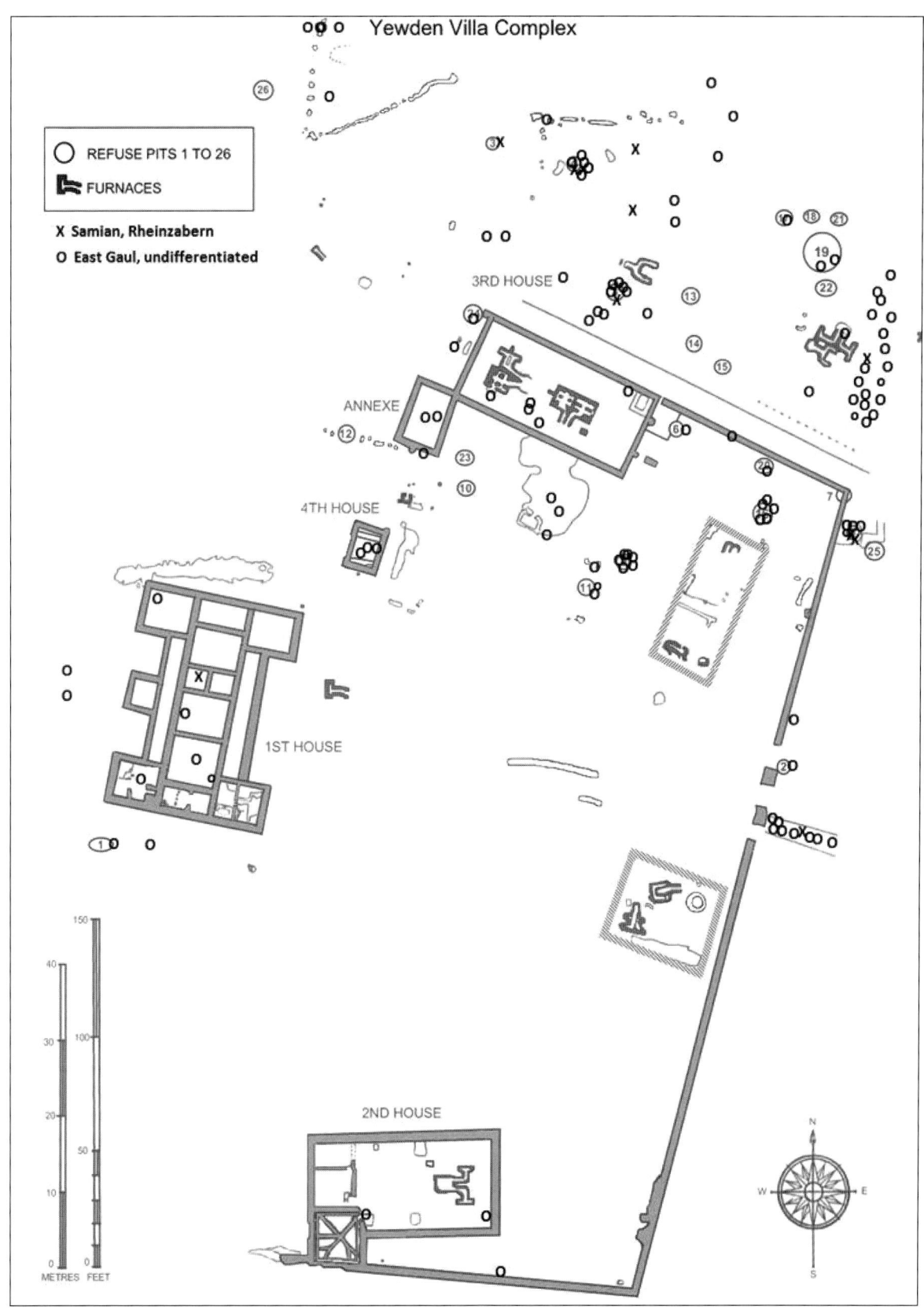

Figure 5.3.11 Finds plot for East Gaulish Samian ware (Rheinzabern and undifferentiated) for the Yewden villa complex.

References

Allen, T. G. 1990. *An Iron Age and Romano-British enclosed settlement at Watkins Farm, Northmoor, Oxon.* Thames Valley Landscape: the Windrush Valley Vol. 1,

Ashcroft, D. 1939. The excavation of a Romano_british villa at Saunderton, Buckinghamshire. *Records of Bucks*, **13(6):** 398-423.

Booth, P. M. 1997. *Asthall, Oxfordshire: excavations in a Roman 'small town', 1992.* Thames Valley Landscapes Monograph No. 9. Oxford Archaeological Unit.

Booth, P. M., Evans, J. And Hiller, J. 2001. *Excavations in the extramural settlement of Roman Alchester, Oxfordshire, 1991.* Oxford Archaeology Monograph No. 1.

Branigan, K. 1971. Latimer: Belgic, Roman, Dark Age and early modern farm. *Proceedings of the Chess Valley Archaeological and Historical Society*, pp. 131-134.

Brodribb, A. C. C, Hands, A. R. And Walker, D. R. 2005. *The Roman Villa at Shakenoak Farm, Oxfordshire. Excaavtions 1960-1976.* BAR British Series **395**.

Brown, Kayt. Somerford Keynes, Neigh Bridge, Finds Report. Downloaded Jan 2011.

Hands, A. R. 2004. *The Romano-British roadside settlement at Wilcote, Oxfordshire III. Excavations 1997-2000.* BAR British Series **370**.

Hartley, B. R. 1959. A Romano-British villa at High Wycombe. *Records of Bucks*, Vol **XVI (4):** 227-257.

Marney, P. T. 1989. *Roman and Belgic pottery from excavations in Milton Keynes 1972-1982.* Buckinghamshire Archaeological Society Monograph Series No.2.

Niblett, R. 1999. *The excavation of a ceremonial site at Folly Lane, Verulamium.* Britannia Monograph Series, No. 14 ,Society for Promotion of Roman Studies.

Philp, B. 1996. *The Roman site at Orpington, Kent.* Seventh Report in the Kent Monograph Series. Kent Archaeological rescue Unit.

Symonds, R. P and Wade, S. 1999. *Roman pottery from excavations in Colchester, 1971-1986.* Colchester Archaeological Report 10.

Williams, R. J. And Zeepvat, R. J. 1994. *Bancroft: a late Bronze Age/Iron Age settlement, Roman villa and temple mausoleum.* Buckinghamshire Archaeological Society Monograph Series No. 7.

Willis, S. 2005. Samian pottery: a resource for the study of Roman Britain and beyond. *Internet Archaeology* **17**. www.intarch.ac.uk

Acknowledgements*: I owe a huge gratitude to Gwladys Monteil who proved an inspiration for work on the Samian pottery and gave so generously of her time. More than half the fabric and form IDs are those of Gwladys' and without her assistance this work could not have been completed. Also, many thanks to John Clutterbuck who assisted with sorting databases and proof-reading, and Lisa Burrup for providing the histograms.*

Chapter 5.4 Samian potters stamps

Jill Eyers and Gwladys Monteil

This catalogue is the complete list of stamps on Samian ware in the BCM Yewden collection from the 1912 excavation. The stamps appear as rubbings or images below unless otherwise specified. There are 47 stamps which are all described here, even if the potter has not yet been identified. The date ranges from the invasion period c. AD 40 to AD 250 as the maximum range, based on the known potter and/or the fabric.

The stamps originate from the following areas

Area:	S. Gaul LGF	C. Gaul Lezoux	C. Gaul LMV	East Gaul
No of stamps	5	34	5	3

Stamps on specimens held at the BCM, Aylesbury or the Technical Centre Halton:

1994.57.2016 Dr38. Whole, restored. Makers name 'PRIVATIM'. **Privatus iii**. Lezoux. AD 160-190

1994.57.2019 Dr31R. Central Gaul, Lezoux. Whole restored. **Illianus**, die 1a. AD 155-180.

1994.57.2022 Dr27. Central Gaul, Lezoux. ALBVCL.OF with AL ligatured, BV ligatured and B retrograde. Die 3a of **Albucius ii**. AD 145-175.

1994.57.2024 Dr33. Central Gaul, Lezoux. ECV.LA.RISF. **Pecularis?** AD 160-170.

Figure 5.4.1 Stamps of Privatus iii (left) and Albucius ii (right).

For a full list of named Samian potters from Yewden (by stamp and decoration) see Appendix 3.

Figure 5.4.2 Stamp of Peculiaris

Stamp list of specimens held at the museum stores, in BCM number order, all of which are prefixed with '1994.57.P.____'

7   Dr37 bowl. Repaired. East Gaul. Mould maker = REP

11   DR31R base. ('Pseudo-Samian' of Cocks 1921). Bowl base. East Gaul? Illiterate stamp AD160-250.

57   Dr33 conical cup. Central Gaul Lezoux. *NIM. AD 120-200.

58   Dr33 conical cup. Central Gaul, Lezoux *VN. AD120-200

59   Dr27g cup. South Gaul, LGF. 'OFPONTI'. **Pontus** AD 65-90.

62   Dr33 conical cup. Central Gaul, Lezoux. *SF. Not illustrated. AD120-200.

64   Dr33 conical cup. Central Gaul, Lezoux. *S. AD 120-200.

100   Dr33 conical cup. Central Gaul, Lezoux. *M*. AD 120-200.

102   Dr33 conical cup. Central Gaul, Lezoux. LITTERAF. **Littera i.** AD120-150.

174   Dr31R dish. Central Gaul, Lezoux *IM. AD 150-200.

720   Dr33 conical cup. Central Gaul, Lezoux. *VSMIM. **Cinstumus i**. AD140-180.

874   Dr27 cup. South Gaul, LGF. Partial. Not illustrated. AD 40-100.

1032   Dr27 cup. Central Gaul, Lezoux. CUCANI? And Graffiti 'R' on other side. **Cucullus**. AD 140-170.

1033   Dr18R plate. South Gaul, LGF. OFRONT*. **Frontinus**. AD 70-95.

1040   Dr18/31 plate. Central Gaul, Les Martres-de-Veyre. *LOSFE. **Paterclus ii**. Not illustrated. AD 110-120

1059   Dr27 cup. Central Gaul, Lezoux. CIRR, **Cirrus i.** AD 130-160.

1060   Dr33 conical cup. Central Gaul, Lezoux. TEDDIL.F. **Tedillus**. AD 125-160.

1061 Dr33 conical cup. Central Gaul, Lezoux. CROBISOM (Maker = **Crobiso**) AD 135-165.

1062 Dr33 conical cup. Lezoux. REBVRRI. **Reburrus ii.** AD 145-170.

1063 Dr33 conical cup. Central Gaul, Lezoux. MVXTVIIIM. **Muxtullus**. AD 140-175.
Not illustrated.

1066 Dr31 dish. Central Gaul, Lezoux. VIM*. **Vertecissa**. AD150-170.

1067 Dr18/31 dish. Central Gaul, Lezoux. DIVICATVS. **Divicatus**. AD 135-165

1121 Dr27 cup. Central Gaul, Lezoux. *VLIM. **Paullus iv**. AD120-180.

1151 Dr27. Central Gaul, LMV. OF*. Not illustrated. AD 100-120.

1209 Lezoux sherd. 8-petal flower. A stamp on a plain vessel (used instead of potter's stamp). Antonine, *c*. AD 150-190.

1210 South Gaul, LGF. *SF. AD 40-100

1211 Dr33 conical cup. Central Gaul, Lezoux. LLIN.X. AD 120-200.

1212 Dr33 conical cup. East Gaul IV_A? **?Lullius viii**. AD 150-250.

1225 Dr31R dish. Central Gaul, Lezoux. *IMA. AD120-200.

1235 Dish. Central Gaul, Lezoux. Triple circle. AD 120-200.

1236 Dr18/31 plate. Central Gaul, Lezoux. *M. AD 120-150.

1240 Dr27? cup. Central Gaul, Lezoux. Single ring. AD 120-200.

1245 Dr18/31? Plate. Central Gaul, LMV. *F. AD 100-120.

1246 Dr31R plate. Central Gaul, Lezoux. *IMPVS. AD 150-200.

1247 Dr33 conical cup base. Central Gaul, Lezoux. VES*. **Vespo.** AD 120-200. Not illustrated.

1265 Dr27 cup. Central Gaul, Lezoux. BICAIII. **Biga**. AD 125-150

1267 Plate base, possibly WA79. Central Gaul, Lezoux. INVI*. AD 120-200.

1268 Dr18/31 plate. LMV, Central Gaul. VIDVCVSF. **Viducus ii.** AD 100-120.

1675 Central Gaul, LMV. Two stamps: 1 illiterate, 1 faint and retrograde. Not illustrated. AD 100-120.

1676 South Gaul, LGF. Three sherds (not illustrated):

*IMI or *IIVII dish. AD 40-100
OF* AD 40-100
*VIM AD 40-100

1773   WA79 plate. Central Gaul, Lezoux. AETE* (in reverse). **Aeternus**
AD 155-180.

1774   Dr33 cup. C. Gaul, Lezoux. Makers mark = *.IM. Not illustrated. AD120-200

1775   Dr37. Central Gaul, Lezoux. *DVOCI* **Advocisus**. AD 160-180

(LMV = Les Martres-de-Veyre; LGF = La Graufesenque)

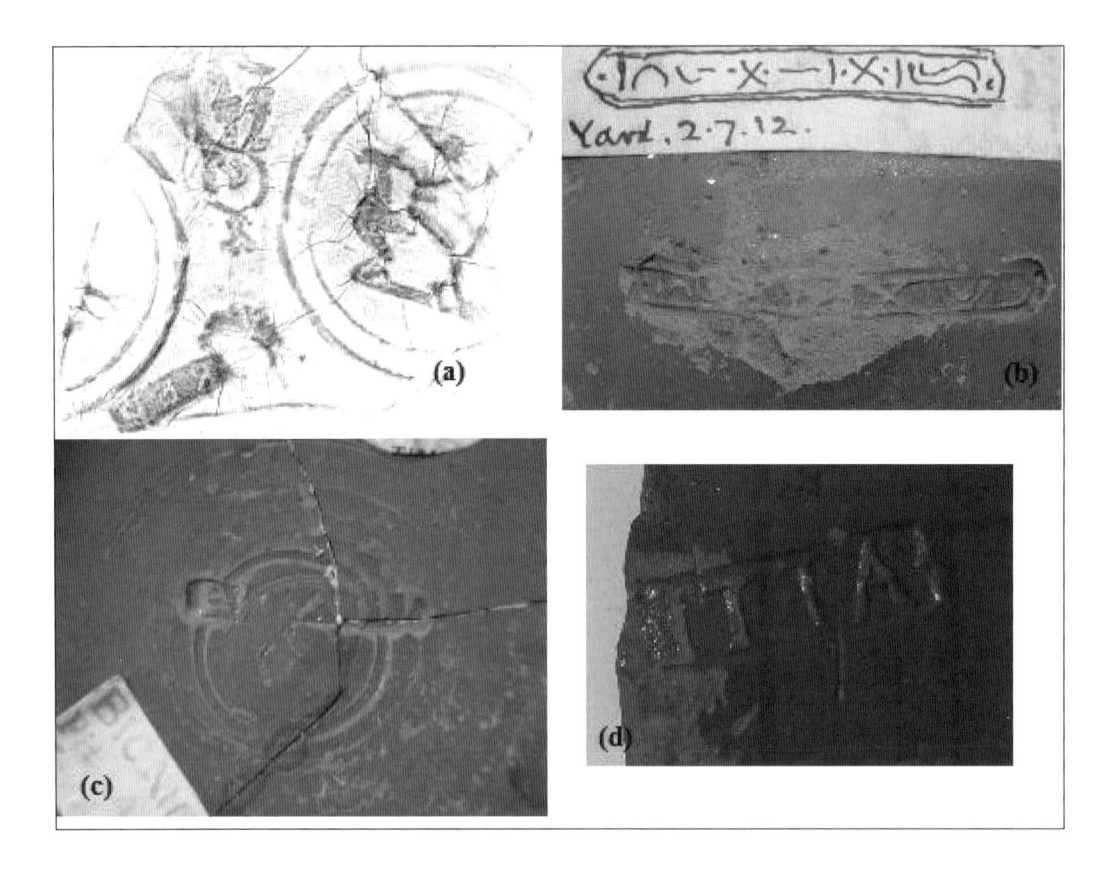

Figure 5.4.3 (a) Mould mark, in reverse (P.7) REP on decorated sherd; (b) illiterate stamp (P.11); (c) Lezoux potter BIGA (P.1265); (d) Aeternus (P.1773).

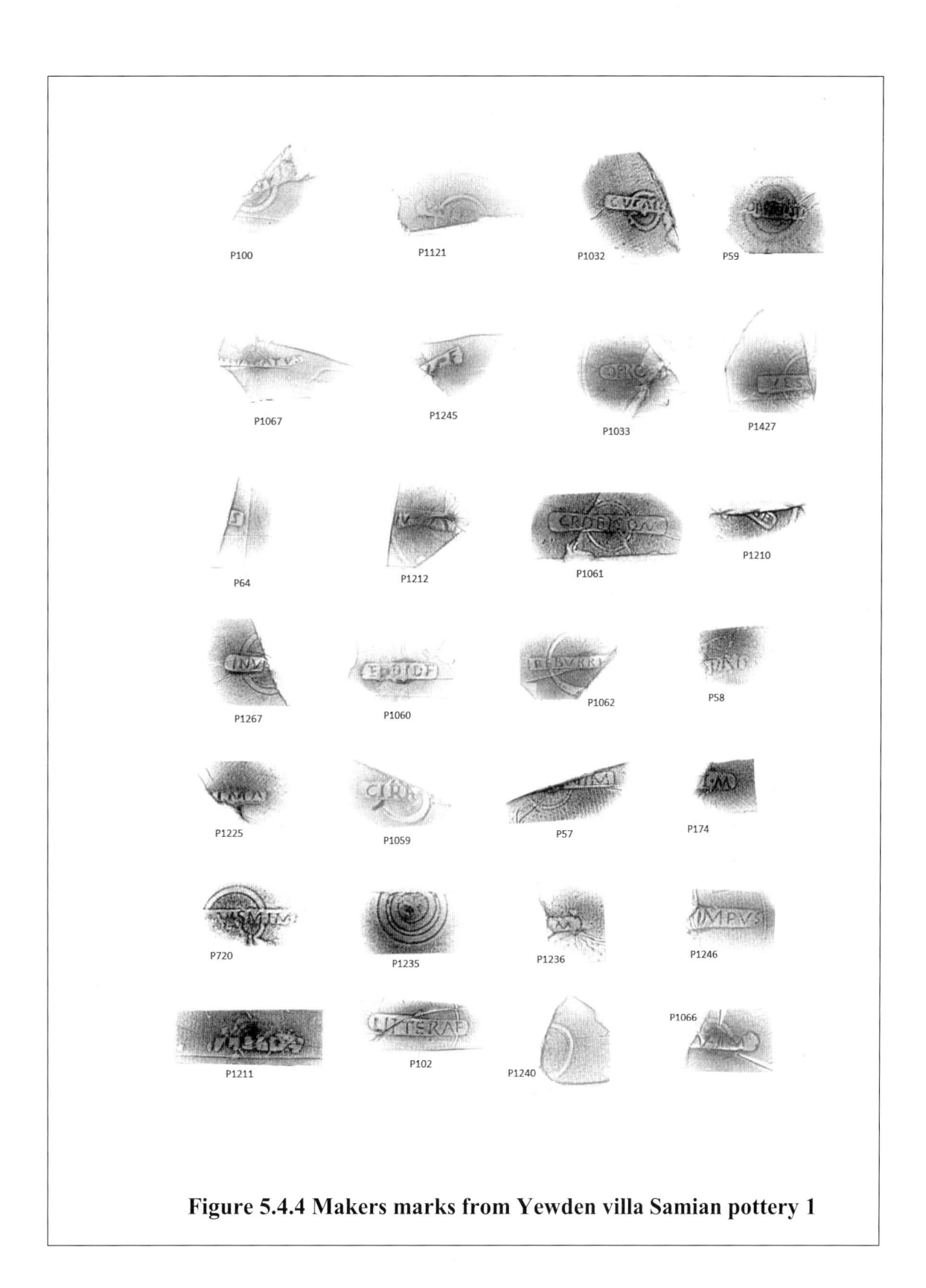

Figure 5.4.4 Makers marks from Yewden villa Samian pottery 1

Figure 5.4.4 Makers stamps from Yewden (continued) 2

Chapter 5.5 Decorated Samian

Jill Eyers

The catalogue of decorated Samian pottery from Yewden villa is presented below in BCM number order (whole vessels from the 1912 excavation start with BCM number 1994.57 and are held at Halton, those sorted and identified within the 2008 to 2010 project start with 1994.57.P…).

Abbreviations:
MON	Montans
LGF	La Graufesenque
LMV	Les Martres-de-Veyre
LEZ	Lezoux
EG	East Gaul
BM	British Museum
BCM	Buckinghamshire County Museum
Dr	Dragendorff
Dech	Déchelette

Figure Types:

O. F. Oswald, *Index of Figure Types on Terra Sigillata*, University of Liverpool Annals of Archaeology & Anthropology, Supplement, 1936-37

Decorative Motifs:

Hermet 1934	Hermet, F. 1934. *La Graufesenque*. Vols I & II. Condatomago, Paris.
Knorr 1919	R. Knorr, *Töpfer und Fabriken verzierter Terra Sigillata des ersten Jahrhunderts*, Stuttgart.
Mees 1995	A.W. Mees, *Modelsignierte Dekorationen auf südgallischer Terra Sigillata*, Forschungen und Berichte zur Vor- und Frühgeschichte in Baden-Württemberg, Band 54, Stuttgart.
Ricken 1948	H. Ricken, *Die Bilderschüsseln der romischen Töpfer von Rheinzabern (Tafelband)*, Speyer.
Rogers	G.B. Rogers, *Poteries Sigillées de la Gaule Centrale I: les motifs non figurés*, Gallia Supplement 28, 1974 (though after the first one or two examples, I have just put the number)
RF	H. Ricken and C. Fischer, *Die Bilderschüsseln der römischen Töpfer von Rheinzabern (Textband)*, Bonn, 1963 (Rheinzabern types and motifs. Companion piece to Ricken 1948 (see end))
S&S	Stanfield, J. A. and Simpson, G. 1958. Central Gaulish potters. Oxford University Press.

For a full list of named Samian potters from Yewden (by stamp and decoration) see Appendix 3.

1994.57.2017
LEZ Dr37 whole vessel (restored)
Censorinus has used almost all the motifs and figures shown in this vessel including the horizontal astralagus border which is typical of his work. However the ovolo are not those of Censorinus. The double bordered slightly squared ovolo with beaded tongue is attributed to **Atilianus** and **Priscus I** (Rogers B.95, although Rogers' sherds were not stamped). Vertical beaded borders, double ridged medallions, small circles and 8-petal flowers, plus the tripod (Rogers Q7) with a male head base are the style of **Censorinus** (S&S 1958). Censorinus also used the Apollo with branch (O.92), the medallion with rosette (Rogers C6), the seated Venus (O.334) on sherds (a) and (d) and Victory (O.812). Censorinus also used a seated Apollo (O.84) which was smaller than that seen on this vessel. A seated Apollo (O.83). A stamped sherd of **Atilianus** shows O.83 with a broken foot (as here) in Rogers 1999, Fig. 7.1. Sherds ibid. Fig. 7.5 and 7.3) show the same ovolo (B95) and the same tripod (Q7) as this Yewden bowl.

It is concluded therefore that that as these potters are all contemporaries in the Paternus Group that they may have copied or borrowed motifs from each other and hence, the bowl is attributable only to the **Paternus Group**, AD 160-200.

Figure 5.5.1 Dr 37 bowl, restored. Paternus Group, Lezoux.

1994.57.2018
LEZ Dr37 whole vessel (restored)
The decoration is a repeating panel of figures comprising a stag (O.1704A), a crouched male figure with club (O.605) and a female figure O.281 The crouched figure is of a style used between the Trajan and Antonine periods, as is the female figure. The stag is Trajan-Hadrianic. The stag is within a single plain line festoon with astragales. The beading (horizontal and vertical from the astragales) and the ovolo style are not diagnostic. Trajan-Hadrian AD 120-170.

Figure 5.5.2 Dr37 bowl restored. Lezoux, Trajan-Hadrian

The numbers below all have a prefix of '**1994.57.P**' on the BCM main database.

3 a, b
LGF   Dr37   4g
Leaf and frond within diagonal borders. In the style of **M. Crestio/Mercator** (Symonds and Wade 1990 (No.277), although not necessarily these potters as the ovolo and motifs on No. 277 are not the same. The saltire decoration was very common in the Flavian period, *c*. AD 80-100.

5 a, b
LGF   Dr29   17g
Vine scroll in the style of **Masclus/Aquitanus?** (Dannell, 1999, p.60, No.408), this is a common form of decoration for the period, hence potter not certain. AD 50-65.

7a
EG   Dr37   46g
Double ridged medallions enclosing figures. The style and stamp decoration is like that of **Comitialis IV** (Bird, 1999, p.116, No.1217), with mould maker's stamp **REP**. Apollo (O.84, RF M72), trophy (RF O160). An almost identical bowl is from Rheinzabern (Ricken 1948, Taf. 90, 14). Same bowl as 7b. Later 2nd – early 3rd century AD.

7b
EG   Dr37   6g
Partial figure within double ridged medallion. **Comitialis IV** workshop? (as for 7a). Medallion with Apollo (O.84). Same bowl as 7a. Later 2nd – early 3rd century AD.

9a, b and c
LEZ   Dr37 bowl   76g
Cinnamus. Ovolo 3. Vertical beading divisions. Double ridged medallions alternating with double ridged festoons. Figures within medallions and between beaded border

1105
LMV   Dr37   15g
Acanthus (Rogers K2) and cornucopiae motif as used by **X.13** (S&S pl. 47, 557). Probably his ovolo (Rogers B7) and row of trifid buds (Rogers G171?) and part of Hercules fighting the snakes. Paler than usual fabric for LMV. AD 100-120.

1106
LGF   Dr30 bowl   5g
Leaping dog (O.2004) within closely spaced wavy line borders, and trident tongued ovolo, possibly of **M. Crestio** (but no evidence for M Crestio using the dog motif). AD 80-100.

1107
LEZ   Dr30 bowl   5g
Saltire with bird. The **Quintilianus** group used saltires like this (S&S pl. 71, 29) and also the bud (Rogers G18). Probably their bird (O.2299) in the lower compartment. AD 125-145.

1108
LEZ   Dr37   7g
Ovolo with beaded lines. **Cinnamus** ovolo 2 (Rogers B231). AD 150-180.

1110
LEZ   Dr37 bowl   89g
Double ridged medallions – one with standing figure with one foot resting on square block (Vulcan, O.66); one with panther running to right (O.1518). Figures and decorative style of **Cinnamus** (S&S, Plates 159, 160, and 161). AD 150-180.

1111
LMV   Dr37   13g
Running figure (satyr O.591). **Drusus** (Potter X.3, S&S 1958, Plate 15, No.190). AD 100-120.

1112
LEZ   Bowl sherd   8g
'Holly' leaf similar in style to **Cinnamus'** (Rogers J93). AD. 150-180.

1113
LMV   Dr37   19g
Basal line of circles within panel. **Ioenalis** and **X-13** both used this ornament (S&S 1958). AD 100-120.

1114a and b
LEZ   Dr37 bowl   8g
Part of leaf, beaded line and stylized dolphin (type uncertain) within double ridged medallion. (a) Leaf (H96) as on 1117, **X9** style, AD 120-135.

1115a, b, c and d
LMV   20g
Floral, medallions and wavy lines decoration. (a) Vertical wavy line with standing nude figure to the right with hands clasped in front; (b) Leaf (J127) in saltire common in the style of the **Rosette Potter** (*cf.* S&S pl. 20, 250 & 252) with wreath of buds

(Rogers G169) below? AD100-120. (c),(d) insufficient detail to determine, different potter.

1117
LMV Dr30 23g
X.9 (Medetus-Ranto) style of floral decoration with 'twist' portions (leaf H96), wavy lines, ovolo (Rogers B38, and ovolo 1 of S&S 1958, Fig. 9; and Plate 32). AD 110-130.

1118
LGF Dr29 3g
Block fill of leaf tips and wavy diagonal lines. Flavian design. AD 70-96.

1119
LGF Dr29 10g
Gadroon with alternating twists and loops. **Maponus** (Polak, 2000, Plate 39). AD 60-80.
(Form 29 ceases to be made *c*. AD 85.)

1120
LMV Dr37 46g
Gladiator fighting panther and decorative detail: shield (U209), bud (G112), astragalus (R91), panther (O.1518), warrior (O.218). All decorative detail first used by Drusus, Potter X.3 of LMV. But Potter X.3 does not use wavy line decoration hence this is likely to be a related potter, **Geminus** (S&S's G.I. Vibius or Gelenus, p.13) who used the same decorative details, warrior and similar panther, cf. S&S pl. 65 for most of the types and details. Geminus worked at LMV *c*.AD 110-130, at Lezoux *c*.AD 125-145. This is LMV fabric hence the date of this sherd is AD 110-130.

1122
LMV Dr37 16g
Decoration with single line festoon interspaced with figure (Hercules O.753) between zigzag line divisions. Ovolo B40. Style of **X9** (Ranto, S&S pl. 34, 402). AD 110-130

1123
LMV Dr37 18g
Female figure (dancer O.363). Ovolo (B56) and decoration in the style of **X.11** (Ioenalis of S&S 1958, Plate 36, No's 422, and 426, and Plate 38). AD 100-120.

1124
LMV Dr37 bowl 8g
Ovolo (probably B7) used by **X13**. AD100-125.

1127 a, b
LEZ Dr37 bowl 32g
(a) Ovolo B28, used at Lezoux by the **Quintilianus** group AD 125-145
(b) Ovolo, dot beading and double ridged medallion. AD 120-200.

1128
LGF Dr37 bowl 6g
Hercules fighting snakes (O.786) (decoration same as P.1104). **Mercator** AD 80-100

1129
LEZ   Dr37 bowl   7g
Line of ovolo, circle stamp, and figure. The decoration suggests that this is the same bowl as 1102. Style typical of Trajanic or Hadrianic period, hence AD 120-138.

1140
LEZ   3g
Double ridge medallion fragment found at same level as 'TV' maker's mark sherd, **Muxtullus**. AD 150-180.

1162a
LEZ   Dr37   7g
Double ridged medallion. Abundance (O.809) used by Cinnamus (and others). **?Cinnamus** AD 150-180.

1162b
LEZ   Dr37   19g
Figures (erotic group) within double ridged medallion, with edge of large leaf (J1) below. In style of **Cinnamus**. AD 150-180.

1162c
LEZ   Dr37   20g
Ovolo with straight plain tongue, dot beaded horizontal line and large leaf below in style of Cinnamus. The ovolo is probably B144 (with beaded tongue) rather than B143 (with diagonal lines across tongue). B144 typical of **Cerialis** - early Cinnamus, AD 135-160.

1198
LEZ   Dr30 bowl   45g
Foot ring of type E (Webster, 1996). Hind (O.1743) used by Cinnamus and others (e.g. S&S 1958, Plate 163, No.74). The wreath medallion is in the style of **Cinnamus**, but the bead rows are not. Antonine, *c.* AD 150-180.

1199
LGF   Dr29   32g
Part of saltire with twist. Early Dr29A (Webster, 1996) *c.* 50-70 AD.

1200
LGF   Dr29   18g
Floral design. Distinct leaf shape of **Mercator** as seen on the Great St Helen's bowl, London, BM). Date also confirmed by Webster 1996; Symonds & Wade 1990. AD 70-85.

1204
LEZ   Dr37 bowl   11g
Wreath medallion (Rogers E16?) and dot beading in the style of **Cinnamus** and **Pugnus**. Hadrianic or Antonine, *c.* AD 150-195.

1206
LGF   Dr 29   8g
Boar (O.1670). AD 70-85.

1284
LGF   Dr29 bowl   9g
Floral scroll and bird of **Modestus** (Dannell, 1999, p.63, No.444). Same as 1285j. AD 50-65.

1285 a, b, c, d, h, i, and j
LGF   Dr29 bowl and 1 sherd Dr30?   35g
Floral design with tendrils. (a) Stirrup leaves in scroll and (j) leaf and bird as 1284, both **Modestus** (Dannell, 1999, p.63, No.444). AD 50-65. Sherd (f) has an ovolo and may be a Dr30. Remaining sherds including further floral designs, leaf tip fillers, wavy diagonal lines, a festoon and pendant are also **Modestus?** AD 50-65.

1286 a, b, c
LGF Dr30 bowl   17g
(a) Floral with edge of a wreathed medallion. Flavian. AD 69-100.
(b) the ovolo and corner tendril are on a bowl signed by **Vitalis** (Mees 1995, Taf. 197, 2) AD 75-95.
(c) a known, but anonymous, South Gaul ovolo, likely to be Flavian, AD 69-100.

1287 a, b
LGF   Dr37 bowl   8g
Ovolo with floral, wavy lines and leaf tip 'filler' decoration. The ovolo on (b) was used by **Memor, Mommo** and **Tetlo.** (The ovolo on (a) appears smaller, but appears to be the same.) A bowl (form 30) from Binchester with a signature of **Tetlo** shows the ovolo and saltire with the same bud. AD 70-90.

1288a
LGF   Dr30   3g
Floral design with ovolo. Tree of the same general type as used by **Germanus** (Mees 1995, Taf. 72), ovolo not known. AD 75-100

1288b
LGF   Dr30   8g
Lion running to the left, as used by **Germanus** (Mees 1995, Taf. 72). Ovolo not known. AD 70-100.

1289
LGF Dr37 bowl   16g
Running figure and floral decoration. **Germanus'** vine and figure on stylised rock (Mees 1995, Taf. 73, 1). AD 70-90.

1290
LGF   Dech 67?   7g
Rear end of running dog, curly tail. Flavian. AD 70-100

1292
LEZ   Bowl sherd   4g
Floral with vertical wavy lines. Trifid buds cf **Quintilianus** (S&S pl. 70. Rogers 1999 pl. 92, 4 shows a vertical row) *c.*AD 125-145.

1293 a, b
LGF   Dr37? Bowl sherds   35g

Floral design, with bud, with part medallion visible, block infill spacers, and S-shaped gadroons at base. The bud was used by **Frontinus, Iucundus** and **Meddillus** (Knorr 1919, Textb. 12). S-shaped gadroons are very common, and certainly used by **Frontinus**. Probably AD 80-100.

1295
LGF   Dech 65 or 67 beaker   6g

Floral. AD70-100.

1299
LMV   Dr37 bowl   77g

Basal wreath of dotted circles. Scroll with spiraled lines of decorative style of **Drusus** (Potter X.3 of S&S 1958, Fig. 4 and Plates 12 and 13). AD 100-120.

1300
LEZ   Dr37 bowl   31g

Part of floral design and decorative detail of **Cinnamus** (S&S 1958, Fig 47 and Plates 161 and 162). AD 150-180.

1301
LMV   Dr37 bowl   45g

Figures and decorative beading. Apollo (O.77) and women conversing (O.970) were both used by **Libertus** and **Butrio**. The (beaded?) point is not known. Probably Trajanic or Hadrianic. (Libertus AD 100-120, Butrio AD 120-140).

1302
LEZ   Dr37 bowl   69g

Lion devouring boar (O.1491) and stag (O.1781). **Cerialis-early Cinnamus** style. AD 135-160.

1303
EG   Dr37 bowl   37g

Warrior (O.230), first used by **Satto** at Chémery (though this is not his style), and later on **Ianus'** style at Heiligenberg and on Ianus' and other styles at Rheinzabern. Multiple ridges like this occur below the decoration on some Ianus style bowls from Rheinzabern (Ricken 1948, Taf. 8-9. Also the warrior on Taf. 8, 1). Antonine *c.*AD 140-190.

1304 a, b
LGF   19g

(a) Trident-tongued ovolo and saltire typical of the period AD 80-100. Only a) is figured.

1305
LMV   Dr37 Bowl   8g

Foot of standing figure with tendrils in small spirals & dotted basal border line in the decorative style of **Drusus** (X.3 of S&S 1958, Plate 14, No's 175, 178). AD 100-120.

1308a
LMV   Bowl sherd   9g
Beaded circles (C294) in basal wreath. **Drusus** (Potter X.3 of S&S 1958). AD 100-120.

1308b
LEZ   Bowl sherd   6g
Row of the twist motif (U103). X11 and X13 both use this motif, but not in vertical rows (see 1468 below, which is X11 style). A potter who does use it in vertical rows is Rogers' **Paternus III**, *cf.* Rogers 1999, pl. 80, AD 135-165.

1309 a, b
LMV   Dr37 bowl   13g
Neither sherd (a) or (b) is typical LMV fabric, but the decoration indicates an LMV source.
(a) Horizontal line of plain circles (as ovolo replacement) with wavy line beneath and a leaf (J33) which was used by **Pugnus** (S&S, 1958, Fig.45 and Plate 153, No.7), by **X5** and **X10** (although none of these appear to use a line of circles as a border). The circle ovolo replacement was used by **X11** and **X13** (Donnaucus and Ioenalis of S&S pl. 37, 429, also with a wavy-line border). AD 100-125.
(b) Rosettes (Rogers C293) and foot of a standing figure above, of the type used by the 'Donnaucus-Ioenalis' group (X11, X13). AD 100-125.

1310a, b and c
LMV   24g
Square and rectangular decoration within wavy lines. AD 100-120.

1311
LGF   Dr37 bowl   18g
Chevron border, *cf.* 1387. AD 80-100

1315 a, c   Dr37 bowl
LEZ   Bowl sherds   21g
(a) Tusked wild boar (O.1666) running to the left in the style of **Attianus** AD 125-145.
(c) Leaf (H58) of the style of **Attianus** AD 125-145..

1315 b
LMV   Dr37 bowl   18g
Style of **Drusus** *cf.* S&S pl. 11, 134 and Fig 4, 18). Leaf H90. AD 100-120. Same as 1325?

1316
LGF   Dech beaker?   6g
Lion running to the right (O.1898) over stylised rocks/grass and leaf. Same vessel as 1324, leaf and ovolo are the same South Gaulish style. Flavian, AD 70-100.

1317
LGF   2g
Leaf scroll and wavy line with floral decoration suggests South Gaul, Flavian-Trajanic, AD 70-100.

1319

LEZ   Dr37 bowl   21g

Style of **Criciro**: caryatid (O.1199), medallion (E26) containing erotic group (O.B), *cf.* S&S pl. 117, 4. AD 135-155.

1320a

LEZ   Dr37 bowl   13g

The standing figure (O.273) and Pan (O.710) were used by several later Antonine potters, including **Severus** and **Servus III**. Rogers 1999, pl. 110, 1 (Servus III) shows both types and the large-beaded borders (one apparently showing a slight bend, as here). However, the ovolo is not his, but the likely date is the 2nd half of the 2nd century, AD 150-200.

1320b

LEZ   Dr37 bowl   21g

Double ridged medallions, dot beading divisional borders and decorative detail (U210) used by **Cinnamus** (S&S 1958) and by **Servus III**. The leaf is not clear enough to identify. Date: 2nd half of 2nd century AD 150-200.

1321

LEZ   Dr37 bowl   20g

Dolphin (O.2328) within double ridged medallion with vertical and horizontal beaded lines possibly in the style of **Cinnamus** (S&S 1958, Plates 159-160) or potter of same date. AD 150-180.

1322a

LEZ   Dr37 bowl   32g

Hind legs of galloping horse (to left). Possibly **Cinnamus** (S&S 1958, Plate 163) or potter of same date. AD 150-180.

1322b

LEZ   Dr37 bowl   21g

Head of panther (O.1512 or 1518?) and hind legs of goat (O.1842). The 4-petalled junction rosette (C23) was used by **Attianus**, who used the panther. (The goat was used by his associate **Sacer**.) AD 125-145

1322c

LEZ   Dr37   14g

Horse galloping to left and looking back to right, with human figure beneath, **Cinnamus**. S&S 1958, Plate 163 and Plate 159, No.26. The leaf-tip filler, bottom left, is characteristic of **Cerialis-early Cinnamus** style, AD 135-160

1323

LEZ   Dr37 bowl   32g

Galloping horse and rider (O.245), ovolo (B231) and filling ornament (N15) of **Cinnamus**. (S&S 1958, Plate 163, No.73). AD 150-180.

1324

LGF   Dech beaker?   10g

Wild boar running to left (O.1682) over stylized rocks/grass with leaf to the right. The leaf is the same as that on 1316, which is likely to be from the same vessel? Flavian. AD 70-100.

1325
LMV Dr37 10g
Ovolo (B28) over sinuous floral decoration. Style of **Drusus**, his ovolo (B28), *cf.* S&S, pl. 11, 134. Paler in colour than many LMV fabrics. Presumably the same bowl as 1315b. AD 100-120.

1330
LMV Dr37 bowl   11g
Diana (O.106), line of ovolo and wavy lines in the style of **X9** (Ranto of S&S 1958, Plate 34). AD 110-130.

1331
LMV Dr37 9g
Standing figure (Pan O.709) and single astralagus within beaded borders under a line of ovolo (probably Rogers B7). AD 100-120. Same bowl as 1023.

1332
LEZ Dr37 bowl   6g
The ovolo appears to be B234, used by **Paternus II** and other late 2nd century potters, though the rosette (not in Rogers) does not match any that he used. Likely to date to 2nd half of 2nd century AD 150-200.

1333a
LMV Dr37 bowl   57g   220mm
Double ridged festoon, wavy lines, 'cushion (U3) and large ovolo of the style of **P9** (Medetus-Ranto of S&S 1958, Plate 32, No.375). AD 110-130.

1333b
LMV Dr37 15g   160 mm
Column top, wavy lines and ovolo of style of **Igocatus (X4).** His ovolo (B37), column (P50) and seven-dot rosette (C280) (S&S pl. 17, 209, 218). AD 110-120.

1334a
LEZ Dr37 7g
Bird (O.2252) within double ridged festoon and beaded lines, with a line of ovolo (B231) with twisted tongues in the style of **Cinnamus** (S&S 1958, Plate 157, No.2). AD 150-180.

1334b
LEZ Dr37 17g
Ovolo (B206) as used by the **Paternus II** group. The tripod (Q16) was used by **Paternus** and **Laxtucissa**. As Laxtucissa also used rosettes at border junctions, this sherd is attributed to him. AD 155-185

1337
LEZ Dr37 36g
A distinctive dog (R4042 – a type, not in O., listed in Rogers 1999) used by **Avitus** (S&S pl. 62, 6). Probably his ovolo (B9). AD 120-150

1386a, b, c and d
LMV Dr37 10g
Various medallion, floral and geometric decoration, (b) wreath of buds (G377), (c) festoon (F74), (d) leaf (H96) all used by **X11** (Ioenalis). AD 100-120.

1387
LGF   6g
Chevron border *cf.*1311. AD 80-100

1388
LGF   3g
Floral decoration. AD 80-100.

1389a, b
LEZ   Bowl sherds   8g
a) Seated Diana (O.111) used by **Cinnamus;** b) stag (O.1732?). AD 150-200.

1390 a, b, c
LEZ   11g
Not from the same vessel.
a) Ovolo with wavy line border, same as 1129 and 1102. Hadrianic? AD 120-138.
b) Uncertain. The style is Hadrianic or Antonine, hence *c.* AD 120-192
c) Large beads suggest AD 160-200

1395 a
LEZ   Dr37 bowl   3g
Standing female figure (caryatid O.1201, 1202 or 1205?) with head of a galloping horse? to the left of the vertical beaded line. Probably Lezoux and Antonine, *c.* AD 140-190

1395 b
LMV   Dr37 bowl   3g
Not figured. Squared ovolo with twist tongue (not found in Rogers) with beaded line beneath. AD 100-120.

1401a, b, c, d
LEZ   Dr37 bowl
a, b, c, and d are from the same bowl.
(a) **5 g**. Winged figure of cupid (O.401) within beaded borders. (b) **9g**. Same, badly damaged **Cinnamus** (S&S 1958, Plate 158, No.16). AD 150-180.
(c) **18g.** Stag running to the right (O.1704) within a single line festoon beneath a row of ovolo (B17). **Cinnamus** (e.g. S&S 1958, Plate 157, No.8). AD 150-180.
(d) **9g 180 mm.** Row of ovolo (B17) with beaded line beneath **Cinnamus**. AD 150-180.

1463
LEZ   Dr37 bowl   9g
Vulcan (O66). Ovolo with twisted tongue to right (B231). **Cinnamus**. (S&S, pl. 159, 23) AD 150-180.

1465
LGF   Dr37 bowl   13g
Festoons with spirals, *cf.* **Biragillus** (Mees 1995, Taf. 14, 1), **Mercator** (*ibid.* Taf.135, 6). A common type of decoration *c.*AD 80-100.

1466
LMV   Dr29?   10g
Trefoil basal wreath and legs of galloping horse in style of either **X12** (Ioenalis) or **X13** (Donnaucus), but decoration not found. AD 100-120.

1468
LMV   Dr37 bowl   7g
Decorative column with tripod (Q21) over twist (U103). Vertical beading. **X12** (Ioenalis of S&S 1958, Plate 36 No's 422, 424, 425). AD 100-120.

1471
LMV   Dr37 bowl   25g
Ovolo (B7) above head of dolphin (O.2384). Style of **X13**, who used the ovolo, and also the dolphin (S&S, pl. 43, 491). AD 100-120.

1472
LGF   Bowl sherd   5g
Figure in beaded medallion (left) and saltire (right). The saltire was common during the Flavian period hence, AD 80-100.

1473
LEZ   Dr37 bowl   10g
This appears to be the same sherd as 1304b. Seated Apollo (O.83) and leaf (J91). Both types were used on **Vegetus** style (Rogers 1999, pl. 119) and this is probably his ovolo (B228). AD 120-140

1474
LGF   Dr37 bowl   11g
Festoon with spiral. A common decoration in the Flavian-Trajanic period (see 1465 above), e.g. **Germanus** (Mees 1995, Taf. 78, 10) where it occurs with similar stylised rocks. AD 75-100.

1475
LEZ   Dr37 bowl   4g
Feet of standing figure in Hadrianic or Antonine style. AD 120-190.

1768
LGF   bowl   4g
Floral design with tendrils. Five-lobed leaf and sinuous tendril in style of **Modestus** or **Crestio?** (Dannell, 1999). AD 50-65.

3100
LGF   Dr30 bowl   9g
A passive lower border with two rabbits facing each other with a tiny floral dot between, and with a chase scene above indicated by galloping horse legs. AD 43-100.

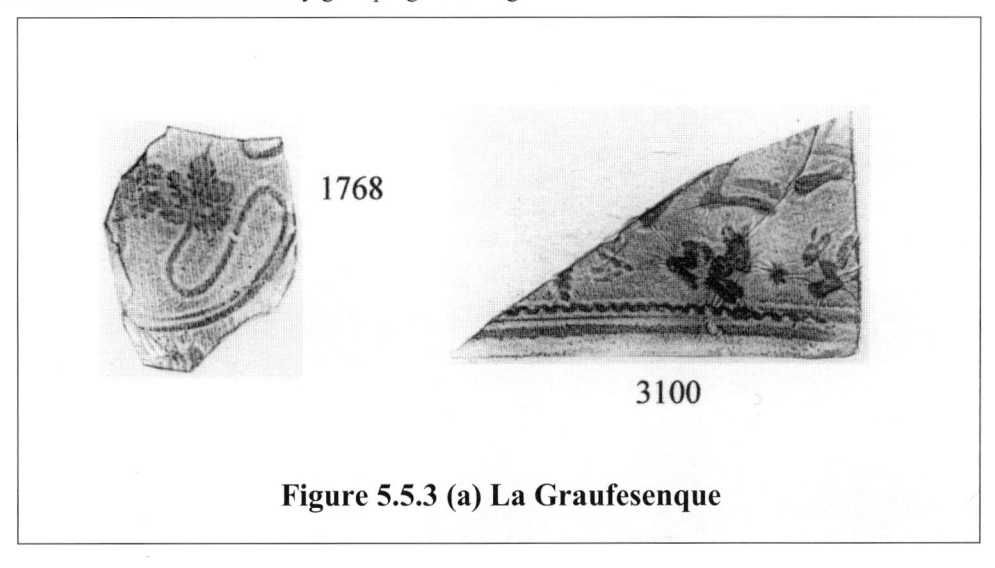

Figure 5.5.3 (a) La Graufesenque

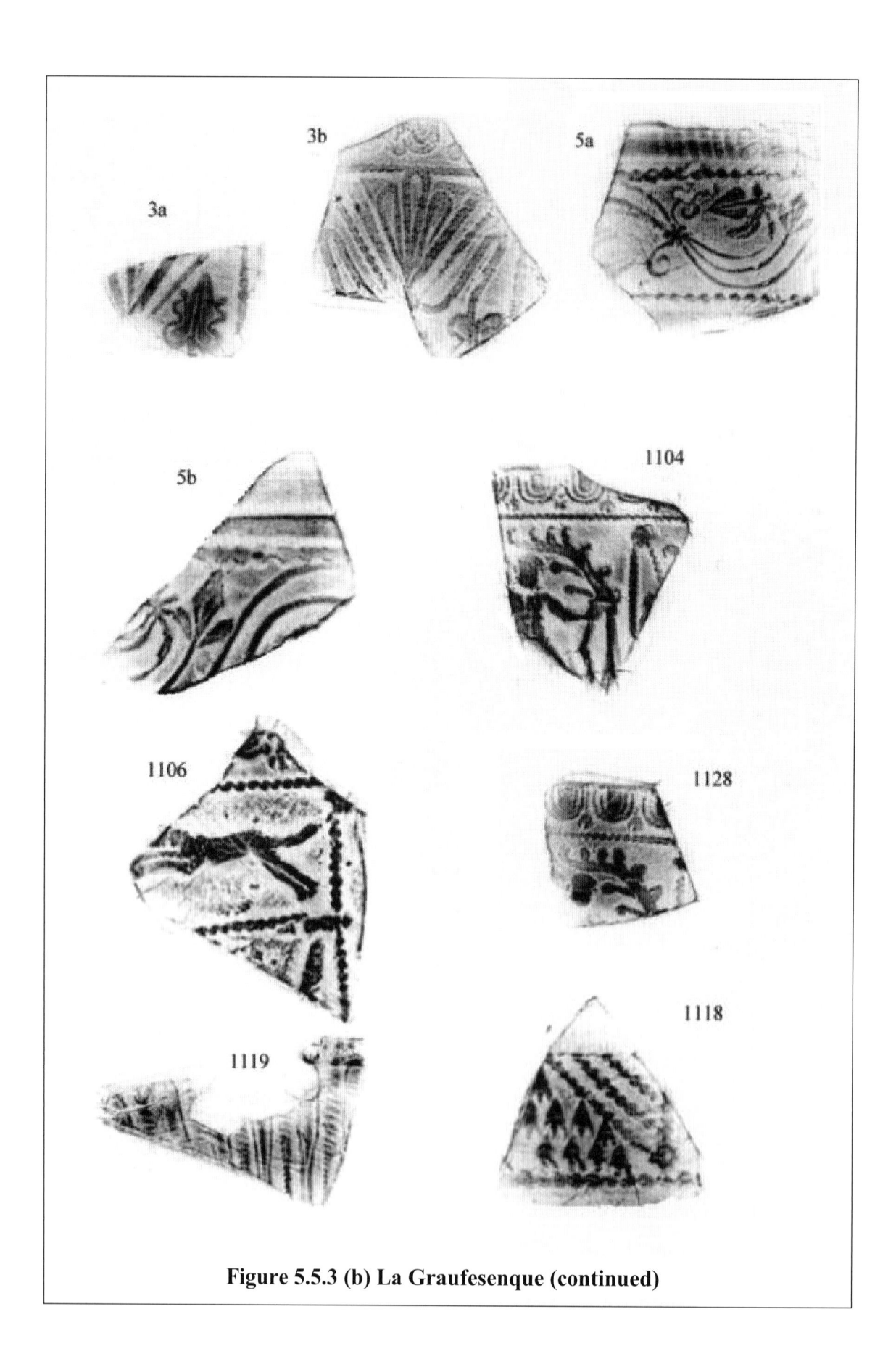

Figure 5.5.3 (b) La Graufesenque (continued)

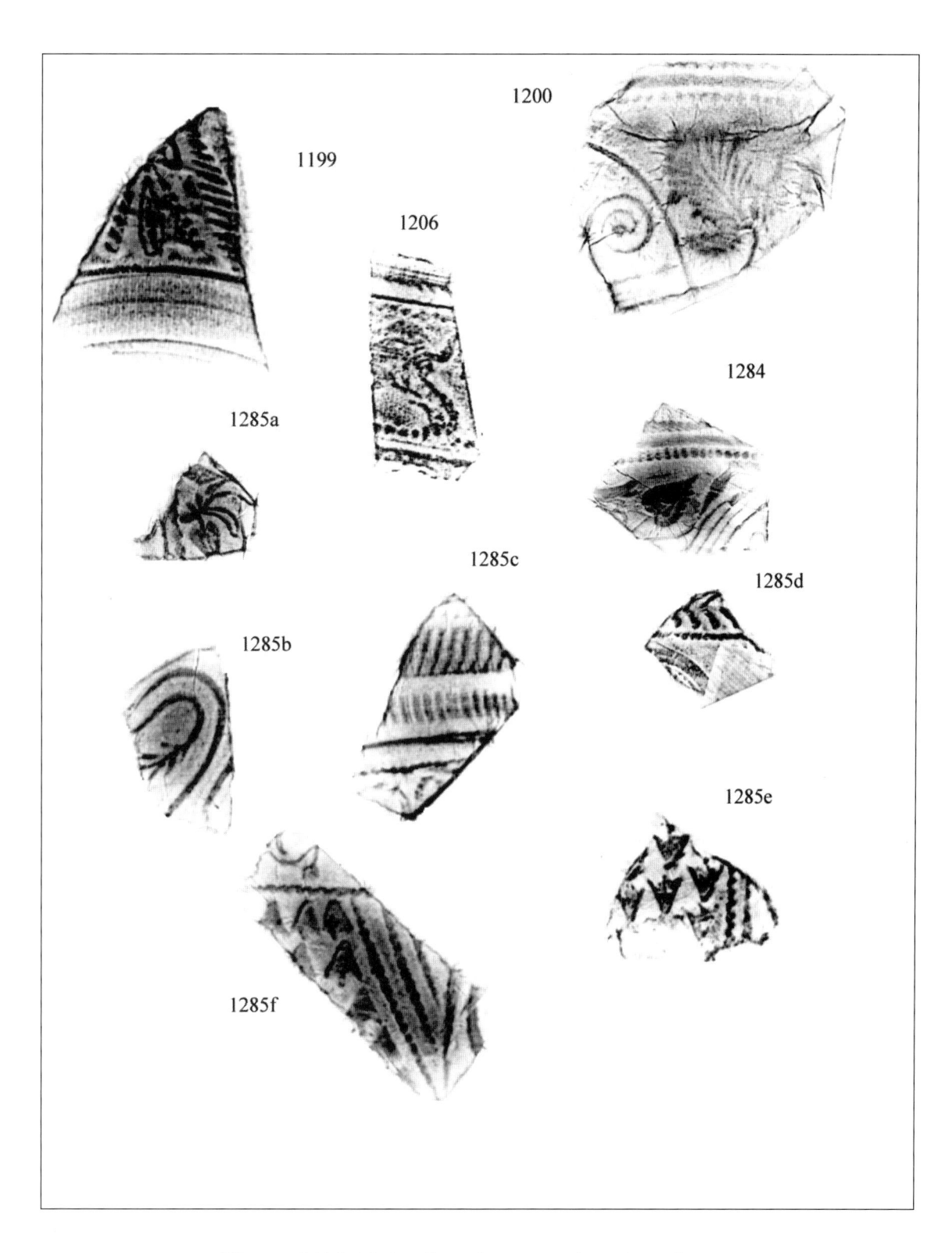

Figure 5.5.3 (c) La Graufesenque (continued)

1285h

1285j

1285g

1285i

1286c

1286a

1286b

1287b

1287a

1288a

1288b

Figure 5.5.3 (d) La Graufesenque (continued)

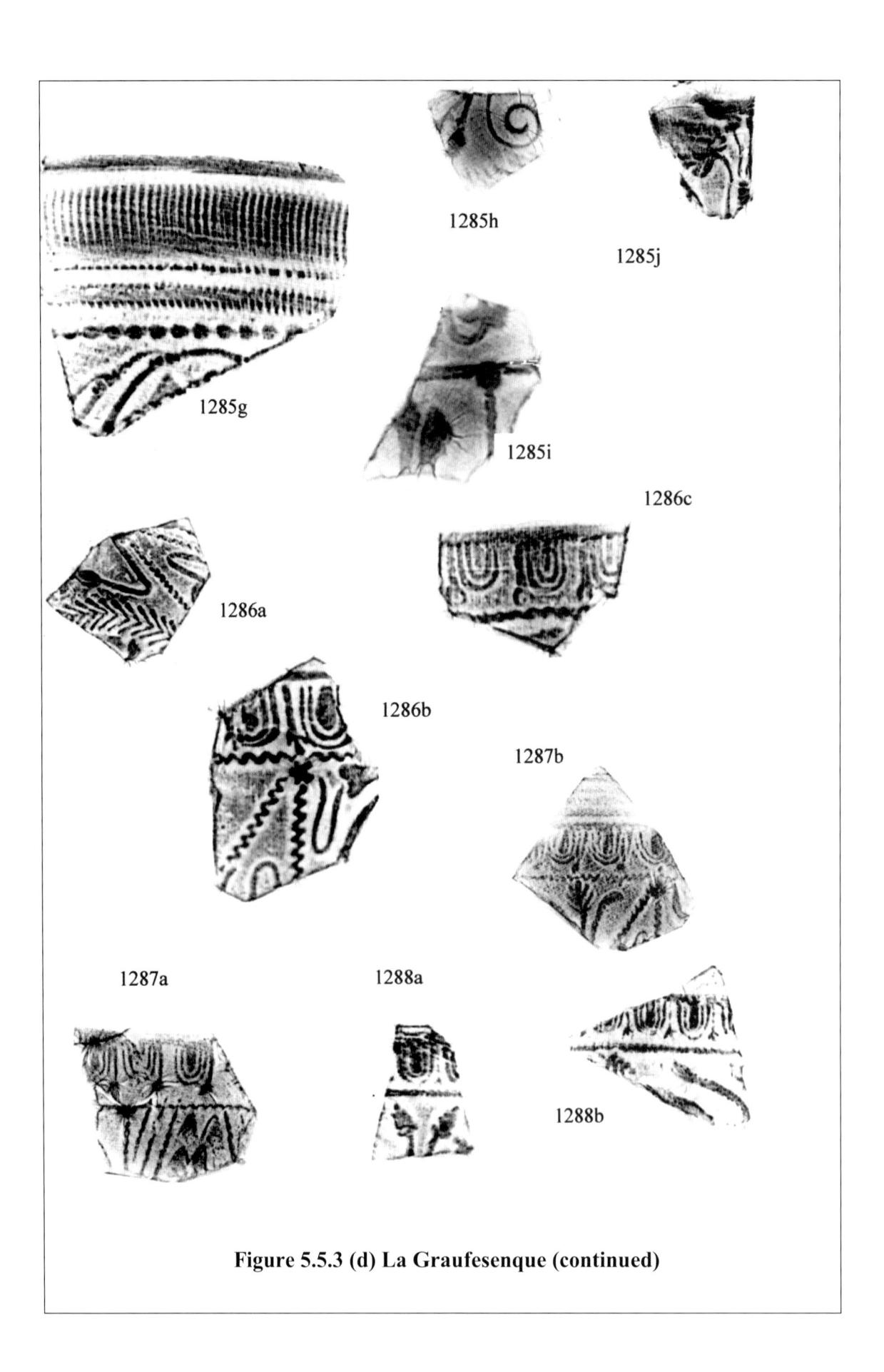

Figure 5.5.3 (e) La Graufesenque (continued)

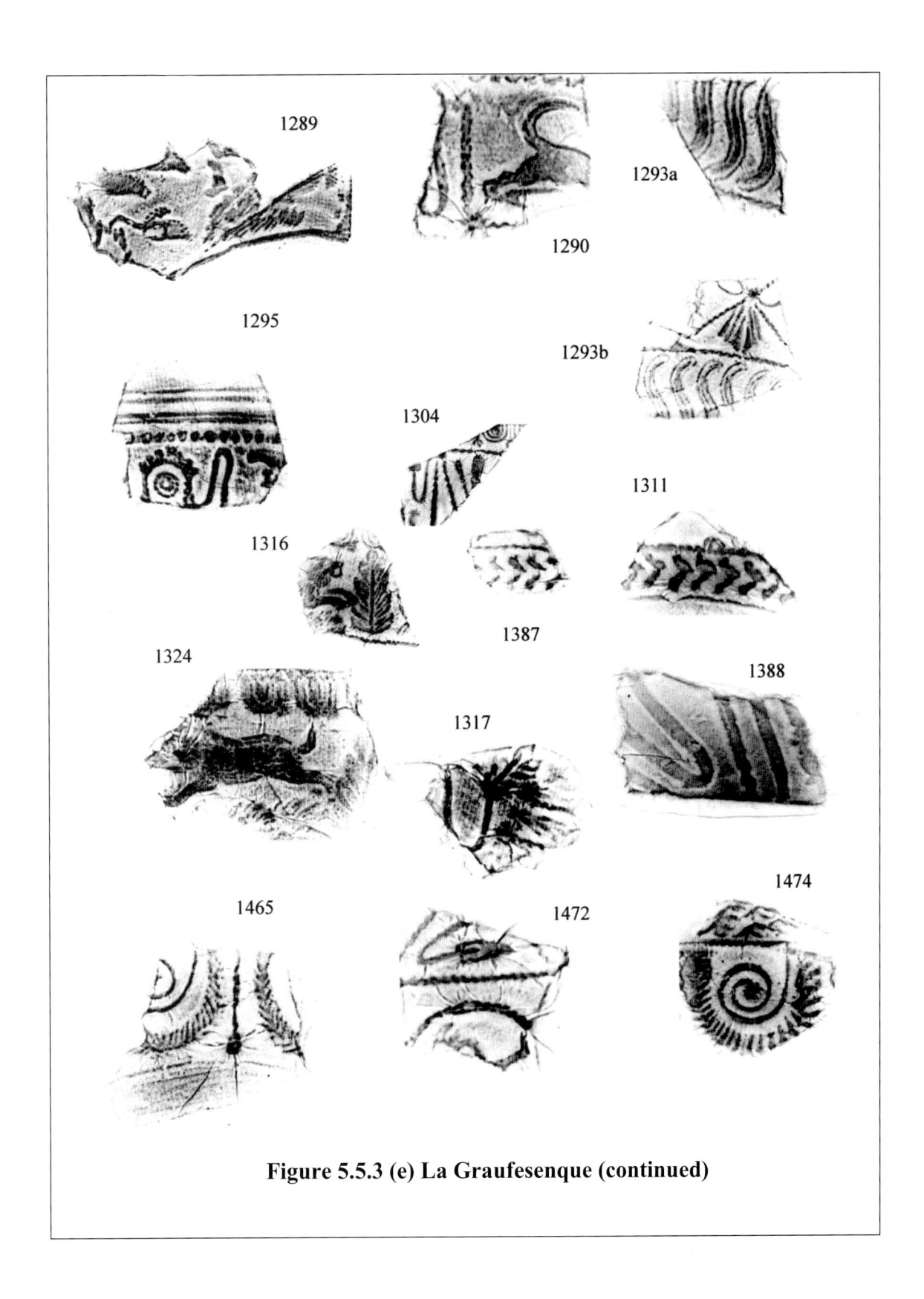

Figure 5.5.4 (a) Les Martres-de-Veyre

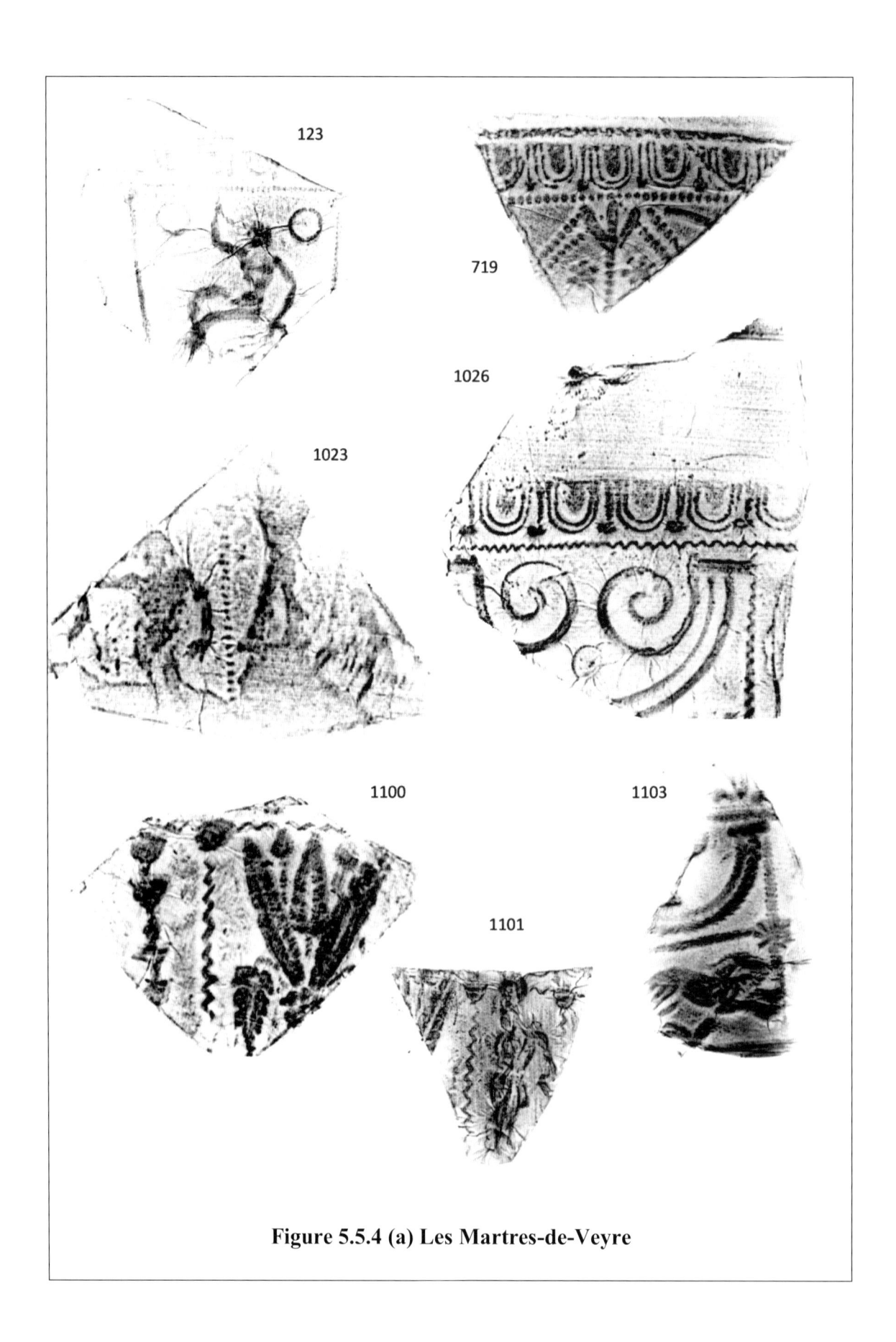

Figure 5.5.4 (b) Les Martres-de-Veyre (continued)

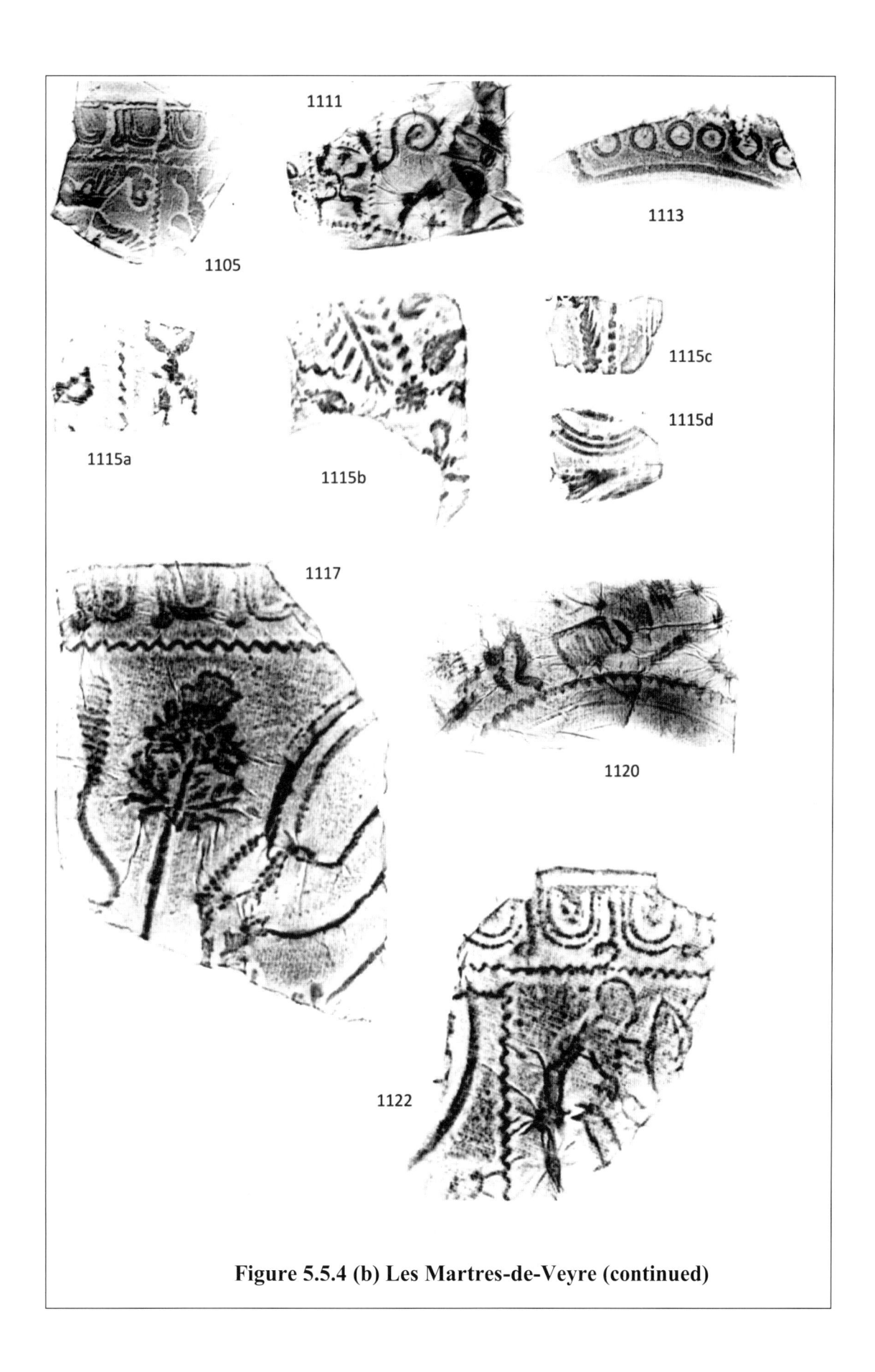

Figure 5.5.4 (c) Les Martres-de-Veyre (continued)

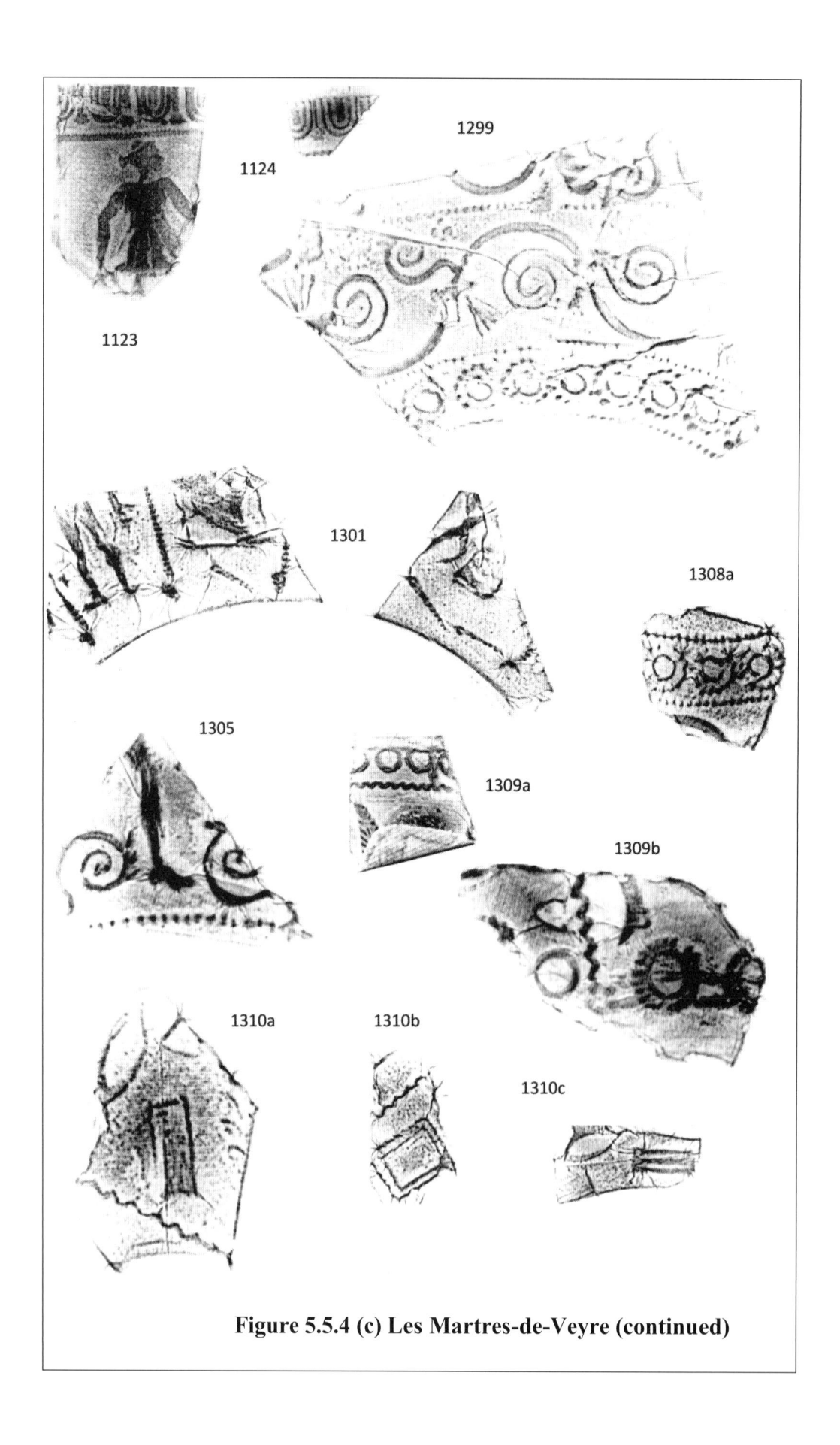

Figure 5.5.4 (d) Les Martres-de-Veyre (continued)

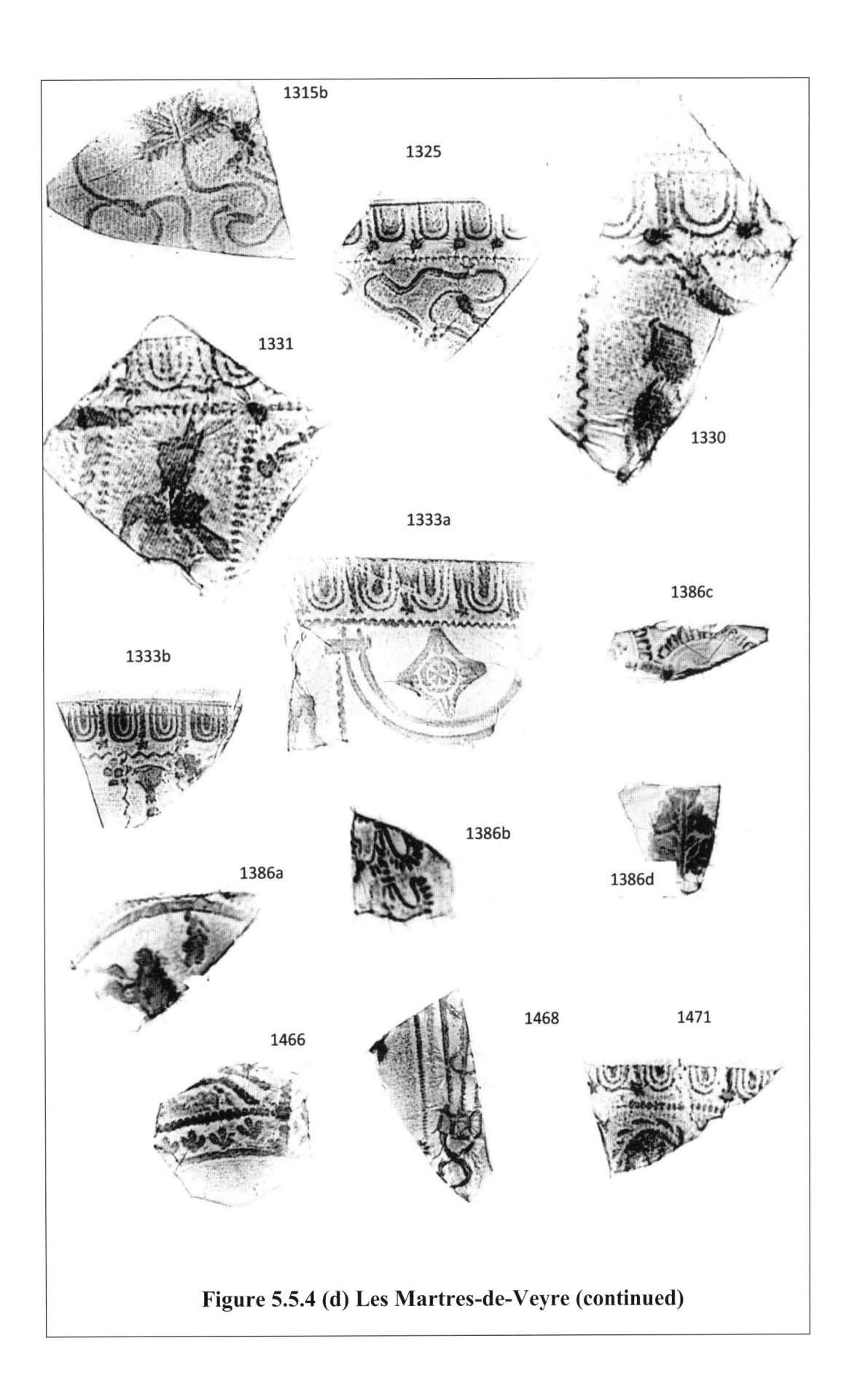

9 a, b, c

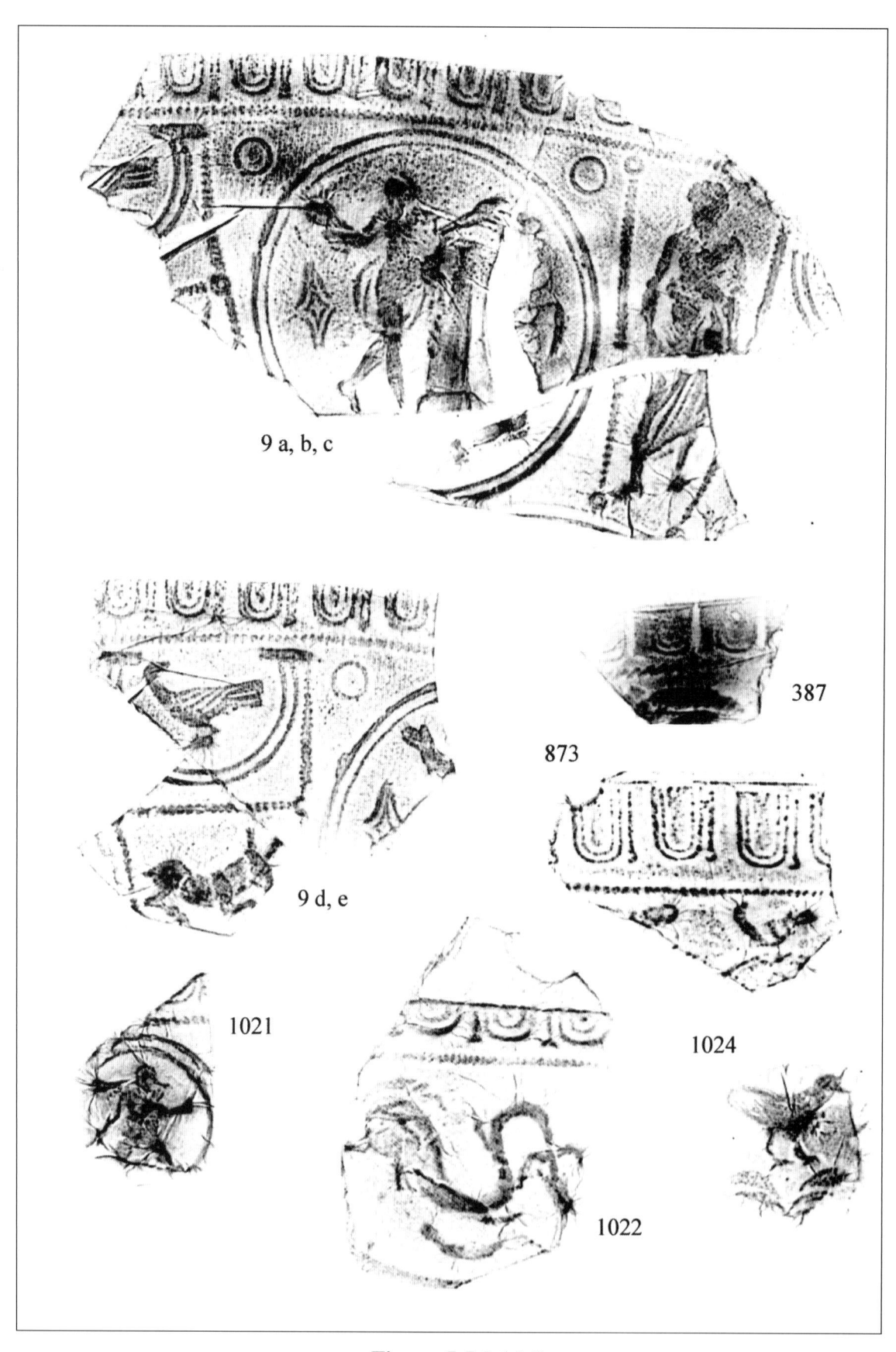

9 d, e

387

873

1021

1024

1022

Figure 5.5.5 (a) Lezoux

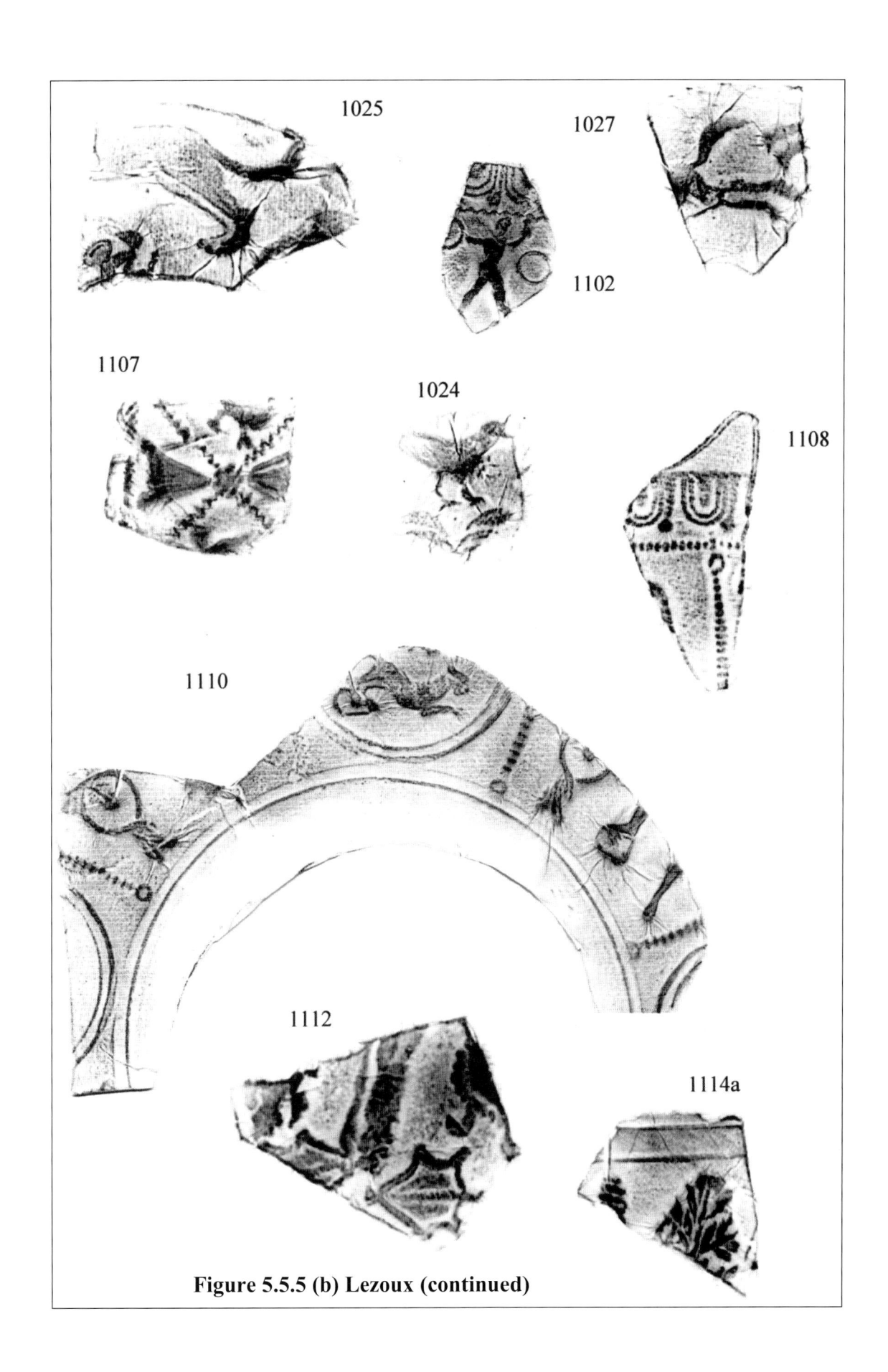

Figure 5.5.5 (b) Lezoux (continued)

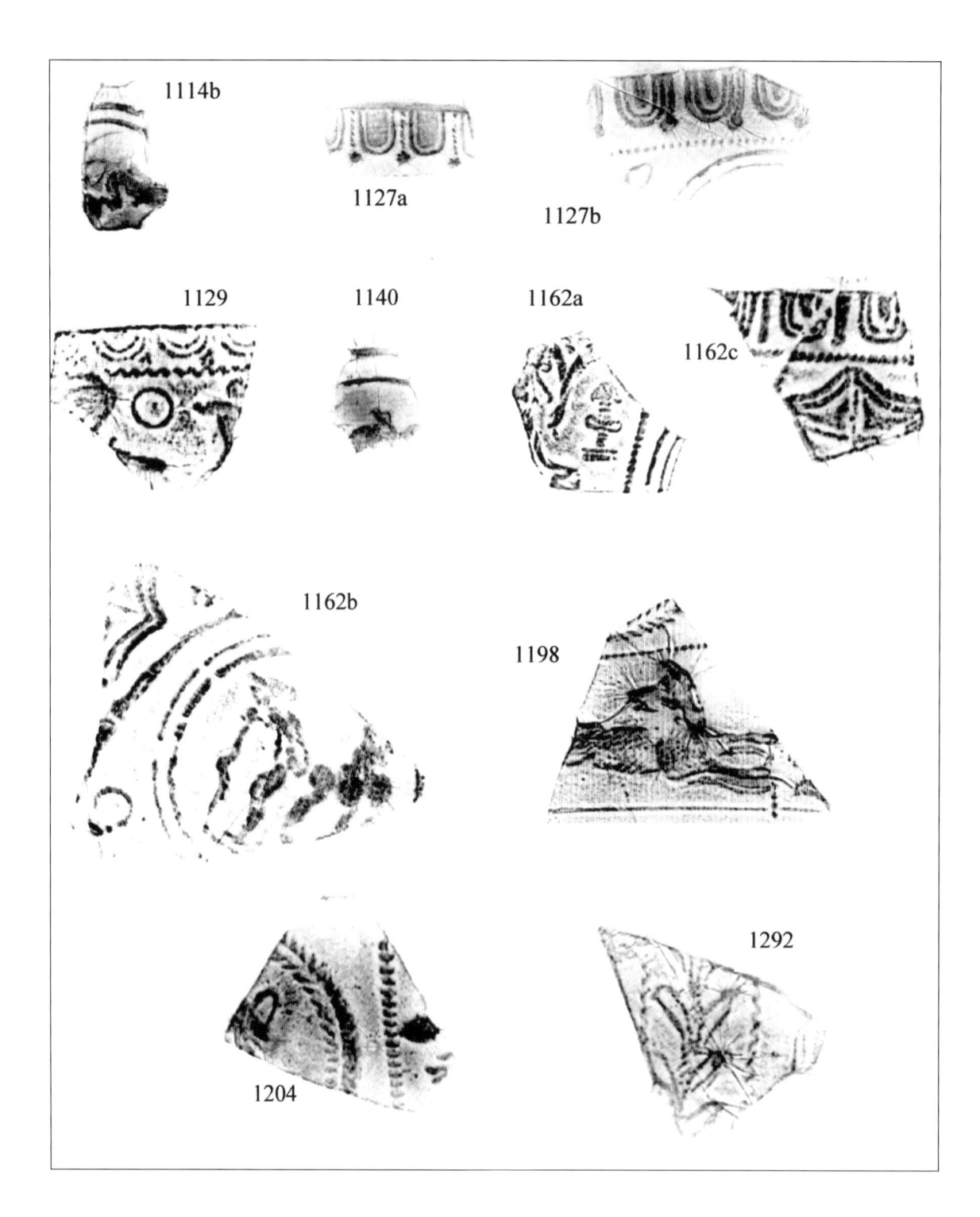

Figure 5.5.5 (c) Lezoux (continued)

Figure 5.5.5 (d) Lezoux (continued)

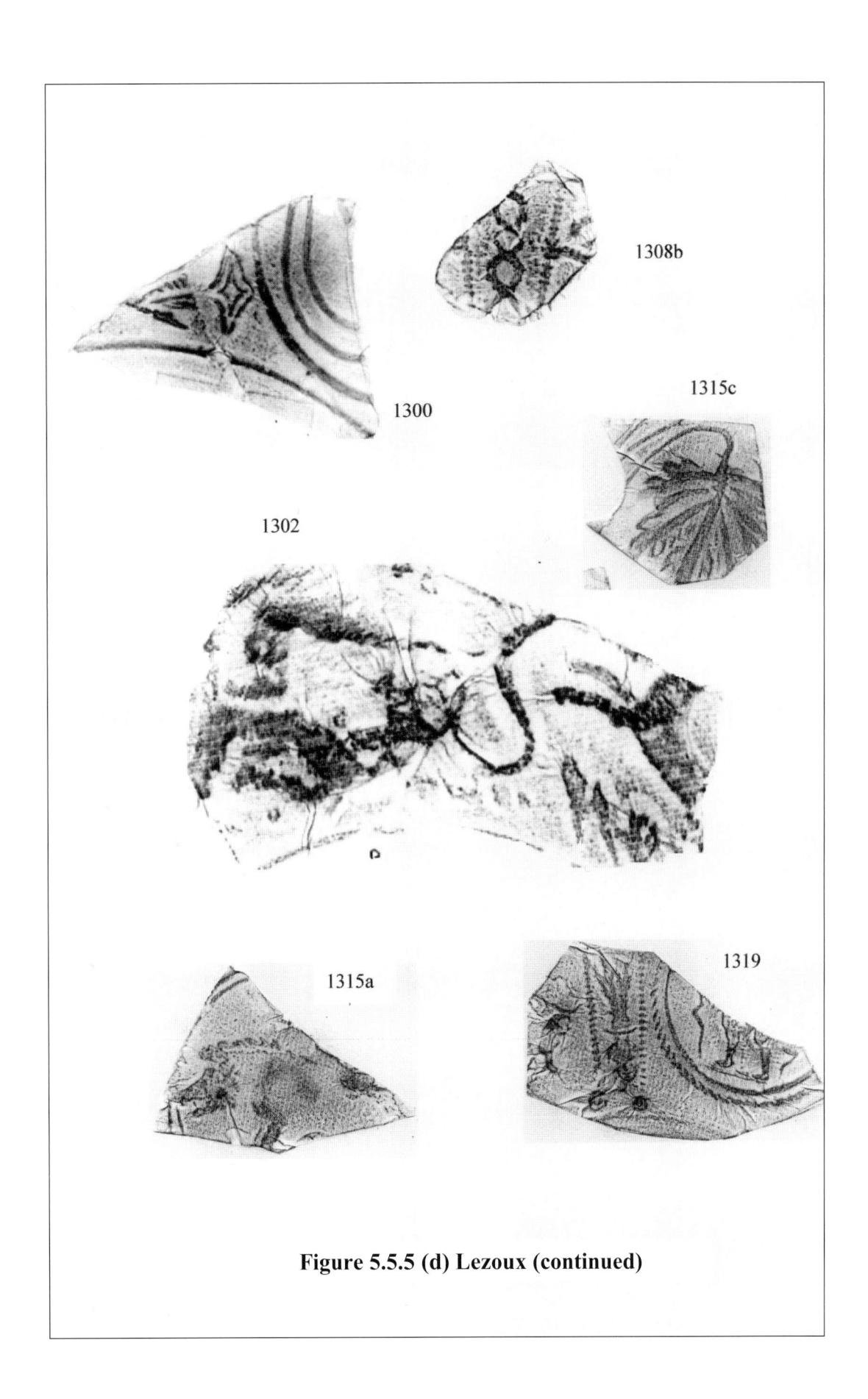

Figure 5.5.5 (e) Lezoux (continued)

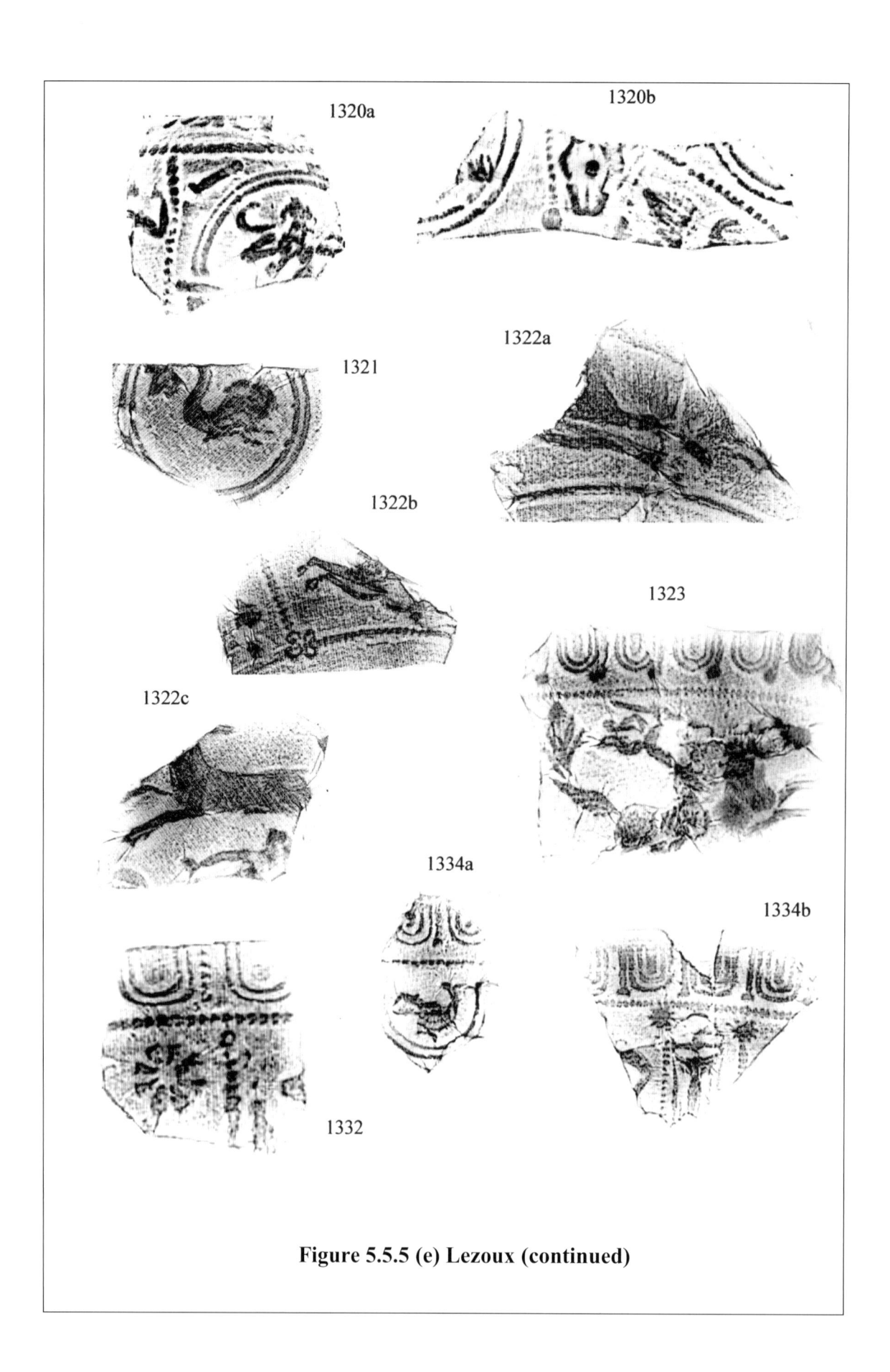

Figure 5.5.5 (f) Lezoux (continued)

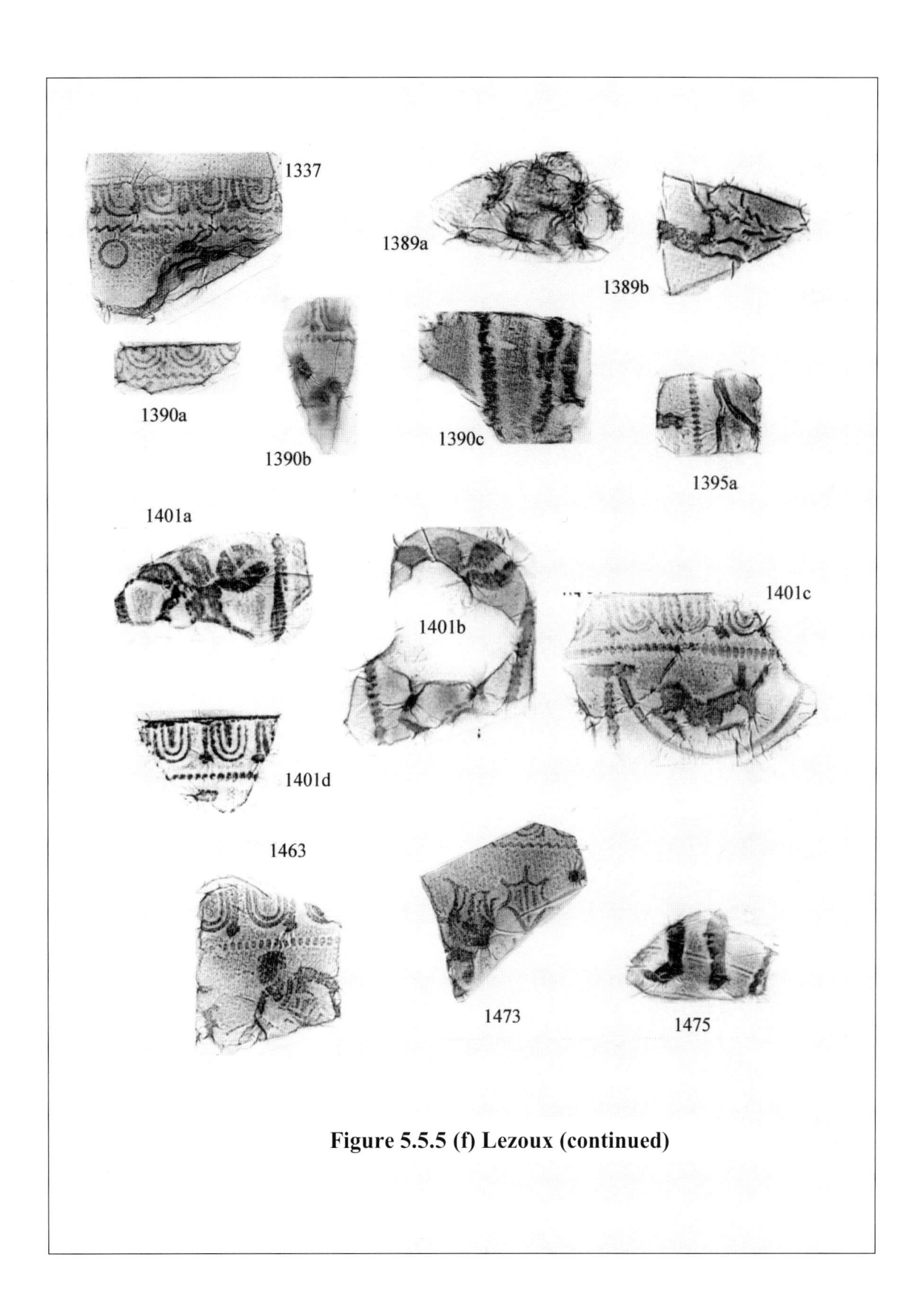

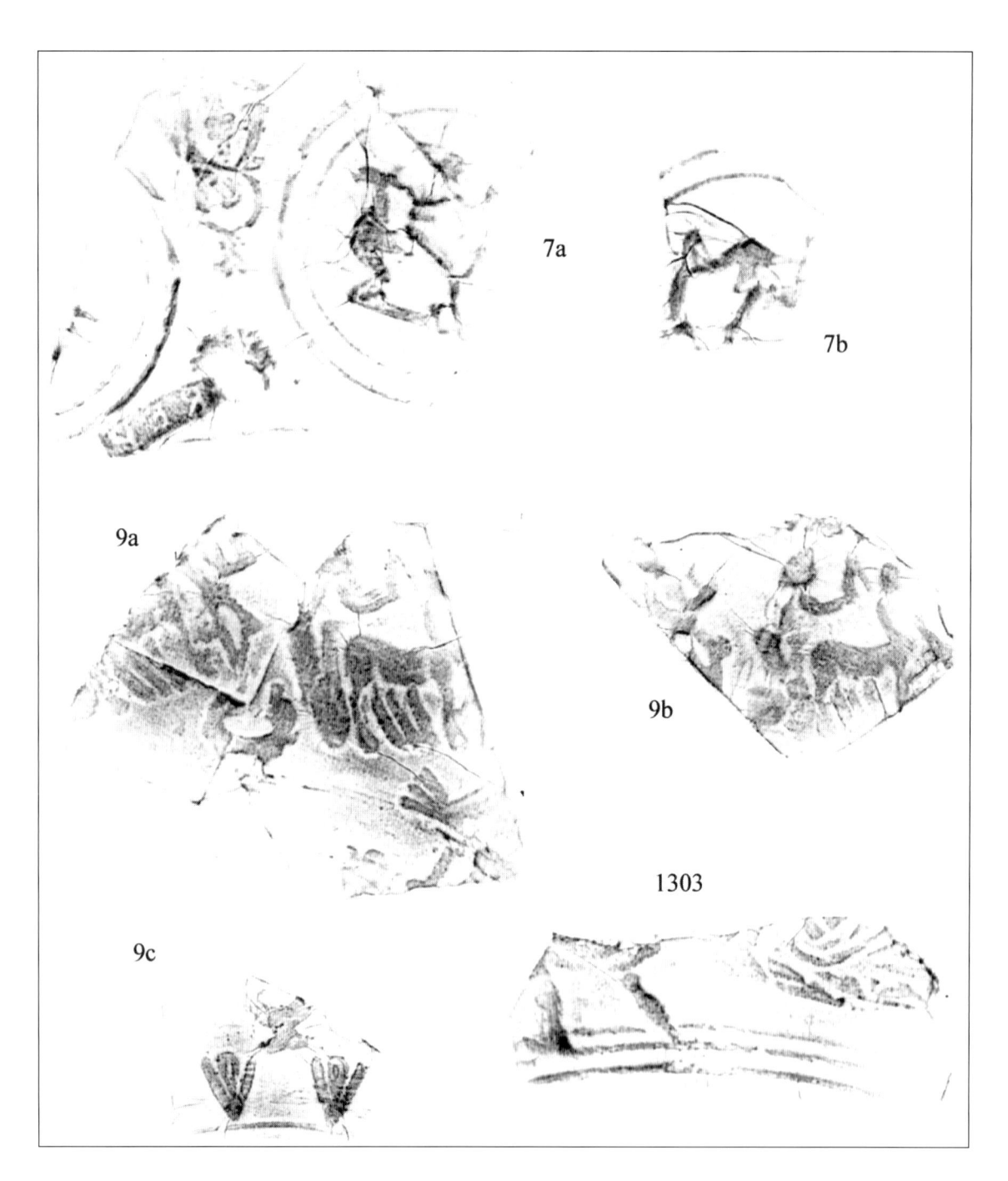

Figure 5.5.6 East Gaul

Acknowledgements: thanks to Gwladys Monteil and Felicity Wild for assistance with the identifications and proof reading, and to the 'black thumb gang' for some enjoyable rubbing sessions.

Chapter 5.6 Roman pottery repairs: some experiments in the replication of repair techniques with reference to Yewden pottery

Rick Magaldi

Introduction

The purpose of this document is to describe and examine the approach employed by Roman craftsmen in the repair of pottery, and then to assess those repairs seen in the Yewden Villa pottery collection. The types of repair tools that would have been available are examined before undertaking a short review of certain aspects of Roman metallurgy which contributed to the metalworking techniques employed in the repair of damaged pottery. Some repair schemes are examined in detail, particularly those described by J. Pena (2007) and S. Willis (2005), and the author's attempts at replicating them are described and discussed.

Roman wood and metalworking tools

A wide range of tools was available to Roman craftsmen including hammers, saws, drills and files (R.B. Ulrich). The basic designs of these tools are familiar in form and function to those in common use today. It is interesting to note that the tools of the Roman period, although somewhat crude by modern standards, were nevertheless highly effective and sufficient for the demands made of them. Since the Roman period the basic designs have undergone refinement rather than any radical change. It is perhaps interesting to note that Egyptian stonemasons used copper saws with sand as an abrasive material to cut large blocks of stone. Copper being a soft ductile material is not one that readily springs to mind when choosing a material to make a saw! However, as inefficient as such saws might have been when compared with modern masonry saws, they were clearly adequate for the task. Skilled use of the tools would have been required at various stages in the pottery repair process. Also required would be a knowledge of jointing materials such as glues, waxes and resins, and a familiarity with the properties of metals such as copper and lead.

Roman metallurgy

It is known that metalworking techniques available to the Romans include the alloying of metals as well as casting and forging. It is perhaps the alloying and casting of metal that are most relevant to the task of pottery repair and restoration. The delicate fabric of pottery requires caution when selecting a repair method suitable for a particular vessel. The use of metal in such a repair requires that the metal can be easily worked with the minimum of hammering, or that it can be melted and bonded with the pottery fabric.

The Romans mined metal ore throughout the empire (Healey, 1978) and developed metal refining processes that they used on the ore to extract gold, silver, copper, tin, lead, iron, zinc, antimony and other metals. Many of the metals were alloyed (the mixing of two or more together) to alter their basic properties and form a product with new qualities. For example, by combining tin and copper to make bronze, or by combining lead with tin to make pewter.

One characteristic of alloys is that their melting point often differs from those of the base metals from which they are formed. The relative proportions of the base metals determine the melting point of alloys. The proportions, at some point, can produce what is known as an eutectic mixture. This particular combination of the base metals gives a melting point for the alloy which is as low as possible, and significantly lower than the melting point of either base metal. (Compare Tables 5.6.1 and 5.6.2).

Metal	Melting Point (degrees C)
Lead – Pb (Plumbum)	327.5 °C
Antimony – Sb (Stibium)	630 °C
Tin – Sn (Stannum)	232 °C
Bismuth - Bi	271 °C

Table 5.6.1 The relative melting points of some pure base metals

Alloy Component added to Lead – (Pb)	Weight of Alloy Component	Melting Point (degrees C)
Antimony – Sb (Stibium)	11%	247 °C
Tin – Sn (Stannum)	61%	187 °C
Bismuth - Bi	60%	125 °C

Table 5.6.2 Eutectic characteristics of various lead alloys

In reality, Roman metallurgy was not able to produce metals of absolute purity, so most metals extracted from ore, with the possible exceptions of copper and gold, would have included small amounts of other elements. Consequently, the physical characteristics of most alloys would have reflected these imperfections. Nevertheless, the extraction, purification and alloying of metals improved over time. The advances would have allowed Roman artisans to both refine and extend their manufacturing and repair techniques. Clearly, available metals such as copper and lead, together with their alloys, had the properties required to be of value in pottery repairs. They are ductile, and so can be hammered and shaped at room temperature, and they also have low melting temperatures for casting (Table 5.6.2). They present ideal materials for the manufacture of wire, staples and rivets.

Figure 5.6.1 illustrates the effect of alloying various metals known to the Romans with lead (Pb). It shows the degree to which the melting temperature of lead can be significantly reduced when lead and another metal are alloyed. The melting temperature of lead in its pure state (325 degrees C), is reduced to 247 degrees C when 11% by weight of Antimony (Sb) is added; 187 degrees C when 61% by weight of Tin (Sn) is added; and 125 degrees C when 60% by weight of Bismuth (Bi) is added. This significant reduction of the melting point, perhaps combined with an extended temperature range over which the alloy melt remains fluid, would have been beneficial in allowing poring and casting of metal during pottery repairs.

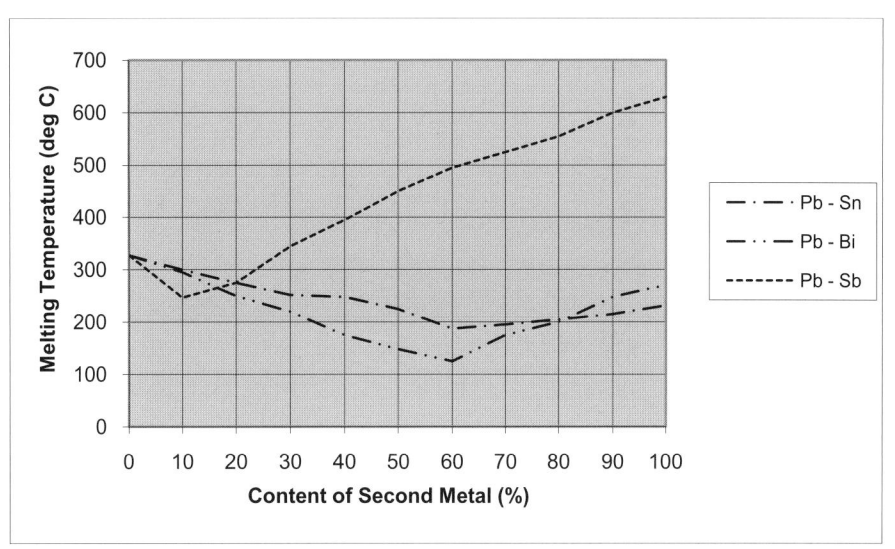

Figure 5.6.1 Eutectic temperatures of the Lead alloys of Tin (Sn), Antimony (Sb) and Bismuth (Bi)

It is interesting to note that both Bismuth and Antimony share the property of expanding when cooling. When alloys that incorporate these metals are used in casting they expand as they cool to fill the mould, and by doing so they produce very clean, well defined castings. The properties of these alloys would have been very useful when carrying out repairs.

When high temperatures were needed outside of a blacksmiths forge, it is possible that knowledge was used passed down from the goldsmiths of ancient Egypt. These craftsmen, when working with precious metal and delicate objects, used spirit or oil lamps together with a blowpipe to achieve the high temperatures required. If Roman craftsmen were familiar with the use of the spirit lamp and blowpipe it is interesting to speculate on the possible application of this technology to pottery repairs. Gold, with a melting point of 1063 °C, can be worked using this technique, so it would have been very easy to work lead and lead alloys which have much lower melting points of between 125 and 327.5 °C.

Figure 5.6.2 Spirit lamp and blowpipe arrangement: possibly used for small pottery repairs

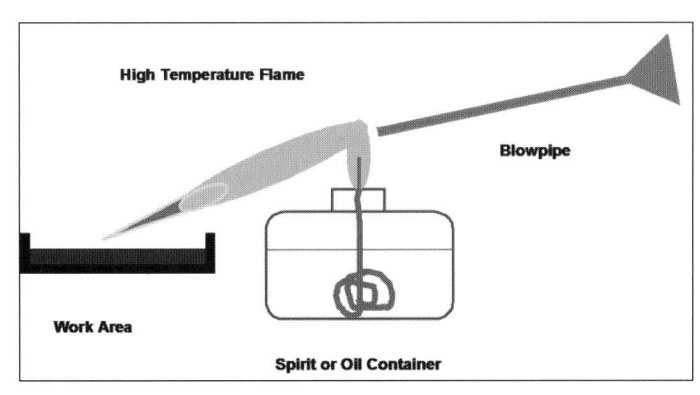

The use of the spirit lamp and blowpipe for repairs to smaller vessels would have provided a portable heat source and precise local heating (Fig. 5.6.2). This would be useful when molten metal was required to strengthen existing metal repairs. However, this approach to repairs would have been time consuming and so costly, and would have been restricted to objects of great scarcity, or of religious or sentimental value.

Cold repair techniques were also employed in the Roman period, particularly to large heavy objects. This approach relied on the properties of white lead (cerussite – lead carbonate) referred to as Cerussa. Cerussite was mixed with linseed oil, or a mixture of calcium carbonate and linseed oil, to form putty that could be applied at ambient temperature. As the linseed oil evaporated the compound hardened to form a rigid joint.

Roman pottery repair methods

Contemporary archaeological literature describes a number of pottery repair methods. Much of the evidence has been accumulated through the examination of pottery sherds, which show either complete or partial repair details. Several different processes and techniques are evident in the repairs such as drilling and boring holes; sawing and cutting of pottery fabric; and the use of metal and other materials for bracing and jointing. The overall repair processes can be classified according to the method employed for the re-joining of the broken vessel pieces. Despite the inconsistent adoption of repair terms by different authors, all repair jointing techniques can be classified as either of the following:

- Stapling/Riveting (hole and clamp)
- Mortise and tenon (cleat jointing)

Stapling and riveting repairs

Stapling, or hole and clamp repairs, are generally found applied to smaller vessels. Fig 5.6.3 shows the nature of a typical hole and clamp repair in which holes have been drilled through the surfaces to be joined. The holes are aligned and then held in place by a thick metal wire formed into a staple and placed through the holes. The surfaces are then locked in position either by hammering the legs of the staple to form a rivet head, or by folding back the legs. Variations of this basic process were employed depending on the nature of vessel usage, its shape, fabric and the region of breakage. For example, if the vessel was required to contain liquid after repair, mechanical stability alone would not be sufficient. Some way of sealing the joined parts would be essential. For this purpose, we know that various waxes and resins such as pine pitch and tars were available (Thornton, 1998; Rosenfeld, 1965). In the case of a repair to a vessel with damage on a delicate part such as the vessel rim, hammering during the repair process could cause further damage. Evidence suggests that a variation of the hole and clamp technique was then used, and the staple was cast *in situ* as shown in Figure 5.6.3.

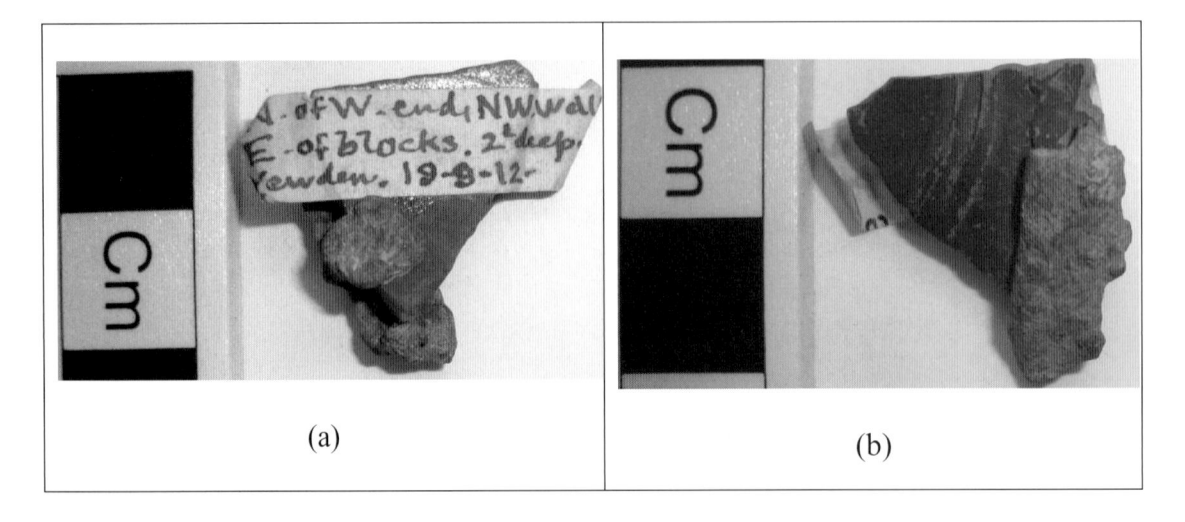

(a)   (b)

Figure 5.6.3 Hole and clamp repair on Yewden Samian sherd 1994.57.P.1391. A Dr37 decorated bowl from La Graufesenque, South Gaul (AD 70-100)

After drilling suitable holes in the vessel walls, a mould would be attached to both the interior and exterior surfaces of the vessel being repaired. Fig 5.6.4 offers an idealised representation of the technique. The mould, probably fashioned from clay, formed a dam which allowed molten metal to adopt the shape of the vessel. The result was a staple that matched the dimensions and contours of the vessel. On completion of this task, the mould would be removed and the cast metal trimmed by cutting and filing. The basic shape of the cast metal would be that of a staple with legs that projected either into the interior or outwards to the exterior of the vessel. The legs could be trimmed to an appropriate length and the ends hammered to form plain rivet heads (Fig. 5.6.5) or, if the pre-drilled holes had been countersunk, hammered to form flush rivet heads (Fig. 5.6.6).

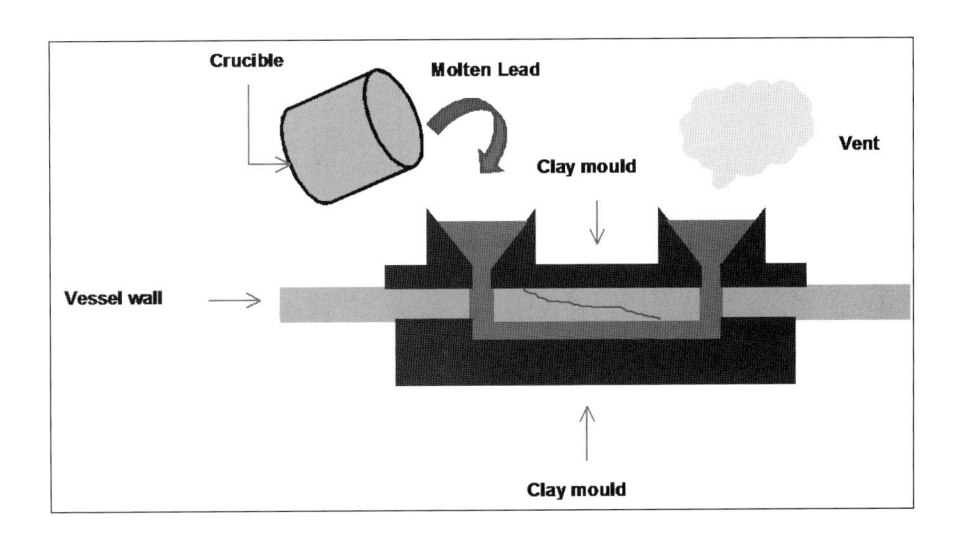

Figure 5.6.4 A possible *in situ* method of casting a staple during pottery repair.

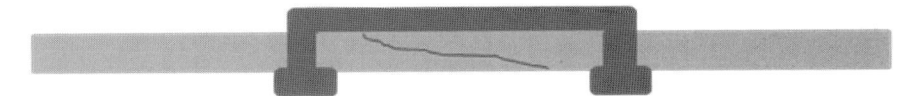

Figure 5.6.5 The completed repair after casting and surface finishing (plain riveted holes)

Figure 5.6.6 The completed repair after casting and surface finishing (countersunk riveted holes)

A less complex repair method involved the use of a lead dowel. The dowel was bent to form a staple to bridge the drilled holes in the vessel. The legs of the staple were passed through the holes and then bent flat and hammered to lock the staple in place

(Fig 5.6.7). A variation on this type of repair included dripping molten lead into the staple holes with the staple in place, or packing the holes with white lead putty prior to, or after, the staple was fitted. This ensured a stable and secure joint. This technique would have been suitable for the more delicate areas of vessels such as rims.

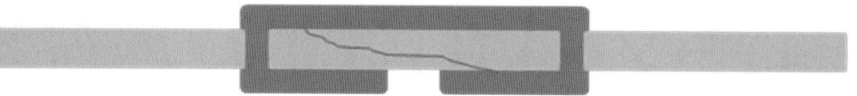

Figure 5.6.7 A basic hole and clamp repair, the staple legs are bent double and hammered

Mortise and tenon repairs

Mortise and tenon repairs are those generally found applied to larger vessels such as Dolia (large wine containers with a capacity of 1,500 litres or more), but have been found used to repair smaller items. This dovetail type of joint locks the joined surfaces together and prevents both lateral and vertical movement of the joined surfaces. However, cutting the pottery fabric is more complicated than drilling holes as in the hole and clamp approach.

The mortise and tenon repair scheme can be broken down into two stages. The first stage requires the dovetails to be cut through the surface of the vessel using either saws or chisels (or both) depending on the thickness of the fabric. This would have placed a degree of stress on the item during repair preparation when the dovetail shapes were cut. Choice of the mortise and tenon repair method would have been influenced by the size, shape and thickness of the vessel in question as well as the ease of access to the damaged area.

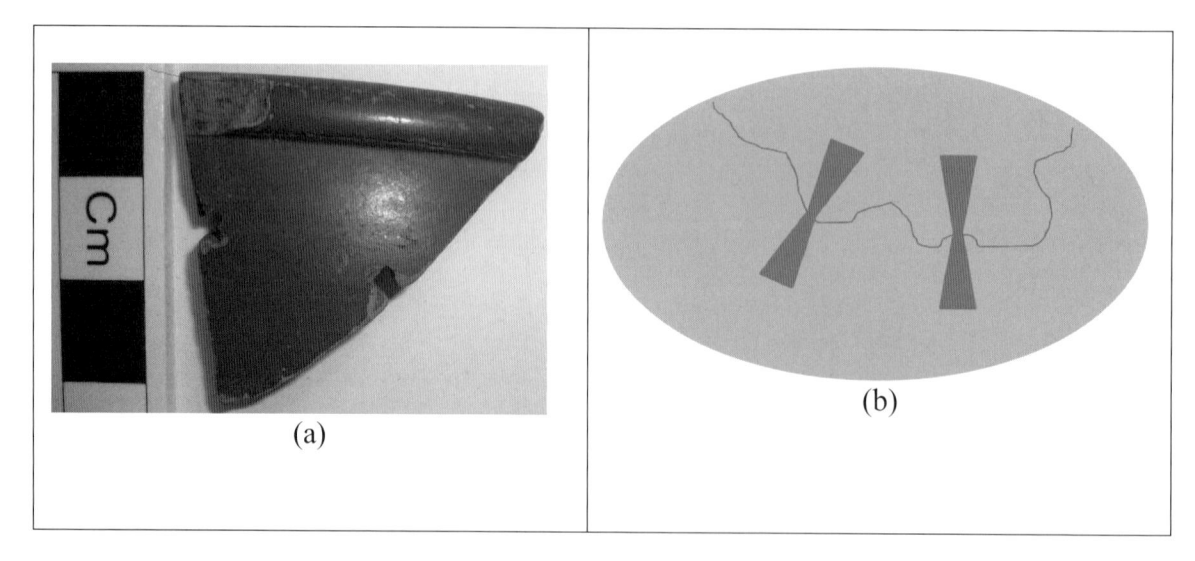

Figure 5.6.8 Single mortise and tenon repair Yewden villa Samian ware sherd 1994.57.P.1410, a Dr38 bowl from Lezoux, Central Gaul (AD120-200).

Once the necessary preparations had been made for the mortise and tenon repair, the second stage was to make the joint. This was done by either pouring molten lead/alloy into the joint or alternatively by the using a cold material such as white lead (cerussite – lead carbonate) mixed with linseed oil which was pressed into the joint. On cooling or hardening, the joint would then be finished by either filing off or chiselling off excess material. A series of oblique indentations would then be hammered into the lead/alloy joint. These indentations served to expand the joint material that may have shrunk on cooling.

Figure 5.6.8 (a) shows a pottery sherd collected from the Yewden villa site that shows dovetails cut into the rim of the sherd suggesting that a mortise and tenon repair had been carried out in the past. Fig 5.6.8 (b) is a stylised representation of such a repair scheme.

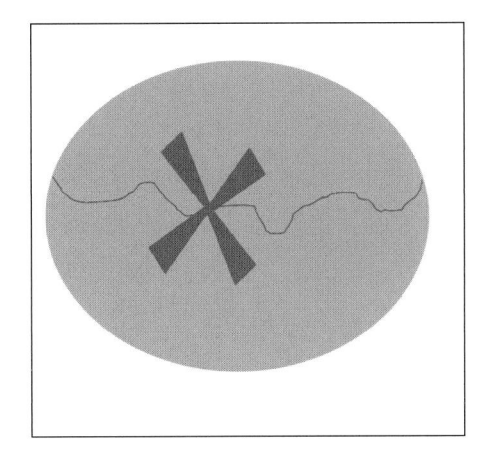

Figure 5.6.9 Double mortise and tenon repair

Large vessels may have been repaired using one of a number of variations on the mortise and tenon technique. For example, a double mortise and tenon repair (see Fig 5.6.9). This approach would have provided even greater strength and stability to the repair of large vessels. It required exactly the same repair techniques as the single mortise and tenon except that an additional pair of dovetails was cut at 90 degrees to the first set. As yet no obvious examples of this type of repair have been found on sherds collected at the Yewden villa site.

Repair replication: some experiments in Roman pottery repair techniques

Given the detailed repair descriptions of Pena 2007, it was decided to attempt to replicate some of the processes described. These included:

- Mortise and tenon jointing (cutting and casting of joints)

- Stapling (the production of staples by casting and hammering to the desired shape)

The vessel used for the experiment was a cheap terracotta pot from a garden centre that had already been broken during use. The fabric of the vessel was fairly uniform with no strengthening material being incorporated into the clay material prior to firing (Figure 5.6.10a).

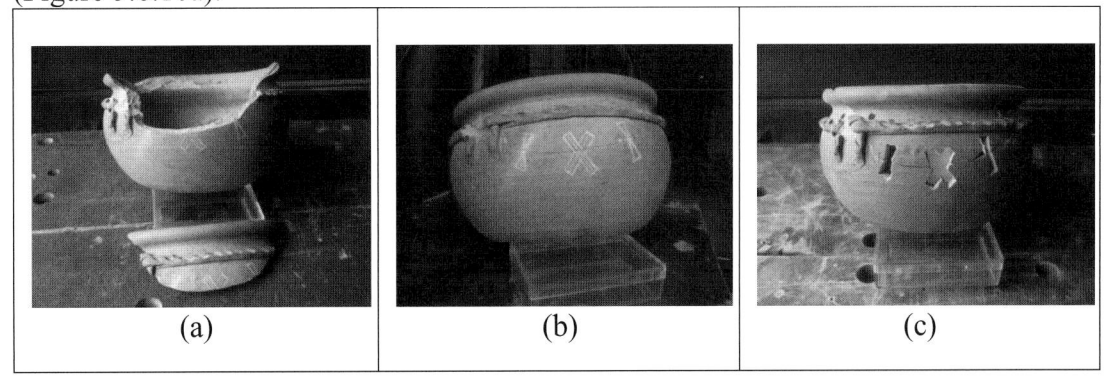

Figure 5.6.10 Initial stages of terracotta pot repair preparation and replication

The first repairs attempted were both single and double mortise and tenon joints. The first stage of the repair was to place the broken part of the pot into its original position. Then by using a scriber (a sharpened piece of metal) and a straight edge to mark the dovetails of one double mortise and tenon and then those of two singles (Figure 5.6.10b). This was easily achieved as the metal scriber cut easily through the glaze and pottery fabric (Figure 5.6.10c).

The second stage of operations was to cut the dovetails as required. This was done by separating the vessel and broken fragment, and then, using an old broken hacksaw blade, making the necessary cuts through the pottery fabric. Again, making the cuts posed no problems. Even saw blades made of a soft metal such as copper would have achieved the same result.

The third stage was to join the two pieces using a temporary glue to hold them together. A water soluble glue was sparingly used to cement the broken halves (the Romans could have used tar or pitch) so clay moulds could attached to the inner and outer surfaces of the vessel (Figs. 5.6.11a, 5.6.11b and 5.6.11c). The clay used was bought from a local craft shop. Both inner and outer moulds were shaped so that an excess of metal would form that, after cooling, could be either filed or hammered to expand the metal plug and tighten the join.

(a) (b) (c)

Figure 5.6.11 Preparation of clay moulds prior to metal pouring

The clay moulds were allowed to air-dry, then the metal was prepared for casting. The metal used was ordinary roof-guttering lead which was cut into small chips and melted in a crucible fashioned from a tin can to which an insulated pouring handle was attached.
After clamping the pot in a suitable position for metal pouring (a large woodworking vice was used), the lead was melted with a blowlamp. The molten lead was poured into each mould and allowed to cool (Fig. 5.6.12a). The vessel was rotated between each pouring operation. After cooling, the clay from each mould was removed exposing the cast mortises and tenons standing proud of the inner and outer vessel surfaces (Fig. 5.6.12b).

(a)	(b)

Figure 5.6.12 Metal casting and the removal of clay moulds

Once the cast mortises and tenons had been exposed, the final stage was to finish the repair. The poor fabric of the pot precluded hammering the lead to expand the casting. However, the metal castings seemed not to have contracted on cooling and the joints formed were very secure. The proud metal surfaces on the pot exterior were filed to the contour of the pot (Figs. 5.6.13a and 5.6.13b) using a rough file of a type that was probably available in the Roman era.

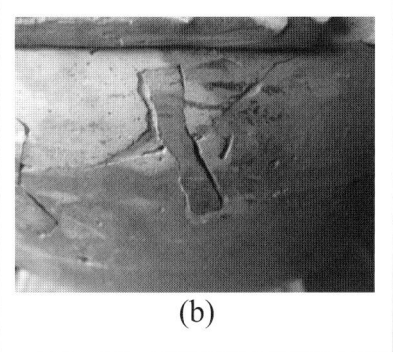

(a)	(b)

Figure 5.6.13 Repair finishing by filing to the exterior contours of the vessel

The next repair attempted used the hole and clamp method. First, a suitable length of lead wire/dowel was prepared by hot metal casting. The mould was built in several stages using wooden dowel to provide an internal mould cavity of the required shape (Figure 5.6.14a). After air drying the mould, the dowels were withdrawn and the ends of the mould sealed and left for a further period of air drying (Fig. 5.6.14b).

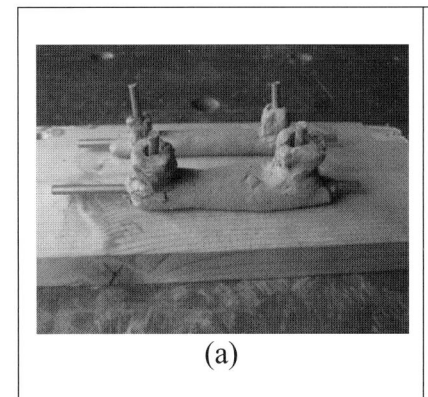

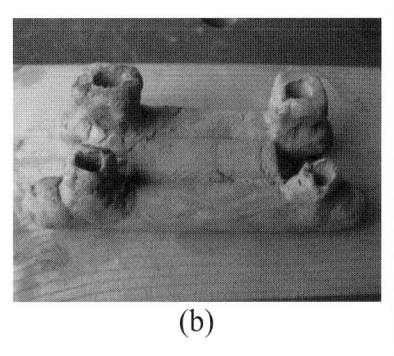

(a)	(b)

Figure 5.6.14 Preparation of moulds for the casting of lead dowel

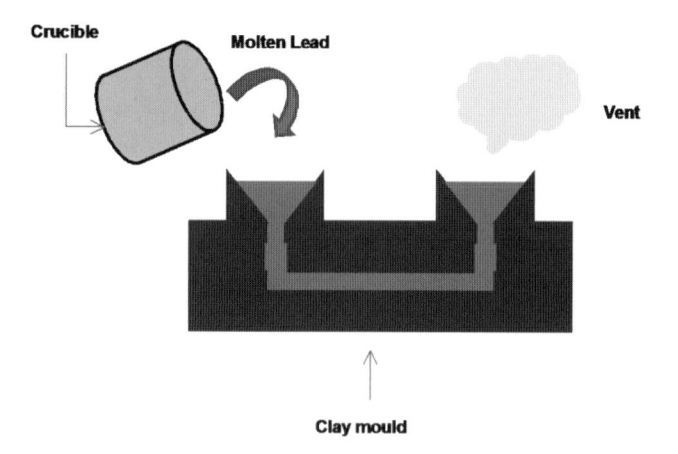

Once dry, the moulds were heated in an oven to drive off any residual moisture. Then a casting was attempted (Fig. 15). The process proved less than satisfactory as the metal cooled too quickly and only very short lengths of dowel could be made. A second attempt at metal casting was then made using an open moulding process.

Figure 5.6.15 Casting of lead dowel

The open mould was made by pressing wooden dowel into a thick sheet of clay and allowing the clay to dry. The dowel was then removed and molten lead poured into the channels left by the dowel in the clay (Figure 5.6.16a). When the lead dowels had cooled, they were removed from the mould (Figure 5.6.16b). The dowels were dressed by hammering a uniform round cross-section along their length. They were then ready to be cut to length for making staples for hole and clamp type repairs.

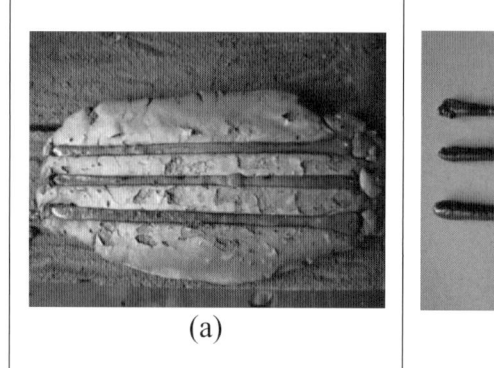

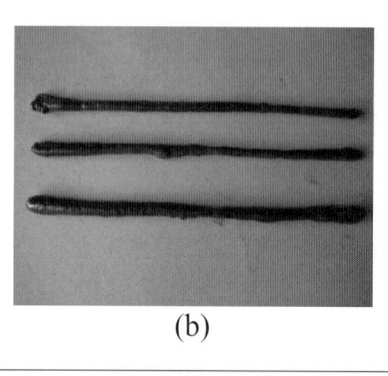

Figure 5.6.16 Open mould casting of lead dowel

The hole and clamp repair replication focussed on the damage to the rim of the terracotta pot already used for the mortise and tenon repair. The cracks terminating at the rim of the vessel either side of the mend were suitable for demonstrating the effectiveness of the hole and clamp technique. To begin, holes of the same diameter as the lead dowel prepared earlier were drilled either side of the crack running through the vessel rim. This was done using a hand brace and a twist drill (time did not allow the construction of a bow-drill). Staples were then made by cutting the lead dowel to a suitable length and bending it to make the legs. The legs of the staple were passed through the previously drilled holes. The legs were then bent over and hammered flat against the interior sidewall/rim of the vessel (Figure 5.6.17).

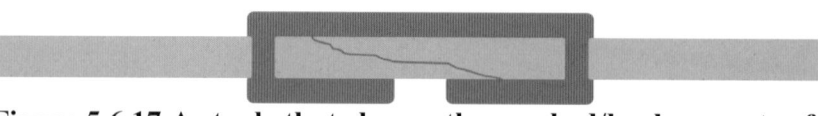

Figure 5.6.17 A staple that clamps the cracked/broken parts of a vessel together

While the staples were hammered, the exterior rim of the vessel was supported with a wooden block. The block spread the load of hammering more evenly. However, because of the delicate fabric of the vessel, further cracks developed around one of the repair areas. This highlighted the limitations inherent in the approach due to the danger of inflicting additional damage during the repair process. No attempt was made to fill any of the gaps surrounding the drilled holes by dripping in molten lead because the crucible available was too large to allow the delicate control necessary to successfully complete such a task.

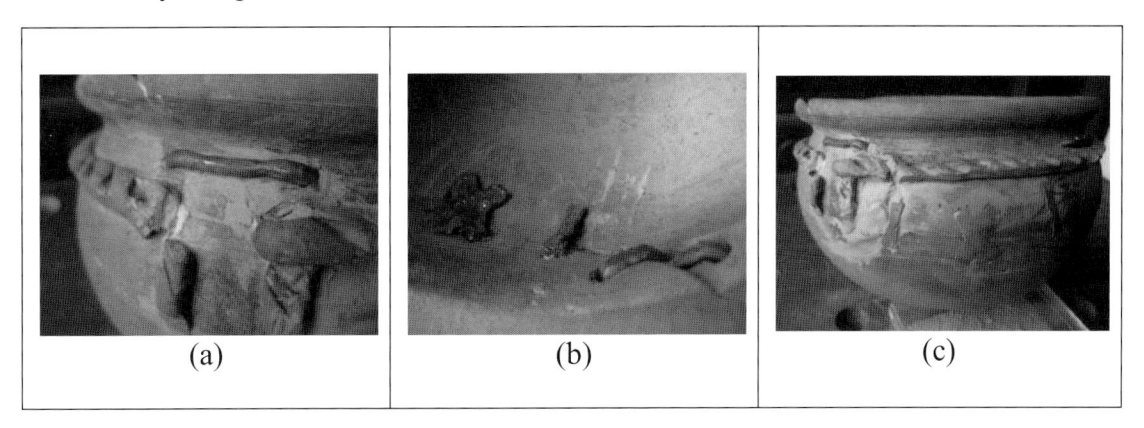

Figure 5.6.18 The hole and clamp method showing both the internal and external feature of the repair method

The results of this repair are shown in Figures 5.6.18a and 5.6.18b. Figure 5.6.18c shows the combined results of both mortise and tenon repairs and also the hole and clamp repair.
The main objective of the exercise was to better understand the application and limitation of Roman repair methods in evidence in the Yewden villa pottery sherds by attempting to replicate the processes.

No repair techniques other than the mortise and tenon and the hole and clamp methods were attempted.

Tools and methods employed by the author during repair replication are summarized in Figure 5.6.19 below.

Conclusions

Attempts by the author to recreate repairs of the types identified and discussed in the archaeological literature gave insight into some of the potential problems and difficulties faced by those of the Roman era when carrying out repairs to pottery fabric. Great care would have been needed when matching a particular repair technique to the object being repaired with respect given to the finish, thickness and quality of the pot fabric.

For example, the hole and clamp method is easily applied and is suitable for delicate fabrics when hammering must be kept to a minimum. But the joins can be unstable. Further reinforcement can be unsightly if aesthetics are a consideration. The mortise and tenon repair is more intricate and takes longer to prepare, but the outcome can be very stable, producing a tight joint that can be blended with the body of the vessel to produce an aesthetically pleasing finish.

The economics of a repair would have to consider the value and utility of the object against the cost of time and materials required to complete the task. The time taken by the author (who is familiar with hand tools and basic metalwork) to accomplish the experimental repairs described was approximately 8-10 hours. No attention was paid to sealing the vessel or to the surface finish. It is likely that skilled Roman artisan would have less time to carry out the same repairs although the basic processes would have been the same.

It is also concluded that in many instances the types of repair that the author attempted would not have required a high level of knowledge of pottery per se in the Roman era, just an appreciation of the constituent materials of the pottery fabric. The craft skills were within the repertoire of woodworkers and blacksmiths of the period and would have been widespread throughout the empire. However, the repair of small objects with great sentimental or religious value which may have had curved surfaces, elaborate rims and delicate fabrics would have required the more refined skills of craftsmen making glassware and jewellery.

The spirit lamp and blowpipe as a compact portable device capable of raising metals to high temperatures is known to have been used by Egyptian goldsmiths. Is there any evidence of such devices being used in Roman era workshops?

The use of metals and metal alloys would have relied either on a local sources of a metal ore, such as lead, or on trade of refined materials throughout the empire. This raises the intriguing question as to what insights could be gained by modern analyses of metal found in repaired pottery of the Roman era and identifying the original source of the ore.

Roman pottery sherds that have been collected in the modern era often show signs of repair using what is presumed to be either lead, copper, iron (or similar) in the form of a rivet, staple or metal jointing. While the implications of the social, organizational, economic and religious significance of such repairs is well discussed in contemporary literature there seems, with certain exceptions, to be few reports of any metallurgical analyses of repairs. Metallurgical studies of the metals/alloys found in repairs might relate repairs to the centres of ore mining (1) in a similar manner to those studies that characterise pottery fabrics and relate them to specific geographical and geological regions (J. Riederer).

Tools:
Hammers
Chisels
Saws
Files
Metal scriber
Metal straight edge

Bow Drill
Tongs
Crucible

Materials:
Lead
Tin/Lead Alloy
Clay
Creosote/Pitch
Wood or metal dowel
Wood supports for riveting

Heat Source
↓
Melt lead in crucible

Select and mark Mortise and Tenon positions
↓
Cut-out mortises using a saw and chisel
↓
On the interior of the vessel build a dam a few mm high around the shape of each cut-out using wet clay. Then, provide a roof over each using wet clay. Then allow to air dry.
↓
On the exterior of the vessel build a dam a few mm high around the shape of each cut-out using wet clay then allow to air dry.
↓
Make moulds for lead staples by pressing dowel into wet clay, then remove. This forms long D-shaped channels for molten metal casting. Allow to air dry
↓
Pour molten lead in to each cut-out allowing lead to cool before rotating the vessel and pouring into the next cut-out. →

Pour molten lead into staple moulds →

Select and mark staple and rivet positions
↓
Drill staple and rivet holes

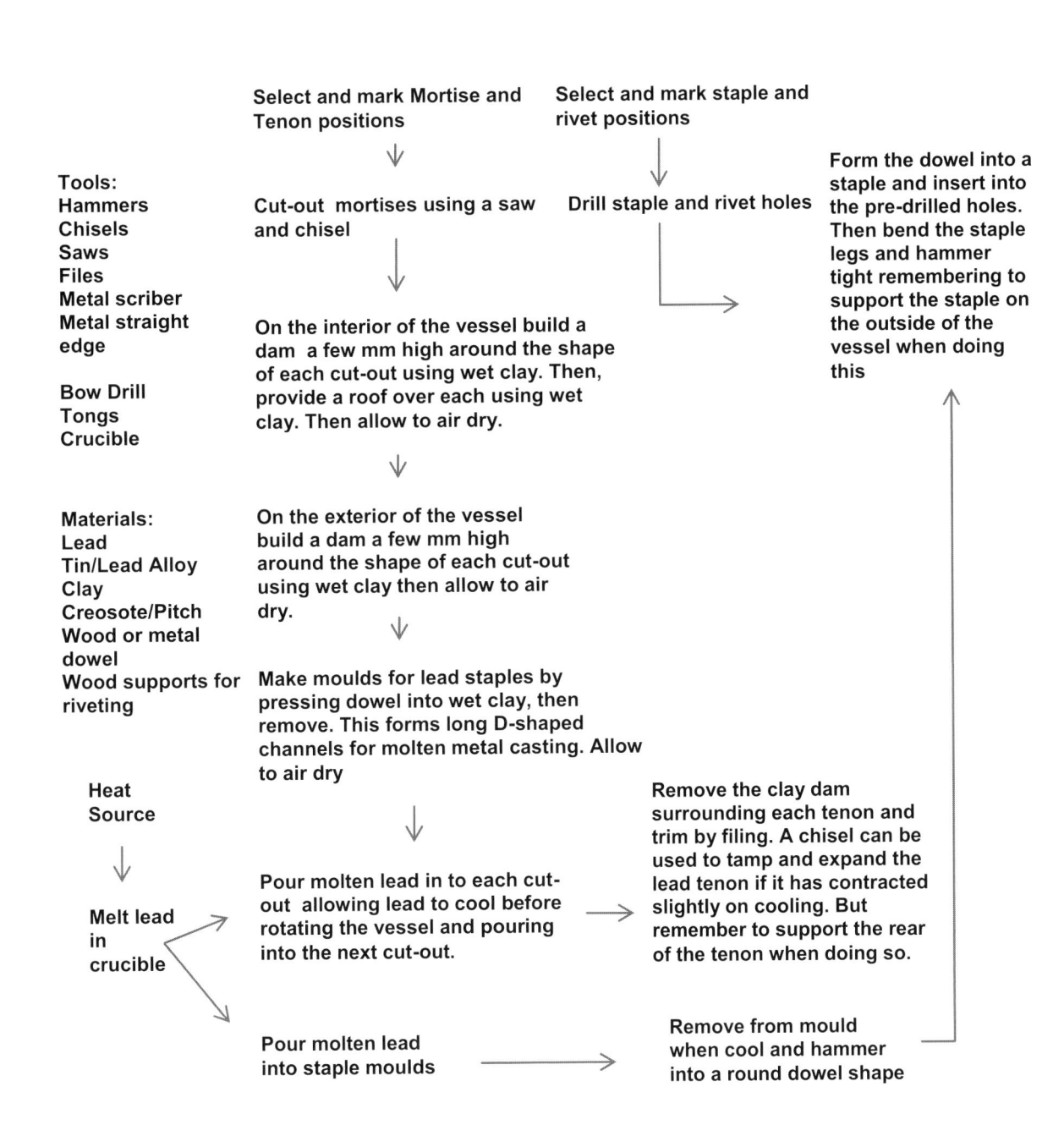

Form the dowel into a staple and insert into the pre-drilled holes. Then bend the staple legs and hammer tight remembering to support the staple on the outside of the vessel when doing this

Remove the clay dam surrounding each tenon and trim by filing. A chisel can be used to tamp and expand the lead tenon if it has contracted slightly on cooling. But remember to support the rear of the tenon when doing so.

Remove from mould when cool and hammer into a round dowel shape

Figure 5.6.19 A summary of the pottery repair stages and processes employed in the replication of Roman pottery repair techniques

Results:
The adult burials

Context: Adult Burial A, Pit 6.
Material: Well-preserved skeleton, approximately 60-80% complete.
Age: About 17-25 years (dental wear – Brothwell, 1981; pubic symphyseal morphology –Brooks & Suchey, 1990)
Sex: Male

Dental formula:

X	.	.	.	.	X	X	-	X	X	-	-	-	-	-
8	7	6	5	4	3	2	1	1	2	3	4	5	6	7	8
8	7	6	5	4	3	2	1	1	2	3	4	5	6	7	8
-	-	-	-	T	-	-	-	-	-	-	-	-	-	-
Left								Right						

Key: X = tooth lost post-mortem; · = tooth present in socket; T = tooth present, socket missing; - = tooth and socket missing.

Stature: 169.5cm.
Notes: The medial side of the proximal metaphysis of the right fibula bears a raised, smooth ridge of bone approximately 3cm long. The long axis of the ridge is aligned with the long-axis of the bone. The inferior end of the ridge is damaged but it had at least one small bony projection pointing distally. Radiography shows that the interior of the lesion is of cancellous bone which is continuous with that of the metaphysis. Probably an osteochondroma (a benign tumour). The adjacent part of the tibial metaphysis is normal.

Context: Adult Burial B, Pit 6.

Material: Well preserved skeleton, about 50% complete
Age: About 17-25 years (dental wear – Brothwell, 1981)
Sex: Male

Dental formula:

X	X	.	X	X	X	X	X	X	X	X	X	X	X	X	X
8	7	6	5	4	3	2	1	1	2	3	4	5	6	7	8
8	7	6	5	4	3	2	1	1	2	3	4	5	6	7	8
.	X	.	.	X	.	.	X	X	X	.	.	.	.	.	X
Left								Right							

Key: X = tooth lost post-mortem; · = tooth present in socket

Stature: 171.1cm
Notes: The medial surface in the middle half of the right tibia bears a well-remodelled deposit of porous new bone. The left tibia is normal. Given the location of the lesion on the subcutaneous surface of the bone, local infection following soft tissue injury is a likely cause.

The lowest sternal segment bears a small cleft in its lower border. This is likely due to incomplete union of left and right halves of the this segment during embryonic life (Barnes, 1994: 221-230).

Context: Adult Burial C, Pit 6.
Material: Well-preserved skeleton, approximately 60-80% complete.

Age: Approximately 25-35 years (dental wear – Brothwell, 1981)
Sex: Female
Stature: 157.8cm

Dental formula:

-	-	X	X	X	X	X	X	X	X	X	X	.	.	X	X
8	7	6	5	4	3	2	1	1	2	3	4	5	6	7	8
8	7	6	5	4	3	2	1	1	2	3	4	5	6	7	8
0	.	*	X	X	X	X	X	-	-	X	.	X	.C	.	0
Left								Right							

Key: X = tooth lost post-mortem; ˙ = tooth present in socket; - = tooth and socket missing; C = caries cavity; * = tooth lost ante-mortem; 0 = tooth congenitally absent.

The Juvenile Burials

Context: 45I(i) / 60, Pit 6.

Material: Contexts 45I(i) and context 60 are bones from a single individual. Those marked 45 appear to have been mislabelled. Well-preserved skeleton, approximately one-third complete.
Age: About 6 years (dental development – Gustafson & Koch, 1974).

Dental formula:

-	-	-	-	-	-	-	-	-	-	-	-	-	-	-	-
8	7	6	5	4	3	2	1	1	2	3	4	5	6	7	8
8	7	6	5	4	3	2	1	1	2	3	4	5	6	7	8
-	-	.E	.d	.d	Xd	Xd	X	.E	Xd	Xd	.d	.d	.	.U	-
Left								Right							

Key: X = tooth lost post-mortem; ˙ = tooth present in socket; d = deciduous tooth; - = tooth and socket missing; E = tooth erupting, U = tooth unerupted

Context: 45I(ii), 'Yard'

Material: Well-preserved skeleton, approximately 20-40% complete.
Age: About 1 year (comparison with pre-modern long-bone bone growth curves – Mays, 2007: Table 26).
Dental formula: no dentition

Context: 46, 'Yard'

Material: Well-preserved skeleton, approximately 60-80% complete
Age: About 1.5 years (dental development (Gustafson & Koch, 1974).

Dental formula:

-	-	UT	.Ud	.d	-	-	dT	dT	dT	Utd	dT	dUT	-	-	-
8	7	6	5	4	3	2	1	1	2	3	4	5	6	7	8
8	7	6	5	4	3	2	1	1	2	3	4	5	6	7	8
-	-	.U	.UdT	.d	.dE	Xd	Xd	-	-	.dE	.d	.dU	.U	-	-
Left								Right							

Key: ˙ = tooth present in socket; d = deciduous tooth; - = tooth and socket missing; E = tooth erupting, U = tooth unerupted; T = tooth present, socket missing

The Perinatal infants

The data for the 35 perinatal infants are summarised in Tables 6.1 and 6.2. The ages at death of those aged using the Scheuer *et al.* (1980) regression equations are depicted in Figure 6.1.

Although the gross preservation of the perinatal material was generally fairly good, with minimal post-depositional erosion of bone surfaces, most skeletons were substantially incomplete, with only long-bones and cranial fragments present. It seems probable that this reflects the nature of bone recovery on site resulting in principally the larger bones and parts thereof being recovered.

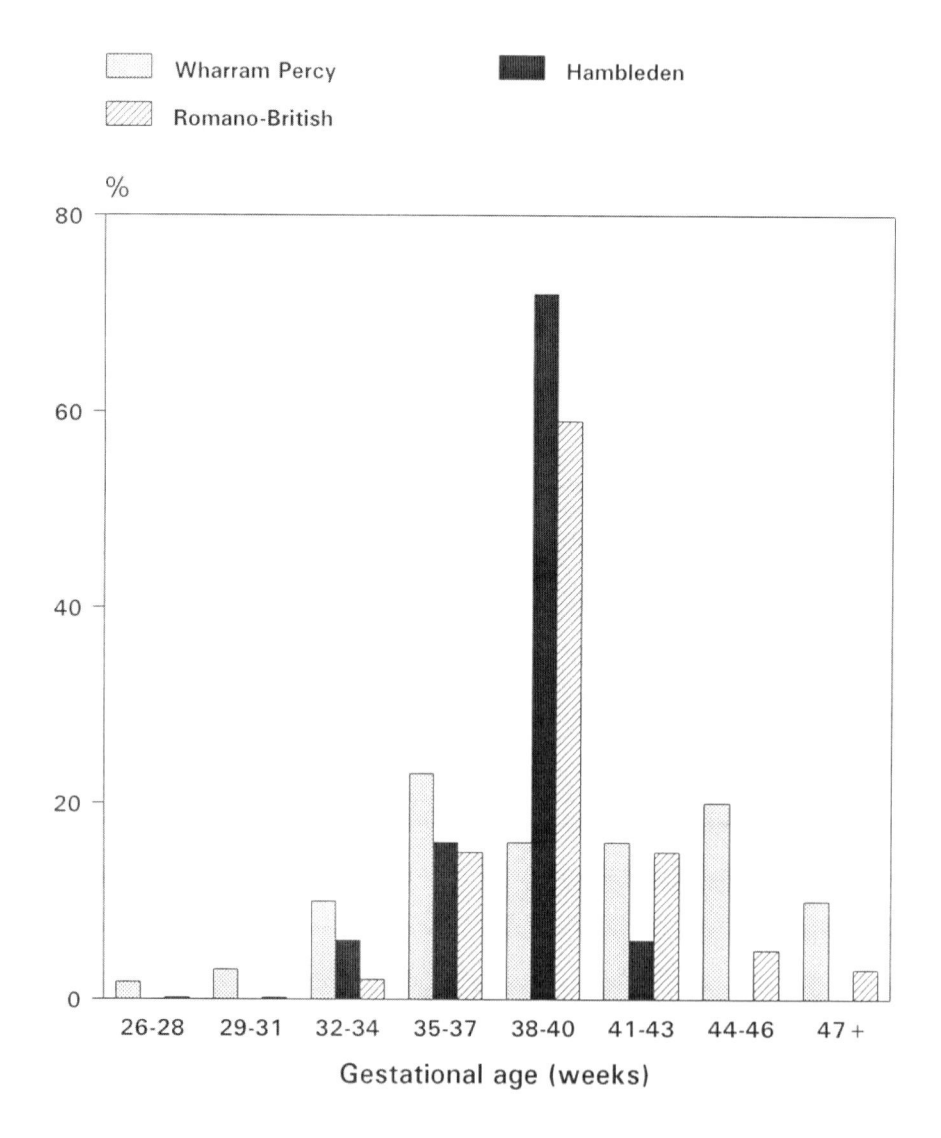

Figure 6.1 Distribution of gestational ages at death of the Hambleden perinatal infants (N=32) aged from long-bone lengths using the Scheuer et al. (1980) BCH equations. Also presented for comparison are age distributions from some other Romano-British sites (N=164 infants), and from Mediaeval Wharram Percy (N=61), also generated from long-bone lengths using the Scheuer et al. BCH equations. Comparative data taken from Mays (1993, 2003).

A bone from burial 38 (aged 35-37 weeks gestation) bears what appear to be cut-marks. They are five in number and are located on the postero-lateral side of the right femur in the subtrochanteric region (Fig. 6.2). The four situated most superiorly run approximately transversely across the bone, with the fifth, most inferior mark being angled at approximately 45 degrees to the rest. The most superiorly located mark is about 3mm long, the remainder about 4mm long. The surfaces of the marks are weathered, and examination under low-power microscope revealed soil particles in the base of the cuts. These observations indicate that the marks were made in antiquity. There is no sign of new bone formation in any of the cuts. They appear consistent with marks made by a metal blade drawn across fresh bone (Greenfield, 1999; Lewis, 2008), and they seem to be perimortal events. They have a fairly uniform appearance suggesting they may have been made by the same blade. Careful examination of the remainder of the skeleton showed no convincing evidence for further cut-marks.

In order to investigate further the morphology of the cut-marks, a μCT scan was taken of the femur from burial 38. To establish the depth and character of the cut-marks several virtual cross-sections through the damaged area were reconstructed. The results show that all the cuts penetrate the full thickness of the cortical bone, but do not extend into the cancellous bone. The cut surfaces are smooth, and the dimensions of the cuts are relatively uniform; mean maximum depth is 545μm (range 478-612μm), and width is 549μm (range 497-602μm). These findings support the gross and low-power microscopic examinations in suggesting the use of a single, non-serrated and probably metal blade.

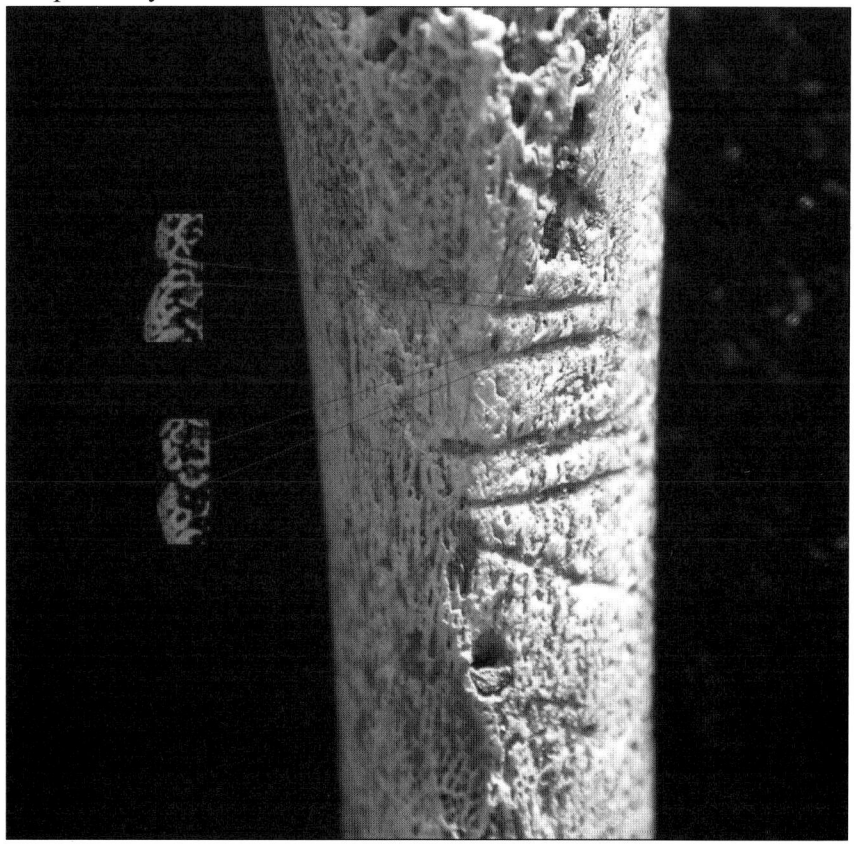

Figure 6.2: Burial 38 posterior surface of the subtrochanteric region of the right femur showing cut-marks and two examples of their cross-sections generated from the μCT scan. The μCT slices have a pixel resolution of 17.55μm.

The disarticulated bone
In addition to the 41 contexts which seem to represent discrete burials there are a further 24 contexts that contain single or some few fragments of human bones, often in association with small amounts of animal bone. The identification of the human elements is listed in the Appendix.

Discussion
One of us (SM) has previously suggested that analysis of the distribution of ages at death (in weeks gestation) of perinatal burials can potentially reveal whether the perinates in an assemblage were predominantly natural deaths or were mainly victims of infanticide, the deliberate killing of unwanted infants (Mays, 1993). Infanticide is normally carried out immediately following birth, and one might therefore expect that the regular practice of infanticide would lead to a perinatal age at death distribution with a strong peak at an age corresponding to a full-term infant (about 38-41 weeks gestation – Tanner, 1989: 43). By contrast, natural deaths show a rather more dispersed distribution. Previous work has shown that perinatal infants from several Romano-British villa, settlement and cemetery sites showed peaked distributions characteristic of infanticide, whereas perinatal infants from a Mediaeval burial ground showed a flatter distribution, with no pronounced peak at full-term, typical of natural deaths (Mays, 1993, 2003).

The age distribution of the Hambleden infants aged using the Scheuer et al. (1980) regression equations (which allow gestational age to be estimated to within about two weeks), together with those from the Roman and Mediaeval data of Mays (1993, 2003), are shown in Fig 6.1. The Hambleden distribution shows a marked peak at 38-40 weeks, an age approximately corresponding to a full-term foetus. In this it resembles other Romano-British data and differs from the natural age at death distribution evidenced by the Mediaeval Wharram Percy data. These results are suggestive of infanticide at Hambleden, and provide further evidence for the practice in Roman Britain. Further regression and Bayesian methods of ageing the Hambleden perinatal infants also point toward infanticide (Mays & Eyers, in press). The results need not, of course, imply that all the perinatal infants at Hambleden were victims of infanticide, but rather that the practice was carried out with sufficient regularity to exert a marked effect on the age at death distribution.

Turning to the cut-marks on the femur of perinatal burial 38, given their location they seem unlikely to have been inflicted with the intent of killing the infant, and the lack of further convincing cuts elsewhere on the skeleton argues against a systematic deflashing process, as has been seen, for example, in a 2nd century AD cranium from Roman Britain (Mays & Steele, 1996). The purpose of the cuts is unclear, but one possibility is that they were a result of an attempted obstetric operation.

Procedures for embryotomy to remove a dead foetus that became stuck in the birth canal were known in the Roman world (Jackson, 1988). In the second century AD, Soranus of Ephesus describes embryotomy using a series of amputations at the joints of a dead foetus, cutting each part as it presents (Molleson & Cox, 1988). If burial 38 was a breech birth (breech presentations occur in about 6-7% of infants of the gestational age of burial 38 (Fox & Chapman, 2006)), and hence stuck in the birth canal, the location of the cuts would be explicable as they would be in an area readily accessible to the surgeon in a breech presentation. The knife-marks may have been adventitious cuts as the surgeon attempted to locate the hip joint. There are no knife marks upon the proximal extremity of the femur, but a successful attempt to amputate through the hip joint could have left marks solely upon the pelvic bones (missing in the burial 38) or it may have solely involved slicing periarticular elements unmineralised in late foetal life. That the type of embryotomy by dismemberment described by Soranus was practiced in Britain when it was a province of the Roman empire is evidenced by the dismembered foetus from Poundbury, Dorset (Molleson & Cox, 1988; Molleson, 1993).

Two infants from the 'yard' area show supra-condyloid process of the humerus. This is a minor anatomical variant. Its frequency in recent Europeans is generally less than about 2% (Natsis, 2008), and systematic studies on large archaeological skeletal collections from Britain produce similar frequencies (e.g. Cox, 1989; Mays, 1991, 2007; Waldron, 2007). The causation of the variant is not well-understood, but there is some evidence for a familial occurrence (Finnegan, 1976). That two of the Hambleden infants show the trait may therefore suggest a close genetic relationship between them.

References

Barnes, E. 1994. *Developmental defects of the axial skeleton*. University Press of Colorado, Niwot.

Berry, A.C. and Berry, R.J. 1967. Epigenetic variation in the human cranium. *Journal of Anatomy* 101: 361-379.

Brooks, S. and Suchey, J.M. 1990. Skeletal age determination based on the os pubis: a comparison of the Acsádi-Nemeskéri and Suchey-Brooks methods. *Human Evolution* 5: 227-238.

Brothwell, D.R. 1981. *Digging up bones*, 3rd edition. Oxford University Press / British Museum (Natural History), Oxford.

Cox, M. 1989. *The human bones from Ancaster*. AML Report 93/89. English Heritage, London.

Fazekas, I.G. and Kosa, F. 1978. *Forensic Foetal Osteology*. Akademiai Kiado, Budapest.

Finnegan, M. 1976. Walnut Creek massacre: identification and analysis. *American Journal of Physical Anthropology* 45: 737-742.

Finnegan, M. 1978. Non-metric variation of the infra-cranial skeleton. *Journal of Anatomy* 125: 23-37.

Fox, A.J. and Chapman, M.G. 2006. Longitudinal ultrasound assessment of fetal presentation: a review of 1010 consecutive cases. *Australian and New Zealand Journal of Obstetrics and Gynaecology* 46: 341-344.

Greenfield, H.J. 1999. The origins of metallurgy: distinguishing stone from metal cut-marks on bones from archaeological sites. *Journal of Archaeological Science* 26: 797-808.

Gustafson, G. and Koch, G. 1974. Age estimation up to 16 years of age based on dental development. *Odontologisk Revy* 25: 297-306.

Jackson, R. 1988. *Doctors and diseases in the Roman Empire*. British Museum, London.

Lewis, J.E. 2008. Identifying sword marks on bone: criteria for distinguishing between cut marks made by different classes of bladed weapons. *Journal of Archaeological Science* 35: 2001-2008.

Mays, S.A. 1991. *The Mediaeval burials from the Blackfriars Friary, School Street, Ipswich, Suffolk*. AML Report 16/91. English Heritage, London.

Mays, S. 1993. Infanticide in Roman Britain. *Antiquity* 67: 883-888.

Mays, S. 2003. Comment on 'A Bayesian approach to ageing perinatal skeletal material from archaeological sites: implications for evidence for infanticide in Roman Britain' by R.L. Gowland and A.T. Chamberlain. *Journal of Archaeological Science* 30: 1695-1700.

Mays, S. 2007. The Human Remains. In (Mays, S., Harding, C. and Heighway, C.) *Wharram XI: The churchayard*. Wharram: a study of settlement on the Yorkshire Wolds XI. York University Press, York, pp. 77-192, 337-397.

Mays, S. and Eyers, J. in press. Perinatal infant death at the Roman villa site at Hambleden, Buckinghamshire, England. *Journal of Archaeological Science*

Mays, S. and Steele, J. 1996. A mutilated skull from Roman St Albans. *Antiquity* 70: 155-161.

Molleson, T. 1993. The human remains. In (Farwell, D.E. and Molleson, T.I.), *Excavations at Poundbury 1966-80, Volume 2: The cemeteries*. Dorset Natural History and Archaeological Society Monograph Series 11. Dorset Natural History and Archaeological Society, Dorchester, pp. 142-214.

Molleson, T. and Cox, M. 1988. A neonate with cut bones from Poundbury Camp. *Bulletin de la Société Royale Belge d'Anthropologie et Préhistoire* 99: 53-59.

Natsis, K. 2008. Supracondylar process of the humerus. Study on 375 Caucasian subjects in Cologne, Germany. *Clinical Anatomy* 21: 138-141.

Pounder, D.J., Sim, L.J. 2011. Virtual casting of stab wounds in cartilage using micro-computed tomography. *American Journal of Forensic Medicine and Pathology* doi:10.1097/PAF.obo13e3182186f37.

Robson Brown, K., Silver, I.A., Musgrave, J.H., Roberts, A.M. 2010. The use of μCT technology to identify skull fracture in a case involving blunt force trauma. *Forensic Science International* 201: http://dx.doi.org/10.1016/j.forsciint.2010.06.013.

Scheuer, J.L., Musgrave, J.H. and Evans, S.P. 1980. Estimation of late foetal and perinatal age from limb bone lengths by linear and logarithmic regression. *Annals of Human Biology* 7: 257-265.

Sherwood, R.J., Meindl, R.S., Robinson, H.B. and May, R.L. 2000. Fetal age: methods of estimation and effects of pathology. *American Journal of Physical Anthropology* 113: 305-315.

Tanner, J.M. 1989. *Foetus into man*, 2nd edition. Castlemead, Ware.

Thali, M.J., Taubenreuther, U., Karolczak, M., Braun, M., Brueschweiler, W., Kalender, W.W., Dironhofer, R. 2003. Forensic microradiology: micro-computed tomography (micro-CT) and analysis of patterned injuries inside of bone. *Journal of Forensic Sciences* 48: 1336–1342.

Trotter, M. and Gleser, G.C. 1952. Estimation of stature from long-bones of American Whites and Negroes. *American Journal of Physical Anthropology* 10: 463-514.

Trotter, M. and Gleser, G.C. 1958. A re-evaluation of 'Estimation of stature from long-bones of American Whites and Negroes', American Journal of Physical Anthropology (1952). *American Journal of Physical Anthropology* 16: 79-123.

Trotter, M. and Gleser, G.C. 1977. Corrigienda to 'Estimation of stature from long-bones of American Whites and Negroes', American Journal of Physical Anthropology (1952). *American Journal of Physical Anthropology* 47: 355-356.

Waldron, T. 2007. *St Peter's Barton-Upon-Humber, Lincolnshire. A parish church and its community. Volume 2: The human remains*. Oxbow, Oxford.

Wood, R.E. 2006. Forensic aspects of maxillofacial radiology. *Forensic Science International* 159S: S47–S55.

Appendix: list of identifications of disarticulated bone

All remains are of perinatal size unless stated. Measurements taken according to Fazekas & Kosa (1978).

Context 11: Parietal bone fragment.

Context 21: Left deciduous maxillary first molar (roots incomplete), cranial vault, base and facial bone fragments, mental eminence of mandible (symphysis fused). The molar development suggests an age at death of about 1 year; the bony remains are consistent with this. Parietal, sphenoid, rib and scapula fragments from an adult skeleton.

Context 29: Cranial base and vault fragments. R *pars lateralis* of occipital bone, length=28mm, width=14.

Context 32: Greater wing left sphenoid (width 20mm, length 32mm), fragment of cranial vault.

Context 34: Distal 70% of left humerus.

Context 36: Left humerus (length 64mm).

Context 37: Midshaft 50% left humerus, smaller than perinatal.

Context 39: Right tibia, length approx 58mm.

Context 44: Proximal 50% right femur.

Context 47: Left ilium, length 35mm, width 31mm.

Context 48: Proximal 10% right tibia, proximal 50% left radius, midshaft 50% right femur, 2 fragments of unidentified longbones.

Context 49: proximal 25% ?right humerus

Context 50: Distal 70% right humerus, proximal 50% right tibia, midshaft 50% right femur, parts of two further unidentified longbones.

Context 51: Tibia.

Context 52: Right femur, length 80mm.

Context 53: right tibia (length approx. 52mm), right humerus (length approx. 67mm).

Context 54: Midshaft 70% right tibia, proximal 70% left femur, distal 50% right femur. The two femurs are not a pair.

Context 55: Right humerus, length approx. 56mm – smaller than perinatal.

Context 56: Proximal 50% right femur.

Context 57: Right radius (length 53mm), left humerus (length approx. 66mm). Proximal 70% left ulna, probably slightly older than perinatal.

Context 58: Left tibia (length 69mm), distal 80% right humerus.

Context 59: Right ilium (length 54mm, width 47mm), age about 8-17months (cf Spitalfields growth data – Molleson & Cox, 1993: Table 10.4). Probably part of burial 45I(ii).

Context 61: Frontal bone fragment including supra-orbital region, adult male.
Context 62: Four fragments of an adult left parietal bone.

Table 6.1: Osteological data for perinatal skeletons.
Preservation scored on a subjective basis as good, moderate or poor based on the degree of soil erosion of bone surfaces. Skeletal completeness scored according to the approximate percentage of the skeleton present. Age given as weeks gestation, estimated from long-bone lengths using the Scheuer et al. (1980) BCH linear regression equations, except *, estimated from long-bone lengths using the Sherwood et al. (2000) regression equations. Burial 16, age estimated as perinatal using dental development (Gustafson & Koch, 1974) and sphenoid dimensions (body length 10mm, lesser wing length 16mm – Fazekas & Kosa, 1978). Burial 31, mixed bones of perinate (dental development - Gustafson & Koch, 1974) and 4-6 month (dental development – Gustafson & Koch, 1974) infant.

Context	Preservation	Completeness	Age at death	Notes
1	Moderate	40-60%	41-43	
2	Moderate	20-40%	38-40	
3	Good	20-40%	38-40	
4	Good	40-60%	38-40	
5	Good	20-40%	38-40	
6	Good	40-60%	32-34	
7	Good	40-60%	38-40	
8	Moderate	40-60%	38-40	
9(I)	Good	<20%	38-40	Burial 9 is mixed bones of two individuals, here called 9(I) and 9(II). Only bones that could be reliably assigned to one or other individual are recorded
9(II)	Good	<20%	35-37	
10	Good	20-40%	32-34	
12	Good	40-60%	38-40	
13	Moderate	<20%	38-40	Bones from burials 13 and 14 were mixed. Only bones that could be reliably assigned to one or other individual are recorded
14	Moderate	<20%	38-40	
15	Good	<20%	35-37	
16	Good	<20%		
17	Good	20-40%	38-40	Burials 17 and 18 were located close together on site and the bones were recovered mixed. Only bones that could be reliably assigned to one or other individual are recorded
18	Good	20-40%	38-40	
19	Good	40-60%	38-40	
20	Good	20-40%	38-40	
22	Good	60-80%	38-40	The right humerus bears a small supra-condyloid process
23	Good	<20%	38-40	Bones from burials 23 and 24 were mixed. Only bones that could be reliably assigned to one or other individual are recorded
24	Moderate	<20%	38-40	

25	Moderate	<20%	38-40	
26	Good	<20%	35-37	
27	Good	<20%	38-40	
28	Good	40-60%	38-40	
30	Moderate	20-40%	38-40	The left humerus bears a supra-condyloid process
31	Good	20-40%		
35	Good	<20%	38-40*	
38	Good	60-80%	35-37	Knife-marks on right femur
40	Good	40-60%	38-40	
42	Good	40-60%	41-43	
43	Good	40-60%	35-37	
45(II)	Good	60-80%	38-40	

Table 6.2 Diaphyseal long-bone lengths for perinatal burials

Context	Fem l	Fem r	Tib l	Tib r	Fib l	Fib r	Hum l	Hum r	Rad l	Rad r	Ulna l	Ulna r	Clav l	Clav r
1	83		70	70						55		62		
2	80													
3	77		67			63	66			53				
4							66		53	53	61			
5	76	76	67	66			64							
6	64	63	55	56	53	53		57		48	54	54	39	39
7	76	76	66	65	61							58		
8							67	67	51			59		
9(I)		79					67							
9(II)		71					63							
10	60						55			46				
12	76						65	55	54					
13		74												
14	74													
15								49						
16														
17			67				68			62				
18	73	73	63	64			63					56		
19	75	75	62	62	60	60	64			48		56		
20									53	61				
22	74	73	62	63		60	64	64			59		44	
23	76	76					67	67						
24	75	75												
25										52		61		
26	69	69												
27							66							
28	76		67			63	66		53		60		45	45
30										54				
31														
35			64											

38	70	69	62	62			61	60	50	49	56		40	40
40				65				65						
42	83	82	70	70		67				56	64	64		
43	70	71	61	62		58	61	61	50		57			44
45(II)	74	74	65	65	62		67			52		61		44

Chapter 7 The environmental evidence

Chapter 7.1   Animal bone

There were insufficient funds during this phase of the project to undertake a full assessment and study of the animal bones. There are 45 boxes of bones in the Buckinghamshire County Museum stores. Mr Cocks labelled the bones with their Yewden site location and the whole assemblage is in excellent condition. A study of this collection will prove a valuable future project and would provide useful information not only on the species present and their abundance, but also on butchery techniques and palaeo-pathology, amongst other research areas.

A summary of the animal bones was provided by Cocks (1921, pp. 163-166) and this includes the following species:

	No. of individuals	Location
Wild animals:		
Cat	c. 6	
Pine marten	2?	Pit 4
Polecat	1	
Otter	1	
Badger	2 or 3	
Fox	3 or 4 adults, plus a litter of cubs	
Hare	1 whole, plus bone scatter	Pit 21
Rabbit	1 whole, plus bone scatter	Pit 21
Red deer	c. 12	
Roe deer	c. 6	
Domestic animals:		
Cat		
Dog	Numerous	
Horse	9 to 15 hands, exceptionally numerous	
Pony	1 individual, 9 to 10 hands	
Ox	Very numerous	
Sheep	Numerous	
Goat		
Pig	Fairly numerous, most immature individuals	
Birds:		
Raven	1 bone	
Rook	8 bones +	
Lark	1 bone	
Blackbird	1 bone?	
Goose	Numcrous	
Duck	3 bones	
Woodcock	3 bones	

Dove	2 bones	
Pheasant	11 bones	
'Domestic fowl'	Numerous	

From a pellet of a bird of prey: S. Wall 1st House
    Bank mouse
    Grass mouse
    Field mouse
    Birds, indet.
    Frog
    Toad

Fish:
    Roach   1 bone

Amphibians:
    Frogs
    Toads

Invertebrates:
    Oyster   Hundreds, including one batch unopened. Many shells had no location recorded, but those with details include: 1st House Room C; Trench SE from the Stoke hole of Room A 1st House; Pit 24; 2nd House Stoke hole of the Union Jack Furnace; near the N end of the 2nd House.

    Mussels   c. 12
    Cockles   c. 12

Chapter 7.2 Charred Grain from Yewden Roman Villa

Gill Campbell

Two samples of charred grain were found within the pottery assemblages of Box 2256 and Box 2381. These are labelled as coming from the furnaces and it is likely that both samples were retrieved from one or more of the corn drying ovens. The material in the two samples was identified by the author using a dissecting binocular microscope at magnifications up to x 50, and with reference to the modern comparative collection held at English Heritage, Fort Cumberland. Nomenclature follows Zohary and Hopf (2000, table 3, table 5). The results are presented in Table 1.

Both samples contained spelt wheat *(Triticum spelta)* type grain along with a small amount of hulled six-row barley grain (*Hordeum vulgare*). While spelt wheat cannot be definitively identified from grain alone, the occurrence of spelt wheat chaff in the form of a number of glume bases in one of the samples confirms the presence of this variety of wheat. A large proportion of the grains in both samples showed definite signs of germination and detached cereal sprouts were also present.

Table 7.2.1
Charred grain samples from Yewden villa

Taxa	Boxes 2256	2381
Triticum spelta L.- sprouted grain	15	14 (4)
T. spelta L.- grain	12	2
T. spelta L.- glume base	-	4
T. dicoccum/ spelta -spouted grain	-	3
T. dicoccum/ spelta -grain	1	-
T. dicoccum/ spelta -glume base	-	3
Triticum sp. -grain	8	7
Triticum/ Secale sp. -awn fragment	-	1
Hordeum vulgare L. -part of a spikelet	1	-
Hordeum sp. - sprouted, hulled, straight grain	3	1
Hordeum sp. - sprouted, hulled, twisted grain	(1)	1
Hordeum sp. - hulled, twisted grain		2
Cereales indet. -grain	mni 3	mni 5
Cereales indet. -sprout	1	16

This shows that the spelt wheat, with hulled six-row barley probably present as a contaminant, was being malted at the site. It is likely that the corn drying ovens were used to dry malted grain, and that these assemblages are the result of accidental burning of grain during this process or derive from material that dropped from the floor of the drying ovens into the underlying open flues. However, the ovens were likely to a have been used for a number of other purposes including the drying of grain prior to grinding into flour.

Malted grain is parched in order to stop the germination process. However it is important that the grain is only heated gently, as if it gets too hot the diastase enzymes, become denatured. These enzymes are essential in the brewing process to convert starch into simple sugars (Corran, 1975, 12; Dinley and Dinley, 2001). In Roman Britain, spelt wheat beer was the norm, so these results are consistent with the national picture (Campbell, 2008a; 2008b; Pearson and Robinson, 1994, 583; van der Veen, 1989).

References

Campbell, G, 2008a 'Plant utilisation in the countryside around Danebury: a Roman perspective', *in* B Cunliffe *The Danebury Environs Programme A Wessex landscape in the Roman era Volume 1: Overview* (English Heritage and Oxford University School of Archaeology Monograph **70**), 53-74 and e text

Campbell, G, 2008 'Charred plant remains' *in* B Cunliffe and C Poole *The Danebury Environs Programme A Wessex landscape in the Roman era Volume 2- Part 2: Grateley South, Grateley, Hants, 1998 and 1999* (English Heritage and Oxford University School of Archaeology Monograph **71**) 166-74 and e-text

Corran, H S, 1975 *A History of Brewing*, London: David and Charles

Dinley, M, and Dinley, G, 2001 'Neolithic ale: barley as a source of malt sugars for fermentation', in A S Fairburn (ed) *Plants in the Neolithic and beyond*, Oxford: Oxbow books, 137-53

Pearson, E, and Robinson, M, 1994 'Environmental evidence from the villa', in Williams, R J, and Zeepvat, R J, *Bancroft, a late Bronze Age/Iron Age settlement, Roman villa and temple mausoleum, vol* **2**, *finds and environmental evidence*, Aylesbury: Buckinghamshire Archaeological Society (monograph **7**), 565-84

van der Veen, M, 1989 'Charred grain assemblages from Roman-period corn driers in Britain, in *Archaeol. J.* **146**, 302-19

Zohary, D & Hopf, M 2000 *Domestication of plants in the Old World* 3rd edn. Oxford: Oxford University Press.

Chapter 8 Discussion and conclusions

The flint assemblage indicates a human presence in the Hambleden Valley from the Mesolithic through to the Neolithic and Bronze Age, and a variety of finds and geophysics has provided further evidence of Iron Age and Roman habitation. There was no evidence for Saxon settlement, but the Domesday records would infer a community already in the area with records of a fishing weir and a mill. Norman archaeology is seen today in the modern village, which continued as a settlement from this period to the present-day.

The Iron Age community settled in the west side of the valley (Hog Pit field) with agricultural fields and water meadow adjacent (to the east). Hilltop grazing was also located to the east via the Rotten Row Holloway leading from a square enclosure seen partly lying within the villa complex (the 'V ditch' of Cocks, 1921). This enclosure ditch was proved to date from the Iron Age to the Roman period, possibly earliest 5th century AD, and hence is not the 'temporary military camp' suggested in the scheduling document (NM27160). In addition, there are crop marks visible in drought conditions to the south of the site, nearer to the River Thames. These features form a variety of shapes, indicating further archaeology to the south. One area is clearly Romano-British (Mill End villa), with an enclosure ditch on the north side visible on geophysics (Eyers and Hutt, paper in prep). The size and shape of other nearby features are characteristic of the Iron Age, but could equally well represent mixed archaeology, and may prove to have a component including the Neolithic or Bronze Age (especially as many flints of these eras were found in the surrounding fields). The fields in the southern end of the Hambleden Valley, adjacent to Mill End, would benefit from a continued geophysical survey.

Romano-British occupation at Yewden continued from the Iron Age community on the same site, but migrated southwards. This is shown by the continued fill of pits from the Early and Middle Iron Age, through to Late Iron Age and the 'Belgic' transition into the Roman period. The overlap of the settlement and associated paths and tracks is also shown by geophysics. The huge quantity of finds from the Romano-British period provides a valuable insight into this site, into local and international trade, as well as life and customs in general. Pottery alone provided almost 1 tonne of material!

The buildings and chronology

Buildings of various types were excavated in 1912 and more recently proved by geophysics, which also extended our knowledge of associated archaeology. Roundhouses from the pre-Romano-British community were shown present by geophysics extending from the Yewden site northwards in Hog Pit Field. There is a profusion of pits in this area which, by association with the interpreted Iron Age house structures are inferred to be mostly, if not all, datable to the Iron Age. This is supported by the pottery evidence – Iron Age pottery clusters in the far northern end of the excavation and within the V ditch (which is an Iron Age enclosure ditch). Some Iron Age pottery is present in the fill of those pits within the Yewden excavation area, but lower levels and older pits, tend to show a large proportion of Belgic pottery.

The Yewden building structures embraced Romanization from the invasion period onwards, both in terms of shape and layout. However, the buildings are all wooden structures supporting wattle and daub walls over mortared flint foundations, and either a tiled or a thatched roof. This style is not uncommon in the Chilterns and in parts of Oxfordshire, where good use is made of the locally available materials. In theory, stone from Oxfordshire might have been potentially available, but it was not imported for use in the Yewden buildings, with the exception of some oolitic window surrounds. Pottery was brought in from Oxfordshire in large quantities, so it would appear that the trade route was there, but stone was not available or it was not the preferred building material. Likewise, patterned mosaics were not present. This might reflect the lack of a suitable craftsman for the more elaborate designs, as well-laid tessellated pavements were present in several areas at Yewden.

During the 1st century Romano-British activity is concentrated to the north end of the 1912 excavation and almost certainly continued northwards beyond the excavation area. In this early phase, the 2nd and 3rd Houses were residential, with a possible third dwelling to the north of the site – for which the North Wall may be part of the building structure, and not an enclosure wall. If this is the case, then this building may be circular (similar to an Iron Age hut style) or have curved walls to the broad 'rectangle' shape of a cottage villa as seen in the excavations at Ower, Dorset (a reconstruction can be seen in Upton Country Park by appointment with the Waterfront Museum). In complete contrast, the 3rd House was associated with a large number of high status finds and was the principal dwelling, and the only one at this time with window glass. Associated with these houses in the 1st century were three separate grain driers or malting areas – the Tuning Fork, Shears and the Single T furnaces.

During the 2nd to early 3rd century the 2nd and 3rd Houses continued as residential. However, early in the 3rd century the 3rd House experienced a significant fire within the southern end of the building. At this time a small building appears immediately east of the 3rd House (the Northwest Building of Chapter 3). It has a thatched roof, a hearth and a significant range of pottery and coins proving the residential status. Grain drying and malting was now concentrated in two buildings to the north and east of the site – the Hybrid Furnace and the Well House.

By the mid to end 3rd century, construction of the 1st House had started and the first 'strip villa' phase was built. Both the 3rd House and the new residence of the Northeast Building were converted into workshops. The 2nd House remained residential over this period.

During the 4th century the enclosure wall was built and the 1st House became the only residential building with added wings, extensions and corridors which provided an increased living space and larger bathing area. Interior design was simple and mosaic was restricted to tessellated floors with a very small amount of a simple black and white design. Window glass was also found associated with the 1st House. A large quantity of finds indicates the purpose of certain rooms, and shows a change in function over time. In this respect, it is clear that the kitchen was re-located over time into three different areas, as extensions to the structure were sequentially built. As a result of the 1st House becoming the main residential area, the 2nd and 3rd Houses were converted to grain drying and/or malting areas. The 3rd House also had a grain processing and grinding purpose. The function of the 4th House is not clear, but it appears to have been built at the end of the 3rd century and re-built during the 4th century. Its second use may have been as a shrine, but the evidence is not conclusive.

In conclusion, the buildings show an early embrace of the Roman lifestyle albeit with simple structures making use of mostly local materials. The inhabitants were wealthy, but did not import stone for the main structure or put elegant mosaics in the buildings. This probably relates more to lack of supply and/or lack of the required craftsmen. A house fire in the early 3rd century prompts a shift of residence and activities. This was a time of financial low for the site, but an economic revival is seen from the end of the 3rd into the 4th century with the construction of the 1st House and the new enclosure wall.

Local area and landscape
Yewden villa had an excellent location for many different purposes. It was situated in a small valley with a chalk stream and numerous springs. It had a variety of agricultural land surrounding it including water meadow, good arable soils, slopes for grazing, and hilltop woodland for pigs and timber. The River Thames (just 500 m south) would have functioned as the main transport route for goods and people. It is highly likely that Yewden worked in partnership with Mill End villa, which is situated on the banks of the river. A division of function can be envisaged whereby Yewden fulfils an agricultural and workshop role, whilst Mill End (in its prime riverside location) would have been in an ideal position to control the movement of goods and people. Mill End has never been excavated, but geophysics show no workshops or other features expected of 'normal' villa activities. There is only one enclosure ditch on the north side, but not on the river side. This villa, and its relationship with Yewden, is to be the focus of future research and geophysics results are in hand (Eyers and Hutt, in prep.). A scuba dive is currently being undertaken along the banks of the Thames to search for any remaining infrastructure of quays or locate any finds along the river bed. There have been no significant finds to date, although a track leading from the adjacent marina and Hambleden Mill leads northwards past Yewden and meets up with a wider track running E-W along the north end of the Yewden complex (noted in the excavations of 1912 and seen clearly on aerial photographs and geophysics results). If this track is found to continue in the same westward direction it would run past Bix Roman villa and meet the Fairmile Roman Road that links Henley with Dorchester (Figure 8.1).

The tracks, roads and their link to the river are considered highly significant to understanding Yewden and Mill End villas. Of particular note is the observation that the Thames becomes exceptionally shallow along this stretch. Mid-channel maximum depths of 2.5 m down to 1.2 m were recorded whilst diving in November 2010 and January 2011 (high water periods). In the Roman period the River Thames was not controlled as it is now by the modern river authorities who can adjust water flow very effectively. It is clear that, in Roman times, at low water this section would have been highly likely to have impeded travel by larger boats, and may even have become fordable. This is true of other sections of the river, but this section also has a high gradient. Under these circumstances, off-loading goods and people at Mill End to travel westwards on the track to the Fairmile, would make the continued journey to Dorchester possible by cutting off a loop of the Thames. This is mentioned again later in an attempt to understand the whole site and valley economics.

commonly encountered distribution, but significantly higher quantities of coins than other villas. This rapid acquisition of wealth and Romanization indicates collaboration with the Roman forces from the outset. During this early phase significant amounts of Samian pottery and other imported vessels are acquired, but this suddenly drops shortly after 60 AD. As the Thames is the main transport route, this drop in imports is interpreted as Boudicca's revolt and the effect this event had on trade passing through London. Following this turbulent period there was an increase in the amount of high status goods to the site, shown clearly by the Samian statistics, with a peak *c.* 80 AD. Subsequent falls in Samian ware from 90-100 AD can be accounted for by changes in the production areas from South to Central Gaul, as clay ran out. Other find categories at Yewden, such as copper alloy and Romano-British pottery, show that the villa continued as a wealthy site during the Trajanic-Hadrianic to Antonine period. The peak in Samian supply from about 150 to 180 AD was undoubtedly due to a strong trade link set up with the large production areas in Lezoux (Central Gaul). This enabled goods from the highly productive workshops of Cinnamus and his contemporaries (150-180 AD) to be imported for those who could afford them. However, there was a distinct 'dip' in Samian imports at *c.* 160 AD, which is not readily explained – a local event perhaps?

After 190 AD Samian and other imports decline dramatically, never to recover. The trade link from Central Gaul had been broken and manufacturing of Samian shifted to East Gaulish traders. Trade links resumed to other Thames Roman sites, e.g. London, but never returned to Yewden. Following this period there was a large increase in the proportion of local goods in assemblages, notably pottery from Oxfordshire. The early 3rd century fire in the 3rd House may in some way explain this, but the decline continued throughout the 3rd century. This is a common feature with many villas. The 3rd century rebellions by tribes throughout the Roman Empire (e.g. by the Goths, Alamanni, Franks, and other groups) disrupted trade and triggered a general economic depression. It coincided with de-basing of the currency and hoards became common as a result. As an example, silver content of the denarius falls from 85% to 5% at this time. Amongst this general economic depression, it is therefore not clear why Yewden shows remarkable activity (coin evidence) at 260-275 AD.

During the time of Diocletian (284-305 AD) a recovery started in agricultural production, manufacturing and trade. Hence, by Constantine's reign in the 4th century, a stable government had resumed trade connections to the Empire, including Britain. Yewden showed an economic revival during the 4th century with the building and extending of the 1st House, the development of the enclosure with two large malting buildings and grain preparation areas. The coin evidence also supports this economic revival. This end-3rd to 4th century revival is echoed all over southern England e.g. Bignor (Sussex), Witcombe and Froster Court villas (Gloucestershire), North Leigh and Wilcote (Oxfordshire). In each case, an increase in agriculture and trade was the key to their success.

Religion and ritual

There is evidence for religious and ritual activities associated with Yewden and this comes from structures and finds. Evidence from structures includes:

- **A temple in Horseleys Field?** The square within a square feature seen in the geophysics survey, east of Yewden and near the Hamble Brook, represents a classic plan of a Roman-British temple inner and outer precinct. Close proximity (overhanging) the original location for the stream in the Roman period, and association with water retaining features (one inside and one outside, wells?), plus a nearby spring, all suggests the involvement of a water deity. The site has not been excavated and no finds have been reported to the SMR/HER office.

- **A temple west of Yewden?** This structure is clear from crop marks which show a small square structure in the middle of the field above Bath Ponds west of Yewden. The magnetometry results show a pipeline has since gone directly over the structure. It is included in the reconstructions of Figures 8.2 and 8.4 below. Supporting evidence of the interpretation of a temple came from a metal detectorist who was encountered during the project. He reported verbally that this area had produced a good number of coins and other finds. One of the other finds was a statuette, since sold, and not photographed. The description of the item very closely matched that of Harpocrates (the Greek Horas), son of Isis. This cannot be proved as the item was not traceable. However, if correct this is an interesting find as it links to another 1912 find in the collection, notably the scarab beetle representing Isis, found in the 1st House. Isis is sometimes presented as a figure nursing Harpocrates as a baby at her breast.

- **A shrine within the Yewden enclosure?** The small 4th building, with its tessellated flooring, is suggested as a shrine which is operational during the end 3rd to 4th century. Abraded finds associated with it are from earlier settlement. Contemporary finds include beakers and a pommel from a dagger.

- **Furnaces.** Several furnaces have Samian wares recorded from the stoke holes the information coming either from the labelled finds or within Cocks (1921). Despite these records it was not possible to find all sherds reported or to work out which sherds were found within the stoke hole, or how many. One exception was the Drag.36 dish in the Single T furnace described below. Unburnt objects of this nature are interpreted as a closure of the furnace.

Figure 8.2 Reconstruction of the view to the field west of Yewden villa showing the location of a square structure interpreted as a temple. The E-W track is running across the lower left. Looking approximately to the northwest. © Alison Jewsbury

Objects found within the 1912 collections that might relate to religious or ritual activity:
- **A broken Drag. 43 mortarium placed at the top of Pit 3.** This mortarium (from Rheinzabern, see the back cover image and Fig.3.19) was cleanly broken into three pieces, and the fragments are now re-joined to present a perfect vessel on display at the BCM. The grits are not worn and there is no wear on the vessel body. This is regarded as a votive or ritual breakage as an act of closure for the pit. This item would have been of considerable value to the dedicant, making this act of great importance. It is decorated with symbolic images of trailing ivy leaves and peacocks – imagery often associated with Juno. Juno has many functions as a goddess. One of her main roles is protector of the community, but she is more often associated with women and fertility. In this respect she is known to take several guises from goddess of marriage to being the spirit of youthfulness and strength, linked to cyclical renewal (Basanoff, 1974). In this last role she is sometimes linked to her epithet *Lucina* and the moon, along with female sexuality (Palmer, 1974). Linked to this is her use as protector of women in childbirth. Juno and Hercules share the role of protector of the newborn. Hercules appears as one of the designs on decorated Samian ware at Yewden – an interesting observation, although not necessarily linked to Juno or to the newborn infants discussed next, but it is compelling to have so much imagery relating to women at Yewden. The date of production of the mortarium is 170-230 AD, but a *terminus post quem* is provided *c*. 1 m below by a Gallic Empire radiate coin of 268-286 AD. It is also

270

associated with an uncommon New Forest mortarium dating 260-370 AD, and hence this confirms the pit closure as the end of the 3rd century.

- **A samian flanged bowl (Drag38) broken and with half a quern stone in the stoke hole of the Single T furnace (fIV)**. An act of closure of the furnace.
- **Venus figurine in Pit 8**. A pipe-clay head of Venus (Fig.4.8.4) was found at c. 4.5 m (between 14 and 15 ft) depth. According to Green (1978) these cheap pipe-clay versions of Venus (in comparison to the bronze figurines) were likely to "belong to women, perhaps as fertility symbols, or to bring luck in childbirth". It can be dated by the pottery assemblage at this level to early-mid 3rd century.
- **Votives**. Three votive spears and an axe, all worked bone items, were found in Room H of the 1st House (p.196, Cocks, 1912). These were not located during this study. Also found in Room H were a number of bone carvings, a buckle, a bucket and 3 spoon bowls. As these objects were found beneath the concrete floor it suggests a household shrine in an early phase, hence datable to the end 3rd to 4th century. A votive figurine arm and a bronze votive axe have been reported by a metal detectorist to the PAS as found close to Yewden villa. Votives are not religious items, but they are used by the votary to request a favour from the gods. Often body part votives are used to request the healing of that part offered. It has often been suggested that votive tools represent the profession of the dedicant. However, given the vast number of miniature spears and axes at many different locations, this seems unlikely. Green (1975; 1981) saw them as a dedication to a Celtic deity. Indeed these votives have been used from the Iron Age and represent a continuation of a Celtic tradition. Henig (1984) has argued that they represent the axes used in animal sacrifice. Both interpretations may be correct (in different situations) or they simply may represent iconography of something protective and strong.
- **Scarab beetle**. A carved stone scarab was found in Room D of the 1st House. The scarab is linked to the cult of Isis and it is a symbol of re-birth. This area dates to the end 3rd and 4th century.
- **Dea Nutrix (the nursing goddess)**. A clay figurine of a nursing female figure was found in the 3rd House. The information is insufficient to date the object or its position. If it relates to the earlier residential phase for the building then it is likely to be a personal possession. If it relates to the later grain drying and malting phase in the 4th century, then it might imply fertility symbolism as a 'mother Earth' figure.
- **Animal remains**. One, possibly two, pine martin skeletons were located in the top of Pit 4. The skeletons occur with a Samian mortarium. The level can be dated on the find assemblage to the 3rd century. Similar to adjacent Pit 3, this deposit is interpreted as a sealing offering for the closure of the pit. A pony skull was placed

at the top of Pit 18 and this is also interpreted as an act of closure, again dating to the 3rd century.
- **Human remains**. Infant burials are almost totally confined to the area north of the 3rd House, which appears to be a special burial area. Some infants are associated with the top of pits, two infant burials just 60 cm from the edge of Pit 6, may represent an act of closure for Pit 6. In addition, there are two infant burials beneath the 2nd House floor which would not appear to have any connection to the rest of the burial practices for infants at the north end of the site. It is a suggestion that these could be a rite of commencement for the building, a common practice in the Romano-British period (Merrifield, 1990).

There may be more examples of ritual deposit at Yewden, but unfortunately the methods of excavation in 1912, together with a lack of both knowledge of stratigraphy and precise recording, hinders a more complete assessment. The term 'ritual' is used here when one or more of the following occurs:
- Completeness of items (e.g. pottery) associated with deliberate breaking and especially if accompanied with other objects in this list;
- Articulation and completeness of skeletons (note: the majority of the animal bone has not been researched and may reveal more information in this regard);
- Unusual nature of the items deposited, such as articulated wild animals with deliberate placement.
- Symbolic potential

Three items were buried with infant burials that are regarded as normal burial practices rather than a 'ritual' significance, see below

Further research into the location and nature of certain classes of finds would provide greater insight into this fascinating subject in the future.

Burial

The Romano-British cemetery for Yewden has never been located. However, there were 5 skeletons found on site in a deep pit or well (Pit 6), further fragments of human adult skulls were found over the site, and 97 infant burials were noted by Cocks (1921) although fewer were located during this study (from which 35 perinatals were selected for research due to completeness of these remains). The infants cluster around the north end of the site and hence this might be interpreted as an infant cemetery, although this area is not confined to being solely used for this function.

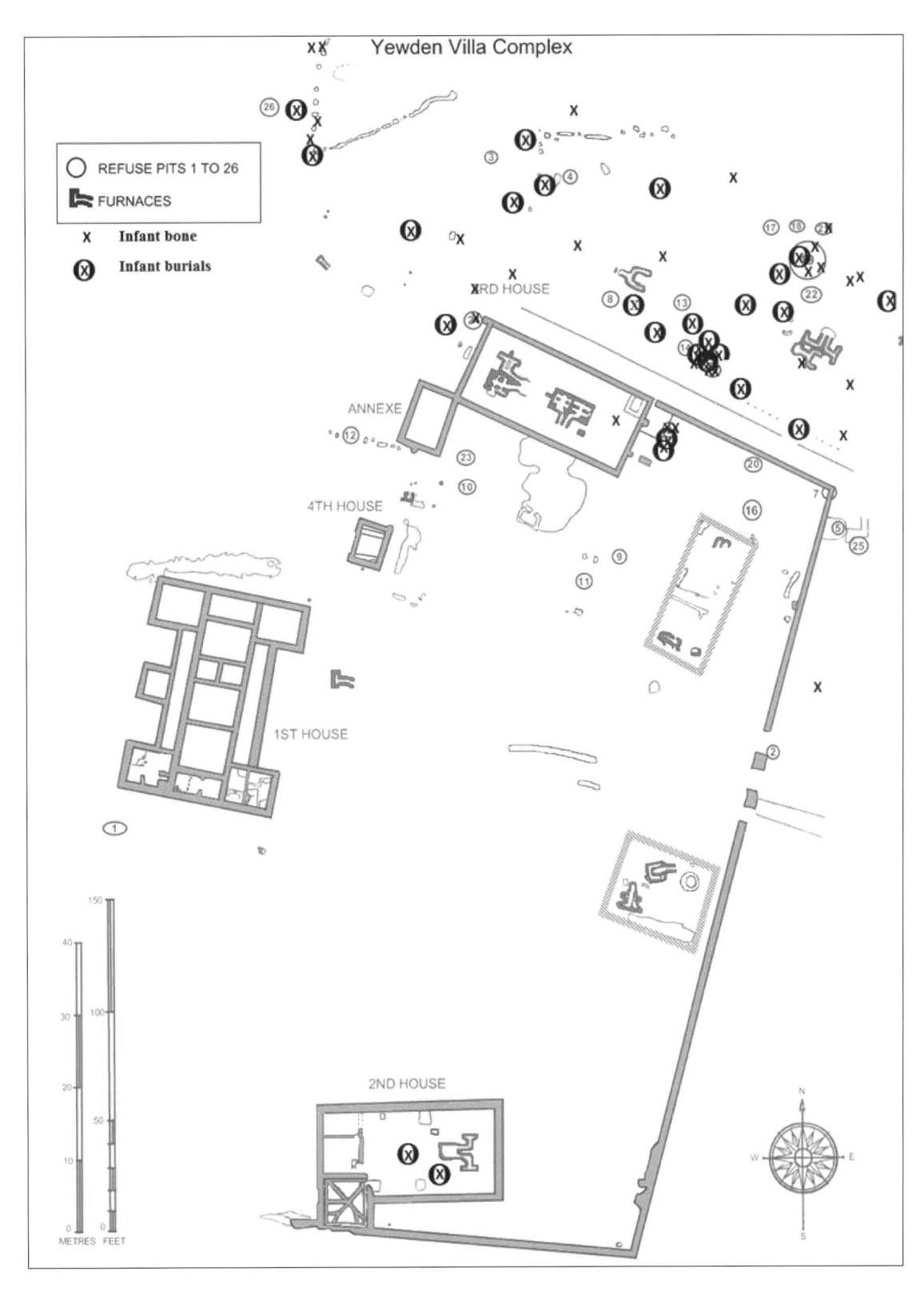

Figure 8.3 Distribution plot of the infant burials. A single x indicates a small amount of bone and uncertainty that this represents an infant burial. Cocks has added notes with these remains (e.g. 'head to the north') so it appears they may be burials, but they are not complete skeletons in the archive collections today. Crosses in circles are infant burials.

The five skeletons in Pit 6 comprised three adults (two males between 17 and 25 years, and one female about 25-35 years) along with two children (a six year old child and another around 15-18 months). There was no sign of trauma observed on these remains, but their location at the bottom of a deep pit or well, below the water table, and covered by a thick deposit of building materials, strongly infers rapid disposal of the victims of murder or infectious disease. It is not uncommon to find skeletons deposited in pits or wells during the Romano-British period, but the depth of the overlying building materials lends itself to the interpretation of a rapid deposition for the bodies and the fill.

The perinatals offered a good dataset for study (Chapter 6 this volume; Mays & Eyers, in press). The results strongly support that the majority of the infants died at or very close to 38-40 weeks gestation, which is the normal age for a full term foetus, and support Mr Cocks' (1921) suggestion that they were the victims of infanticide.

To gain a deeper insight into the reasons for and dating of the infanticide it is first necessary to look at the site distribution (Figure 8.3) and then assess what would be 'normal' practice for the Romano-British period. The site distribution shows the infant burials predominantly in an area to the north of the 3rd House, but with a cluster adjacent to this building and which are associated with Pit 6 (interpreted as a deep shaft or a well). There are several occurrences of bone within pits, some some of these are incomplete and may be reworked material. Where depths were recorded they were at the top of the pits and hence may represent an act of closure. If the burial were placed in the pits merely due to the open pit being a convenient resting place, then some would be found at levels other than the top. Two inhumations have already been mentioned above as having potential as a rite of commencement or 'foundation offering'. Such burials are well recorded from archaeological sites of the majority of countries around the world. They are common throughout the Roman period in Britain (Merrifield, 1990) where they take the form of baby, animal or bird inhumations, or sometimes burials of pots containing food, drink and occasionally coins.

Dating of the burials at Yewden is not possible in many instances as stratigraphic recording was not undertaken during the 1912 excavation. Records of the horizon from which the interment cut was made were not noted. However, in some instances the infant lies within a stratified deposit or the burial was sealed by overlying floors. Dating was thus possible using coins, pottery or other datable objects. No radiocarbon dating was undertaken.

The following BCM numbers for the perinates take the form .xx and are preceded by 1994.57.3606_) and this links with the context number in Chapter 6 Tables 1 and 2. Some perinates listed below were not included in the osteological study, but provide dates.

Dates of interments:
- **2nd House (2 infants, BCM .16 and .19)**. No level or associated finds were recorded. The date can only be confined by the building which is 1st to 4th century. Hence, the date would be 1st century if the burials are interpreted as rite of commencement.
- **3rd House (2 infants, BCM .44 and .54)**. Below the gravel floor AD 150-200. These are not complete skeletons, but the 1912 excavation finds records indicate they were

"buried with" two items. One item was a cut-down jar (thus forming a dish; 1994.57.P.3047) and and another was an Oxford mortarium (M3.7 of Young, 1997 AD 140-200). It is not clear why no further bones were found during the excavation (possibly missed by the rapid collection techniques). If correct, the dating would place them as burials beneath the earlier residential building phase, before re-building as a workshop and grain processing area. The re-build would explain disturbance to floor levels and of objects placed there. The infant bones may have been scattered and damaged, and not noticed by the excavators.

- **Pit 6 (2 infants, BCM .17 and .18)**. These were placed at the edge of the pit, about 60 cm from the edge. Both burials are covered by the gravel and flint floors dating them to AD 150-200.
- **Pit 15 (2 infants, BCM .40, .41)**. Placed at the top of the pit with Cocks' note that the burial is associated with an iron spear head. 1st to 3rd century.
- **Pit 19 (4 infants BCM .32, .34, .35, .37)**. No depth given. Date: mid 2nd to end 4th century. Only infant .35 was part of the osteological study (a confirmed burial) and the remainder may represent re-worked bone from adjacent burials. The evidence is not clear and the collection/recording methods poor.
- **Pit 21 (1 infant .49)**. Depth was not noted. It is not clear if this infant was associated with the bones of hare and rabbit which are recorded with it. This perinate was not included in the osteological study as only one bone was recovered from deposits dating between the 1st to 4th century.
- **Pit 24 (1 infant, BCM .29)**. At the top of the pit. Not a perinate and buried in close proximity, maybe with, a pottery infant feeder (P.272). A partial skeleton (?re-worked) and incorporated into deposits of the 3rd to 4th century.
- **Fill in the Northwest wall (2 infants, BCM .47 and .48)**. Not included in the osteological study. Not complete burials, but isolated bones recoverd from deposits dating between the 1st to 3rd century.
- **The 'Yard' (all remaining infants)**. All remaining infant burials were in the area north of the 3rd House and perimeter wall. Not all of these are likely to represent burials, but are isolated, reworked bone.

Dating evidence for the infant burials remains fairly wide due to lack of depth information and also the longevity of pottery types and coins used for dating in many parts of the site. Where dates can be more closely defined the perinates fall nearer the 2nd century and quite a number are defined as interments of 150-200 AD.

Infanticide – why?

It is clear from the evidence that, although not every infant burial was a perinate, a very high proportion were between gestational ages 38 and 40 weeks. This indicates that even with natural deaths in the infant population, the practice of infanticide skewed the population. Archaeologists have puzzled over this practice for a very long time, but only rarely are the number of remains in a population sufficient for statistics to be applied.

Studies of infanticide do not necessarily need to include a perinate population, which will always be less likely to be preserved, but may focus on cemeteries using the adult and older child population. Studies on skeletons from the Upper Palaeolithic period in Europe show a higher proportion of male to female skeletons (a ratio of *c.* 1.5 to 1) indicating a regular practice of selecting out female infants from the population.

Evidence from written records appears from the Roman period onwards. Plautus refers to the disposing of unwanted babies by exposure as a common practice (*Gasina*, prol. 41, 79). Soranus, a great writer on medical matters, states his method of deducing which babies were worth keeping, was to plunge them into icy water. Those that look sickly after the experience may not be worth rearing (Soranus *Gynecology* II.10). Mays (1995) showed that the number of infant burials found on archaeological sites in Britain, and that display a perinatal age at death, suggested infanticide was widely practised. In addition, the widespread tolerance of infanticide around the world is also shown by Warren (1985) and was a well-attested practice in Roman Britain (Mays 1993).

Evidence from cemetery analysis and tombstones (Collingwood and Wright, 1965) show that the people of Roman Britain limited the size of their families to two children (Allason-Jones, 2005 p.30). Birth control would inevitably have included applications of special preparations such as those advised by Soranus (one example is the mixture of olive oil, alum and vinegar which was still advice given by Marie Stopes in the 1930s). While abortion was certainly supported by medical practitioners in Rome, it seems less likely that this was widely available, if available at all, to the British population. Also, abortion would not be a safe method for the mother. Infanticide was the only method that would be certain and safe for the mother. However, this was not simply a practice used by prehistoric and the Romano-British population. Infanticide remained widespread throughout the Medieval period in Britain and remained so through the 1800s. It no doubt led to the many folklore stories based on 'foundlings'. It was not until 1938 that the Infanticide Act defined infanticide formally and brought in penalties in law. However, even in the early 1960s in Britain, only one of the 72 women found guilty of infanticide was sent to prison. In looking at the many different cultures and at the wide range of time that infanticide has been carried out as birth control, there are a couple of observations. Firstly, that the first emotion from a modern European society is one of horror – but is it the act of an uncaring society, or population control for a family who care very much for their existing children, and who would not be able to provide for more? Secondly, the Roman population under consideration here, may have seen nothing wrong with their judgement that the human as a 'person with rights' does not exist until two years of age. If that were the commonly held view, then disposal of the infant would be seen as a simple means of limiting family growth. Modern British law deems this cut-off point to be 24 weeks of gestation.

It must be stressed that infanticide at Yewden villa is invoked not as a result of a high number of infant burials (97 as recorded by Cocks). A higher number than average excavations would be expected for the large excavation area undertaken. This is especially obvious as the excavation encountered what appears to be a part chosen for the burial area for the infants. The chalky soil at Hambleden also helped preservation of the fragile bones. The evidence for infanticide at Yewden is strong, and it is based on a high peak in the infant burials at 38 to 40 weeks gestation. Burials associated with villas usually have a broader spread of infant age, up to 2 years of age (Mays, 1993). Children older than two years would be found in the main cemetery, but no Romano-British cemetery has yet been located for the Hambleden Valley.

Possible motives for infanticide take many guises, but often include any of the following: lack of money or means of support; selective infanticide (either girls or boys); a desire for no children at all which could include illegitimacy. In relation to this last point, Lindsay-Allason Jones (2005) writes an excellent account which includes reasons why illegitimacy presented no problem to a Romano-British population (also hinted at in various Roman writers' accounts of family relations in Britain). The finds from Yewden prove the site to have had considerable wealth throughout most of the 1st to the end of the 4th century. DNA analyses so far processed to assess gender of the Yewden infants show an equal number of males and females, hence no selectivity with the infanticide (Keri Brown, *pers comm.*). We can therefore rule out illegitimacy, elimination of one sex and lack of money, which leaves the 'require no children' category.

Natural explanations for the high perinate population?

Natural deaths and other reasons for the large number of perinates were considered, and where rejected, the reasons are given below:

- Epidemics or illnesses affecting children would affect all children and increase the population number in older babies and young children at the same time.
- Infant burial area, this explains the large number of infants recovered, but this does not explain the exceptionally high proportion of 38 to 40 week gestation infants. Barton Court had 41 infant burials (Miles, 1986), but the age distribution was not dominated by the 38-40 weeks gestation group. Similarly the Medieval cemetery at Wharram Percy had 61 infant burials (Mays, 2007), but again a much wider age distribution.
- A birthing centre: a neat explanation as healthy babies would leave the site with the mother, but infants dead at birth would be buried on site. However, this is a reasonably isolated site (it would be a long distance to travel in the final stages of pregnancy or when in labour). Also, Soranus specifically advises, and other writers describe the birth process as being "at home with one attendant".
- Congenital illness or problems. None are visible by osteological study.
- A population with a high incidence of the rhesus negative blood group allele would increase the perinate population, if rhesus positive males enter the family (reproductive) group. Mothers that have a blood group that is rhesus negative, will only give birth to one healthy baby if it is rhesus positive. Giving birth will sensatized the mother's immune system and all subsequent pregnancies to rh+ babies result in infants that are dead at birth. This would require previous reproductive isolation to the rh+ allele. The Rh- allele explanation is rejected due to the fact that many of these babies would not reach full term, and some infants that do, will live on for a while in a jaundiced condition. This would result in a wider range of gestational age in the perinate population than that seen at Yewden. It also does not provide an

explanation for all Romano-British sites which have a high proportion of 38-40 week gestation perinates, where infanticide has also been proposed.

The evidence from fieldwork and finds in conjunction with the work on infant burials, shows there is no clear-cut solution to prove the reasons behind the infanticide. In this relation, and linked to the 'require no infants' category, it has been suggested that a brothel may have been located in one or more of the buildings to the north of the enclosure area at Yewden. This alone would warrant a small excavation into the structures located in this part of the site.

At first sight this might present an unlikely suggestion – brothels are almost totally located in towns or with military sites. However, the evidence is listed below:

➢ 97 infant burials, of which a large proportion were perinatal.
➢ Yewden was a wealthy site.
➢ Housing located within the Yewden excavation, in the immediate area and at Mill End, indicates this was not a large population.
➢ Unusual quantities and types of find indicate substantial trade via the River Thames.
➢ Literate individuals were on site (large numbers of styli, an inkwell and graffiti) supporting the suggestion of trading activities and associated people passing through.
➢ A large number of female finds: hairpins, jewellery, brooches and others.
➢ The only religious items relate to female deities: Juno, Isis (and possibly Harpocrates), Venus, and Dea Nutrix,
➢ One Samian bowl with an 'erotic group' decoration (although one erotic vessel does not prove a brothel!)
➢ Suitable location – a shallow section of the river and a series of track connections from the Thames to a notable town (Dorchester) and further Chiltern villas.

The location of Yewden close to the river Thames is a crucial link in this interpretation. It was discovered during exploratory dives 2010 to 2011 that the Thames is exceptionally shallow along parts of this section (1.2 m to 2.2 m in mid channel) as described earlier. It is suggested that river traffic may have been required to unload or reload at this point.This may also explain the close proximity of Mill End and Yewden villas, by virtue of a division of labour – one controlling trade and one undertaking 'normal' villa activities and/or the main high status residence.

A search for infrastructure for a quay has not been successful in the stretches currently accessible. The most likely location for the quay is where the Hambleden marina and mill are sited today. Supporting this statement is the small track leading from the riverside, northwards past Yewden villa, and linking to the main track running E-W past the 3rd House (described earlier). It is possible therefore, but not proven, that some kind of refreshment and brothel activity could have been seasonally active at Yewden as river trade was forced to disembark or load up at this location. Unwanted infants from such liaisons may be represented by the infant burials – the majority of which are on land north of the track and close to buildings that were outside the 1912 excavation area. This suggestion is possible, but it is based only on circumstantial evidence.

The last word

The 1912 excavation has provided an unrivalled assemblage of finds and information which has given a valuable glimpse of life in a rural villa. The whole site excavation method, with retention of all finds, provided a challenging and exciting opportunity. Finds were in good condition as they were collected before damage by the chemicals and machinery used by modern farming methods. Research was sometimes scuppered by inconsistent recording, but it is truly remarkable that such detailed labelling was given to finds from an excavation of this date. The result is a complex picture of life in rural Hambleden. In some ways the villa appears to support the agricultural activities expected of such sites, but in many ways it stands out as exceptionally different to comparable villas in this region. Assemblages of finds record the shift from Iron Age to Romanization, whilst also showing that the population still retained a hold onto some traditional elements. Economic expansions and declines can be deduced from the assemblages – some due to effects of events on site (for instance, the 3rd century fire) and some due to events further afield in the Empire. This is a unique opportunity to explore many aspects of Romano-British life, and death. Still in question is the link to the Thames, trade and the relationship between Mill End villa and Yewden. This monograph is merely the start of much more in-depth research that is now possible, and so it will not be the last word by any means.

Figure 8.4 A reconstruction of the Yewden villa complex looking approximately northwest. © Alison Jewsbury

Figure 8.5 A reconstruction of the Yewden villa complex looking approximately southeast. © Alison Jewsbury

Bibliography

Allason-Jones, L. 2005. *Women in Roman Britain*. CBA, York.
Basanoff, V. 1974. *Les dieux des Romains*. In: Palmer, 1974.
Cocks, A. H. 1921. A Romano-British homestead in the Hambleden Valley, Bucks. *Archaeologia* 71, 141-198.
Collingwood, R. and **Wright**, R. 1965. *The Roman inscriptions of Britain*. Clarendon, Oxford.
Green, M. 1975. Romano-British non-ceramic model objects in south-east Britain. *Antiq. J* 132, 54-70.
Green, M. Model objects from military regions of Roman Britain. *Britannia* 12, 253-269.
Green, M. J. 1978. *Small cult objects from military areas of Roman Britain*. BAR, British Series, 52, Oxford.
Henig, M. 1984. *Religion in Roman Britain*. Batsford, London.
Mays, S. 1993. Infanticide in Roman Britain. *Antiquity*. 67, 883-888.
Mays, S. 1995. Killing the unwanted child. *British Archaeology* 2, 8-9.
Mays, S. 2007. The Human Remains. *In*: Mays S., Harding, C. and Heighway, C. *Wharram XI: The Churchyard*. Wharram: a study of settlement on the Yorkshire Wolds XI. York University Press, pp. 77-192, 337-397.
Merrifield, R. 1990. *The archaeology of ritual and magic*. New Amsterdam Books.
Miles, D. 1986. *Archaeology at Barton Court Farm, Abingdon, Oxon*. Oxford Archaeological Unit Report 3. CBA Research Report 50.Palmer, R.E.A. 1974. Roman religion and Roman Empire. 5 essays. Philadelphia.
Warren, M. A. 1985. Reconsidering the ethics of infanticide. *Philosophical Books* 26, 1-9.

Appendix 1   Yewden Villa glass record

Record number	Object name	Context	Weight (g)	No of items	Colour	Thickness/notes
1994.57.1811.1	Glass & vessel & rim	3rd house above platform inside S & W walls	3	1	Greyish green (10GY 5/2)	Body 2 mm thick; rim 4mm.
1994.57.1811.2	Glass & vessel	3rd house above platform inside S & W walls	1	1	Pale green (10G 6/2)	1 mm thick
1994.57.1812.1	Glass & vessel	Yard E at 1.5 ft	2	1	Greyish blue-green 5BG 5/2	4 mm thick, diameter c. 80 mm
1994.57.1813.1	Glass & vessel	E of enclosure wall, S of urn hole at 2 ft deep	1	1	Colourless, blue tint	1 mm thick
1994.57.1813.2	Glass & vessel & cup	E of enclosure wall, S of urn hole at 2 ft deep	2	1	Pale green 5G 6/2)	Cup or bowl with vertical ribs
1994.57.1814	Glass & vessel & rim	N of NW wall	8	1	Greyish green (5G 5/2)	Rim c. 3 mm thick.
1994.57.1815	Glass & vessel & rim	30 ft N of enclosure wall	3	1	Greyish green (5G 5/2)	
1994.57.1816	Glass & vessel & rim	Pit 9 at 12 ft deep	3	1	Greyish yellow-green (5GY 7/2)	Body = 1 mm thick.
1994.57.1817.1	Glass & cullet	5ft E of edge of Pit 6	11	1	Greenish grey (5G 5/2)	
1994.57.1817.2	Glass & vessel	5ft E of edge of Pit 6	2	1	Greenish grey (5G 5/2)	2 mm thick.
1994.57.1818	Glass & vessel & rim	Pit 23 at 1.5 ft deep	1	1	Colourless, blue tint	2 mm thick
1994.57.1819	Glass & vessel	Pit 23 at 1.5 ft deep	1	1	Colourless, green tint	1.5 mm thick
1994.57.1820	Glass & vessel & rim	Close to Hybrid furnace 45ft NW of enclosure wall at 1.5 ft	2	1	Dusky yellow-green 5Y 6/4	
1994.57.1821	Glass & vessel & base	Pit 19 at 3 ft	2	1	Greyish olive 10Y 4/2	

1994.57.1822.1	Glass & vessel & rim	N of 4th block of NW wall	4	1	Greyish blue-green 5BG 5/2	
1994.57.1822.2	Glass & vessel	N of 4th block of NW wall	1	1	Colourless	0.5 mm thick
1994.57.1823.1	Glass & vessel	3rd House W end	1	1	corroded	0.5 mm thick
1994.57.1823.2	Glass & vessel	3rd House W end	2	1	Greenish grey (5BG 7/1)	2 mm thick
1994.57.1823.3	Glass & vessel	3rd House W end	1	1	Light greenish grey 10Y 7/1	1 mm thick
1994.57.1824	Glass & vessel	Over clinker wall N of W end of NW wall at 2 ft	0.5	1	Colourless	1 mm thick
1994.57.1825	Glass & vessel & cup	Pit 1	1	1	Colourless	1 mm thick; with Aes of Claudius Grothicus (No3)
1994.57.1826	Glass & vessel	Pit 16 at 4 ft deep	1	2	Pale green (10G 6/2)	
1994.57.1827.1	Glass & vessel	N of NW wall E of detached blocks at 2 ft	3	1	Pale blue green 5BG 6/2	
1994.57.1827.2	Glass & window	N of NW wall E of detached blocks at 2 ft	2	1	Dusky yellow-green 5GY 5/2	
1994.57.1828	Glass & vessel	90 ft N of enclosure wall	1	1	Pale blue green 5BG 7/2	1 mm thick; ridged decoration
1994.57.1829	Glass & vessel	Built in, W end of NW wall of Yard	4	1	Greyish green 10GY 5/2	6 mm thick
1994.57.1830	Glass & vessel	10 ft E of Hybrid furnace at 1.5 ft	4	1	Greyish green 5G 5/2	
1994.57.1831	Glass & cullet	Pit 16 at 4 ft deep	3	1	Greyish green 5G 5/2	Worn, fractured
1994.57.1832	Glass & vessel & bottle & rim	3rd House NW corner	1	1	Pale green (10G 6/2)	Rim c. 4 mm thick
1994.57.1833	Glass & vessel & rim	2nd House SW corner	1	1	Greyish green 5G 5/2	Rim c. 4 mm thick
1994.57.1834.1	Glass & window	30 ft N of enclosure wall at 1.5 ft deep	1	1	Pale olive 10Y 6/2	2 mm thick

1994.57.1835	Glass & vessel & rim	15 ft N of NE angle of enclosure wall	3	1	Dusky yellow green 5GY 5/2	4 mm thick, cup or bowl.
1994.57.1836	Glass & vessel & rim	20 ft N of NE angle of enclosure wall	0.5	1	Colourless	1 mm thick
1994.57.1837	Glass & vessel	1st House heap by Room O	2	1	Colourless	1 mm thick
1994.57.1838.1	Glass & vessel	S of mortar floor at 2 ft	9	1	Moderate yellow green 5GY 7/4	6 mm thick
1994.57.1838.2	Glass & vessel	S of mortar floor at 2 ft	1	1	Pale yellowish green 10GY 7/2	1 mm thick
1994.57.1839.1	Glass & vessel & rim	7 yards W of Pit 3	4	1	Greyish green 5G 5/2	2 mm thick
1994.57.1839.2	Glass & vessel	7 yards W of Pit 3	1	1	Greyish green 5G 5/2	2 mm thick; corroded
1994.57.1840.1	Glass & vessel & rim	S edge of Pit 20	3	1	Moderate yellow 5Y 7/6	6 mm thick; 100 mm radius vessel
1994.57.1841	Glass & vessel	4 ft E of 7th detached block N of W end of NW wall	4	3	Greenish grey 5G 5/2	2 mm thick
1994.57.1842	Glass & vessel & rim	N of 8th block NW wall	3	2	Greenish grey 5G 6/1	2 mm thick
1994.57.1843.1	Glass & vessel & rim	5 ft NE of Pit 18 at 1.5 ft deep	4	1	Greyish blue-green 5BG 5/2	4 mm thick
1994.57.1843.2	Glass & vessel	5 ft NE of Pit 18 at 1.5 ft deep	3	1	Greyish blue-green 5BG 5/2	4 mm thick
1994.57.1844.1	Glass & cullet	Pit 12 at 1.5 ft	8	1	Greyish green 5G 5/2	
1994.57.1844.2	Glass & vessel	Pit 12 at 1.5 ft	4	1	Pale green (10G 6/2)	6 mm thick
1994.57.1845	Glass & vessel	Pit 19 at 2.5 ft	2	1	Colourless	Body 22 mm thick, rim 5 mm thick
1994.57.1846	Glass & vessel & rim	Pit 8 at 15 ft	7	1	Dark brown 7.5YR 3/4	2 mm thick
1994.57.1847.1	Glass & vessel	Pit 22 at 2 ft deep	15	1	Greyish blue-green 5BG 5/2	3 mm thick

1994.57.1847.2	Glass & vessel	Pit 22 at 2 ft deep	10	1	Greyish blue-green 5BG 5/2	
1994.57.1848.1	Glass & vessel	Quern hole	9	1	Pale green (10G 6/2)	5 mm thick
1994.57.1848.2	Glass & vessel	Quern hole	1	1	Pale green (10G 6/2)	5 mm thick
1994.57.1849.1	Glass & vessel	N of W end of NW wall W of detached blocks at 2 ft	4	1	Pale green (10G 6/2)	2.5 mm thick
1994.57.1849.2	Glass & vessel	N of W end of NW wall W of detached blocks at 2 ft	3	1	Pale green (10G 6/2)	2.5 mm thick
1994.57.1849.3	Glass & vessel	N of W end of NW wall W of detached blocks at 2 ft	4	1	Greyish green 5G 5/2	5 mm thick
1994.57.1850.1	Glass & vessel & neck	By 9th block 18 ft NW of 8th block NW wall	8	1	Greyish green 5G 5/2	4 mm thick
1994.57.1850.2	Glass & vessel	By 9th block 18 ft NW of 8th block NW wall	3	1	Light greenish grey 5G 7/1	2 mm thick
1994.57.1851	Glass & cullet	NW wall 3 ft W of middle line of blocks	9	4	Greyish green 5G 5/2	Heavily patinated
1994.57.1852.1	Glass & cullet	35 ft N of enclosure wall	7	1	Greyish green 10G 4/2	
1994.57.1852.2	Glass & cullet	35 ft N of enclosure wall	8	1	Greyish green 5G 5/2	
1994.57.1853	Glass & cullet	44 ft N of enclosure wall at 1.5 ft deep	29	1	Greyish green 5G 5/2	
1994.57.1854	Glass & vessel	2nd House NE corner of Union Jack furnace	3	2	Colourless	Patinated, 1 mm thick
1994.57.1855.1	Glass & vessel	Top Pit 4	4	1	Light olive grey 5Y 5/2	2 mm thick
1994.57.1855.2	Glass & vessel	Top Pit 4	1	1	Light olive grey 5Y 5/2	2 mm thick
1994.57.1855.3	Glass & vessel	Top Pit 4	3	1	Light olive grey 5Y 5/2	2 mm thick
1994.57.1856.1	Glass & vessel	Yard E 30 ft E of tuing fork furnace	2	3	Dark brown with gold patination	May be Medieval
1994.57.1856.2.1	Glass & vessel	Yard E 30 ft E of tuing fork furnace	2	1	Colourless	3 mm thick
1994.57.1856.2.2	Glass & vessel	Yard E 30 ft E of tuing fork furnace	2	1	Pale olive 5Y 6/4	1 mm thick

1994.57.1856.2.3	Glass & vessel	Yard E 30 ft E of tuing fork furnace	2	1	Greenish grey 5G 6/1	2 mm thick
1994.57.1857.1	Glass & vessel	1st House on long pavement	6	2		Heavily patinated
1994.57.1857.2	Glass & vessel & rim	1st House	1	1	Light greenish grey 5G 8/1	4 mm thick
1994.57.1857.3	Glass & vessel	1st House	0.5	1	Light olive brown 5Y 5/6	3 mm thick
1994.57.1857.4	Glass & vessel	1st House	0.5	1	Colourless	1 mm thick
1994.57.1858	Glass & vessel & bottle	Quern hole at 1 ft deep	155	26	Light blue green 5BG 6/6	c. 3 mm thick mostly; some square bottle fragments
1994.57.1859.1	Glass & vessel	Between Pits 6 and 20 at 2 ft deep	7	1	Dark green	Devitrifying, 5 mm thick, Medieval/post-Medieval?
1994.57.1859.2	Glass & vessel	Between Pits 6 and 20 at 2 ft deep	3	1	Light greenish grey 5GY 7/1	Medieval/post-Medieval?
1994.57.1859.3	Glass & vessel	Between Pits 6 and 20 at 2 ft deep	5	1	Pale green 5G 7/2	Medieval/post-Medieval?
1994.57.1861.1	Glass & vessel & bottle	Between Pits 6 and 20 at 1.5 ft deep	58	5	Greyish green 5G 5/2	5 mm thick, square bottle with slightly curved vertical ribs.
1994.57.1861.2	Glass & vessel	1st House Room H	11	9	Colourless, blue tint	
1994.57.1861.3	Glass & window	1st House Room H	7	5	Colourless	1 mm thick.
1994.57.1862.1	Glass & vessel	Fill in 2nd House	32	4	Greenish grey 5GY 5/1	2 mm and 4 mm thick
1994.57.1862.2	Glass & vessel	Fill in 2nd House	7	1	Dark green	5 mm thick, Medieval/post-Medieval?
1994.57.1863.1	Glass & cullet	Pit 4	4	1	Greenish grey 5G 5/2	
1994.57.1863.2	Glass & vessel	Pit 4	1	1	Colourless	1 mm thick.
1994.57.1863.3	Glass & vessel	Pit 4	15	6	Pale green 5G 6/2	1 rim; 1 cut decoration.
1994.57.1863.4	Glass	Pit 4	1	1	Colourless	Highly fractured

1994.57.1864.1	Glass & vessel	1st House Room H below floor	2	1	Dusky yellow green 5GY 5/2	5 mm thick.
1994.57.1864.2	Glass & window	1st House Room H below floor	9	11	Colourless, green tint	
1994.57.1865	Glass & vessel & base	Pit 4	28	7	Pale green 5G 6/2	Basal ring.
1994.57.G.001	Glass & window	Between 3rd House and Pit 8	2	1	Dusky yellow green (5GY 5/2)	2.5mm thick
1994.57.G.002	Glass & vessel		1	1	Light olive grey (5Y 5/2)	1.5 mm thick
1994.57.G.003	Glass & vessel		10	1	Greyish olive (10Y 4/2)	4mm thick
1994.57.G.004	Glass & vessel	Pit 1	1	1	colourless to very pale green	1mm thick
1994.57.G.005	Glass & vessel		15	1	Greyish blue (5PB 5/2)	5mm thick, circular decorative or base
1994.57.G.006	Glass & vessel			1	Greenish grey (5GY 6/1)	sherd
1994.57.G.007	Glass & vessel	On cream pans floor	4	1	Royal blue	3mm thick
1994.57.G.008	Glass & window	Pit 20 at 1.5ft; Pit 8 at 15ft; Pit 25 at 1.5ft; 1st House below wall of NE wing	31	4	Pale green (10G 6/2)	3mm thick
1994.57.G.009	Glass & window	S of 1st house opposite Rom C; yard E of shed 1.5ft; Pit W of 3rd House?; v-drain	34	5	very pale blue-green	2.5mm thick (1 piece 1mm)
1994.57.G.010	Glass & vessel	Fill in 1st house	5	1	Blue-green (5BG 4/6)	2mm thick, with rim, high quality, 7 cm diameter
1994.57.G.011	Glass & vessel	Pit 9 at 3.5ft; Pit 22; v-drain; Pit to N of W end of 3rd House; N of W end of NW wall at 2ft	176	12	blue-green (5BG 5/2)	3mm to 6 mm thick; one piece with pattern
1994.57.G.012	Glass & vessel	Pit 8 at 15ft; v-drain; E of tuning fork furnace	6	3	brown (5YR 4/4)	1mm thick
1994.57.G.013	Glass & vessel	Pit 24 at 3ft	9	1	Pale green (10G 6/2)	4 to 5mm thick

1994.57.G.014	Glass & vessel	2nd house N wall; ?	9	5	colourless to very pale green	1mm thick
1994.57.G.015	Glass & vessel	Pit 16 at 3ft;Yard N; E edge Pit 20 at 1.5 ft	15	4	Greyish green (5GY 5/2)	2mm to 5 mm thick
1994.57.G.016	Glass & vessel		10	1	Colourless, very pale green	4mm thick
1994.57.G.017	Glass & vessel & handle	3rd house S wall	9	1	Greyish green (5G 5/2)	5mm thick, groove down centre
1994.57.G.018	Glass & vessel		3	2	Royal blue	1mm thick
1994.57.G.019	Glass & vessel	1st house	5	1	Heavily patinated	3mm thick; see BCM 2008.25.G.2
1994.57.G.020	Glass & vessel	N Cream pan; 3rd house s wall; E of 3rd house at 1.5ft	8	3	blue-green (5BG 5/2)	4mm thick
1994.57.G.021	Glass & waste	E of N cream pan at 1.5ft; Yard E of Pits 3 & 4	21	2	Greyish green (5G 5/2)	molten lump
1994.57.G.022	Glass & vessel	By 6th block N of W. end of NW wall at 1.5 ft	7	1	Pale olive (10Y 6/2)	2mm thick
1994.57.G.023	Glass & vessel		16	3	Blue-green (5BG 4/6)	2mm & 4 mm thick
1994.57.G.024	Glass & vessel	Between N and S cream pan	12	1	Blue-green (5BG 5/2)	9mm thick
1994.57.G.025	Glass & vessel	Pit 4	6	1	Greyish green (5G 5/2)	10mm to 5 mm thick
1994.57.G.026	Glass & vessel	Yard E; V-drain; E of 2 detached blocks N of W end of NW wall at 1.5 ft	15	5	Pale green (5G 7/2)	7mm thick
1994.57.G.027	Glass & vessel	Pit 22 at 12 ft; W of N cream pan at 1.5ft; N edge Pit 16	22	6	Light blue (5B 7/6)	4mm to 2 mm thick
1994.57.G.028	Glass & vessel	Between pits 6 and 20 at 1.5 ft	13	1	Dusky yellow green (5GY 5/2)	
1994.57.G.029	Glass & vessel	Pit 8 at 15ft	1	1	colourless	1mm thick
1994.57.G.030	Glass & vessel	Near end of 2nd house	8	2	Pale green (5G 6/2)	5mm thick
1994.57.G.031	Glass & vessel	Pit 16 at 3ft	4	1	Pale green (5G 7/2)	
1994.57.G.032	Glass & vessel	W edge of Pit 16 at 1.5 ft	2	1		3mm thick
1994.57.G.033	Glass & vessel	By 6th block N of W. end of NW wall at 2 ft	5	1	Heavily patinated	6 mm thick

1994.57.G.034	Glass & vessel	Pit 24	1	1	Pale green (5G 7/2)	6 mm thick
1994.57.G.035	Glass & window	2nd House	4	1	Greyish green (5G 5/2)	4 mm thick
1994.57.G.036	Glass & vessel	Pit 1	1	1	Pale green (5G 6/2)	3 mm thick
1994.57.G.037	Glass & window	10 ft E of Pit 6 at 1.5ft deep	6	1	Greenish grey (5GY 6/1)	2 mm thick
1994.57.G.038	Glass & vessel & bottle	1st House Room F	16	1	Green?	Flanged neck bottle rim. Completely covered in devitrifying residue. Unlikely to be Roman - Post Med?.
1994.57.G.039	Glass & vessel	1st House?	1	1	Clear	Devitrifying. Very thin glass vessel.
1994.57.G.040	Glass & vessel	Pit 15	3	1	Blue green	Rim
1994.57.G.041	Glass & window	Pit 15	1	1	Pale Green	1 mm thick
1994.57.G.042	Glass & vessel	3rd House 3ft W & 6ft S of NW angle	4	1	Green	2mm to 3 mm thick. Indent betw neck and shoulder. Heavy patination
1994.57.G.043	Glass & vessel	1st House SW corner Room J	7	1	Pale green	3 mm thick

Appendix 2

Yewden Villa Iron Age Pottery Analysis

Bag No.	Ware	Form	No. sherds	Weight (g)	Rim count	Diameter	Rim EVE's	Wear	Decoration	Record date	Comments
1994.57.P.0015	Grog tempered	Bead-rimmed cooking pot	2 CJ	38	2	160mm	0.17	abraded	none	LIA	possibly wheel turned
1994.57.P.0029	Flint tempered 1 - 4mm	Body	1	20					none	LIA	
1994.57.P.0154	Fine shell & grog	Chinnor-Wandlebury group jar	2 CJ	148	2	200mm	0.19	abraded	scratched	EIA	hand made
1994.57.P.0157	Flint tempered 1 - 4mm	Base	1	130						MIA	hand made
1994.57.P.0494	Sand tempered	Base	1	220					finger marked	Early 1st C. AD	wheel turned transition period
1994.57.P.0798	Fine sand & grog	Bead-rimmed bulbous bowl	1	72	1	180mm	0.02	v. abraded	geometric	LIA	hand made
1994.57.P.2094	Grog tempered	Bead-rimmed jar	1	22	1	180mm	0.1	abraded	none	LIA	hand made
1994.57.P.2115	Sand tempered	Body	2 CJ	40				v. abraded	none	LIA	burnished
1994.57.P.2147	Sand & grog	Carinated bowl	1	98	1	180mm	0.17	v. abraded	none	Early 1st C. AD	transition period
1994.57.P.2155	Fine sand & grog	Bead-rimmed bulbous bowl	1	34				v. abraded	incised	LIA	
1994.57.P.2268	Fine shell & grog	Bead-rimmed bulbous bowl	7	262	3	160mm	0.35	v. abraded	burnished	LIA	Simple bead-rimmed
1994.57.P.2573	Grog tempered	Body- possible saucepan	5	130				v. abraded	none	MIA	hand made
1994.57.P.2576	Grog tempered	Body Saucepan	3	104				v. abraded	none	LIA	hand made
1994.57.P.2592	Sand, flint & grog	Bowl	2 CJ	150	2	280mm	0.13	abraded	none	LIA	Lid-seated bowl
1994.57.P.2743	Flint tempered 1 - 4mm	Bead-rimmed bulbous bowl	2	50	2	280mm	0.12	v. abraded	burnished	LIA	
1994.57.P.2743	Grog tempered	Bead-rimmed bulbous bowl	2	110	1	260mm	0.17	v. abraded	none	LIA	
1994.57.P.2743	Sand & grog	Bead-rimmed bulbous bowl	2	158	2	260mm	0.09	v. abraded	wiped	LIA	
1994.57.P.2811	BB1?	Body	1	14					lattice	c. AD 220-400	
1994.57.P.2812	Sand tempered	Base	1	18					lattice	1st - 2nd C. AD	local wheel turned?
1994.57.P.2814	Flint tempered 1 - 4mm	Body	1	14				v. abraded	none	EIA	or Saxon!
1994.57.P.2927	Flint tempered 1 - 4mm	Body	1	20				v. abraded	none	LIA	hand made
1994.57.P.2936	Grog tempered,v.sparse flint	Body	1	12				v. abraded	haematite ?	EIA	hand made
1994.57.P.3000	Grog tempered,v.sparse flint	Jar	1	22	1	200mm	0.09	v. abraded	none	Early 1st C. AD	wheel turned
1994.57.P.3011	Shell tempered	Base	1	26				v. abraded	none	4th C. AD	wheel turned
1994.57.P.3013	Flint tempered 1 - 4mm	Body Saucepan	4	132				v. abraded	none	MIA	hand made
1994.57.P.3066	Fine sand tempered	Body	1	18				v. abraded	none	LIA	hand made
1994.57.P.3101	Flint tempered 1 - 4mm	Body	1	14				v. abraded	none	LIA	hand made
1994.57.P.3168	Fine sand tempered	Jar	1	50	1	160mm	0.14	abraded	none	LIA	hand made
1994.57.P.3180	Flint tempered 1 - 4mm	Body Saucepan	8	338				v. abraded	none	MIA	hand made

Jonathan Dicks

Appendix 3: Named potters of Samian ware, Yewden Villa

Name	No of vessels	Form	Source area	Edate	Ldate
Advocisus (S)	1	DR37	Lezoux	160	180
Aeternus (S)	1	WA79	Lezoux	155	180
Albucius ii (S)	1	DR27	Lezoux	145	175
Attianus (D)	3	2 x DR37	Lezoux	125	145
Avitus (D)	1	DR37	Lezoux	125	150
Biga (S)	1	DR27	Lezoux	125	150
Biragillus/Mercator(D)	1	DR37	La Graufesenque	80	100
Casurius (D)	1	DR37	Lezoux	160	190
Cerialis (D)	3	DR37	Lezoux	135	160
Cinnamus (D)	18	17 x DR37	Lezoux	150	180
Cinnamus/Pugnus (D)	1	DR37	Lezoux	150	195
Cinstumus i (S)	1	DR33	Lezoux	140	180
Cirrus i (S)	1	DR27	LMV	130	160
Comitialis IV ? (D)	2	DR37	Rheinzabern	170	260
Criciro (D)	1	DR37	Lezoux	135	155
Crobiso (S)	1	DR33	Lezoux	135	165
Cucalus (S)	1	DR27	Lezoux	140	170
Divicatus (S)	1	DR18/31	Lezoux	135	165
Drusus (D)	6	3 x DR37 & 3x DR18R	LMV	100	120
Frontinus (S)	3	DR18R & 2x DR37	La Graufesenque	70	100
Geminus (D)	1	DR37	LMV	100	130
Germanus (D)	4	2 x DR30 & 2 x DR37	La Graufesenque	75	100
Ianus (D)	1	DR37	Indet. E. Gaul	140	190
Igocatus (D)	3	3 x DR37	LMV	100	120
Illianus (S)	1	DR31R	Lezoux	150	180
Ioenalis or X13 (D)	2	DR30 & 1 bowl	LMV	100	120
Laxtucissa (D)	1	DR37	Lezoux	155	185
Libertus/Butrio (D)	1	DR37	LMV	100	120
Littera i (S)	1	DR33	Lezoux	120	150
M. Crestio ? (D)	1	DR30	La Graufesenque	80	100
Maponus (D)	1	DR29	La Graufesenque	60	80
Masclus/Aquitanus? (D)	1	DR29	La Graufesenque	50	65
Memor, Mommo, Tetlo (D)	3	DR37, DR29 & DR30	La Graufesenque	70	90
Mercator (D)	3	DR37	La Graufesenque	70	85

Modestus (D)	2	DR29	La Graufesenque	50	65
Muxtullus (S & D)	2	DR33	Lezoux	150	180
Paterclus ii ? (S)	1	DR18/31	Lezoux	120	150
Paternus II (D)	3	3 x DR37	Lezoux	160	195
Paternus III (D)	1	bowl	Lezoux	135	165
Paternus group (D)	2	DR37	Lezoux	160	200
Paullus iv (S)	1	DR27	Lezoux	120	180
Pecularis? (S)	1	DR33	Lezoux	120	200
Pontus (S)	1	DR27g	La Graufesenque	65	90
Privatus iii (S)	1	DR38	Lezoux	160	190
Quintilianus (D)	3	DR30, DR37, bowl	Lezoux	125	145
Reburrus ii (S)	1	DR33	Lezoux	145	170
Rosette Potter (D)	2	2 bowls	LMV	100	120
Teddillus (S)	1	DR33	Lezoux	125	160
Vegetus ? (D)	1	DR37	Lezoux	120	140
Vertecissa (S)	1	DR31	Lezoux	150	170
Viducus ii (S)	1	DR18/31	LMV	100	120
Vitalis (D)	1	DR30	La Graufesenque	75	95
P9 (D)	1	DR37	LMV	110	130
X9 (D)	3	DR37	LMV	115	120
X9 (D)	2	DR37	Lezoux	120	135
X11 (D)	1	DR37	LMV	100	120
X11/X13 (D)	1	DR37	LMV	100	125
X12 (D)	1	DR37	LMV	100	120
X12 or X13 (D)	1	DR37	LMV	100	120
X13 (D)	6	DR30 & 5 x DR37	LMV	100	120

Total

57 potters   **114 vessels**

Notes:
S & D = potter identified by stamp (S) or by decoration (D)
LMV = Les Martres-de-Veyre

Appendix 4 a
Samian forms present in the Yewden assemblage, vessel numbers

Form	Montans	LGF	MLEZ	LMV	LEZOUX	East Gaul	EG RHZ	Total Vessels (Min)
CU11		1			1			2
CU15		1			1	1		3
CU21					1	1		2
CU23					1			1
De67		1	1					2
De72					1			1
DR15/17		1						1
DR15/31					1			1
DR17				1				1
DR18		4		1				5
DR18R		2						2
DR18/31		1		1	4			6
DR18/31R				1	1	1		3
DR23		1						1
DR24/25		1						1
DR27	1	7		2	6		1	17
DR29		4						4
DR30	1	4		2	1			8
DR30R					1	1		2
DR31				1	7	2		10
DR31R					2	1	1	4
DR32					1	1		2
DR33		1		1	16	3		21
DR33a		1						1
DR35		1		1	1			3
DR36		2		1	3	1		7
DR37		5		14	15	1	1	36
DR38				1	2	1		4
DR40						1		1
DR42		1		1	1			3
DR43					1		1	2
DR44				1				1
DR45					3	1		4
LUD					1			1
LUD Tg					1			1
LUD Sn							1	1

Form									
LUD Tx					1				1
RT12		1							1
RT13		1							1
WA79					1				1
WA79R					1				1
WA80					1				1
cup		1		1	1	1			4
beaker					1	1			2
bowl		1		4	4	1	1		11
dish		1		1	1	1			4
mortaria					2	1			3
plate		1		1					2
platter					2	1			3
Indet. form		1		1	3		2		7
Indet. fabric									4
Total	2	46	1	37	91	22	8		211

Appendix 4b
Samian forms present in the Yewden assemblage as EVEs

Form	Montans	LGF	MLEZ	LMV	LEZOUX	East Gaul	EG RHZ	Total Rim EVEs	
								EVE	(EVE %)
CU11		0.03			0.39			**0.42**	**(0.5%)**
CU15		0.07			0.22	0.12		**0.41**	**(0.5%)**
CU21					0.2	0.02		**0.22**	**(0.3%)**
CU23		0.06			0.52			**0.58**	**(0.7%)**
De67		P	0.02					**0.02**	**(0.02%)**
De72					P				
DR15/17		0.75						**0.75**	**(0.9%)**
DR15/31					0.28			**0.28**	**(0.03%)**
DR17				0.01				**0.01**	**(0.01%)**
DR18		3.74		0.09				**3.83**	**(4.5%)**
DR18R		1.1						**1.1**	**(1.3%)**
DR18/31		0.38		0.83	3.89	0.17		**5.27**	**(6.2%)**
DR18/31R				P	0.09		P	**0.09**	**(0.1%)**
DR23		0.35						**0.35**	**(0.4%)**
DR24/25		0.05						**0.05**	**(0.06%)**
DR27	0.1	5.55		1.39	5.21		0.05	**12.3**	**(14.6%)**
DR29		0.11						**0.11**	**(0.13%)**
DR30	P	0.19		0.02	0.3			**0.51**	**(0.6%)**
DR30R					0.08	0.03		**0.11**	**(0.13%)**
DR31				0.03	6.46	1.23		**7.72**	**(9.1%)**

DR31R					1.82	P		**1.82**	**(2.2%)**
DR32					0.05	0.27		**0.32**	**(0.4%)**
DR33		0.05		0.63	15.74	2.18		**18.6**	**(22%)**
DR33a		0.25						**0.25**	**(0.3%)**
DR35		0.37		0.35	0.47			**1.19**	**(1.4%)**
DR36		2.01		0.18	2.22	0.06		**4.47**	**(5.3%)**
DR37		0.62		0.4	3.78	0.13	P	**4.93**	**(5.8%)**
DR38				P	1.62	P		**1.62**	**(1.9%)**
DR40						0.05		**0.05**	**(0.06%)**
DR42		0.08		0.26	0.05			**0.39**	**(0.5%)**
DR43					P		1	**1**	**(1.2%)**
DR44				P					
DR45					2.3	0.1		**2.4**	**(2.8%)**
LUD					0.05			**0.05**	**(0.06%)**
LUD Tg					0.24			**0.24**	**(0.3%)**
LUD Sn							0.07	**0.07**	**(0.08%)**
LUD Tx					P				
RT12		P							
RT13		P							
WA79					0.5			**0.5**	**(0.6%)**
WA79R					P				
WA80					0.38			**0.38**	**(0.4%)**
cup		0.42		P	0.34	P		**0.76**	**(0.9%)**
beaker					0.57	P		**0.57**	**(0.7%)**
bowl		0.05		P	1.71	0.18	P	**1.94**	**(2.3%)**
dish		0.09		P	0.65	P		**0.74**	**(0.9%)**
mortaria					1.25	P		**1.25**	**(1.5%)**
plate		P		0.21				**0.21**	**(0.3%)**
platter					1.62	P		**1.62**	**(1.9%)**
indet		0.08		P	0.41	4.54	P	**5.03**	**(5.9%)**
Total EVEs	**0.1**	**16.4**	**0.02**	**4.4**	**53.41**	**4.54**	**1.12**	**84.53**	**(100.05%)**

The percentages are rim EVEs of total Samian rim EVEs. P = body sherds present, no rim.

Appendix 5
Catalogue of Roman pottery fabrics (non-Samian)

The Roman pottery list uses the Oxford Archaeological Unit's fabric code. The percent values are of the whole Yewden Roman pottery assemblage. Fabrics as a percentage within each group are shown in the tables presented in Chapter 5.2. Percentages are not shown if they are less than 0.1%

Fabric	Sherd No (%)	Weight, g (%)	EVE (%)
Fine ware			
F10 Gallo-Belgic ware	3	75	0.2
F20 Glazed fabric	19	182	-
F30 & 31 mica dusted	33 (0.1%)	667 (0.1%)	2.2 (0.4%)
F43 Central Gaulish CC	189 (0.5%)	858 (0.1%)	1 (0.2%)
F44 Moselkeramik	32 (0.1%)	124	0.4
F50 Romano-British CC	216 (0.6%)	3671 (0.4%)	6 (1%)
F51 Oxford CC	1320 (3.5%)	18804 (2%)	19.7 (3.3%)
F52 Nene Valley CC	157 (0.4%)	2084 (0.2%)	2.2 (0.4%)
F53 New Forest CC Fabric 1a	2	51	-
F54 & 57 New Forest 1a & 1b	3	59	-
F59 Oxford early CC	7	136	0.9 (0.2%)
Mortaria			
M20 white fabric (indet.)	80 (0.2%)	6246 (0.7%)	-
M21 Verulamium region	55 (0.2%)	5272 (0.5%)	-
M22 Oxfordshire, white fabric	647 (1.7%)	39040 (4.2%)	16.5 (2.8%)
M25 New Forest	8	905 (0.1%)	0.6 (0.1%)
M30/31 Oxidised with white slip/Oxfordshire	46 (0.1%)	1434 (0.1%)	1.6 (0.3%)
M36 S. England, oxidised with pale grey core	2	228	-
M41 Oxfordshire, oxidised with red colour coat	80 (0.2%)	2339 (0.2%)	1 (0.2%)
M50 oxidised	7	458	0.1
S Samian mortaria	34 (0.1%)	4925 (0.5%)	3.6 (0.6%)
White ware			
W10 Fine white fabric, indet.	144 (0.4%)	1645 (0.2%)	1.2 (0.2%)
W11 Oxfordshire Parchment	10	357	0.3
W12 Oxfordshire fine white	68 (0.2%)	957 (0.1%)	12.5 (2.1%)
W20 Sandy white fabric, indet	700 (1.9%)	16083 (1.7%)	11.5 (1.9%)
W21 Verulamium region	160 (0.4%)	4979 (0.5%)	4.7 (0.8%)
W22 Oxfordshire sandy white ware	504 (1.3%)	10446 (1.1%)	10.8 (1.8%)
White slipped ware			
Q20 Oxidised white slipped, indet	73 (0.2%)	1644 (0.2%)	1.5 (0.3%)

Q21 Oxfordshire oxidised white slipped	106	(0.3%)	1892	(0.2%)	8.3	(1.4%)
Q30 Reduced, white slipped fabric	33	(0.1%)	919	(0.1%)	3.2	(0.5%)
Oxidised ware						
O10 Fine fabric, indet.	190	(0.5%)	2226	(0.2%)	1.3	(0.2%)
O11 Oxfordshire fine fabric	65	(0.2%)	1052	(0.1%)	1.4	(0.2%)
O14 fine, very micaceous	3		94		0.2	
O20 Sandy, indet.	387	(1.0%)	6591	(0.7%)	6.2	(1.0%)
O21 Oxfordshire sandy	42	(0.1%)	1077	(0.1%)	1.3	(0.2%)
O24 Overwey 'Portchester D' type	119	(0.3%)	2685	(0.3%)	2.1	(0.4%)
O80 coarse grog tempered	2429	(6.4%)	114409	(12.2%)	11.0	(1.8%)
Reduced ware						
R10 Fine reduced ware	1854	(4.9%)	23744	(2.5%)	40.2	(6.7%)
R11 Oxford fine reduced	86	(0.2%)	1642	(0.2%)	3.2	(0.5%)
R20 sandy reduced ware	11301	(30%)	256847	(27.5%)	142.2	(23.8%)
R30 Medium reduced ware	3257	(9%)	64032	(6.8%)	95.7	(16%)
R37 Fine sandy, black incl.	29	(0.1%)	807	(0.1%)	1.0	(0.2%)
R39 Alice Holt fine sandy	237	(0.6%)	7776	(0.8%)	13.9	(2.3%)
R90 Coarse tempered fabric	1965	(5.2%)	107547	(11.5%)	18.7	(3.1%)
R91 Coarse with orange & grey grog	126	(0.3%)	6441	(0.7%)	0.5	(0.1%)
Calcareous tempered ware						
C11 Late Roman shell tempered fabric	18		383		0.3	
C13 abundant shell tempered fabric, reduced	268	(0.7%)	8631	(0.9%)	11.6	(1.9%)
Late Iron Age-early Roman 'Belgic' ware						
E20 Fine sand tempered	47	(0.1%)	1370	(0.1%)	0.4	(0.1%)
E30 Med-coarse sand tempered ware	531	(1.4%)	17606	(1.9%)	11.7	(1.9%)
E80 Grog tempered ware	519	(1.4%)	18638	(2%)	12.7	(2.1%)
E810 Grog & sand temper	299	(0.8%)	10899	(1.2%)	10.0	(1.7%)